# A COMPANION TO GOWER

Chaucer, Gower and Lydgate were the three poets of their time considered to have founded the English poetic tradition. Gower, like Lydgate, eventually fell victim to changing tastes but is now enjoying renewed scholarly attention. Current work in manuscript studies, linguistic studies, vernacularity, translation, politics, and the contexts of literary production has found a rich source in Gower's trilingual, learned, and politically engaged corpus. This *Companion to Gower* offers essays by scholars from Britain and North America, covering Gower's works in all three of his languages; they consider his relationships to his literary sources, and to his social, material and historical contexts; and they offer an overview of the manuscript, linguistic, and editorial traditions. Five essays concentrate specifically on the *Confessio Amantis*, Gower's major Middle English work, reading it in terms of its relationship to vernacular and classical models, its poetic style, and its treatment of such themes as politics, kingship, gender, sexuality, authority, authorship and self-governance. A reference bibliography, arranged as a chronology of criticism, concludes the volume.

SIÂN ECHARD is Associate Professor in the Department of English at the University of British Columbia.

# A COMPANION TO GOWER

EDITED BY

Siân Echard

D. S. BREWER

First published 2004
D. S. Brewer, Cambridge


ISBN  1 84384 000 6




D. S. Brewer is an imprint of Boydell & Brewer Ltd
PO Box 9, Woodbridge, Suffolk IP12 3DF, UK
and of Boydell & Brewer Inc.
PO Box 41026, Rochester, NY 14604–4126, USA
website: www.boydell.co.uk




A catalogue record for this title is available
from the British Library

Library of Congress Cataloging-in-Publication Data
A companion to Gower / edited by Siân Echard.
    p. cm.
Includes bibliographical references and index.
    ISBN 1–84384–000–6 (alk. paper)
1. Gower, John, 1325?–1408 – Criticism and interpretation.   2. Love
poetry, English (Middle) – History and criticism.   3. Gower, John,
1325?–1408. Confessio Amantis.   4. Poetry, Medieval – History and
criticism.   5. Christian ethics in literature.   6. Courtly love in literature.
7. Rhetoric, Medieval.   I. Echard, Siân.
    PR1987.C66 2004
    821'.1 – dc22                                                            2003017979




This publication is printed on acid-free paper

Printed in Great Britain by
Antony Rowe Ltd, Chippenham, Wiltshire

# Contents

# Illustrations

# *Acknowledgements*

This collection has been a long time in the making, and so there are many debts to record. I was introduced to John Gower while I was a graduate student at the Centre for Medieval Studies at the University of Toronto, and so my first thanks must go to the teachers responsible for that introduction, Patricia Eberle and George Rigg. Also at Toronto, I began my Gowerian collaborations with Claire Fanger, and she remains my most valued reader. I remember first discussing the possibility of a Gower companion at Kalamazoo some years ago, with Pete Wetherbee and Elizabeth Archibald; and then the conversation happened again at another Kalamazoo, this time with Bob Yeager, Ad Putter and Caroline Palmer. Many thanks are due to Ad and Caroline for allowing me to use them as a sounding board for my ideas about the shape of the volume. Ad also found a few key contributors, and Caroline has put up cheerfully with endless questions. The contributors to this volume were of course crucial to the success of the project, and I feel privileged to have worked with them all. I have also benefited from the advice of Gower scholars who do not appear in the volume – Peter Nicholson and Tamara O'Callaghan both answered questions for me as the project was underway. Colleagues at the University of British Columbia – particularly my lunchtime crew of Patricia Badir, Miranda Burgess, Sandra Tome and Judy Segal – provided endless support, as did my husband, Eric Fergusson, and my children, Patrick and Catherine. Finally, my superb research assistant, Julie Lanz, made the whole process of stitching together work by diverse hands as painless as possible, and I am glad to be able to take this opportunity to thank her publicly.

Much of the research which underlies my own contributions to this collection was funded in part by the Social Sciences and Humanities Research Council of Canada, and I am very grateful for that support.

# Abbreviations

| | |
|---|---|
| CA | *Confessio Amantis* |
| MO | *Mirour de l'Omme* |
| VC | *Vox Clamantis* |
| EETS | Early English Text Society |
| ELS | *English Literary Studies* |
| MED | *Middle English Dictionary* |
| OED | *Oxford English Dictionary* |
| PMLA | *Publications of the Modern Language Association* |
| RES | *Review of English Studies* |

# Introduction:
## Gower's Reputation

### SIÂN ECHARD

> Whate'er a man may write, it's Nature writes the end;
> Who like a shadow flees, nor, fleeing, e'er returns.
> She's dealt my end to me; I'm blind; and nevermore
> And nowhere will I write – for though my will remains,
> My power's gone, and all I long for, she denies.[1]

One of John Gower's last works was the short Latin poem 'Quicquid homo scribat', a lament for the poet's failing eyesight and health, and also, it seems, for the uncertainty which attends the poetic future of even so careful a poet as Gower. As the essay on Gower's life and tomb in this volume records, much of what we know about John Gower comes from the arrangements he made for his own death and burial, and Gower was similarly meticulous in the manuscripts of his works, recording again and again in colophons the order and content of his major poetic pieces. Whereas in other places Gower seems to express confidence in the perpetuation of his poetic voice, the merging of physical with poetic death implied by the opening line of the Latin poem suggests a pessimism about any kind of survival, a pessimism which Gower's subsequent critical fate seems to justify. While today there is indeed a renewal of interest in this major Middle English poet – a renewal which brought forth this *Companion* – I wish to begin by tracing some of what precedes that renewal and the present collection.

There are two major accounts of Gower's reputation. The first is John Fisher's opening chapter in his *John Gower: Moral Philosopher and Friend of Chaucer*.[2] Fisher's 1964 book was the first full-length study of Gower's life and works. He opened by remarking that 'T.S. Eliot has admonished us that "to bring the poet back to life is the great and perennial task of criticism". No English poet is more

---

[1] John Gower, 'Quicquid homo scribat', in *The Complete Works of John Gower*, ed. G.C. Macaulay, 4 vols (Oxford, 1899–1902), IV.365:
> Quicquid homo scribat, finem natura ministrat,
> Que velut vmbra fugit, nec fugiendo redit;
> Illa michi finem posuit, quo scribere quicquam
> Vlterius nequio, sum quia cecus ego.
> Posse meum transit, quamuis michi velle remansit;
> Amplius vt scribat hoc michi posse negat.
All translations from Latin and French are my own.

[2] John H. Fisher, *John Gower: Moral Philosopher and Friend of Chaucer* (New York, 1964), pp. 1–36.

badly in need of such resuscitation than John Gower.'[3] Fisher began by tracing
Gower's decline from his late-medieval position in the Chaucer-Gower-Lydgate
laureate triumvirate, to the nadir of 'the stereotypes of the brilliant Chaucer and
dull Gower bequeathed us by Taine, Lowell, and the superficial critical tradition
of the 19th century'.[4] Almost twenty years later, Derek Pearsall's essay on 'The
Gower Tradition' revisited the early references, and carried the story through to
various twentieth-century critics.[5] The story as Pearsall tells it is concerned with
the initial disjunction between Gower's apparently high literary reputation and
his lack of literary influence. Pearsall points out, for example, that the references
to Gower are usually considerably more perfunctory than are those to Chaucer.[6]
Thus even as the story is carried into the present, in an important collection
which is one of the early signs of the Gower revival,[7] what Pearsall calls the
'odour of unsuccess' which surrounded Gower in the nineteenth century seems
still to linger.[8] Both Fisher and Pearsall offer coherent accounts of this decline;
what I would like to do here is to pick out some of the themes in those early
references to the poet, and trace how they played out through the centuries, and
how they appear now, in the contributions to this collection.

The thematic threads to be taken up in what follows are Gower's famous
epithet 'moral Gower'; his politics; his language; his use of sources; and his relationship with Chaucer. This journey will inevitably involve revisiting the many
signposts, documented by others, of Gower's decline in critical reputation, and I
could well be accused, given that many critics in recent years have energetically
challenged these older stereotypes, of setting up straw men. But I believe it is
crucial, in order to move Gower forward into the twenty-first century, to under-

---

3   Ibid., p. v.
4   Ibid., p. 36.
5   Derek Pearsall, 'The Gower Tradition', Gower's Confessio Amantis: Responses and Reassess-
    ments, ed. Alastair J. Minnis (Cambridge, 1983), pp. 179–97.
6   Ibid., p. 185. Pearsall notes, however, that Gower is frequently cited in Ben Jonson's English
    Grammar (p. 191); see also R.F. Yeager, 'Ben Jonson's English Grammar and John Gower's
    Reception in the Seventeenth Century', The Endless Knot: Essays on Old and Middle English in
    Honor of Marie Borroff, eds. M. Teresa Tavormina and R.F. Yeager (Cambridge, 1995),
    pp. 227–39. Pearsall also points out that the Confessio was the first major English poem to be
    translated into a foreign language (into Portuguese, by Robert Payne, canon of Lisbon
    Cathedral; a Castilian version was made from the Portuguese by Juan de Cuenca in the first
    half of the fifteenth century, and this survives to us as Madrid, Escorial Library, MS g.ii.19,
    p. 184. G.C. Macaulay called these 'facts to be reckoned with' in any serious assessment of
    Gower's place in English literature: Complete Works, II.x.
7   The full contents of the collection are as follows: J.A. Burrow, 'The Portrayal of Amans in
    Confessio Amantis'; Christopher Ricks, 'Metamorphosis in Other Words'; Alastair Minnis,
    ' "Moral Gower" and Medieval Literary Theory'; Paul Miller, 'John Gower, Satiric Poet';
    Charles Runacres, 'Art and Ethics in the Exempla of Confessio Amantis'; Elizabeth Porter,
    'Gower's Ethical Microcosm and Political Macrocosm'; Jeremy Griffiths, 'Confessio Amantis:
    The Poem and its Pictures'; Derek Pearsall, 'The Gower Tradition'. Since 1983, collections of
    essays on the poet have been produced with increasing frequency: see the full list of contents
    in the 'Chronology of Criticism' for R.F. Yeager, ed., John Gower: Recent Readings (Kalamazoo,
    MI, 1989); R.F. Yeager, ed., Chaucer and Gower: Difference, Mutuality, Exchange (Victoria, B.C,
    1991); R.F. Yeager, ed., Mediaevalia 16 (1993 for 1990), a special issue for John Hurt Fisher; and
    R.F. Yeager, ed., Re-Visioning Gower (Asheville, NC, 1998).
8   Pearsall, 'Gower Tradition', p. 194.

stand fully the lines of critical influence which stretch back to the poet's own day. It is also important to understand the extent to which Gower has not simply been acted upon. I will argue that much of his subsequent history is the inevitable result of a clash between his own self-fashioning and the expectations of later eras. Gower crafted his own reputation as carefully as he evidently planned his tomb, and as all of our new encounters will inevitably be mediated through the reputations which have followed the poet down the centuries, it is worth revisiting their roots here in what follows.

### 'Moral Gower'

> O moral Gower, this book I directe
> To the and to the, philosophical Strode,
> To vouchen sauf, ther nede is, to correcte,
> Of youre benignites and zeles goode.[9]

> And write in such a maner wise,
> Which may be wisdom to the wise
> And pley to hem that lust to pleye.[10]

The first epigraph to this section is Chaucer's famous direction, at the end of *Troilus and Criseyde*, of his book to 'moral Gower'. As we shall see below, this single reference has been the linchpin for the pairing of Chaucer with Gower throughout the whole of Gower's critical history, a pairing which was either a boon or a curse, depending on the tastes of the age which repeated it. We will consider how the connection works out in the critical history in due course, but I would first draw attention to the second epigraph – Gower's own characterisation, at the start of the Ricardian[11] version of the *Confessio*, of his work as 'pley to hem that lust to pleye'. Play is not something traditionally associated with Gower, and this particular line, one of my own favourites, is removed in the Henrician version, though the description of the *Confessio* as a poem which offers 'somwhat of lust, somwhat of lore' (Prol. 19) stands. The *Confessio* is indeed sometimes playful – in the interaction between Genius and the frequently befuddled Amans; in the description of Florent's wedding night; or in the gleeful account of Faunus's attempt to have sex with a cross-dressed Hercules. There is play of another kind as well, in the complex interactions between the various voices, Latin and vernacular, on the page, and in Gower's

---

[9] Geoffrey Chaucer, *Troilus and Criseyde*, in Larry D. Benson, ed., *The Riverside Chaucer* (Boston, 1987), V.1856–9.

[10] John Gower, *Confessio Amantis*, in *The English Works of John Gower*, ed. G.C. Macaulay, EETS, es nos. 81 and 82 (1900–1901), Prol. *83–5. All further references to the *Confessio* are to this edition, and book and line numbers are indicated within parentheses in the text.

[11] Derek Pearsall's essay on the Gower manuscripts in this volume discusses the various stages of rewriting through which the poem progressed, which Macaulay called the three recensions of the poem. The Ricardian version includes the commission story in the Prologue, in which Gower says that he met Richard while boating on the Thames, and that Richard requested that he write a new poem. It also includes praise of the king at the opening and closing of the poem; these elements have been removed and/ or replaced in the Henrician version of the poem.

evident delight in linguistic games and punning, across his works and his languages. Nor should we be surprised to find this kind of playfulness in Gower: *ludus* is, as C. Stephen Jaeger has demonstrated, a necessary characteristic of the Latin court writers who originated the genre of the mirror for princes, a genre which is clearly part of the literary ancestry of the *Confessio*.[12] *Ludus* and *moralitas* (or *sentencia*) are not mutually exclusive, and Gower certainly knows his Horace – he makes it clear from the start of the *Confessio* that too much wisdom 'dulleth ofte a mannes wit' (Prol. 14), and so he proposes, not merely to produce a variety of *exempla*, but also to mix Genius's moral instruction with the pleasures of narrative. Chaucer, for his part, was for a long time also read as a 'moral' poet, as for example in these lines from Stephen Hawes' *The Pastime of Pleasure* (1517):

> As morall gower / whose sentencyous dewe
> Adowne reflayreth / with fayre golden beames
> And after Chaucers / all abrode doth shewe
> Our vyces to clense / his depared stremes
> Kyndlynge our hertes / with the fyry leames
> Of morall vertue / as is probable
> In all his bokes / so swete and prouffytable.[13]

Gower pairs lust with lore, wisdom with play; Chaucer famously combines earnest with game, and both, for Hawes, offer works of 'morall vertue'. How then is it that Gower's morality becomes such an albatross in his later history?

For George Ellis in his influential *Specimens of the Early English Poets* (1801), it is not morality which makes Gower dull, but rather narrative:

> While he is satisfied with being 'the moral Gower', he always appears to advantage: he is wise, impressive, and sometimes almost sublime. The good sense and benevolence of his precepts, the solemnity with which they are enforced, the variety of learning by which they are illustrated, make us forget that he is preaching in masquerade, and that our excellent instructor is a priest of Venus. But his narrative is often quite petrifying.[14]

Ironically, it is Gower's self-conscious blending of instruction with storytelling which leads to Ellis's condemnation. It is easy to be sidetracked at this point into a discussion of whether or not Gower was a good storyteller, but the important point here is that Gower's careful framing and announcing of his plan in the Prologue to the *Confessio* sets him up for the assessments, positive and negative, which will dog his subsequent critical reputation. He looks back to a time when 'bokes weren levere' (Prol. 37), when they showed the world good and bad

---

12  See C. Stephen Jaeger, *The Origins of Courtliness: Civilizing Trends and the Formation of Courtly Ideals, 939–1210* (Philadelphia, 1985).
13  Stephen Hawes, *The Pastime of Pleasure: A literal reprint of the earliest complete copy (1517), with variant readings from the editions of 1509, 1554, and 1555, together with introduction, notes, glossary and indexes, by William Edward Mead*, EETS, os no. 173 (London, 1928), lines 1317–23.
14  George Ellis, *Specimens of the Early English Poets, to which is prefixed an historical sketch of the rise and progress of the English Poetry and Language; in three volumes* (London: W. Bulmer for G. and W. Nicol, 1801), p. 177.

examples from which to learn. He then inserts himself (via the traditional modesty topos) into that tradition:

> Thus I, which am a burel clerk,
> Purpose forto wryte a bok
> After the world that whilom tok
> Long tyme in olde daies passed:
> Bot for men sein it is now lassed,
> In worse plit than it was tho,
> I thenke forto touche also
> The world which neweth every dai,
> So as I can, so as I mai. (Prol. 52–60)

His 'bisinesse', he says, is to write something by which 'The wyse man mai ben avised' (Prol. 63, 65). Once the Prologue is done, 'This bok schal afterward ben ended/ Of love, which doth many a wonder/ And many a wys man hath put under' (Prol. 74–6). The reader, then, is invited to consider what follows in terms which set high conditions for success – the wedding of the political with the personal, as well as of the moral with the pleasurable. In her essay in this collection, Helen Cooper suggests that Gower's appearance in Shakespeare's *Pericles*, a play marked by what she calls an 'in your face' theatricality, is testament to the playwright's delight in Gower's storytelling and in his *insistence* on storytelling. Gower announces his 'business' at the outset of the *Confessio* – and I deliberately invoke here our own sense of the word, along with the Middle English emphasis on effort and care. Later generations have taken up the challenge presented by that self-conscious announcement, and the way is thus paved for the shifting assessments of Gower's achievement, according to shifting tastes regarding lust and lore. The point here is that, as with many aspects of his history, Gower invites the scrutiny which later, sometimes, turns against him.

As the quotation from Ellis above illustrates, 'moral' did not necessarily equal 'dull' for the eighteenth century – but as time went by, the two terms gradually came to fuse. Fisher's survey of Gower's declining reputation includes James Russell Lowell's 1887 assertion that Gower has 'positively raised tediousness to the precision of science'.[15] What happened? Fisher suggests that, in part, people actually began to read Gower:

> The reputation of Gower in the 19th century is paradoxical. The cynic might observe that his reputation for dullness grew almost in direct proportion as his works became accessible; that so long as he was little more than a name he fared reasonably well, but that as soon as he could be read people began to find what he was really like.[16]

The revival of interest in Gower, to which the 'Chronology of Criticism' in this volume attests, suggests, on the contrary, that once critics began to read Gower again, they did indeed discover 'what he was really like' – and it was not, any longer, what he had been *assumed* to be like. The epithet 'moral', for example,

---

[15] Fisher, *John Gower*, p. 2; quoting from *My Study Windows*, p. 258.
[16] Ibid., p. 28.

can be revisited in terms of a commitment to right rule and the public realm – a direction recognised by George Coffman in the 1940s and pursued by Russell Peck in the 1970s, as well as in the latter's contribution to this collection. Several of the essays to follow have something to say about 'moral Gower'. The discussion of Gower's arrangements for his tomb by John Hines, Nathalie Cohen and Simon Roffey points out that this activity is both intensely pious and intensely proud. Ardis Butterfield argues that the confessional model is one of both self-revelation and self-concealment, of affirmation and shame; it is a complex vehicle for self-exploration. Winthrop Wetherbee writes that the mimicry of glossed schooltexts in the bilingual structure of the *Confessio* is a criticism of moralising allegory in a work whose main debt to the Boethian tradition is in its constant questioning of authority. And Diane Watt contends that Gower's attitude towards the women of the *Confessio* is part of his general emphasis on the individual as a rational moral agent. That individual is also embedded in the state, and so I turn to my second thread, Gower's politics.

### Political Gower

> Wise men beware, who read this here:
> If living ill, earth's rulers will
> Endure God's hate. No king is he
> Whom sin doth win; by Richard's test,
> It's manifest: his vaunting pomp's
> Reduced to naught; such was his life.
> His pride has died; this cronique stands.[17]

In addition to the obsession with a possible quarrel with Chaucer, discussed further below, criticism of Gower in the seminal eighteenth and nineteenth centuries focused on his politics. The lines which open this section are drawn from Gower's *Cronica Tripertita*, the poet's retrospective, condemnatory account of Richard's reign. By the time of the *Cronica*, G.C. Macaulay argues, 'Gower has in the end brought himself to think that the misfortunes of the earlier part of Richard's reign were intended as a special warning to the youthful king'; a warning Richard ignored.[18] Macaulay goes on to argue that this change of mind explains the changes in the account of Gower's books with which so many of his manuscripts end. And of course, Gower most famously retooled the beginning and end of the *Confessio Amantis*, removing praise of Richard and inserting praise of Henry. These shifts were the source for the frequently repeated contention that Gower was a political turncoat; and he was compared in this regard

---

[17] John Gower, *Cronica Tripertita*, in *Complete Works* IV, iii. 484–9:
　　　Hoc concernentes caueant qui sunt sapientes,
　　　Nam male viuentes deus odit in orbe regentes:
　　　Est qui peccator, non esse potest dominator;
　　　Ricardo teste, finis probat hoc manifeste:
　　　Post sua demerita periit sua pompa sopita;
　　　Qualis erat vita, cronica stabit ita.
[18] Macaulay, *Complete Works*, IV.lvii.

unfavourably to Chaucer. Fisher traces the turn in perceptions of Gower's political career to the life of Chaucer written by Thomas Hearne and prefaced to
Urry's 1721 edition of Chaucer, and he establishes clearly how common it was to
move 'from personal to literary denigration' in the criticism of the eighteenth
and nineteenth centuries.[19] There are many instances of this kind of assessment.
I have chosen just one, from Charles Cowden-Clarke's *The Riches of Chaucer*
(1835). In this popularising work, Cowden-Clarke responds to William
Godwin's defence of Gower in his 1803 *Life of Chaucer* by remarking contemptu-
ously that:

> Gower, . . . with the callous selfishness that not unfrequently accompanies a blind
> old age, was among the first to welcome the new sovereign, spurning at the same
> time his fallen master and patron. We may conceive how the generous and noble
> soul of Chaucer must have revolted at such miserable ingratitude in a brother
> poet.[20]

This popular judgement of Gower's behaviour was frequently repeated,
including in Cowden-Clarke's own version of Chaucer for children. The pairing
of Chaucer and Gower discussed further below kept such assessments and their
consequences alive.

Gower's politics continued to be a problem for readers after the nineteenth
century. While earlier critics concerned themselves with negative descriptions of
Gower's shift from Richard to Henry, twentieth-century critics sometimes
collected from Gower all his remarks about peasants who refuse to keep their
place – so that recently, for example, David Aers has argued that in Gower's
bestialisation of the participants in the Peasants' Revolt, 'the poet implies that
even if the current policy is as corrupt as his own satire of the 1370s might have
seemed to suggest, any actual alternative is infinitely worse'.[21] I would argue
that part of the problem has to do with a conflict between Gower's own creation
of his poetic position, and how later generations have reacted to that position. It
is obvious that Gower concerned himself with right rule, of the individual and
of the state, throughout his poetic career and in all his languages. It is clear that
he is a staunch royalist. And he is politically and socially conservative. But these
positions, as Gower would have understood them and inherited them from the
literary traditions on which he drew, did not require blind allegiance to one
particular ruler, nor did they limit their criticisms to members of a particular
class. The political Latin tradition which underpins Gower's own version of the
mirror for princes is indeed focused on kings – but that hardly precludes criticism of the king, or even the idea that it can be licit to remove a bad king. John of
Salisbury, for example, insists that the distinction between a good king and a
tyrant is to be found in respect for the law:

---

[19] Fisher, *John Gower*: discussion pp. 22–8, quotation p. 28.
[20] Charles Cowden-Clarke, *The Riches of Chaucer: in which his impurities have been expunged; his
spelling modernised; his rhythm accentuated; and his obsolete terms explained*, 2 vols (London,
1835), I.36.
[21] David Aers, '*Vox populi* and the Literature of 1381', *The Cambridge History of Medieval English
Literature*, ed. David Wallace (Cambridge, 1999), p. 441.

And this therefore is the difference between the tyrant and the prince, that the latter observes the law, and rules his people by its will, whose servant he believes himself to be, and all the business and duties which must be undertaken he performs with the support of the law[.][22]

And the law applies up and down the social ladder: reading across Gower's works, one finds kings, nobles, knights, bishops, priests, lawyers, merchants and peasants subject to criticism. I quote here a few lines from the *Mirour de l'Omme*:

> Ah World, I will not lie to you:
> For if these ills to you are due,
> Then I'll complain about your might . . .
> Ah World, answer, speak to me,
> Some answers I demand of thee,
> The whole truth you must tell to me.
> What's the reason, tell me, do
> People speak so ill of you?[23]

The voice adopted here is the voice of the complaint genre, a genre of moral lament or outrage. The few lines quoted address the world, but if one searches the poem, vocatives are widely scattered, applied to bishops (line 19,069 etc.), foolish priests (line 20,461 etc.), Fortune (line 22,081 etc.), the king (line 22,273 etc.), the nobles (line 23,329 etc.), the knights (line 23,893 etc.), judges (line 24,733 etc.), wool (line 25,369 etc.) and man (line 27,121 etc.). This challenging voice is the voice of the prophet-poet, the *vox clamantis* which also gives the title to Gower's most political poem. It is also an outsider's voice. Despite putting himself on the river with Richard at the outset of the *Confessio*, despite writing in not one but two elite languages, Gower's frequent position is as the observer who stands somewhat apart from the world he records. He is to some extent in the world – in this collection, for example, Jeremy Smith remarks on his apparent attachment to the professional classes, R.F. Yeager on his use of French to address the culture of the court, and Derek Pearsall on the Lancastrian associ-

---

[22] John of Salisbury, *Policraticus*, in *Joannis Saresberiensis Opera Omnia*, ed. J.-P. Migne, *Patrologia Latina* 199 (1855), IV.i:
> Est ergo tyranni et principis haec differentia sola, quod hic legi obtemperat, et ejus arbitrio populum regit, cujus se credit ministrum, et in reipublicae muneribus exercendis, et oneribus subeundis, legis beneficio sibi primum vindicat . . .

[23] John Gower, *Mirour de l'Omme*, in *Complete Works*, Vol. I:
> He, Siecle, ne t'en quier mentir,
> Si tu ces mals fais avenir,
> Je me compleigns de ta vertu. (lines 26,518–20)

> He, Siecle, responetz a moy,
> De ce que je demander doy
> La verité tout plain me dy:
> Quelle est la cause et le pour qoy
> Dont l'en parolt si mal de toy? (lines 26,605–9)

I have had to take a few liberties in this translation in order to produce some representation of Gower's rhyming practice. It is also not possible – at least in rhyme – to represent fully such features as Gower's punning use of 'vertu'; the speaker actually complains about both the strength and the virtue (that is, the lack of it), of the world.

ations of some of the manuscripts of the *Confessio*. But just as Langland critics have in recent years complicated their perception of the poet's self-declared outsider status with a growing understanding of his place in London's literary culture, so too Gower critics have been revisiting their poet's associations with the court and with the city, a tendency seen in this volume when both Hines and Epstein remark on Gower's association with Southwark. For Hines, Cohen and Roffey, this place, that is both on and off the map of the city, is the stage on which Gower can most suitably perform his life. For Epstein, Gower moves through a world of urban coterie culture, and yet does not directly place himself in it. Epstein suggests a similar detachment from the court, remarking that the *Confessio* is a mirror for princes without the prince – a recognition of the insider/ outsider role which helps us to understand Gower's political poetry.

Whatever one thinks of his politics, Gower is a supremely political poet. And his politics, like his poetics, are complex. In their essay on Gower's Latin works, A.G. Rigg and Edward Moore trace the tradition in which Gower worked, and argue that the Latin poetry, in keeping with the Latin tradition, is more declarative and public than Gower's vernacular work. They point to a new trend in the fourteenth century – the heraldic use of Latin poetry for political and public ends. They also argue that the self-consciousness seen as an innovation in Ricardian writers of English has its antecedents in the Latin tradition, a tradition of political advice and complaint which structures Gower's self-presentation. Wetherbee's delineation of Gower's deployment of the Boethian tradition to question and explore the limits of authority pursues a similar trajectory. Butterfield adds the French tradition to this picture, pointing to the exploration of authority – of what it means to be an author – in the courtly French texts which cooperated with various Latin works to give Gower his Genius and Amans. As for Gower's English work, it too is engaged, as Peck says, with 'dom' – with judgement in rule, both personal and political. Peck shows how the two are tied, and Watt, too, remarks on the connection between personal and parental or political rule, when she points out that Gower's incest stories concern the relationships of kings to their children.

Gower's poetics and his politics are intimately linked. He engaged in a life-long search for the place from which, and the voice in which, to speak. That search involved different languages and different genres, and involved Gower in choices which later were not always well understood. In his essay on Gower's English style, John Burrow shows how the poet avoids oral formulae, alliterative decoration, and words that might appear archaic. Gower is searching, Burrow argues, for a plain style – because good speech is plain speech. This is, as Burrow notes, a good long-poem style, and he remarks that a declining taste for narrative poetry leads, regrettably, to a declining appreciation of Gower's stylistic achievement. I would add that Gower's English style also speaks to the poet's ideas about good political speech, as represented, for example, in his condemnation of Hypocrisy in the *Vox Clamantis*:

> Many such there are who colour words;
> Who stuff our ears with aureate-sounding speech,

·

> Their words burst forth with leaves, but there's no fruit;
> Sweet talk is all, to move the innocent.[24]

We have seen that for Gower, a poet must please and he must persuade. Yet both pleasing and persuading are, potentially at least, suspect. Typically, Gower invites his audience to examine his position. Also typically, that position can be pieced together completely only if we pay attention to more than just the English works.

## English Gower

> And for that fewe men endite
> In oure englissh, I thenke make
> A boke for Engelondes sake. (Prol. 22–4)

In the opening of the *Confessio Amantis*, Gower announces his decision to write in English. He had already composed major works in Latin and in French, and in the Ricardian version of the Prologue to the *Confessio*, he describes his English poem as a 'newe thing' (Prol. *51) requested by the king himself, to whom, rather than to 'Engelonde', the first version of the poem was dedicated. Thus Gower presents his English work as a novelty, produced at the command of the king or, in the later redaction we now call the third recension or the Henrician version, for the benefit of the nation. Later medieval and early modern references to the poet agree on the importance of this decision to write in English, though how they gloss it differs – and in rather interesting ways, as we shall see shortly. For its part the critical tradition took the cue of the early references in concentrating on Gower's English works – so that when Maria Wickert's *Studien zu John Gower* appeared in 1953, J.A.W. Bennett remarked 'That the first monograph devoted to Gower should concentrate attention on his least-read work – the *Vox Clamantis* – seems odd today.' Yet Bennett went on to call the *Confessio* 'merely an experimental diversion in the vernacular'.[25] Gower's self-conscious deployment of all his languages is crucial to his poetic project, and in this section I will argue that current critical interest in vernacularity has allowed readers at last to recognise that fact.

Around 1475, George Ashby's *Active Policy of a Prince* praised Gower, Chaucer and Lydgate for contributing to the creation of 'douce' English:

> Maisters Gower, Chauucer & Lydgate,
> Primier poetes of this nacion,
> Embelysshing oure englisshe tendure algate,
> Firste finders to oure consolacion

---

24 John Gower, *Vox Clamantis*, in *Complete Works* IV, xxii, 1065–80:
   Sunt etenim multi tales qui verba colorant,
   Qui pascunt aures, aurea verba sonant,
   Verbis frondescunt, set non est fructus in actu,
   Simplicium mentes dulce loquendo mouent.
25 J.A.W. Bennett, '*Studien zu John Gower*, by Maria Wickert, p. 204, Köln: Unversitäts-Verlag, 1953', *Review of English Studies* 8:29 (1957), p. 54.

Off fresshe, douce englisshe and formacion
Of newe balades, not vsed before,
By whome we all may haue lernyng and lore.[26]

Ashby's vocabulary suggests a French influence – 'douce' English, new 'balades' – even as he praises the nation-building qualities of these poets. The reference to embellishment is reflected in other writers' remarks on the rhetorical qualities of the medieval triumvirate: thus William Dunbar's famous reference to Chaucer, Gower, and Lydgate in *The Goldyn Targe* (c. 1508) praises the poets for their contributions to the development of 'oure speche' in terms that stress the decorative and the ornate:

Your angel mouthis most mellifluate
Oure rude langage has clere illumynate,
And faire ourgilt oure spech, that imperfyte
Stude or your goldyn pennis schupe to write;
This ile before was bare and desolate
Off rethorike, or lusty fresch endyte.[27]

Compare, then, Thomas Berthelette's address to Henry VIII at the opening of his printing of the *Confessio*: 'There is to my dome/ no man/ but that he may bi reding of this warke get right great knowlege/ as wel for the vnderstandyng of many <u>and</u> diuers autors/ . . . / as for the plenty of englysshe wordes and vulgars/ . . . Whiche olde englysshe wordes and vulgars no wyse man/ bycause of theyr antiquite/ wyll throwe asyde.' In a world where writers ransack 'latyne/ frenche/ and other langages' for 'newe termes', Gower is presented as a 'lanterne' for the aspiring English poet: Gower will 'gyue hym lyghte to wryte counnyngly/ and to garnysshe his sentencis in our vulgar tonge'. Where the praise of Ashby and Dunbar focuses on Gower's abilities to produce ornate language (reflected here as well in words such as 'garnysshe'), Berthelette also uses the poet to counter the foreign coinings and difficult expressions currently fashionable: the 'worthy olde wryter' represents a solid, indigenous strain of language.[28]

This attitude towards Gower's English has both positive and negative reflexes in later centuries, depending, perhaps, on the tastes and sensibilities of the commentator. Thomas Warton's late eighteenth-century account of Gower is largely a sympathetic one – his is the famous remark, 'If Chaucer had not existed, the compositions of John Gower, the next poet in succession, would alone have been sufficient to rescue the reigns of Edward the third and Richard the second from the imputation of barbarism.' Yet this positive assessment soon gives way to a rather tepid praise of Gower for, one might say, holding the vernacular fort until the arrival of Chaucer:

[26] George Ashby, *Active Policy of a Prince*, in *George Ashby's Poems*, ed. Mary Bateson, EETS, es no. 76 (London 1899), Prol. 1–7.
[27] William Dunbar, *The Goldyn Targe*, in *The Poems of William Dunbar*, ed. James Kinsley (Oxford, 1979), lines 265–70.
[28] Thomas Berthelette, *Jo. Gower de Confessione Amantis* (London, 1532), aa.ii.v.

By a critical cultivation of his native language, he laboured to reform its irregularities, and to establish an English style. In these respects he resembled his friend and contemporary Chaucer: but he participated no considerable portion of Chaucer's spirit, imagination, and elegance.[29]

Warton does not define 'elegance' here, though it is noteworthy that he is the first to print examples of Gower's French verse. Whatever he may have been thinking, it is clear that Ellis, whose *Specimens of the Early English Poets* followed on from Warton's and was often twinned with it in nineteenth-century accounts of Gower, actually favoured Gower's other vernacular, his French – or at least, some of it. Of the *Balades*, he writes: 'These juvenile productions are more poetical and more elegant, than any of his subsequent compositions in his native language.'[30] Ellis's admiration for the *Confessio*, by contrast, appears to be undermined by its length: 'although few modern readers will be tempted to peruse a poem of more than thirty thousand verses, written in obsolete English, without being allured by the hopes of more entertainment than can easily be derived from the *Confessio Amantis*, there are parts of the work which might very probably be reprinted with advantage'.[31]

Other commentators were highly critical of Gower's adventures in languages other than English. Berthelette's dislike of foreign tongues has an echo, for example, in Alexander Chalmers' *Life*, preceding his reprinting of Berthelette's edition of the *Confessio*: 'Chaucer had the courage to emancipate his muse from the trammels of French, in which it was the fashion to write, and the genius to lay the foundation of English poetry, taste and imagination. Gower, probably from his closer intimacy with the French and Latin poets, found it more easy to follow the beaten track.'[32] The same attitude which imagines Chaucer proceeding through 'French' and 'Italian' phases to his final, 'English' phase in the *Canterbury Tales* informs much of the commentary on Gower's poetry as well, as Yeager's essay in this collection points out.

For the anonymous writer of the *British Quarterly Review* essay of 1858, Gower's particular achievement was to bring the English language to the acceptance of the aristocracy:

Gower led the despised language of the commons into the very presence-chamber of royalty, and proved to knight and noble, and high-born lady, how far in copiousness and power that 'English tongue' surpassed the long-cherished language of France – that 'English tongue' whose 'words have gone forth even to the ends of the world'.[33]

[29] Thomas Warton, *The History of English Poetry from the Close of the Eleventh to the Commencement of the Eighteenth Century*, Vol. II (London, 1778), pp. 1–2.
[30] Ellis, *Specimens*, p. 170.
[31] Ibid., p. 178.
[32] Alexander Chalmers, *The Works of the English Poets, from Chaucer to Cowper; including the Series Edited with Prefaces, Biographical and Critical, by Dr. Samuel Johnson: and The Most Approved Translations* (London, 1810), II.iv.
[33] 'John Gower and his Works', *The British Quarterly Review*, no. 53, Jan. 1 (1858), p. 8.

But Gower's appeal is not merely to the upper classes; in a striking echo of Berthelette, as filtered perhaps through Wordsworthian attitudes, the essay goes on to remark that:

> Gower . . . is very fond of our old homely proverbs, and frequently introduces them with much humour. Indeed, in adopting the English language, nothing seems to have been farther from his thoughts, than to bring into use a kind of fine-gentleman phraseology, which should cast aside the forcible words and forcible modes of speech of the common people. There were no sickly notions in the minds either of him or Chaucer about the courtly, or the super-refined in phraseology but like every great writer since their days, they were well content to use 'market language'.[34]

It is perhaps no surprise, then, to find Gower's chief editor, G.C. Macaulay, repeatedly praising Gower's style in similar terms: Gower has a 'simple direct-ness of narrative style'; his expression is 'perfectly simple and natural'; he exhibits 'technical skill . . . rare among the writers of the time' and 'surprising in that age of half-developed English style, and in a man who had trained himself rather in French and Latin than in English composition'.[35] Gower is here presented as the straightforward technician of new English. But Macaulay's praise continues with the familiar comparison to Chaucer:

> Chaucer had wider aims, and being an artist of an altogether superior kind, he at-tains, when at his best, to a higher level of achievement in versification as in other things; but he is continually attempting more than he can perform, he often aims at the million and misses the unit. His command over his materials is evidently incomplete, and he has not troubled himself to acquire perfection of craftsman-ship, knowing that other things are more important.[36]

Chaucer is Michelangelo to Gower's Andrea del Sarto, and Gower's technical mastery becomes a mark of his inferiority – just as, we shall see below, the tradi-tional praise for Gower's learning undergoes a similar transformation when the understanding of 'invention' shifts to mean creation.

Like Ellis, Macaulay had some degree of admiration for Gower's lyric French style, though little for the style of the much longer *Mirour de l'Omme*:

> If however we must on the whole pronounce the literary value of the *Speculum Meditantis* to be small, the case is quite different with regard to the *Balades* . . . they are for the most part remarkably good, better indeed than anything of their kind which was produced in England at that period.[37]

By contrast, Macaulay has little time for Gower's Latin. Part of this distaste has to do with Gower's use of source materials, discussed further below, but even when estimating Gower's 'own style of versification', Macaulay's praise is tepid at best:

---

34  Ibid., p. 31.
35  Macaulay, *English Works*, I.xiv, xvii.
36  Ibid., I.xvii.
37  Macaulay, *Complete Works*, I.xiii.

If we take into account the fact that the Latin is not classical but medieval, and that certain licences of prosody were regularly admitted by medieval writers of Latin verse, we shall not find the performance very bad.[38]

Echoes of these assessments of Gower's languages can be heard even as Fisher attempts to 'resuscitate' Gower: in his Preface, he outlines his practice with respect to Gower's languages:

Although Gower was a reasonably effective Latin stylist and much is lost in translation, the gain in intelligibility is so great that I have felt no qualms about Englishing the Latin throughout and omitting the original. On the other hand, I could not bring myself so to deal with the French.[39]

Today, renewed interest in the polyglot nature of England in the fourteenth century, along with the current fascination with the political and ideological implications of 'Englishing', have led readers back to Gower, where they have found their preoccupations anticipated. The contributors to this collection encounter Gower's linguistic complexity in a variety of ways, some of them technical, some of them social and political. Burrow follows Macaulay in observing that Gower's style in the *Confessio Amantis* combines the English metrical system with the French syllabic system, and he goes on to note that a French taste for purity and simplicity, along with a firm grasp of the rules of Latin grammar, are key elements in Gower's English style. The importance of language, or languages, to current studies of Gower is in fact reflected in many different ways in the contributions to follow. Smith remarks on the social dynamism of London in Gower's day, and on the ways in which the manuscript evidence suggests that we can understand Gower's language as a kind of norm or type in this world – remarks which connect neatly to Pearsall's detection, in the regularity of many *Confessio* manuscripts, of a fifteenth-century campaign to promote vernacular literature. This campaign is of course political as well as literary, reminding us of the degree to which Gower's linguistic uses are also political. My own essay, which documents the sidelining in print of Gower's non-English writing (even in an English poem like the *Confessio Amantis*), shows how some of the negative perceptions of Gower's achievements – linguistic and otherwise – were conditioned by the limited print tradition which they then fed, in a seemingly endless and destructive loop. Yeager notes that while Gower's courtly French was limited as to audience, it was the perfect tool for turning the assumptions of French courtly culture against itself, and in a different recognition of the linking of poetics to politics, Rigg and Moore point out that Gower makes his strongest political statements in Latin, a language with a particularly rich tradition of political satire. Peck, too, asserts that Gower's Latin political poetry is a necessary context for understanding the politics of his English work. For Wetherbee, in order to understand the complex dynamic of the *Confessio*, we must understand the dialectic between the love-cult of courtly (French) poetry and the cosmic idealism of the Boethian (Latin) tradition. These essays are not

---

[38] Macaulay, *Complete Works*, IV.xxxiii.
[39] Fisher, *John Gower*, p. vi.

always concerned with language on the level of style, as is Burrow's, but they all reflect the extent to which current readers of Gower range across the poet's languages and works. On Gower's tomb, the poet's head rests on three books, in three languages. The 'Quia vnusquisque', the list of works which is appended to so many of the manuscripts of his poetry, also emphasises the three books and the three tongues. Gower's various monuments tell us something about how he wanted to be read; the contributors to this volume accept that triple challenge.

*Learned Gower*

> Wherof, if that the list to wite
> In a Cronique as it is write,
> A gret ensample thou myht fynde,
> Which now is come to my mynde.    (I.1403–6)

Ellis ended his brief discussion of Gower's work in the *Specimens of the Early English Poets* with a long extract from Gower's 'Tale of Florent', commenting, by way of introduction, that

> It is usual to couple the names of Gower and Chaucer, as if these contemporary poets had possessed similar talents: the fairest method, therefore, to form an estimate of both, will be to give from one, a subject which has been attempted by the other.[40]

Ellis does not express his own conclusion overtly, but it is quite clear what the reader is meant to decide as to the relative merits of the two poets. Ellis's concern is not with the decision to tell a story told before; rather, it is with the differences in execution. His chosen example, which he says shows both Gower and Chaucer adapting a Latin tale, is in keeping with early perceptions of the nature of the two poets' achievements – achievements which at first were understood precisely in terms of literal and cultural translation. George Ashby's *Active Policy of a Prince*, to which I have already referred, prays that Chaucer, Gower and Lydgate may receive heavenly recompense for the work they have undertaken:

> But sithe we all be dedly and mortal,
> And no man may eschewe this egression,
> I beseche almyghty god eternal
> To pardon you all / youre transgression,
> That ye may dwelle in heuenly mansion,
> In recompense of many a scripture
> That ye haue englisshede without lesure.[41]

The three poets are praised for 'Englishing' other written texts. Gower frequently figures as one who carries words from the *scriptura* of the past into his present, as for example in the prologue to the *Vox Clamantis*:

---

[40] Ellis, *Specimens*, p. 178.
[41] George Ashby, Prologue to *Active Policy of a Prince*, lines 15–21.

> From varied blooms the honey's gathered in,
> And shells are caught from many varied shores –
> So thus this work's the work of many mouths,
> And many visions too produce this book.
> My songs are fortified by men of old,
> I wrote my words to their examples' form.[42]

Throughout the *Confessio*, too, Genius makes constant reference to the sources of his tales: 'In a Cronique' (I.1404), 'In Metamor' (I.389), 'in poesie' (IV.1038), 'Ovide telleth' (IV.3317) – the examples could be multiplied endlessly. In the same address to Henry VIII in which he praised Gower's simple 'vulgar', Berthelette also praised the *Confessio* precisely because it was 'plentifully stuffed' with *exempla* and stories taken from old books and from scripture. Cooper's essay in this collection quotes Berthelette on this subject, and there are many other examples of later writers praising Gower as a transmitter of stories and knowledge. Thomas Freeman's *Epigram 14* (1614), for example, says that Chaucer, Lydgate and Gower:

> equal'd all the Sages
> Of these, their owne, of former Ages,
> And did their learned Lights aduance
> In times of darkest ignorance,
> When palpable impurity
> Kept knowledge in obscurity.[43]

For Ashby, Berthelette, and Freeman, then, Gower's achievement rests in good part on his 'Englishing' of old texts, on his role as the translator and transmitter of old matter in new wise. As was the case with language, this praise remains in Macaulay's influential account of Gower's abilities: 'The materials of course are not original, but Gower is by no means a slavish follower in detail of his authorities; the proportions and arrangement of the stories are usually his own and often show good judgement.'[44] It is curious, given this willingness to grant Gower his sources in English, that Macaulay should disapprove so vehemently of Gower's use of lines of Latin verse in the *Vox*:

> The extracts from medieval authors are to some extent tolerable, because they are usually given in a connected and intelligible shape, but the perpetual borrowing of isolated lines or couplets from Ovid, often without regard to their appropriate-

---

[42] *Vox* II. Prol. 75–82:
> Non tamen ex propriis dicam que verba sequntur,
> Set velut instructus nuncius illa fero.
> Lectus vt est variis florum de germine fauus,
> Lectaque diuerso litore concha venit,
> Sic michi diuersa tribuerunt hoc opus ora,
> Et visus varii sunt michi causa libri:
> Doctorum veterum mea carmina fortificando
> Pluribus exemplis scripta fuisse reor.

[43] Thomas Freeman, *Rubbe, and a Great Cast: Epigrams* (London, 1614), *Epigram 14*, lines 3–8.
[44] Macaulay, *English Works*, I.xii.

ness or their original meaning, often makes the style, of the first books especially, nearly as bad as it can be.[45]

Perhaps the difficulty is that Gower is actually taking lines rather than story ideas; but other critics also speak disapprovingly of Gower's treatment of Ovid. Ellis, for example, suggests that, 'when we read in his work the tales with which we had been familiarized in the poems of Ovid, we feel a mixture of surprise and despair, at the perverse industry employed in removing every detail, on which the imagination had been accustomed to fasten'.[46]

The characterisation of Gower's recourse to past texts as a kind of 'perverse industry' demonstrates again the odd alchemy which bedevils Gower, by which the qualities that he made central in his own poetic ethos themselves become the evidence for his lack of poetry. Thus Gower's learning, like his command of his unique metrical style, is a double-edged sword. Stephen Hawes' *The Conforte of Louers* (1515?) figures both Gower and Chaucer as 'philosophers' writing big books:

> Fyrst noble Gower/moralytees dyde endyte
> And after hym Cauncers/grete bokes delectable
> Lyke a good phylosophre/meruaylously dyde wryte.[47]

But in later eras, while Gower remains wedded to his learning (just as his effigy's head continues to lie on that pile of books), Chaucer is liberated from this increasingly problematic, 'bookish' association. Warton, for example, excuses rather than praises Gower's learning, giving us again the contrast between stolid Gower and brilliant Chaucer:

> . . . when books began to grow fashionable, and the reputation of learning con-
> ferred the highest honour, poets became ambitious of being thought scholars;
> and sacrificed their native powers of invention to the ostentation of displaying
> an extensive course of reading, and to the pride of profound erudition. . . . Chau-
> cer is an exception to this observation: whose original feelings were too strong to
> be suppressed by books, and whose learning was overbalanced by genius.[48]

As feeling and, eventually, creation *ex nihilo* come to be the hallmarks of poetic genius, a work such as Gower's, so thoroughly medieval in its avowed indebt-edness to old books, is bound to appear something of a relic. Ezekiel Sanford's life of Gower in the first volume (1819) of the series *The Works of the British Poets* reads Gower's recourse to classical stories as symptomatic of a general tendency in the period to slavish imitation of the foreign, rather than a healthy cultivation of native originality:

> All the earlier English poets only trod in the steps of foreigners; and, along with
> the other parts of their literature, they imported the continental mania for classic
> lore. . . . This exclusive devotion to ancient literature brought all native genius

---

[45] Macaulay, *Complete Works*, IV.xxxiii.
[46] Ellis, *Specimens*, p. 177.
[47] Stephen Hawes, *The Conforte of Louers*, in *Stephen Hawes: The Minor Poems*, ed. Florence W. Gluck and Alice B. Morgan, EETS, os no. 271 (London, 1974), lines 22–24.
[48] Warton, *History of English Poetry*, II.31.

into discredit. Imitation took the place of originality; and, so extravagant was the admiration in which the learned languages were held, that nothing could be thought excellent which was not in Greek or Latin.[49]

Sanford's criticism is directed as much at Gower's audience, of course, as at the poet himself, and this tendency to characterise the admiration of medieval readers for the learning displayed by Gower as, at best, rather charmingly naive appears over and over again in the criticism of the nineteenth century. Thus for example the indulgent tone of the *British Quarterly Review* article of 1858, which develops the contrast between Gower's imagined audience and the modern one:

> Let not the reader, however, imagine that the *Confessio Amantis* would be found so delightful to *him*. . . . Gower's simple and undramatic way of telling his stories, his lengthened moralizations, which in these days of railroad speed we can willingly spare, and his many dissertations on all manner of subjects . . . will ever prevent the worthy old poet from again becoming popular.[50]

The days of 'railroad speed' have no time for Gower's treasure-trove; but the process of excerpting Gower is one which may be traced back to his earliest readers, for in the manuscript record one finds both excerpts and indications of readerly 'sampling' (see Pearsall's essay on the manuscript tradition for further details). I am not arguing that people *used* to read the whole of Gower's works, or that the process of skimming them is a recent innovation.[51] I do wish however to delineate how the very elements upon which Gower's early reputation rested have become the markers of his inferiority and inaccessibility. The paragraph from the *Review* article just quoted picks out in particular the contents of Book VII of the *Confessio*, and one need only look at twentieth-century criticism to see that the place of this section in the work as a whole has perplexed generations of critics. Fisher's defence of Gower's constant recourse to moralised stories and to encyclopedic lore does not deny their lack of appeal to the railroad age; rather, he writes of Gower's works that 'Their dullness cannot be palliated, but it must be recognized for what it is – not failure, but success in its intended genre.'[52]

---

[49] Ezekiel Sanford, ed., *The Works of the British Poets*, Vol. I (Philadelphia, 1819), pp. 220–1. This collection is peculiar among those that excerpt Gower in choosing most often to print Genius's definitions of the sins, rather than the stories he tells to illustrate them: see the essay on 'Gower in Print' later in this volume.

[50] 'John Gower and his Works', p. 27.

[51] For more on the reading of Gower see, in addition to the essays in this collection, Kate Harris, 'John Gower's *Confessio Amantis*: The Virtues of Bad Texts', *Manuscripts and Readers in Fifteenth-Century England: The Literary Implications of Manuscript Study*, ed. Derek Pearsall (Cambridge, 1983), pp. 26–40; and Joyce Coleman, 'Lay Readers and Hard Latin: How Gower May Have Intended the *Confessio Amantis* to Be Read', *Studies in the Age of Chaucer* 24 (2002), pp. 209–35, among others.

[52] Fisher, *John Gower*, p. 2. David Lawton, in an important piece which assesses the posture of dullness assumed by many of the fifteenth-century writers we have seen praising the Chaucer-Gower-Lydgate triumvirate, remarks at the outset on the reputation of the fifteenth century in terms which apply equally well to Gower criticism: 'the very scholars who have found it interesting enough to work on have been the first to assure us that it is dull'; 'Dullness and the Fifteenth Century', *English Literary History* 54.4 (1987), p. 761. Lawton argues, in ways which remind one of Fisher on Gower, that 'the dullness of the fifteenth century is a willed, self-conscious and ostensible dullness. It is the social mask of a Renaissance poet', p. 791.

Certainly critics did not turn aside from Gower in the twentieth century, simply because of his recourse to old stories; however, the inherited notion of schoolmasterly dullness may well have something to do with the tendency of many studies to stick fairly closely to the identification of sources and analogues – a glance at the 'Chronology of Criticism' with which this volume concludes will show just how prevalent such study was, particularly in the first half of the twentieth century. In the present collection, Cooper's essay cites Ben Jonson's warning that young readers spending long periods of time with Chaucer and Gower might 'fall too much in love with Antiquity'; the attitudes of succeeding generations to antiquity govern many post-medieval assessments of Gower's achievements.

Thus far we have seen later ages responding to Gower the storyteller; sometimes with praise for his narrative art, sometimes with unflattering comparisons between his use of his sources and Chaucer's – and the injunction to undergraduates to 'compare and contrast Gower's 'Tale of Florent' with Chaucer's *Wife of Bath's Tale'* tends to suggest that we have not moved as far beyond Ellis as we might like to think. But there is another problem in the emphasis – and I grant that it is a medieval as well as a later one – on Gower's stories. What happens to those works which are not built around stories? An emphasis on narrative fits awkwardly with such works as the *Vox Clamantis* and the *Cronica Tripertita*, for example. And further, what happens to Gower's careful framing of his stories in the *Confessio*? The tendency to overlook Gower's Latin, outlined in the section on language above, coupled with the emphasis, positive or negative, on Gower's storytelling, leaves the framing of the *Confessio* out of the discussion. Quite often, as my essay on Gower in print shows, that framing is literally left off the page. A significant movement in Gower criticism has been the return to a recognition of the importance of Gower's Latinity. In the present collection, Rigg and Moore, Wetherbee, and Peck all emphasise the Latin tradition of political poetry which Gower inherited and which clearly frames his work in the *Confessio*. Wetherbee shows how Gower mobilises the Boethian tradition, with its ongoing dialogue between poetry and the conventions that determine its role in medieval thought, to structure the *Confessio Amantis*. In his view, the failure of communication between Genius and Amans is an impasse between the Latin and vernacular traditions; thus Gower's use of Latin source material becomes, not mindless repetition, but a complex exploration of the outlines and limits of the authority of tradition. Similarly, Watt shows that the changes which Gower makes to his Latin source materials in his incest tales reflect careful refashioning of those materials to serve Gower's own emphasis on the primacy of personal responsibility, for both men and women.

As for Latin, so for French: recent criticism has also returned to Gower's French works and to Gower's debts to the French tradition. Yeager argues that the eclecticism and freedom which characterise Gower's use of source materials in the *Mirour de l'Omme* indicate his attempt to write a new poem – as Milton was later to do, he was, in effect, trying 'things unattempted yet in verse or rhyme'. For Butterfield, Gower found in the French tradition a central analogy – the Author as Lover – which allowed him entry into the *Confessio*'s exploration of poetics and authority. De Meun, Froissart, and Machaut, whom Butterfield argues all underpin Gower's creation, contribute differently to the destabilisation and problematisation of poetic authority which is central to the *Confessio*, and Gower's deft use of their differing resources, his sophisticated reworking of their central symbols, demonstrates the poet's complex relationship to his source materials. The contributors to this collection, in other words, show Gower engaging critically with his source materials as he explores what it means to be a poet. Ellis invited a reader to compare Chaucer and Gower under the heading of the use of sources; these readers have not come to the negative conclusion Ellis clearly expected.

### Chaucer's Gower

> And gret wel Chaucer whan ye mete,
> As mi disciple and mi poete:
> For in the floures of his youthe
> In sondri wise, as he wel couthe,
> Of Ditees and of songes glade,
> The whiche he for mi sake made,
> The lond fulfild is overal:
> Wherof to him in special
> Above alle othre I am most holde.
> For thi now in hise daies olde
> Thow schalt him telle this message,
> That he upon his latere age,
> To sette an ende of alle his werk,
> As he which is myn owne clerk,
> Do make his testament of love,
> As thou has do thi schrifte above,
> So that mi Court it mai recorde  (VIII.*2941–57)

The 'Chaucer greeting' at the end of the *Confessio Amantis* is another piece that has disappeared in the move from Ricardian to Henrician versions, but despite its demotion 'below the line' in Macaulay's edition, it has, like the envoy to *Troilus*, governed much of Gower's critical history. I have already had occasion to refer to many examples of the Chaucer-Gower pairing. These have been, by and large, conventionalised representations of poetic excellence. But there is also a long tradition of discussing the exact nature of the relationship between Chaucer and Gower. Readers of Elias Ashmole's curious *Theatrum Chemicum Britannicum* of 1652 might be surprised to read that Chaucer and Gower were both initiates in the hermetic arts, and that indeed the older Gower initiated his friend Chaucer into the mysteries:

> Now as Concerning *Chaucer* (the *Author* of this *Tale*) [the *Canon's Yeoman's Tale*] he is ranked amongst the *Hermetick Philosophers*, and his *Master* in this *Science* was Sir *John Gower*, whose familiar and neere acquaintance began at the *Inner Temple* upon *Chaucer's* returne into *England*.

> This *Piece* is the *Worke* of Sir *John Gower*, and Collected out of his *Booke* (I) *De Confessione Amantis*. He is placed in the *Register* of our *Hermetique Philosophers*:

and one that adopted into the Inheritance of this *Mistery*, our famous *English Poet, Geoffry Chaucer*.[53]

Ashmole's notes are unusual in dwelling as they do on an apparent non-poetic relationship between the two men, but in their assertion of a kind of discipleship they align with most portrayals of the relationship from the sixteenth century on. Fisher has pointed out that much of the discussion departed from a misreading of the Chaucer greeting; in Gower's poem, it is Venus who addresses Chaucer as her disciple, but in the Gower/Chaucer tradition, those words were soon understood to be Gower's own.[54] Once a mentor/apprentice relationship had been understood, it seemed inevitable that a comparison of the pupil with the master would follow. That comparison did not necessarily leave only one of the two poets behind. Alexander Chalmers, for example, while he was clear that 'as an English poet Gower was far inferior to his great contemporary',[55] had his doubts about the reception of Chaucer, too: 'His language will still remain an unsurmountable obstacle with that numerous class of readers to whom poets must look for universal reputation. Poetry is the art of pleasing; but pleasure, as generally understood, admits of very little that deserves the name of study.'[56] Nevertheless, generally speaking, Gower has come out of all such comparisons rather the worse for wear. Macaulay has argued that the tendency to link Chaucer and Gower, from the fifteenth century on, did the latter no good:

> The uncritical exaggeration of Gower's literary merits, which formerly pre-vailed, has been of some disadvantage to him in modern times. The comparison with Chaucer, which was so repeatedly suggested, could not but be unfavour-able to him; and modern critics, instead of endeavouring to appreciate fairly such merits as he has, have often felt called upon to offer him up as a sacrifice to the honour of Chaucer.[57]

The sacrifice is often made in an assessment of the poets' politics, as we have seen, but what I would stress here is the amount of critical energy devoted, es-pecially in the eighteenth and nineteenth centuries, to working out the exact nature of the personal relationship and particularly, to arguing as to whether or not the two men quarrelled. Evidence commonly offered for the latter position includes the omission of the Chaucer greeting in the Henrician version of the *Confessio*, and the remarks of the Man of Law about the 'wikke ensample' of

---

[53] Elias Ashmole, *Theatrum Chemicum Britannicum* (London, 1652), pp. 470, 484. Ashmole drew for his biographies of the poets on Thomas Speght's introduction to his 1598 edition of Chaucer; John Bale's *Catalogus Scriptorum Illustrium Maioris Brytannie* (Basle, 1557); John Pits's *De Illustribus scriptoribus Britanniae* (1619); and John Stow, citing both his *Survey of London* (1598) and his *Annales of England* (1600).

[54] See for example Fisher on William Thynne: 'All in all, Thynne did much to straighten out the Gower tradition. But at the same time, he reinforced Leland's misreading of the Chaucer greeting as an expression of Gower's own feelings, and brought to final expression the notion that Gower was Chaucer's mentor', *John Gower*, p. 18.

[55] Chalmers, *Works of the English Poets*, II.iii.

[56] Ibid., I.xv.

[57] Macaulay, *English Works*, I.ix–x.

Canacee, which he says Chaucer (unlike, we assume, Gower) refuses to tell.[58] What is important about this preoccupation is not merely that it tends, as Macaulay and Fisher have both rightly pointed out, to be decided in favour of Chaucer. It also matters that the focus on the Chaucer-Gower relationship over-emphasised the biographical in many early discussions of Gower. And once again, Gower may be said to have cooperated, even to have invited, the attention which subsequently caused him so much harm. His favoured poetic *personae* are first-person narrators. He delights in impersonation, whether as the 'voice of one crying' or as the poet who, as his Latin gloss to the opening of Book I of the *Confessio* famously announces, 'feigns himself to be a lover'.[59] He also continually tells us that he is old, or blind, or sick, or weak – Butterfield's essay explores how the various facets of Gower's *persona* in the *Confessio* contribute to his exploration of poetic authority. And he crafts a final mask – literally this time – in his tomb effigy and the associated instructions for his afterlife. Chaucer is of course also a master of masks; for a time some of his *personae* were taken at face value, and readers scoured his poetry for clues to his biography. But while the biographical impulse is not limited to Gower criticism, the relative thinness of the Gowerian critical tradition, alongside the powerful attraction of Chaucer, have tended together to magnify the effects of this kind of reading.

This collection does contain both some attention to biography and some attention to the legacy of the Chaucer-Gower pairing, but these have been refocused. In the first case – the biographical – Hines/ Cohen/ Roffey, Smith, and Epstein all emphasise Gower's specific place as a locus for understanding his work and his self-presentation. Southwark, the law courts, and the royal and noble courts are all shown to be important in 'placing' Gower in his proper relationship to the world through which Chaucer also moved – and to which he spoke rather differently than did his contemporary. As for the legacy of the Chaucer-Gower pairing, Cooper argues that it was not particularly important to the early modern period – though indeed its appearances could well work to Gower's advantage. Robert Greene, for example, stages a debate on the value of literature by means of a storytelling competition between Gower and Chaucer, a competition which Gower wins – because of his morality! Cooper also points out that Shakespeare treats Gower with unique distinction: the Gower of *Pericles* is the only source author whom Shakespeare makes a major figure in one of his plays. Finally, this Introduction also has occasional recourse to the comparison with Chaucer – for he, too, is part of Gower's context, both in the fourteenth century, and in all the centuries thereafter.

---

[58] Geoffrey Chaucer, *Canterbury Tales*, Prologue to *Man of Law*, line 78. The Man of Law notes that Chaucer also refused to tell the story of Apollonius; these tales are 'unkynde abhomynacions', line 88. See Fisher, *John Gower*, pp. 26–36, for the history of this particular strand of criticism, originating in Thomas Tyrwhitt's 1775–78 edition of Chaucer.

[59] '. . . fingens se auctor esse Amantem', at I.60. For discussion of this feigning, see Siân Echard, 'With Carmen's Help: Latin Authorities in the *Confessio Amantis*', *Studies in Philology* 95 (1998), pp. 1–41, and Ardis Butterfield, 'Articulating the Author: Gower and the French Vernacular Codex', *Yearbook of English Studies* 33 (2003), pp. 80–96.

# 1

# Iohannes Gower, Armiger, Poeta:
## Records and Memorials of his Life and Death

JOHN HINES, NATHALIE COHEN AND SIMON ROFFEY

## Biography

John Gower rightly commands the interest of posterity as a major late medieval author. We have, fortunately, now passed beyond the short and negative phase of critical fashion in which the Barthes-derived 'death of the author', a hangover of the Parisian egoism and nihilism of 1968, meant a blanket refusal to take any scholarly interest in the historical circumstances from which texts derived, least of all the biographies of their authors. It nevertheless remains a debatable point how far such information is relevant to literary study and appreciation, and the case for its importance has to be explored and made in every case. As with their literary output, so with their life records: a comparison between Gower and his more celebrated contemporary Geoffrey Chaucer is both inevitable and invidious. We have far less material on Gower, and what we have paints a considerably less colourful picture.[1] The most substantial surviving sources reflect Gower in his old age and the arrangements for his death and obsequies. Yet these are far from insignificant, in that they show us the man constructing an image and a role for himself, and attempting to control the posterity both of his mortal heritage and of his immortal soul. In Gower's case, the death of the author was truly a phenomenon that reinstates individuality and agency as central factors and topics. None of this can be irrelevant to the study of a creative artist.

Two previous works of modern scholarship have published and discussed what they called the Gower life records: G.C. Macaulay in the introduction to his edition of Gower's Latin writings in 1902, and John H. Fisher in a chapter of his historically structured critical study of Gower, published in 1964–65.[2] While Macaulay presented the original records in a thorough and methodical manner, Fisher sorted out some surprisingly naïve historical interpretations and suggestions by Macaulay to clarify Gower's family background (to the limited degree that was possible), and to make more sense of property dealings in the 1360s and

---

1   Cf. Derek Pearsall, *The Life of Geoffrey Chaucer*, Blackwell Critical Biographies I (Oxford, 1992).
2   G.C. Macaulay, ed., *The Complete Works of John Gower*, 4 vols (Oxford, 1900–02), Vol. IV: *The Latin Works*, pp. vii–xxx; John H. Fisher, *John Gower: Moral Philosopher and Friend of Chaucer* (New York, 1964; London, 1965), pp. 37–69. Macaulay's edition of Gower's works in English was simultaneously published as *The English Works of John Gower*, EETS, es nos. 81 and 82 (London, 1900–1901).

1370s. These constitute virtually the entirety of what we know about Gower until his serious writing career began with the *Mirour de l'Omme* of the middle to later 1370s.[3]

When and where Gower was born, and who his parents were, are all unknown to us. According to an epitaph on his tomb recorded in the late seventeenth century, he lived in the reigns of Edward III and Richard II, which implies that he was born after Edward's succession in 1327.[4] Past attempts to situate him genealogically have been confused by the existence of several Gower families in fourteenth-century records, none of them of any very special rank or historical importance, and therefore all of them imperfectly traceable in the surviving sources. The single most important clue on this question is the coat of arms associated with Gower, carved and painted on his tomb monument in what is now Southwark Cathedral, and also appearing in a manuscript of *Vox Clamantis* and the *Cronica Tripertita* that seems to have been being copied at the time of Gower's death in 1408.[5] The earliest description of the blazon on the tomb comes from Stow, in his *Survey of London* of 1598,[6] describing and identifying three gold leopards' heads on a blue chevron upon a silver field. These arms can also be associated with a Sir Robert Gower who died in 1349 and whose tomb in Brabourne, south-eastern Kent, they also adorn, as well as with a Gower family in the wapentake of Langbargh between Teesside and the Cleveland Hills in northern Yorkshire. The records associated with this family provide no information on the parentage and upbringing of John Gower the poet, but do identify him as the scion of a gentry family whose fortunes generally prospered through their involvement in military service and the baronial and royal politics of England and Scotland in the fourteenth century. Through his service to the Earl of Athol in the 1330s, Sir Robert Gower obtained significant property interests in manors in Suffolk, and holdings in both East Anglia and Kent were to remain a feature of Gower the poet's practical affairs.

While having a family background that would have conferred favourable connections and moderately high aspirations upon him, John Gower had no pre-ordained social role or station to succeed to, and had largely to make his own way in the world. This helps us to understand the diverse sequence of property deals recorded against his name from the 1360s to the 1380s – the earliest datable evidence of his life. In 1365 he purchased the manor of

---

3    To say this assumes that if Gower's *Cinkante Balades* are the *fols ditz d'amours* ('foolish poems of love') referred to as the poet's earlier compositions towards the end of *Mirour de l'Omme* (line 27,340), we can follow him in not counting them as products of his *serious* writing career. See Fisher, *John Gower*, pp. 70–88.

4    Richard Rawlinson, *The Natural History and Antiquities of the County of Surrey: Begun in the Year 1673, By John Aubrey, Esq; F.R.S. and Continued to the Present Time*, 5 vols (London, 1718–19), V.202–5. Remarkably, no early record of this epitaph includes the nine years Gower lived into the reign of Henry IV, although that king's reign has been added to it on the modern restoration of the tomb. Cf. John Stow, *A Survey of London*, ed. Charles Lethbridge Kingsford, rpt. from the text of 1603, 2 vols (Oxford, 1908), II.57–8; Mr Urban, 'On the Disregard paid to Ancient Monuments', *Gentleman's Magazine* 34 ([August] 1764), pp. 359–60; Richard Gough, *Sepulchral Monuments in Great Britain*, 2 vols (London, 1786–96), Vol. II, Part II, pp. 24–6 and pl. VIII, p. 25.

5    Glasgow, University Library Hunterian, MS T.2.17 ; Fisher, *John Gower*, pp. 38–41.

6    Stow, *Survey of London*, II.57–8.

Aldington Septvauns, apparently the place of that name in north Kent, not the archiepiscopal demesne close to Brabourne, taking care to proceed cautiously in a transaction where, as it proved, the question of whether or not the vendor was of age and therefore had a right to sell could be disputed. (This is the case in which Macaulay concluded that the John Gower concerned was a 'villainous misleader of youth', and therefore could not possibly be our moral poet!) It is highly plausible that part of the younger Gower's education would have taken place in the Inns of Court of London, and a famous reference in *Mirour de l'homme*, in which he declares that he wears a garment with striped sleeves, apparently as some form of recognisable professional garb, has reasonably been linked to the wearing of rayed garments in the law courts and taken as evidence that Gower pursued a legal career.[7] He was evidently a successful and affluent man in this period, as records indicate that he acquired (though he also sometimes disposed of) further property in Kent, London, Essex and East Anglia.

There is no sign, however, of his holdings outside London ever being more to him than an investment and security, and a source of income. Evidence of the London circles in which he moved appears from 1378, when he and Richard Forester, another London lawyer, took upon themselves a power of attorney for Chaucer when the latter had to spend the summer on an embassy to Bernabò Visconti in Milan.[8] The personal compliment implicit in this trust was made more explicit by Chaucer in the mid-1380s, when he dedicated his completed *Troilus and Criseyde* to 'moral Gower' and the 'philosophical Strode' – Ralph Strode, yet another London lawyer and man of letters.[9] By this date Gower might just have begun *Confessio Amantis*, but the epithet – if it was a literary-critical categorisation at all, rather than a personal evaluation – must refer to his *Mirour de l'Omme* and *Vox Clamantis*, a response to the Peasants' Revolt of 1381. Fisher conjectures that Gower had retired from his inferred legal career and taken up residence in the precincts of the priory of St Mary Overie in Southwark by the time he completed *Mirour de l'Omme* in the later 1370s.[10] That would have afforded him access to both a library and a scriptorium. It is, however, impossible to be certain how early Gower's close involvement with the priory may have begun, and what stages it may have passed through. Such arrangements were clearly not an absolute precondition for Gower's literary output, as the parallel career of Chaucer demonstrates.

In the 1380s and 1390s Gower most certainly was not cloistered away from the outside world and public life. The original version of the Prologue to *Confessio Amantis* contains the claim that the work was composed 'for King Richardes sake' at the bidding of Richard II, whom Gower ostensibly encountered by chance while passing along or across the Thames.[11] Exactly when such a commission may have been issued we cannot tell, let alone in what form it was

---

7   *Mirour de l'Omme*, lines 21,772–4; cf. Laura F. Hodges, *Chaucer and Costume: The Secular Pilgrims in the General Prologue* (Cambridge, 2000), pp. 101–25, esp. pp. 112–19.
8   Pearsall, *Life of Geoffrey Chaucer*, pp. 106–9.
9   *Troilus and Criseyde* V.1856–7; Fisher, *John Gower*, pp. 61–2; Pearsall, *Life of Geoffrey Chaucer*, pp. 133–4.
10  Fisher, *John Gower*, pp. 58–60.
11  Macaulay, *English Works*, Prol. 22–92*.

contrived, but we can at least be sure that it represents a relationship of royal notice and patronage which was accepted by the poet some time in the middle to later 1380s, as a date of 1390 appears in the margin of manuscripts of the earliest versions of the entire *Confessio*.[12] Fisher observed parallels between Chaucer's *Legend of Good Women* – in, for instance, the commission from a King and Queen of Love, and the requirement that the poet do penance – and argued that they therefore sprang from the same situation and so should have been started simultaneously. The composition of Chaucer's *Legend of Good Women* must follow that of *Troilus and Criseyde* and is generally accepted as dating to 1386–87.[13] The general agreement of dates and events here is unobjectionable, but we cannot assume an absolute synchronisation of the two poets' efforts, and that a single starting pistol set Chaucer off on the *Legend* and Gower on the *Confessio* at exactly the same time.

Between 1390 and 1393, and particularly in the period of 1392–93, when Richard II was involved in a bitter conflict with the authorities of the City of London, references within successive revisions of *Confessio Amantis* track Gower's withdrawal of support from the king and growing allegiance to Henry, Earl of Derby – later Duke of Lancaster and in 1399 to usurp the throne as King Henry IV. Late in 1393 Henry's own papers record the expense of replacing a collar for one Richard d'Ancaster because of a collar given to Gower – one that was previously in d'Ancaster's possession, we can surmise. The issuing of livery apparel and badges as marks of social allegiance was a common and significant practice of this period. Richard II's particular token at this time was his famous white hart symbol. Gower continued to be closely associated with this collar and the loyalty it implied. It was to appear in a portrait of Gower at the beginning of the Fairfax manuscript of *Confessio Amantis*,[14] and on his tomb effigy (below). On the latter it also carries a pendant jewel in the form of a swan, a motif adopted by Henry from 1380, reflecting his connection with an idealised Knight of the Swan through his marriage to Mary de Bohun.[15] Gower maintained his support for Henry in the *Cronica Tripertita* after the latter's seizure of the kingship, and was rewarded with an annual grant of two pipes of Gascon wine. Though we cannot identify Gower as a conspicuous dissident through the increasingly dangerous late years of Richard's reign in the 1390s, even a tacit and passive loyalty to Henry's cause would be a position requiring some courage, and may, as Fisher notes, explain a protective writ for Gower against a certain canon of the priory of St Mary Overie, issued in December 1397.[16]

Meanwhile, in 1398, Gower married a woman named Agnes Groundolf. This is recorded in a licence issued by the Bishop of Winchester, in whose diocese Southwark lay, permitting the marriage to take place in Gower's lodgings by St Mary's priory rather than at the parish church close by. There is no evidence that

[12] Macaulay, *English Works*, Prol. 331; ibid., Vol. I, pp. xxi–xxiii; Fisher, *John Gower*, pp. 116–22.
[13] Fisher, *John Gower*, pp. 235–50; Pearsall, *Life of Geoffrey Chaucer*, pp. 191–8.
[14] Oxford, Bodleian Library, MS Fairfax 3.
[15] Nigel Saul, 'The Commons and the abolition of badges', *Parliamentary History* 9 (1990), pp. 302–15, esp. pp. 307–8; Jonathan Alexander and Paul Binski, eds., *Age of Chivalry: Art in Plantagenet England* (London, 1987), pp. 487–8.
[16] Fisher, *John Gower*, p. 69.

Gower had been married before; no issue are referred to in his will. By this time Gower would have been an old man, certainly in his sixties, possibly around seventy. A prefatory verse epistle associated with a copy of *Vox Clamantis* sent to Thomas Arundel, Archbishop of Canterbury (1396–97 and 1399–1414), contains Gower's description of himself as old and blind, sick and wretched.[17] Old age and infirmity offer an ample explanation of all the arrangements for the wedding and marriage, if we understand that Agnes was to live with Gower in the priory precincts essentially in the capacity of nurse. An epitaph on her tomb, which once stood by Gower's in the priory church, referred to her charity and chastity.[18]

Agnes had to care for John Gower for more than ten years until he died. The date on the probate of his will is 24 October 1408. This will is the most extensive and detailed document that survives, linking Gower directly to his real and personal circumstances.[19] It provides unambiguous information on several significant matters. It demonstrates the arrangements he had made for the performance of his funeral and his commemoration, including burial within the priory church, in an already appointed place within the chapel of St John the Baptist. Bequests were made for funeral prayers to be said in the priory church and the conjoined parochial chapel of St Mary Magdalene – that of which Gower and his wife were parishioners – as well as in Southwark's three other parish churches. Further bequests specified are of a more charitable nature, to hospitals and leper houses in and around Southwark and London, although it is made explicit that these too were made in return for the prayers of those establishments. There are also material bequests to the church: vestments and a chalice are provided for the chapel of St John the Baptist, as well as a missal and a *martilogium* – a calendar recording the days for celebrating saints and other pious benefactors, provided on the condition that the donor (Gower) be remembered in the prayers every day. A chalice and vestments were also left for the separate oratory of his lodgings. More practical bequests were made to his widow: money, the rights to income from his property, furniture and some form of coverlet, cutlery, vessels and utensils. Agnes herself was one of six executors, who also included Sir Arnold Savage, another man with connections both in Kent and with the Inns of Court.

As has already been noted at intervals, the generally sparse and fragmentary records directly associated with Gower and deriving from his own lifetime are usefully supplemented by evidence from manuscripts of his works, and by the writings of antiquarians such as Leland and Stow from the sixteenth century and further scholars of the seventeenth and eighteenth centuries. These early

---

[17] Oxford, All Souls College, MS 98 (Macaulay, *Complete Works*, IV.1). As this manuscript contains the complete *Cronica Tripertita*, it must post-date Henry's accession and Arundel's restoration to the archbishopric.

[18] Macaulay, *Complete Works*, IV.lix, quoting unpublished papers of the sixteenth-century scholar, John Bale. An earlier sixteenth-century antiquarian, John Leland, on whom Bale otherwise largely depends for what he wrote about Gower, also testifies that Gower's wife was buried in the same church: John Leland, *De Scriptoribus Britannicis*, ed. Anthony Hall (Oxford, 1709), pp. 414–16.

[19] The Latin text of the will is printed by Gough, *Sepulchral Monuments in Great Britain*, pp. 25–6, and is translated by Macaulay, *Complete Works*, IV. xvii–xviii.

historians consistently link their anecdotes about Gower to references to, and partial descriptions of, his substantial tomb monument in the church of the priory of St Mary Overie, now Southwark Cathedral. These sources are the principal basis of the most recent restoration of the tomb, in 1958, which put it into the form in which it can be viewed today. As we can now show, in important respects this does allow us to approach the monument as an authentic representation of the memorial Gower himself arranged to have.

### Gower's Southwark and the Priory of St Mary Overie

Southwark Cathedral is situated south of the River Thames, opposite the formerly walled City of London (Figs 1 and 2). From the Dissolution (1540) until 1905 it was known as the parish church of St Saviour. The priory of St Mary on this site was founded in 1106, and was London's first Augustinian house.[20] On the opposite bank of the Thames, the houses of Holy Trinity and St Bartholomew were founded in 1107–08 and 1123 respectively.[21] Like many medieval religious foundations, the earlier history of the house of St Mary is obscure. Tradition has it that there was a nunnery on the site, founded in the seventh century and converted in the ninth century by St Swithun, Bishop of Winchester, into a secular college – a story that reflects the early association of the site with the diocese of Winchester.[22] The London palace of the Bishops of Winchester was located just to the west of the priory. Although archaeological excavations in the crypt of Southwark Cathedral and on surrounding sites have demonstrated Roman settlement in the area,[23] no indication of occupation of the site for most of the Anglo-Saxon period has yet been discovered. Excavations in Montague Close to the north of the priory church have produced evidence for occupation here during the late Saxon period, in the form of pits, and linear features that may be the remains of a timber-framed building.[24] Chalk walls observed in this area may also be features from the pre-Conquest period.[25] Whatever the earlier history of building here, the Domesday Book of 1086 records a *monasterium* on the site, said to have been in existence during the reign of Edward the Confessor (1042–66),[26] and it would appear that it was this establishment that was refounded as an Augustinian secular priory in 1106 by two Norman knights, William de Pont de l'Arche, Sheriff of Hampshire and Royal Treasurer, and

20  Henry Richards Luard, ed., *Annales Monastici*, Vol. III (London, 1866), p. 430.
21  John Schofield and Richard Lea, *Excavations at Holy Trinity Priory, Aldgate, London* (in prep., MoLAS Monograph Series); Mary Lobel, ed., *The City of London from Prehistoric Times to c. 1520* (Oxford, 1989), p. 86.
22  Stow, *Survey of London*, II, p. 56.
23  M. Hammerson, 'Excavations beneath the Choir of Southwark Cathedral', *London Archaeologist* 3 (1978), pp. 206–12.
24  D. Divers, 'Excavations at Southwark Cathedral' (unpublished post-excavation assessment report, Pre-Construct Archaeology, London, 2001), p. 47.
25  G.J. Dawson, 'Montague Close excavations 1969–73: Part 1 – A general survey', *Research Volume of the Surrey Archaelogical Society No. 3* (Guildford, 1976), pp. 37–59 (p. 49).
26  It is listed amongst the holdings of the Bishop of Bayeux in Kingston Hundred, linked to a 'tideway' (*aque fluctu[s]*): John Morris, ed. and trans., *Domesday Book. 3: Surrey* (Chichester, 1975), fol. 32a.

William Dauncey. By the early 1120s this was transformed from a secular foundation to a regular house of canons, following a more formalised monastic rule, probably under the influence of William Giffard, then Bishop of Winchester.[27]

Recent analysis of the surviving medieval fabric of the cathedral building has suggested that the priory was subjected to a building campaign from the second quarter of the twelfth century, which included the construction of the cloister to the north and extensive rebuilding of parts of the church, namely extensions at both the eastern and western ends.[28] It has been suggested that this work was carried out after the style of the French-influenced 'Canterbury' school of architecture.[29]

In 1207, however, a disastrous fire destroyed much of this new work, leading to a further, prolonged building campaign, which was still incomplete at the end of the thirteenth century.[30] That century also saw the construction of the parochial chapel of St Mary Magdalene on the south side of the priory church, a foundation of Peter des Roches, Bishop of Winchester from 1205 to 1243.[31] In addition to the destruction of parts of the priory by fire, its riverside location rendered the priory buildings vulnerable to encroachments by the Thames. The structure as it survives today shows evidence of subsidence in several places, and the excavations in Montague Close revealed traces of flood damage from two separate inundations in the early and later thirteenth century.[32] Disaster struck again in the 1390s when fire damaged the south transept and parts of the choir. This was repaired under the direct supervision of Cardinal Henry Beaufort, Bishop of Winchester.[33] It was during the fourteenth century that the priory became known as St Mary Overie ('over the river'), encapsulating its relationship to the City of London. In 1469 the nave roof collapsed and was rebuilt in timber. One of the surviving fifteenth-century roof bosses carries a rebus containing the elements 'burr' and 'tun', referring to the contemporary prior Henry Burton (1462–86). There were formerly many examples of this type of imagery on the roof bosses.[34]

In 1539, Bartholomew Linsted, the last prior, surrendered the building to King Henry VIII, and he and the remaining twelve canons were pensioned off. The priory church then became, by Act of Parliament, the parish church of St Saviour. By the early seventeenth century the church and the former monastic buildings had fallen into decay. Some alterations and repair work were conse-

---

[27] Simon Roffey, 'The early history and development of St Marie Overie Priory, Southwark: the twelfth century chapel of St John', *London Archaeologist* 8 (1998), pp. 255–62 (p. 260).

[28] A report on the recent programme of archaeological investigations at Southwark Cathedral by N. Cohen, D. Divers, C. Mayo and S. Roffey is in preparation (Pre-Construct Archaeology Monograph Series).

[29] W.R. Lethaby, 'The cloister of Southwark Priory and other early cloisters', *Archaeological Journal* 71 (1914), pp. 155–60.

[30] Luard, *Annales Monastici*, p. 451.

[31] Martha Carlin, *Medieval Southwark* (London, 1996), p. 20.

[32] Dawson, 'Montague Close excavations 1969–73', p. 50.

[33] Carlin, *Medieval Southwark*, pp. 70–2. The arms of Cardinal Beaufort are preserved on the eastern side of the south transept of the cathedral and their presence probably reflects the cardinal's involvement. The building style of the south transept also implies early fifteenth-century construction.

[34] F.T. Dollman, *The Priory of St Mary Overie* (London, 1881), p. 6.

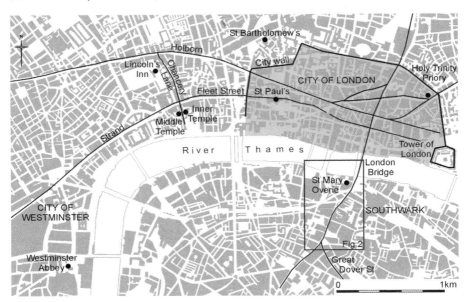

Figure 1. The Cities of Westminster and London, and the suburb of Southwark, in the time of Gower. Prepared by Jon Sygrave; copyright Museum of London Archaeology Service (MOLAS).

quently carried out by the parishioners during the seventeenth and eighteenth centuries,[35] but it was not until the nineteenth century that the church was thoroughly restored. Renovation began at the east end of the former priory church in 1818–23, and the chapel of St Mary Magdalene was demolished at this time.[36] In 1838 the now roofless nave was pulled down and rebuilt by Henry Rose.[37] This was subsequently replaced by a new nave in the Victorian Gothic style, designed by Sir Arthur Bloomfield and built by Thomas Rider (1890–97). In 1905, diocesan reorganisation saw the parish church become a cathedral and regain its earlier dedication as the Cathedral and Collegiate Church of St Saviour and St Mary Overie.

During the period of Gower's residence here in the late fourteenth and early fifteenth centuries, the priory was at the heart of a growing and affluent Southwark. Formally under the control of the Bishop of Winchester, Southwark's character was that of an alternative, and somewhat counter-cultural, suburb of the Cities of London and Westminster. Here, on the south bank of the Thames, across London Bridge and at the starting point for the pilgrims' route to Canterbury, were four parish churches (of St Mary Magdalene, St Olave, St Margaret and St George) and the priory hospital of St Thomas, to all of which Gower made bequests. Of these, St Margaret's and St Mary Magdalene's belonged to

---

[35] Ibid., p. 16.
[36] Royal Commission on Historical Monuments (England), *London: East*, Vol. 5 (London, 1930), p. 59.
[37] Bridget Cherry and Nikolaus Pevsner, *'London, 2: South'*, The Buildings of England (Harmondsworth, 1983), p. 564.

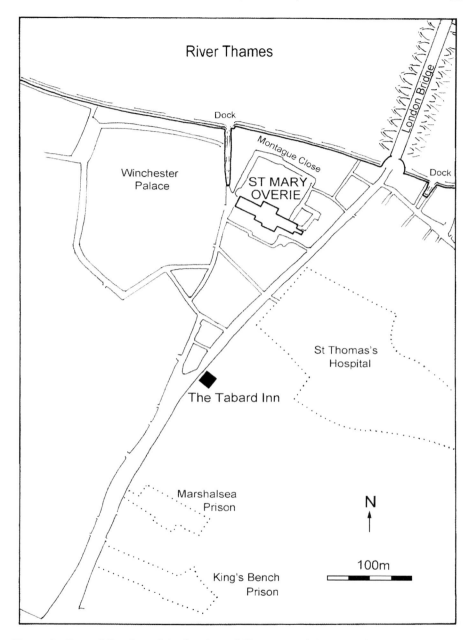

Figure 2. Central Southwark in the time of Chaucer and Gower. After Carlin, *Medieval Southwark*.

the priory. St Margaret's appears to be a foundation linked to the early history of the priory, as Bishop William Giffard (1107–29) certified the priory's owner-ship.[38]

The establishment of major ecclesiastical residences such as the sumptuous palace of the Bishop of Winchester from the thirteenth century onwards had encouraged further residential development, and a distinctive feature of four-teenth-century Southwark was the acquisition of houses by lay magnates and gentry. The construction of a moated residence known as 'Le Rosere' in Horselydown to the east of the priory by Edward II in 1324–25 encouraged knights, earls, countesses and other peers of the realm to purchase property in Southwark.[39] Residences established here during these centuries included those of the Earl of Surrey, the Abbots of Battle, Beaulieu, Waverley, Hyde and St Augustine's Canterbury, and the Prior of Lewes.[40]

The population of the area in the late fourteenth and early fifteenth centuries was gradually recovering from the devastating effects of the Black Death. The nature of local trade and industry was changing too: the expensive and cumber-some tide-mills of the Southwark shore were falling out of use, although the 1381 Poll Tax return still recorded a large percentage of householders described as 'Victuallers' – a category which included millers.[41] During the fourteenth century the High Street began to take the form that still survives, to an extent, today, with the establishment of inns and hostelries. Other industries in the area included those more 'anti-social' occupations characteristic of medieval suburbs, such as tanning. In all, more than a hundred different occupations were listed, including prostitution, for which the Bankside area was to become notorious. Southwark also had five prisons by the late Middle Ages: the Marshalsea, the King's Bench, the Counter, the White Lion (Surrey County Prison) and the Clink. Here also was London's largest immigrant population, mainly Dutch and German, many of them escaping legal and guild-based discrimination in the city.[42] And here, at the heart of this social melting pot, was the priory, the setting for many major social as well as religious events, such as the marriage of Edmund, Earl of Kent, to the daughter of the Duke of Milan in 1406.

It is likely that the house in which Gower lodged was in the western part of the priory precinct, close to the main gate and the Thames shoreline. Ease of access to this gate and to the dock of St Mary Overie (now St Saviour's Dock), also to the west, seems to have meant that this was the part of the priory precinct used to lodge important visitors and residents. Later (sixteenth-century) docu-mentary and cartographic sources depict the area as one of 'lofty and important' houses.[43]

The construction and siting of Gower's tomb, and the other funerary and

38  Carlin, *Medieval Southwark*, p. 89.
39  Dick Bluer, 'Excavations at Abbots Lane, Southwark', *London Archaeologist* 7 (1993), pp. 59–66 (p. 61).
40  Carlin, *Medieval Southwark*, pp. 26–8.
41  Ibid., p. 170.
42  Ibid., pp. 136–67.
43  W. Taylor, *Annals of St Mary Overy: An Historical and Descriptive Account of St Saviour's Church and Parish* (London, 1833), p. 133.

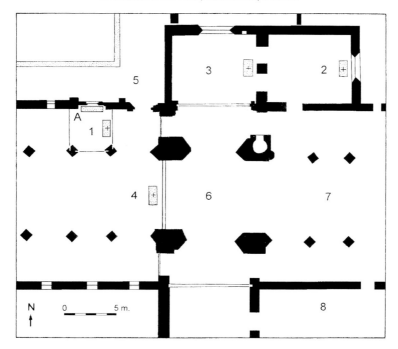

Figure 3. Plan of the interior of Southwark Cathedral, formerly the priory church of St Mary Overie. Drawn by Simon Roffey.

1: The Chapel of St John the Baptist; A: Gower's tomb. 2: Chapel of St John the Evangelist. 3: Chapel of St Peter. 4: Nave altar and rood screen. 5: Cloister. 6: Choir. 7: Sanctuary. 8: Chapel of St Mary Magdalene.

commemorative provisions revealed in his will, provide a fine insight into the operation of the late medieval chantry system. A chantry was essentially the foundation and endowment of a Mass by one or more benefactors, to be celebrated at an altar for the souls of the founders and other specified persons. The most splendidly and expensively endowed chantries had purposely constructed chapels, such as that of Henry Beaufort himself in Winchester Cathedral from the early fifteenth century,[44] whilst many, as apparently in the case of Gower, used existing altars.

The chapel of St John the Baptist was situated at the eastern end of the north aisle of the nave. It is almost certain that this chapel existed prior to the foundation of the Gower chantry. It is also quite possible that the tomb had been constructed and put in place before Gower's death. This was not a particularly unusual phenomenon for that time: many chantries of the Bishops of Winchester in Winchester Cathedral were constructed and in use before the decease of the founder. The practice can be understood in terms of the provision of a *memento mori*: a context for pious reflection, prayer and Eucharistic worship, focusing particularly on the nexus of death and salvation.

[44] G.H. Cook, *Medieval Chantries and Chantry Chapels* (London, 1947), pp. 89–96.

The chapel was likely to have been screened, probably with a wooden parclose, and its altar would have been on the eastern side (Fig. 3). It is also likely that the chantry was served by one of the existing priory canons, possibly one who already had special responsibility for the chapel of St John the Baptist, and the first priest may indeed have been known to the poet himself. Compared with, say, the bishops' chantries in Winchester Cathedral, Gower's chantry might appear modest. Apart from the impact of the tomb and its distinctive features (below), there would have been little to distinguish this from several other examples of the period. However, the location of the chapel itself is of interest. Spatial analysis of chantry altars and chapels and their visual associations can reveal much about the role of chantries in pre-Reformation society, and about their place in the church as a whole.[45]

Although the majority of chantries were ritual and physical monuments of private piety focused on individualised intercession, chantries often had a more public role. Charitable provision was frequently a feature of their endowments, as in Gower's case. Some chantry chapels were endowed and sponsored by guilds, as in the case of the chapel of St John the Baptist in St Laurence's parish church, Ludlow (Shropshire), maintained by the Palmers' Guild of the town.[46] The location of the chantries, which was often in the nave aisles or side chapels of churches, could also bring the mysteries of Christ's Passion closer to the worshippers by moving the celebration of the Mass, that most vital of Christian rites, out of the exclusive confines of the choirs and chancels and into the body of the church itself. Often the chantry would be the site of the 'morrow Mass' – a Mass held at dawn and attended largely by those who would be working during the day, when the High Mass was normally celebrated. It may therefore have been the performance of the ritual witnessed by a considerable majority of the laity. Thomas Berthelette reported that Gower's Mass was still said daily, and his yearly obit read, in 1532.[47]

The chantry was an embodiment and a focus of both public and private piety, and its primary function presupposed the formation of a relationship between the founder and a wider public: a relationship using the Mass as its pivotal ritual medium. The foundation of chantries multiplied the provision of Masses in a period when Eucharistic rituals and their associated doctrine were becoming especially prominent.[48] The prayers of the community were relied upon by the dead: the more prayers, the more powerful the intercession. In return, the public benefited from the spiritual efficacy and protection of the Mass.

[45] Simon Roffey, 'Deconstructing a symbolic world: the Reformation and the English medieval parish chantry', *The Archaeology of Reformation: 1480–1580*, Society for Post-Medieval Archaeology Monograph 1, eds. David Gaimster and Roberta Gilchrist (Leeds, 2003), pp. 341–55.

[46] Michael Faraday, *Ludlow 1085–1660: A Social, Economic and Political History* (Chichester, 1991), pp. 77–95; Christian Liddy, 'The Palmers' gild window, St Lawrence's [*sic*] Church, Ludlow: a study in the construction of gild identity in medieval stained glass', *Transactions of the Shropshire Archaeological and Historical Society* 72 (1997), pp. 26–37.

[47] Thomas Berthelette, 'To the reder', 2–4 [unnumbered pages] in *Jo. Gower de Confessione Amantis* (London, 1532).

[48] J. Bossy, 'The Mass as a social institution 1200–1700', *Past and Present* 100 (1983), pp. 29–61.

The placing of the altar at which the chantry was performed was therefore of prime importance. The chapel of St John the Baptist in which Gower was commemorated would have been highly visible and accessible to the most public areas of the nave. It was also next to what is now known as the prior's doorway – the main entrance to the body of the church from the cloister. The chapel and tomb would therefore be passed and noticed by the brothers as they filed through for their regular daily observances within the church. The power of the tomb as memorial and of the chantry as a vehicle for intercession would then be enhanced by the obligatory attention, and hoped-for respect, of the religious community.

No less important was the internal layout of chantry chapels themselves – the placing of tombs and memorials such as heraldic devices on conspicuous lines of direct sight, often juxtaposed with the altar or with other symbols or imagery of an intercessionary character. In the case of Gower, the tomb itself must have been immediately alongside the altar, with a heraldic device at the eastern end of the tomb recess visible to the altar's left. It is possible that the window above the tomb was inserted or replaced during Gower's lifetime to act as a suitable backdrop to the tomb and chapel. Drawings of the nave before its demolition in the nineteenth century show a window slightly different in design to that which was constructed during the Victorian restoration, and late fourteenth- or early fifteenth-century in style. This could have contained some form of memorial glass.[49] Dollman also records a fragment of an altar said to have been associated with the chapel of St John the Baptist, and a panel and niche that may testify to the reworking of one of the aisle piers in order further to distinguish the chantry area at the same date.[50]

All that now survives of the chapel is the tomb, discussed in more detail in the next section. The aisled nave in which it was situated was totally rebuilt in the late nineteenth century. However, the form and layout of the Victorian reconstruction reflect those of the fifteenth century. While this rebuilding was in progress the tomb-monument was removed to the south transept, and it was moved back to its original position and restored in 1894 by the poet's then namesake, Earl Gower.

The priory church constructed in the twelfth and thirteenth centuries included an aisled nave of seven bays, a central crossing tower, and north and south transepts. Both transepts may originally have had projecting chapels, of which one still survives in the form of the Harvard Chapel off the north transept. This was originally built with an apsidal end and was later converted into a square-ended chapel. Any chapel on the south side would have been demolished to make way for the construction of the parochial chapel of St Mary Magdalene. The eastern end of the church was probably also originally apsidal in form, later replaced by an aisled square-ended choir of five bays and the three-bay retrochoir or ambulatory. An important detail is that the bays of the nave aisle arcades are not of consistent size. This strongly supports the belief that not only does the Victorian rebuilding mirror the building's medieval

[49] Dollman, *Priory of St Mary Overie*, pl. 13.
[50] Ibid., p. 37.

proportions, but also that the chapel of St John the Baptist was in existence prior to the establishment of the Gower chantry. The fact that the tomb fits precisely into its current location suggests that its dimensions were dictated by the original proportions of the chapel, and further that it was put back into the correct location after the rebuilding and its restoration. The bay in which the tomb is located (see Fig. 4) is in fact the narrowest of the whole nave aisle, measuring 4.10m E.–W. from the centre of the first pier to that of the second.

## Gower's Tomb

Gower's tomb is represented by a carved stone monument, 4.06m high, 2.44m broad and 0.85m deep. It was first described in detail by John Stow at the end of the sixteenth century, and our earliest drawing of it was published in volume II of Richard Gough's *Sepulchral Monuments* in 1796.[51] The whole monument takes the form of a three-arched recess above a tomb-chest or altar-tomb, upon which lies a supine effigy of the deceased, clothed in a long, buttoned tunic and with his hands held above his chest in prayer. His feet lie upon a lion and his head is pillowed by three books. The upper edge of the tomb carries the painted Latin epitaph noted above as first recorded in the late seventeenth century, and now reconstructed as:

> Hic iacet I. Gower Arm. Angl. Poeta celeberrimus ac huic sacro edificio benefac. insignis. Vixit temporibus Edw. III et Ric. II et Henr. IV

> [Here lies John Gower, Esquire, a most famous English poet and distinguished benefactor of this building. He lived in the reigns of Edward III, Richard II and Henry IV.]

On the back panel of the recess above the effigy, Berthelette, followed by Stow, records the depiction of three maidens, identified as the virtues of Charity, Mercy and Pity, and associated with three Old French couplets:

> En toy que es fitz de dieu le pere
> Sauvé soit, que gist souz cest piere.
>
> (Charitie)
>
> [In Thee who art the Son of God the Father
> may he who lies beneath this stone be saved.]
>
> O bone Jesu fait ta mercy
> Al alme, dont le corps gist icy.
>
> (Mercye)
>
> [O good Jesus, show Thy mercy
> to the soul whose body lies here.]
>
> Pur ta pité Jesu regarde
> Et met cest alme en sauve garde.
>
> (Pite)
>
> [For your pity, Jesus, take heed,
> and place this soul in [Thy] safe-keeping.]

---

[51] Stow, *Survey of London*, Vol. II, pp. 57–8.

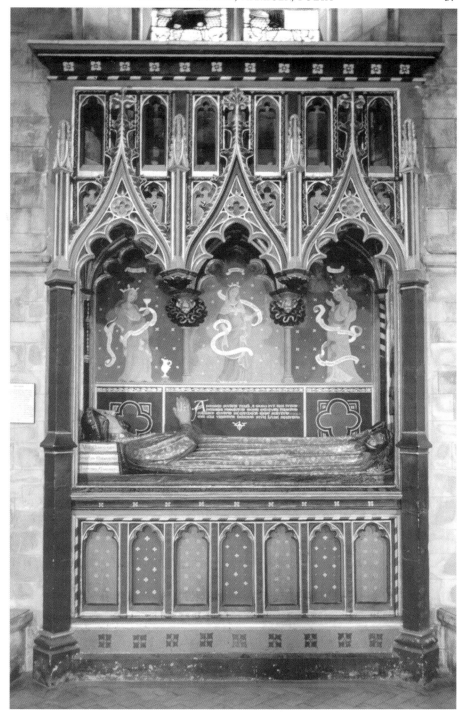

Figure 4. The tomb of John Gower, January 2003. Photograph: John Hines.

Below these on the same wall is now painted a set of four Latin hexameters, verses that are found in the manuscript of Gower's *Vox Clamantis* and other Latin works dated to around the time of his death,[52] and which Stow also indicated were found on the tomb:

> Armigeri scutum nichil ammodo fert sibi tutum.
> Rediddit immo lutum morti generale tributum.
> Spiritus exutum se gaudeat esse solutum.
> Est ubi virtutum regnum sine labe statutum.

> [The shield of the armed man now brings no safety to him.
> Rather, the clay has paid the common tributes to death.
> The spirit may rejoice to be freed from the exhausted corpse.
> It is in the realm of virtues established not to fail [*or* spotless].][53]

The side wall at the eastern end of the recess, above the feet, carries the carved achievement of arms, the painted symbols on which were also recorded by Stow. The blazon (shield) is, as one would expect, surmounted by a helm and crest, crowned by a talbot (a form of hunting dog). Rawlinson, in 1719, recorded that the arms were flanked by angels as supporters – presumably painted figures that have since been obliterated. Stow also records that the effigy had brown hair, long to his shoulders and curling up, a purple garment (recorded as 'scarlet' by Rawlinson and Urban, but purple again by Gough), and that the collar 'of Esses' was gold. He describes the effigy as having a forked beard, of which there is now no sign, although it is still depicted in Gough's engraving of the end of the eighteenth century. Stow's later *Annales of England* testifies that the maidens on the back panel had been painted over and the nose and hands of the effigy struck off.[54] This could have taken place by 1600; the damage and defacement have since been restored. There is a remarkable diversity of descriptions of the chaplet around the poet's head. Leland described it as an ivy wreath, appropriate to a poet; Stow 'like a coronet of foure Roses'; Rawlinson as 'a Chaplet, or Diadem of Gold ... on which are set at equal Distances, four white Quaterfoyles'. It is now a plain band, with no detectable signs of carved ivy leaves, with five rosettes (one of which is hidden at the back of the effigy) painted red. The state of the stone beneath its present paint layer would reveal the full extent of modification and repairs to the tomb that have been undertaken over the centuries, but such investigation remains to be undertaken.

Despite the uncertainties over the precise form and decoration of the original tomb, we can identify and discuss several important elements of its symbolism and significance. The tomb would have filled the recessed space between the piers in the north wall of the chapel in which it stood, close by the altar (Fig. 3),

---

[52] Hunterian MS T.2.17; Fisher, *John Gower*, pp. 38–41.
[53] The grammar of these verses is rendered particularly convoluted by the internal rhyme on *-utum* in each line, and a number of alternative translations could be offered.
[54] John Stow, *Annales*, s.a. 1400. Edition consulted: *Annales, or, A Generall Chronicle of England. Begun by Iohn Stow: Continued and Augmented with matters Foreigne and Domestique, Ancient and Moderne, unto the end of this present yeare, 1631, By Edmund Howes, Gent.* (London, 1631), p. 326.

and would thus have dominated the chapel itself, as it was intended to. It constituted an unambiguous statement of the wealth and importance of the man
commemorated, and was a physical embodiment of his connection with the
place – one, indeed, that was commensurate· with the quantitative value of his
investment in that church, as is explicitly recorded in the epitaph. As indicated
by the introduction to the chantry phenomenon, above, the appropriation of the
physical and ritual space of the church, and of commanding visual positions
both from which to see and in which to be seen, was a dynamic and major
element in medieval church archaeology and architecture. A closely comparable
parallel of equal interest from the perspective of medieval English studies was
the anchoritic movement, with the imposition of anchor-cells on a number of
parish churches.

The religious symbolism of the tomb is rich but unremarkable. There is a
particularly strong emphasis upon triplets, as in the three arches of the canopy, a
large number of trefoil mouldings, and even the three maidens, with obvious
Trinitarian implications. The three books beneath the poet's head extend this
theme in a neat manner. The cross, too, is of course properly represented: not
just in quatrefoils above the three arches, but nicely too in the patterns of rosette
bosses placed at the intersections of the ribs of the vaults above the tomb-effigy,
and which the recumbent figure thus seems to contemplate. The symbolic
significance of the seven panels in the front side of the tomb-chest may originally have been made explicit by figures painted in them – possibly seven
Virtues[55] – but we have no record of anything that was depicted here.

The helm, crest and blazon that make up the achievement of arms at the foot
end make direct allusion to the strong tradition of constructing similar tombs for
lay men and women of high rank, usually presented in effigy as knights in
armour and their ladies. These details emphasise the secular status of the man
entombed and commemorated, as well as asserting the dignity of his own family
line. A recent study has noted that conspicuous tomb-monuments such as this
are often associated with men who died without an heir, so that the assertion of
the lineage in fact coincides with its effective demise.[56]

The production of sculpted secular funerary effigies reached a peak in the
fourteenth century. That the figure lies supine, in prayer, and with his feet upon
a lion (the devil trampled under foot) are common features. That the head rests
upon the stack of three volumes is, by contrast, a peculiar and special allusion to
Gower's adopted identity as a writer.[57] Stow and all the subsequent antiquaries
record the books as being labelled, in order, as *Speculum Meditantis*, *Vox
Clamantis* and *Confessio Amantis* – the order, indeed, of their composition. On the
tomb as now repainted the *Vox* is at the top, above the *Speculum* and followed by

---

55  Cf. Anne-Marie Bouché, 'The Spirit in the world: the Virtues of the Floreffe Bible frontispiece:
    British Library, Add. Ms. 17738, fols 3v–4r', *Virtue and Vice: The Personifications in the Index of
    Christian Art*, ed. Colum Hourihane (Princeton, NJ, 2000), pp. 42–65 (p. 46).
56  Brian and Moira Gittos, 'Motivation and choice: the selection of medieval secular effigies',
    *Heraldry, Pageantry and Social Display in Medieval England*, eds. Peter Coss and Maureen Keen
    (Woodbridge, 2002), pp. 143–67, esp. pp. 144–5.
57  See John Hines, *Voices in the Past: English Literature and Archaeology* (Woodbridge, 2004),
    pp. 127–36.

the *Confessio*. All three of these titles occur in a Latin colophon to the *Confessio Amantis*; in the earliest versions of that colophon from 1390, however, *Speculum Hominis* ('The Mirror of Man' = *Mirour de l'Omme*) is found: this was changed to *Speculum Meditantis* ('The Mirror of One Thinking') by the 1392–93 versions. As Leland noted, there is an elegant grammatical harmony between these three titles (head noun plus genitive singular of the present participle) that forms them into a triad: a model course, perhaps, from contemplation, through crying in anxiety and as a warning, before reaching true love; and also from reflection to confession.

Leland also perceived and commented on the symbolism of two items of Gower's dress: the chaplet around his head, which he described as an ivy crown interset with roses, and the collar. These he interpreted as the insignia of the poet and the knight respectively. The collar, as we have noted, does represent secular allegiance and service, to Henry, Earl of Derby, later King Henry IV. The chaplet has five rosettes on it, which might be interpreted in many ways, for instance as the five wounds of Christ borne constantly in the pious man's mind – not least as identical rosettes form crosses before the same pious figure's eyes. The chaplet now bears a further prayer for the soul of the deceased, included in Gough's illustration: *D[o]m[inu]s merci Ih[esu]s*. The dress of the figure is otherwise simple: a body-length tunic, buttoned down the front. Although it has enough folds in it to convey amplitude and a basic sense of realism, it is presented in a distinctly shapeless style. The garment itself is an entirely appropriate one for a professional, clerical layman: knights of this date are typically portrayed in armour, and churchmen in vestments. On the evidence of Stow's account, this garment was probably sumptuously painted from the beginning. Other than that, however, the emphasis in this element of the effigy would appear to lie on material simplicity of life; perhaps a simplicity deliberately espoused despite the means that were evidently at the dead man's disposal.

While rich in the visual symbolism and imagery characteristic not only of late medieval Christian art but of the material culture of that time generally, in keeping with the particular commemoration of Gower as a writer there are several different texts to read on the monument. These are all either quoted or alluded to in records from the sixteenth century, and we can cautiously take them all to have been original. If they are all, like the four Latin hexameters, Gower's compositions, they reflect his full submission to conventional Christian expressions and sentiments towards the end of his life. The French couplets associated with the maidens are straightforward, if eloquent, prayers for mercy and salvation. The hexameters draw a thoughtful and suitable contrast between the limited protection afforded by the knight's shield and worldly dignity, and the joy of the soul removed to the secure Kingdom of Heaven. Again, though, this sentiment simply demands acceptance and compliance: it neither seeks nor provokes surprise, thought or even admiration in the critical reader.

The tomb thus represents a range of facets of a contemporary perception of Gower; several, perhaps all of them, his own model of how he saw himself, or wished to be portrayed. The tomb has to be understood as a thoroughly pious, and in that sense humble, monument: it reflects the ageing medieval poet's intense desire to do all that he could to intercede for his soul after death and ensure his salvation. Yet it could be proud and secular at the same time – revealing for us the complexity of categories in medieval ideology and culture, not a damning inconsistency at the heart of Gower's actions. At the heart of that complexity are the particular needs of a pious layman seeking to secure his place within a divinely ordained scheme of things, represented on Earth, where his mortal life was lived, by the Church. He clearly believed that he could accommodate his career as a public writer within that order. His tomb continued to advertise both his consciousness of his personal identity as an author, and his desire to address all constituencies of the reading public he knew: clerical and lay, Francophone and Anglophone.

Chaucer's selection of the Tabard Inn in Southwark High Street as the starting point of his Canterbury pilgrimage can be explained as an entirely realistic and pragmatic matter. Nevertheless, the special suburban character of Southwark – its proximity to the Cities of London and Westminster, and yet its freedom from the control of the city authorities; plus the sense of division created by the river, not least when Southwark was also the natural node of routes to London Bridge from the prosperous south, reflected in the cluster of magnates' houses there – saw it add to that the character of a special literary and artistic quarter which it retains to the present day. This is especially manifest in the Elizabethan period, when the great new theatres such as the Swan, Rose and Globe succeeded to the bear pits there. Southwark Cathedral also houses monuments to Philip Henslowe, the Elizabethan and Jacobean theatre-owner, the playwrights John Fletcher and Philip Massinger, and Shakespeare's brother Edmund. Gower the literary artist, who increasingly became a character in his own compositions and who carefully organised his own late days and obsequies, rightly recognised this area as a suitable and ready stage on which he could perform the final acts of this life, just as he wished to.

# 2

## London, Southwark, Westminster: Gower's Urban Contexts

### ROBERT EPSTEIN

One of the most familiar images of John Gower appears at the beginning of some of the earliest manuscripts of *Vox Clamantis*.[1] Gower is shown drawing back a bow to aim an arrow at the world, which hovers before him like a spheroid piñata (Fig. 2, p. 85). Frequently reproduced, in manuscript as well as print, the image has seemed to many of Gower's readers an apt depiction of the author. It gives him a distinctly gaunt and world-weary appearance, and it captures the dogged and pointed nature of his satire, the universality of its vision and the imperiousness of its opinions. The image is made even more appropriate, though, by a coincidence of medieval artistic convention. Though the entire globe is Gower's target, he stands on an indeterminate piece of turf. He defines himself through his profound and intense engagement with the world, and yet, at the same time, he stands in some ill-defined position apart from it. He is of the world, but he is not in it.

Gower seems to have lived nearly his entire life in and around the City of London and to have composed his voluminous work there, constantly taking the measure of the world and responding to it. While the poetry is always politically engaged, though, Gower himself can often seem to stand at a remove, particularly from the life of the city. This chapter seeks to take account of Gower's urban environment as well as its presence in, and its more conspicuous absence from, his written work.

### London

London in the fourteenth century resembled in size and in commercial traffic major cities of northern Europe like Cologne and Ghent.[2] In England, it had no rivals, being three times larger and perhaps five times wealthier than its nearest

---

1    The illustration occurs in Glasgow, University Library, Hunterian MS T.2.17 and London, British Library, MS Cotton Tiberius A.iv, both of them associated with Gower's scriptorium, and in many manuscripts derived from them. See John H. Fisher, *John Gower: Moral Philosopher and Friend of Chaucer* (New York, 1964), pp. 145–7, and Derek Pearsall's essay in this volume.
2    Derek Keene, 'Medieval London and its Region', *The London Journal* 14 (1989), pp. 99–111 (p. 102).

competitors, Bristol and York.[3] International trade, sponsored by a large and
dynamic merchant class, gave it diversity and continental sophistication as well
as prosperity.[4] Just as important to the growth of the city, though, was the
ever-expanding 'public sector'. Traditionally, the business of the crown was
conducted by branches of the 'royal household'. Its home was in the court, and
the court was wherever the king was. Gradually, these various functions of royal
administration developed into established bureaucracies.[5] By the 1340s, the judicial and administrative branches – the Exchequer, the Court of Common Pleas,
the Chancery – had settled permanently into homes in Westminster.[6] There, with
the inexorability explained by Weber, they expanded, becoming an integral
portion of the economy of greater London.[7] Just as inevitably, the legal profession grew up to serve the royal courts as well as the criminal, administrative and
commercial proceedings of the city. Lawyers and clerks clustered around Chancery Lane on the Westminster-London line of the ward of Farringdon Without
(that is, outside the western walls of the city), and it was there in mid-century
that the first Inns of Court, Lincoln's Inn and the Temple, were founded.[8]

When John Gower came to London, probably in the 1360s, this nexus of
commerce, royal service, public administration and law provided him with both
a livelihood and his first audience. The precise nature of Gower's occupation is
not certain, but references in his poetry and his life records point to the world of
law.[9] It would seem that he spent his London years overseeing transactions of
land and wealth while accumulating a good bit of his own.

The city also generated a critical mass of readers sufficient to support a
vernacular literary culture. In particular, Gower's texts may have found an
important early audience through his connection to the legal culture of Chancery Lane. Kathryn Kerby-Fulton and Steven Justice have recently noted that the
work of two particularly important scribes (partners or competitors), known as
Scribe D and Scribe Delta, is weighted heavily towards the works of Gower.[10]

---

3   Ibid., p. 99. Estimates of the post-plague population vary widely but generally fall between
    thirty thousand and fifty thousand. See Stephen Inwood, *A History of London* (New York,
    1998), pp. 113–15.
4   See Sylvia L. Thrupp, *The Merchant Class of Medieval London* (Ann Arbor, 1948; rpt. 1989). See
    also A.R. Myers, *London in the Age of Chaucer* (Norman, 1972), and Derek Pearsall, *The Life of
    Geoffrey Chaucer: A Critical Biography* (Oxford, 1992), pp. 17–23.
5   See Chris Given-Wilson, *The Royal Household and the King's Affinity: Service, Politics and Finance
    in England 1360–1413* (New Haven, 1986).
6   See Myers, *London*, pp. 30–34.
7   Gervase Rosser, 'London and Westminster: The Suburb in the Urban Economy in the Later
    Middle Ages', *Towns and Townspeople in the Fifteenth Century*, ed. John A.F. Thomson (Glou-
    cester, 1988), pp. 45–61.
8   See Myers, *London*, pp. 35–8; Inwood, *History of London*, pp. 126–7.
9   See Fisher, *John Gower*, pp. 55–8; see also the contribution of John Hines, Nathalie Cohen, and
    Simon Roffey to this volume, p. 1.
10  Of the manuscripts attributed to Scribe D and Scribe Delta, eight are Gowers, four Trevisas,
    two Chaucers and one Langland. See Kathryn Kerby-Fulton and Steven Justice, 'Scribe D and
    the Making of Ricardian Literature', *The Medieval Professional Reader at Work: Evidence from
    Manuscripts of Chaucer, Langland, Kempe, and Gower*, ed. Kathryn Kerby-Fulton and Maidie
    Hilmo, *ELS* 85 (Victoria, 2001), pp. 217–37 (p. 223). On these two scribes, see also A.I. Doyle
    and Malcolm B. Parkes, 'The Production of Copies of the *Canterbury Tales* and the *Confessio
    Amantis* in the Early Fifteenth Century', *Medieval Scribes, Manuscripts and Libraries: Essays Pres-*

Kerby-Fulton and Justice argue that the community of scribes and other literate civil servants fostered by Chancery took an active role in fashioning contemporary tastes by creating texts for 'a self-conscious, connected, knowing circle of committed and active, perhaps politically active, readers alert to every new development'.[11]

If this hypothesis of early literary production is accurate, it places Gower at the centre of a significant new vernacular literature and an extensive lay readership. Naturally, though, there are problems. First, this expansive model of audience seems at odds with the evidence of the original owners of Scribe D's work, among whom, A.I. Doyle and M.B. Parkes find, 'armigerous classes predominated'.[12] Second, the high number of surviving manuscripts is the only evidence for the expansion of Gower's audience. As Derek Pearsall has shown, in the fifteenth century 'brief and respectful allusions to the poet Gower are more common than evidence he was much read or imitated'.[13] There is as much evidence for the narrowing of Gower's audience as there is for its widening.[14]

All of this evidence, at any rate, dates from the fifteenth century. There are no explicit references in Gower's work (or Chaucer's) suggesting an expectation of such a broad audience as that hypothesised by Kerby-Fulton and Justice. In reconstructing Gower's readership during his lifetime, criticism has generally described a narrower coterie.

Gower's status and activities in London would have brought him into regular association with professionals, civil servants, and minor aristocrats in royal service. This is the same class of citizens that seems to have provided Geoffrey Chaucer with a literary community. Chaucer's first audience is assumed to be a coterie of friends and associates, and Gower has always been central to the definition of this group. Paul Strohm has carefully identified the most likely members of the 'Chaucer circle':

> Such a 'core' might consist of several knights in royal service whom Chaucer knew in the 1370s and 1380s, including William Beauchamp, Lewis Clifford, Philip la Vache, John Clanvowe, William Nevill, and Richard Stury; London acquaintances of the 1380s, including Ralph Strode and (with certain exceptions) John Gower; and newcomers of the 1390s, including Henry Scogan and Peter Bukton.[15]

ented to N.R. Ker, ed. Malcolm B. Parkes and Andrew G. Watson (London, 1978), pp. 163–210, particularly pp. 206–8.

11  Kerby-Fulton and Justice, 'Scribe D', p. 222. See also the same authors' 'Langlandian Reading Circles and the Civil Service in London and Dublin, 1380–1427', New Medieval Literatures, ed. Wendy Scase, Rita Copeland and David Lawton (Oxford, 1997), pp. 59–83.

12  Doyle and Parkes, 'Production of Copies', p. 208.

13  Derek Pearsall, 'The Gower Tradition', Gower's Confessio Amantis: Responses and Reassessments, ed. A.J. Minnis (Cambridge, 1983), pp. 179–97 (p. 185).

14  Pearsall, 'The Gower Tradition', admits that this is 'puzzling' and offers no definite solution: 'Perhaps a larger proportion than usual of the manuscripts of the Confessio went out of circulation early into the homes of the well-to-do; perhaps the poem was in some ways resistant to imitation, or was not "moral" enough for the fifteenth century, which liked its morality in heavy doses' (p. 187). Fisher and others have also suggested that many Gower manuscripts survive precisely because they lay unread.

15  Paul Strohm, Social Chaucer (Cambridge, 1989), p. 42.

The common denominators of this group are identifiable literary interests and close links to Chaucer, for both of which Gower is most conspicuous. Some critics have therefore referred to a 'Chaucer-Gower circle'. As Strohm hints in his parenthetical remark, however, there are a number of problems with including Gower as a member of such an assumed literary society.

Gower stands out primarily for the relative independence of his professional status. All of the knights on Strohm's list spent their careers in royal service and are associated with the 'king's affinity' and with the Ricardian faction in London politics.[16] Gower, though probably connected to an aristocratic family, always maintained the rank of esquire, like Chaucer. Chaucer, however, was apparently placed in the court as a young page, received his education there, spent his entire adult life serving in various capacities in the royal administration and the civil bureaucracy, and benefited from the king's patronage.[17] He showed himself capable, when the need arose, of putting his poetic gifts to the service of Ricardian interests. The figure mentioned by Strohm whose status was closest to Gower's is Ralph Strode, who was apparently an Oxford theologian before becoming a lawyer for the City of London. But Strode was much more active in support of the Ricardian faction; records show his close ties to the ill-fated Ricardian mayor Nicholas Brembre.[18] Gower, on the other hand, seems never to have been in royal service, working instead in law and business and purchasing land for rental income. He offered praise and advice for the young Richard II throughout the 1380s, but there is no sign that he ever received any patronage from Richard, and when he became disillusioned he switched political allegiance and became a notoriously harsh critic of the king. Though he did receive some compensation as well as recognition from Henry of Derby, Gower's political opinions seem to be voiced out of conviction rather than necessity.[19] Far from being dependent on patronage, he provided for his own retirement and endowed religious institutions as well.[20]

At least as significant as Gower's apparent political independence is the fact that, other than Chaucer himself, none of the conjectural members of the Chaucer circle appear anywhere in Gower's life records – that is, unless one counts Chaucer's poetry among them, in which case Gower is linked to Strode, his co-dedicatee of the *Troilus*. In fact, the only non-poetic text linking Gower to Chaucer is the 1378 document in which Chaucer grants power of attorney to Gower and another London lawyer, Richard Forester, before one of his diplo-

---

[16] Ibid., pp. 25–34.

[17] See Pearsall, *Geoffrey Chaucer*.

[18] Strohm, *Social Chaucer*, p. 32.

[19] Henry apparently gave Gower a collar of S's (one of his heraldic trappings) in thanks for a presentation copy of the revised *Confessio*, and a grant of two pipes of Gascon wine per year for the extravagantly propagandistic *Cronica Tripertita*. See Fisher, *John Gower*, p. 68.

[20] After arranging for the maintenance of his wife, Gower left the bulk of his wealth to the priory of St Mary Overie and to the establishment of a chantry. See Fisher, *John Gower*, pp. 65–6, and Hines, Cohen, and Roffey, pp. 23–41. This kind of dispersal was not extraordinary for a wealthy, middle-class Londoner. Thrupp, *Merchant Class*, p. 312, observes that successful merchants customarily left at least a third of their estates to religious charities; their sons, by and large, had to use business contacts to establish wealth of their own.

matic journeys to Italy. If it were not for their poetry, Gower would be no more linked to Chaucer than Forester is.

Indeed, the very idea of a 'Chaucer circle' is a product of Chaucer's poetry. Strohm cautions that the acquaintances he enumerates knew Chaucer in different periods of his life. Some are friends from the halcyon days of Richard's minority; others are mentioned only in the 1390s. It must therefore have been a series of friends, floating in and out of the Ricardian affinity. The impression of such a literary coterie – a group of men of roughly equal status, like-minded, literary, convivial, mutually supportive – derives from the allusions in Chaucer's verse. There is the envoy of the *Troilus*, in which Chaucer dedicates his largest complete work not to a prince or benefactor but to personal friends in recognition of their qualities and accomplishments and with the expectation that they are the poem's best audience: 'O moral Gowe, this book I directe/ to the and to the, philosophical Strode,/ To vouchen sauf, ther nede is, to correcte,/ Of youre benignites and zeles goode' (lines 1856–9).[21] There are the needling allusions to *Confessio Amantis* in the *Man of Law*'s Prologue.[22] There are, above all, Chaucer's verse epistles to Philip la Vache, Henry Scogan and Peter Bukton. The *Envoy to Bukton*, a rueful toast to Bukton on his wedding, cites the Wife of Bath as an authority on 'wo that is in mariage'.[23] It thereby describes the circulation of portions of Chaucer's *magnum opus* in progress among a group of friends – the very definition of a coterie readership.

If Gower was a member of such a convivial literary fraternity, there is little evidence of it in his own poetry. Gower's only reference to a personal acquaintance occurs near the end of the 1390 version of the *Confessio*. Venus, speaking to Gower as poet, adds one last injunction before she leaves:

> 'And gret wel Chaucer whan ye mete,
> As mi disciple and mi poete . . .
> Thow shalt him telle this message,
> That he upon his latere age,
> To sette an ende of alle his werk,
> As he which is myn owne clerk,
> Do make his testament of love,
> As thou hast do thi schrifte above,
> So that mi Court it mai recorde.'
> "Madame, I can me wel acorde",
> Quod I, 'to telle as ye me bidde.' (lines 2941–2, 2951–9)[24]

[21] All quotations of Chaucer's verse are cited from *The Riverside Chaucer*, gen. ed. Larry D. Benson (Boston, 1987).

[22] Pearsall, *Geoffrey Chaucer*, p. 133. Steven Justice, in *Writing and Rebellion: England in 1381* (Berkeley, 1994), pp. 207–13, reads *The Nun's Priest's Tale* as a burlesque of the first book of *Vox Clamantis*. See also Ian Bishop, '*The Nun's Priest's Tale* and the Liberal Arts', *RES* n.s. 30 (1979), pp. 257–67.

[23] Strohm (*Social Chaucer*, p. 45) notes that this poem is the only evidence of Chaucer's association with Sir Peter Bukton; Pearsall (*Geoffrey Chaucer*, p. 184), however, observes that both Chaucer and Bukton were witnesses at the Scropes-Grosvenor trial.

[24] Quotations of Gower's verse are taken from *The Complete Works of John Gower*, ed. G.C. Macaulay, 4 vols (Oxford, 1899–1902).

This poetic command comes from a very royal goddess and is intended for the glorification of 'mi Court'. The gesture towards the fellow-poet is therefore more mediated than Chaucer's, and its context is more courtly and hierarchical than private and convivial. In agreeing to give Chaucer the goddess' message when he sees him, though, Gower is emphasising that the two are personal friends, while the reference to Chaucer's 'testament of love' (presumably the *Legend of Good Women*) shows that Gower and Chaucer share work in progress and exchange encouragement.[25] This passage, though, for reasons that may be political, personal or merely scribal, disappears from subsequent recensions of the *Confessio*.[26] All of Gower's other references to readership are to kings or other aristocratic patrons. It is easy to imagine Chaucer reading his envoys to a group of London friends as post-prandial entertainment. It is easier to imagine Gower scribbling his verses alone in a monastic cloister – which, in fact, he probably did.

This is not to say that there was no Chaucer circle. Chaucer surely had a circle of friends of the kind implied in his short poems, and the poems are valid enough evidence that they constituted the first audience for much of his work. Gower does not come across, by and large, as the kind of hale fellow that Bukton or Scogan are suggested to be, but there are also plenty of suggestions in Gower's and Chaucer's texts that both poets shared this original audience. Just as Chaucer imagines Scogan mocking his desire to remain true to Venus despite his advancing years by crying, 'Lo, olde Grisel lyst to ryme and playe!' (line 35), so Venus, in the extended debate at the conclusion of the *Confessio* over Gower's fate as lover, chides, 'It sheweth wel be the visage / That olde grisel is no fole' (VIII.2406–7).

There are, however, significant differences between Gower's and Chaucer's representations of audience. Chaucer regularly chooses to represent poetry as the product of an urban community of voluntary association, and Gower does not. Chaucer's epistles to Scogan and Vache make reference to his residence in Kent; the envoys to Scogan and Bukton (this last one dating from around 1396) thematise the poet's old age. Chaucer, therefore, evokes his London community when it is most remote in time and place. Gower's anomalous reference to Chaucer drops out of the text, along with the dedication to Richard II, and is not replaced. What remains is the dedication to Henry of Derby, to whom Gower presented the revised version. Gower's last works are addressed to Henry after his ascension to the throne. Gower does not evoke an egalitarian community of readers and writers, not even as a memory.

---

[25] Gower's mention of Chaucer's 'testament of love' led to Thomas Usk's prose complaint by that name being ascribed to Chaucer for centuries. Anne Middleton has recently argued that Gower was in fact referring to Usk, though in a veiled manner necessitated by the anti-Ricardian politics that also claimed Usk's life. Gower's allusion, then, would be to a broad and complex urban audience of non-aristocratic and non-clerical writers and readers of vernacular poetry. See 'Thomas Usk's "Perdurable Letters": The *Testament of Love* from Script to Print', *Studies in Bibliography* 51 (1998), pp. 63–116. Strohm (*Social Chaucer*, p. 42), however, doubts Usk's association with Chaucer's coterie and counts him only as a 'self-nominated' member of the circle.

[26] On the revisions of the *Confessio*, see Fisher, *John Gower*, pp. 116–27; Peter Nicholson, 'The Dedications of Gower's *Confessio Amantis*', *Mediaevalia* 10 (1984), pp. 159–80.

Gower's failure to represent a reading community for his work also elides his connection to the urban community. For such a prolific writer, who spent virtually his entire life in the London metropolis, Gower only rarely represents the city. He is capable, however, of depicting the city with considerable specificity and vivacity. His earliest work, the *Mirour de l'Omme*, consists largely of rather vague and inert semi-allegorical satire of the estates, but the poem comes alive when it arrives at the professional classes of the city.[27] After the tellingly detailed indictment of lawyers and judges (lines 24,181–25,176), Gower turns to merchants, craftsmen and retailers. His criticism is not of commerce *per se*; merchants, he says, are ordained by God to assure that no one country becomes too proud with hoarded wealth.[28] Gower ascribes the commercial vices to Fraud ('Triche'), who is a world traveller:

> Triche a Florence et a Venise
> Ad son recet et sa franchise,
> Si ad a Brugges at a Gant;
> A son agard auci s'est mise
> La noble Cité sur Tamise,
> La quelle Brutus fuist fondant;
> Mais Triche la vait confondant[.]  (lines 25,248–55)

> In Florence and in Venice Fraud has his fortress and his licence, and at Bruges and at Ghent likewise. Under his care also is placed the noble city on the Thames, which Brutus founded; but Fraud is bringing it to ruin[.][29]

There is an ironic but unmistakable note of civic pride in this critique; the arrival of Fraud in London signals the city's emergence as a major center of European trade. Gower is not always so cosmopolitan and is capable of some homegrown xenophobia; he includes a protracted tirade against the predatory practices of the Italian banking communities in London (lines 25,429–500). But Gower's Fraud is explicitly a London type. When he is a draper (lines 25,309–44) he confuses you with complex bargaining so that you overpay; when he is a goldsmith (lines 25,513–60) he mixes base metals into his gold; when he is an apothecary (lines 25,597–680) he conspires with physicians to swindle you while making you sick; and so on. The climax of this section of the *Mirour*, and to some extent of the poem as a whole, is a sixty–line apostrophe in which Fraud finds his Lady Meed in the one commodity most essential to the English economy and London commerce:

> O belle, o blanche, o bien delie,
> L'amour de toy tant point et lie,
> Que ne se porront deslier
> Les cuers qui font la marchandie
> De toy; ainz mainte tricherie

---

27  See Fisher's discussion, *John Gower*, pp. 95–9.
28  See lines 25,189–97.
29  Translations of *Mirour de l'Omme* are taken from *Mirour de l'Omme (The Mirror of Mankind)*, trans. William Burton Wilson, revised by Nancy Wilson Van Baak (East Lansing, 1992).

> Et maint engin font compasser
> Comment te porront amasser:
> Et puis te font la mer passer,
> Comme celle q'es de leur navie
> La droite dame, et pour gaigner
> Les gens te vienont bargainer
> Par covoitise et par envie. (lines 25,405–16)

> [O beautiful, white, delicate Wool, love of you pierces and binds the
> hearts of those who trade in you so that they cannot unbind them-
> selves. On the contrary, they contrive all kinds of trickery and conspir-
> acy in order to collect great quantities of you. And then they take you
> overseas as if you were the mistress of their ships. And, in order to get
> you, the people come to bargain in covetousness and envy.]

Such passages must derive from first-hand observation of the bustle of fourteenth-century London. The perspective, mixing pride and fascination with
xenophobia and a complex moral ambivalence, is not perfectly aligned with any
one civic or political discourse but is very close to that of the city's ascendant
merchant class.[30]

This portion of the *Mirour*, however, is the high water mark of Gower's representation of the city. In *Vox Clamantis*, he reprises his complaints against men of
law (Book VI, Chapters 1–7) and against merchants (Book V, Chapters 11–15),
but in much more general terms. Fraud returns, but her dealings (Latin *Fraus* is
feminine) are less vividly rendered: 'Fraus et ab vrbe venit campestres querere
lanas,/ Ex quibis in stapula post parat acta sua' (V.773–4). ['And Fraud comes
out of the city to get wool from the country, with which she afterwards engages
in dealings in the market.'][31] More specific is the figure of Susurrus, the Whis-
perer, 'linguosus . . . inter conciues seminator discordiarum' ['a prattling sower
of discord among his fellow citizens'],[32] through whom Gower figures the city as
a place of ubiquitous rumour. By way of criticising the city, however, Gower
exhibits a rare possessiveness towards it. He notes that Athens prospered until it
was riven by schism, but he hopes: 'Sors tamen illa deo mediante recedat ab
vrbe/ Nostra, que magno fulsit honore diu' (V.1015–16). ['But with God's help,
may that fate withdraw from our city, which long shone with great honour.']

Even rarer is Gower's discussion of the government of London. It may seem
that his attack on an unnamed mayor displays an unaccustomed factionalism,
but his criticisms are so vague that no specific target has been identified, and
none may have been intended.[33] The root of his complaint, though, is telling:

---

[30] Fisher (*John Gower*, p. 98) calls the paean to wool 'patriotic', but it is the kind of patriotism that
Dante expresses in the *Inferno*: 'Godi, Fiorenza, poi che se' sì grande/ che per mare e per terra
batti l'ali,/ e per lo 'nferno tuo nome si spande!' (XXVI.1–3). 'Rejoice, O Florence, since you
are so great that over sea and land you beat your wings, and your name is spread through
Hell!' *The Divine Comedy*, trans. Charles S. Singleton (Princeton, 1970).

[31] Translations of *Vox Clamantis* are quoted from *The Major Latin Works of John Gower*, trans. Eric
W. Stockton (Seattle, 1962).

[32] Stockton, *Major Latin Works*, Book 5, Chapter 15, headnote. Stockton translates Susurrus as
'Talebearer'.

[33] Stockton, *Major Latin Works*, p. 438. In the *Cronica* (I.154–9) Gower excoriates Brembre, but this

Mutatis subito rebus natura gemescit,
Et magis insolita de nouitate dolet,
Sorte repentina dum pauper in vrbe leuatur,
Et licet indignus culmen honoris habet.
Vrbis nobilitas poterit tunc dampna timere,
Cum noua stultorum gloria laudat eum[.]  (V.845–50)

[When a poor man is elevated in the city through an unexpected fate, and the unworthy creature is allowed to reach the height of honour, then Nature suddenly groans at the changed state of things and grieves at the unaccustomed rarity. When the new-found adulation of fools praises him, then the city's nobility can fear misfortune.]

Gower here repudiates the very social fluidity and economic opportunity that were the city's most distinctive social features and, to most of its citizens, its greatest promise. He is more specifically distancing himself from the ethos and experiences of the merchant class from which the mayors were drawn, which, as Thrupp says, 'were the opposite of static' and 'fixed in a pattern that fostered ambition in the individual'.[34]

The *Mirour* and the *Vox*, therefore, contain significant but not extensive representations of the city; they exhibit, to a certain extent, an urban perspective, but they also remain aloof from the city. Gower's perspective seems that of a London writer but one somewhat marginal to the city. It may be significant, then, that by the time Gower wrote these French and Latin verses (c. 1377–81) he was marginal to the city geographically. He was living in Southwark.[35]

## Southwark

Given the area's reputation from Chaucer's time well into the modern age, there is a certain incongruity to the thought that Gower spent nearly half his life in Southwark – though, from another perspective, it is the ideal home for a moralist. A short alley connected the priory to High Street, the main southern approach to the bridge and the city, which was lined with dozens of taverns and inns, including the Tabard. Just east along the river was Bankside and, bounded by Love Lane and Maiden Lane, the Stews, the most notorious red-light district of the medieval metropolis.

In fact, however, Southwark was not lawless. It was, rather, a patchwork of

is long after his death, in a virulently anti-Ricardian text, and the details of the *Vox* passage do not seem to fit Brembre.
34  Thrupp, *Merchant Class*, p. 311. It is hard to say what Gower means by 'urbis nobilitas', but there was a significant class difference between Gower and men like Brembre. Gower was not an aristocrat and apparently avoided knighthood, but he was from a noble family and, as Thrupp notes (p. 318), such families guided their sons towards the law rather than trade. He dealt with the merchant class but was himself part of a professional caste.
35  On London's southern suburb, see Martha Carlin, *Medieval Southwark* (London, 1996). On Gower's residence there, see Fisher, *John Gower*, pp. 58–61, and John Hines, Nathalie Cohen and Simon Roffey's contribution to this volume.

jurisdictions, what Martha Carlin calls an 'administrative jungle'.[36] The area essentially comprised five manors, four of them under ecclesiastical control. Each manor had its own judicial courts. The brothels of the Stews were within the manor of the Bishop of Winchester; they were licensed and subject to taxation, regulation and occasional efforts at reform.[37] One parcel of Bankside, including at least one brothel, the Unicorn, was owned by the prioress and nuns of Stratford-at-Bow.[38] If Gower had walked from his home in the priory of St Mary Overie to the Stews (assuming he was so inclined), he would have passed the area of the bishop's prison, known by the sixteenth century as the Clink. When he walked down Pepper Lane he would have encountered, before reaching the bridge or the taverns lining the road out of town, the pillory in the middle of High Street.[39]

Southwark was not, then, merely a frontier of lawlessness and vice; it was, rather, largely beyond the legal control of London. It was not only prostitutes and thieves who found refuge in Southwark but also craftsmen avoiding the controls of guilds and markets skirting the city's cartels.[40] From the twelfth century on the London authorities sought to gain greater control over the growing community south of the Thames. They justified their claims with allegations of unrestrained criminality, but their true intentions were to protect the exclusive and protectionist structures of London commerce. St Mary Overie was in the Guildable manor, the area nearest the bridge. Officially the demesne of the king, the city gained the right to collect tolls and revenues in the manor in 1327, and for the centuries following it regularly attempted to expand its control.[41] Gower's home was in a contested space, simultaneously in the city and outside it. In a broader sense, Southwark as a whole was as integral to the city as anything within the walls. A part of London's urban sprawl, it allowed for the unregulated growth required to support the burgeoning metropolis.

In a well-known essay, David Wallace figures London as the 'absent city' of Chaucer's poetry. Wallace maintains that Chaucer almost never represents London because the city resists representation: 'There is no idea of a city for all the inhabitants of a space called London to pay allegiance to; there are only conflicts of associational, hierarchical, and anti-associational discourses, acted

---

36 Carlin, *Medieval Southwark*, p. 101.

37 Ibid., pp. 211–19. A London ordinance of 1393 officially restricted prostitutes to Smithfield and Southwark, but, as Perkyn Revelour well knew, there were always prostitutes in the city. See Inwood, *History of London*, p. 130; David Wallace, 'Chaucer and the Absent City', *Chaucer's England: Literature in Historical Context*, ed. Barbara Hanawalt (Minneapolis, 1992), pp. 59–90 (p. 74).

38 Carlin, p. 213, n. 23. As Hines, Cohen, and Roffey emphasise, Southwark was as notable for its ecclesiastical residences as for its brothels.

39 On the manor courts and the bishop's prison, see Carlin, *Medieval Southwark*, pp. 112–13. On the pillory, see Carlin, Fig. 9 (p. 39) and p. 61, n. 206. See also Thrupp, *Merchant Class*, p. 24 and C. David Benson, '*Piers Plowman* as Poetic Pillory: The Pillory and the Cross', *Medieval Literature and Historical Inquiry: Essays in Honor of Derek Pearsall*, ed. David Aers (Cambridge, 2000), pp. 31–54. Benson's analogy of the use of the pillory to punish 'social crimes, lies and commercial fraud against others' (p. 43) to the social criticism of *Piers Plowman* could be extended to Gower's satire in portions of the *Mirour* and the *Vox*.

40 Carlin, *Medieval Southwark*, pp. 119–20.

41 Ibid., pp. 120–7.

out within and across the boundaries of a city wall or the fragments of a text called *The Canterbury Tales*.'[42] The clearest instance of this elision is that his Canterbury pilgrimage begins not in London but in Southwark. Chaucer, however, gives a vivid impression of contemporary Southwark: the crowds, the taverns, the variety of characters of different stations intermingling outside one of the city's main portals. Here Chaucer does figure the kind of 'associational forms' that Wallace finds lacking in London's medieval imagination and in Chaucer's representation of it.

Gower, for all his years in the thick of this suburban milieu, depicts almost none of it. Neither the Stews nor the inns figure in his verse. Gower is a censor, but unlike Chaucer's Pardoner he is not particularly interested in the 'tavern vices'. Nor does he much notice commoners below the level of merchants and guildsmen. 'Vrbs stat communis de gentibus ecce duabis,/ Sunt Mercatores, sunt simul artifices' (V.663–4), he observes in the *Vox*. ['The ordinary city depends on two groups of people: there are the merchants and there are likewise artisans.'] Of the more than 2300 lines of the *Mirour* devoted to the estate of the commons, only ninety-six address 'le commun de gent petit,/ Qui labourier sont appellé' (lines 26,429–30) ['the common little people who are called labourers']. He makes no clear distinction between urban and rural labourers. His main concerns are that they not demand too much compensation for their labour and that they not rebel against their station.

This attitude helps to explain Gower's hysterical reaction when the 'common little people' rebelled against their stations most aggressively.[43] Living in St Mary Overie, Gower could have witnessed the Kentish rebels' forced entrance over London Bridge in 1381.[44] In Book I of *Vox Clamantis*, added after the completion of the rest of the poem, Gower recounts the rebels' attack on London. It is not reportage, though, but rather a nightmare of a London apocalypse. Not only is it notably less accurate than the major chronicle accounts, sometimes libellously so, it also forgoes realistic representation in favour of allegorical dream-vision. The book actually consists of three visions: the depiction of the rebels as beasts; the vision of the besieged city as Troy; the ship, figuring the Tower of London, endangered by a whirlpool. Some portions – the flight into the woods in Chapter 16, the refuge in the Tower of London in Chapter 17 – have been taken as autobiographical, but it is unlikely that they are. The book is particularly thick with lines adapted from Ovid; Stockton, its translator, calls it 'bookish, almost a gallimaufry of literary motifs'.[45] It was clearly not Gower's intention to record a momentous event in the life of the city.

After this obscure vision, London and urban life virtually disappear from Gower's poetry. The review of the estates in the Prologue to *Confessio Amantis* is much briefer and less specific than the extensive satires of his earlier poems. The

---

42 Wallace, 'Chaucer and the Absent City', p. 84.
43 See Justice, *Writing and Rebellion*, pp. 207–13 on Gower's response to the rebellion. As Justice observes, Gower equates his *Vox Clamantis* with the *vox populi*, but 'he promotes the interests of a particular clientele as the interests of the realm at large' (p. 210).
44 See Fisher, *John Gower*, p. 60; Janet Coleman, *Medieval Readers and Writers, 1350–1400* (New York, 1981), p. 129.
45 Stockton, *Major Latin Works*, p. 16.

'commune' (line 499) is undifferentiated, and Gower does not cite specific vices as he does with the clergy. He stresses personal responsibility, but first and foremost the need that people be constrained by strong laws, lest they burst like a barrel with weak bands: 'Wher lawe lacketh, errour groweth,/ He is noght wys who that ne troweth' (lines 511–12). The first recension of the Prologue, though, does contain Gower's best-known depiction of London. It is the scene in which Richard II requests the composition of the poem:

> As it bifel upon a tyde,
> Under the toun of newe Troye,
> Which tok of Brut his ferste joye,
> In Temse whan it was flowende
> As I be bote cam rowende,
> So as fortune hir tyme sette,
> My liege lord par chaunce I mette;
> And so befel, as I cam nyh,
> Out of my bot, whan he me syh,
> He bad me come in to his barge.
> And whan I was with him at large,
> Amonges othre thinges seid
> He hath this charge upon me leid,
> And bad me doo my besynesse
> That to his hihe worthinesse
> Som newe thing I scholde boke,
> That he himself it mihte loke
> After the forme of my writynge.  (Prol. 35*–53*)

This vignette has frequently been taken as a factual depiction of the poem's origins, and it is the one passage most likely to make readers think of Gower as a city poet.[46] As Frank Grady has recently explained, however, other than Gower's claim to have taken to the river 'whan it was flowende', the passage offers almost no specific description of the city or the river. 'The Thames, then as now, is a commercial waterway,' Grady observes, 'but Gower gives no sense that it is crowded or noisy or smelly; indeed, the river seems quite oddly empty but for the royal barge and Gower's now-abandoned boat.' The scene of patronage 'works to suppress the presence of contemporary London'.[47]

In *La Male Regle*, Thomas Hoccleve, recalling a time very close to that of Gower's presumed encounter with Richard, describes hiring a boat at London Bridge. Hoccleve's London is a thronging place, full of taverners and wafer–vendors and wayward clerks and young women grateful to have their drinks purchased. When Hoccleve decides to hire a boat, the boatmen at the bridge fight for his business – 'With hem was I I-tugged to and fro' (line 197) –

---

[46] See Fisher, *John Gower*, p. 236. The scene has been offered as the historical source of the poem's composition as recently as Russell A. Peck's Introduction to *Confessio Amantis*, Vol. I (Kalamazoo, 2000), p. 25.

[47] Frank Grady, 'Gower's Boat, Richard's Barge, and the True Story of the *Confessio Amantis*: Text and Gloss', *Texas Studies in Literature and Language* 44 (2002), pp. 1–15 (p. 5).

and flatter him by calling him 'maistir' (line 201).[48] In comparison, Gower's city is vacant and his river crossing thinly imagined. Whatever the reliability of Gower's story as an actual explanation of the poem's genesis, it gives no sense of the quality of urban life.

This is London's only appearance in the *Confessio*. None of the 150 tales in the collection depicts contemporary England.[49] On the other hand, Gower's meeting with King Richard occurs 'Under the toun of newe Troye' (*37); Gower might have represented London in the guise of Troy, as he does in Book I of the *Vox* and as Chaucer clearly does in *Troilus and Criseyde*. There are dozens of references to Troy in the *Confessio*, but most of them come in legends of Greeks on their way to or from the war. Only a few tales are set in Troy itself, such as the stories of the Trojan horse (I.1077–1189), an *exemplum* of hypocrisy, and Paris and Helen (V.7195–7590), an *exemplum* of sacrilege, and none devote much attention to city life or betray any urban consciousness.

Of course, Troy is not the only city in the *Confessio*. In these ancient tales, characters are constantly washing up in various Mediterranean city-states, and there are occasions when these towns are invested with a feeling of civic life, as when the Tyreans discover the sudden departure of their prince Appolinus, who is fleeing the murderous wrath of Antiochus:

> For unlust of that aventure
> Ther was noman which tok tonsure,
> In doelful clothes thei hem clothe,
> The bathes and the Stwes bothe
> Thei schetten in be every weie;
> There was no lif which leste pleie
> Ne take of eny joie kepe,
> Bot for here liege lord to wepe;
> And every wyht seide as he couthe,
> 'Helas, the lusti flour of youthe,
> Our Prince, oure heved, our governour,
> Thurgh whom we stoden in honour,
> Withoute the comun assent
> Thus sodeinliche is fro ous went!'
> Such was the clamour of hem alle.  (VIII.481–95)

It is a striking detail that the citizens in their grief shutter 'the bathes and the Stwes bothe', all the more for Gower's use of the word most associated with the brothels of his home town. Equally notable is their complaint that their beloved prince has left 'Withoute the comun assent'; they seem aggrieved not just by their loss but also by this abrogation of their political rights as citizens.

When Appolinus returns to Tyre, however, he shows little deference to the public common voice:

[48] Frederick J. Furnivall, ed., *Hoccleve's Works: I. The Minor Poems*, EETS, es no. 61 (London, 1892).
[49] Stockton, *Major Latin Works*, p. 21.

> The king, as he well couthe and sholde,
> Makth to his poeple riht good chiere;
> And after sone, as thou schalt hiere,
> A parlement he hath summoned,
> Wher he his doghter hath coroned
> Forth with the lord of Mitelene,
> That on is king, that other queene:
> And thus the fadres ordinance
> This lond hath set in governance[.]  (VIII.1912–20)

A parliament is called, but only in order to receive the orders of the paternal prince.[50]

Of course, the *Confessio* consists almost entirely of ancient *exempla* and offers almost no fresh depictions of contemporary reality. As Derek Pearsall has observed, Gower brings to these classical stories a 'finite moral pattern' reinforced by 'a uniformity of social setting'.[51] The city is occasionally represented as a corporate concept or will, as is almost unavoidably the case when Gower tells the Roman republican foundation-myths. At the end of the Rape of Lucrece 'al the toun' cries: 'Awey, awey the tirannie/ Of lecherie and covoitise!' (VII.5117–19); the tale of Virginia concludes: 'Thurgh comun conseil of hem alle/ Thei have here wrongfull king deposed' (VII.5294–5). But neither Rome nor the other cities are much more differentiated or dramatised than this. In a book that is political on every page, depictions of the *polis*, as human environment or as political entity, are few and far between.

There is one other occasion when Gower's identification with the City of London is assumed to have significantly informed his poetic expression. In 1392, London refused a loan to Richard II. Richard's retaliation included the removal of the Chancery, the Exchequer and the Court of Common Pleas to York; he also imprisoned the mayor and sheriffs and essentially took over the government of

---

50  In contrast, even Chaucer's most autocratic princes are more beholden to the popular will. Theseus arranges the marriage of Emily and Palamon only after the Athenian parliament decides: 'To have with certein contrees alliaunce,/ And have fully of Thebans obeisaunce' (I.2973–4), while Walter never would have married Griselda at all had he not heeded the concerns of the people of Saluces. Chaucer's Troy is a notably democratic place, where the exchanging of Criseyde is decided in the Book IV parliament. Gower's tale of Paris and Helen includes a Trojan parliament, too. Only Hector and Paris speak, but in the end Gower, like Chaucer, makes sure that the people are complicit in their own destruction: 'And every man tho seide his,/ And sundri causes thei recorde,/ Bot ate laste thei acorde/ That Paris schal to Grece wende,/ And thus the parlement tok ende' (V.7436–40). For a representation of a truly urban perspective in public debate, however, we may have to look to Chaucer's parliament of birds. Craig E. Bertolet has recently argued that the depiction of the less courtly birds in the *Parlement of Foules* – ducks and geese and other plain-spoken, time-conscious, egalitarian species – reveals Chaucer's 'understanding of the rising social importance of urban culture in England'. See ' "My Wit is Sharp; I Love No Taryinge": Urban Poetry and the *Parlement of Foules*', *Studies in Philology* 93 (1996), pp. 365–89. The closest analogue in Gower to such contentious dream-debate is Cupid's parliament in the conclusion of the *Confessio* (VIII.2450–2807). The point of dispute is Gower's fate as a lover, and the parliament devolves into a clamorous confrontation of young lovers and old. Riotous though it is, the lovers' parliament does not contain the kind of gradations of class-consciousness that Bertolet finds in the *Parlement of Foules*, and, by and large, this and Gower's other parliaments are contained by hierarchical, monarchical motifs.

51  Pearsall, *Gower and Lydgate* (Harlow, Essex, 1969), p. 20.

the city. The dispute was resolved only with the city's payment of a fine of £100,000.[52] The reconciliation, and the king's victory, were demonstrated in a royal entry and procession through the city.[53] These events are usually characterised as a humiliation of London and often as an important step towards Ricardian absolutism. They are also seen as a key moment in Gower's rejection of Ricardian rule.[54] Fisher notes that from his Southwark home Gower could have witnessed this ritual entry as easily as he could have seen the forced entry of the rebels eleven years earlier.[55] In rejecting Richard's rule and in removing Richard from the *Confessio* and redirecting it to Henry of Derby, Fisher says, 'Gower was merely demonstrating the sentiments of a London citizen'.[56]

There are, however, many possible explanations for Gower's change of heart, since there were many reasons for any Englishman to be annoyed with Richard in the early 1390s. R.L. Storey has pointed to Richard's failure to follow through on his promise to the Commons to restrict baronial abuses of livery and maintenance; this would have offended Gower not as a city dweller but as a member of the gentry, an untitled landowner.[57] This could explain the removal of the reference to Chaucer from the *Confessio*, along with the excision of the king, since as Paul Strohm has shown Chaucer acted in 'Lak of Stedfastnesse' as a mouthpiece for Richard's hollow promises for livery reform.[58] Peter Nicholson points out that Gower says nothing about the dispute with the city, neither in the *Confessio* nor in the *Cronica Tripertita*, in which he passes few opportunities to excoriate Richard.[59]

It becomes very difficult to find in Gower's writing any association with the City of London or its suburbs. Wallace demonstrates that, compared to Boccaccio, Chaucer has an underdeveloped 'urban consciousness'. But Chaucer, in Wallace's reading, dramatises in *The Cook's Tale* the anti-associational discourse dominant in London, and in the General Prologue imagines the associational discourse more free to evolve in Southwark. Gower develops neither of these, perhaps because his attention is directed not to the streets of Southwark nor to the city across the bridge but rather upstream, to Westminster.

---

52  See Caroline M. Barron, 'The Quarrel of Richard II with London 1392–97', *The Reign of Richard II: Essays in Honor of May McKisack*, ed. F.R.H. Du Boulay and Caroline M. Barron (London, 1971), pp. 173–201.

53  See Lynn Staley, 'Gower, Richard II, Henry of Derby, and the Business of Making Culture', *Speculum* 75 (2000), pp. 68–96, esp. 79–80.

54  See Staley, p. 80, though she emphasises not the insult to the city as the source of Gower's displeasure but rather Richard's 'emphatically ceremonial, formal, hieratical' mode of self-presentation.

55  Fisher, *John Gower*, pp. 118–19. Fisher also claims that the imprisoned mayor, John Hende, was 'of the Chaucer-Gower circle'.

56  Ibid., p. 122.

57  R.L. Storey, 'Liveries and Commissions of the Peace 1388–90', *The Reign of Richard II*, pp. 131–53, esp. 150.

58  Paul Strohm, 'The Textual Environment of Chaucer's "Lak of Stedfastnesse" ', *Hochon's Arrow: The Social Imagination of Fourteenth-Century Texts* (Princeton, 1992), pp. 57–74.

59  Peter Nicholson, 'The Dedications of Gower's *Confessio Amantis*', *Mediaevalia* 10 (1984), pp. 159–80 (p. 168). Nicholson goes much further, arguing that Gower never changed allegiance at all until after Richard's deposition.

## *Westminster*

Medieval Westminster was a real place, a suburb of London similar to Southwark in its relationship to the city and even in its reputation.[60] But Gower was no more interested in this suburb than in his own. When I say that Gower was interested in Westminster, I use the name as a metonym for royal power.

Since Anne Middleton cited the *Confessio* along with *Piers Plowman* as the best examples of the 'public poetry' of the Ricardian period – poetry that is 'defined by a constant relation of speaker to audience within an ideally conceived worldly community' and that speaks for 'bourgeois moderation'[61] – discussions of Gower's audience have focused on the middle class. Janet Coleman locates Gower's primary audience in 'the expanded middle estate'.[62] Kerby-Fulton and Justice find that Scribe D reproduced Gower's works for a 'Westminster clientele'.[63]

Certainly, Gower's twin themes are, as the title of Russell Peck's book identifies them, kingship *and* common profit, and the broad appeal and generalised audience of the *Confessio* are indisputable. Still, Gower remained focused on kingship throughout his career, and to a much greater extent than his contemporaries. This is all the more puzzling given that, among the writers and readers with whom he is most associated, Gower is remarkable for his professional self-sufficiency and his independent status. Chaucer was always the king's man and could be called on to compose in the king's interest, as he did in 'Lak of Stedfastnesse'. For the most part, however, he did not have to and did not choose to. The envoy to 'Lak' represents the only time in Chaucer's career that he directly addressed Richard II.[64] The prologue to the *Legend of Good Women* hints at a command performance, but the work is aborted; the *Troilus* barely engages the political world at all, and in the end is dedicated to personal friends; in the *Canterbury Tales*, only the Knight, the Monk, the Clerk and Chaucer in the Melibee address themes of kingship, while the pilgrims themselves forge a diverse, self-governing, egalitarian community.

Gower, on the other hand, who had few visible ties to Ricardian factionalism and lived for most of his writing career in semi-retirement in a religious community on private wealth, addressed Richard II at length in the *Vox* and in the first recension of the *Confessio*. His change of allegiance is presumed to be in response to some element of Richard's absolutist tendencies; the Richard of the *Cronica* begins 'amore remotus' (I.4) in 1387 and moves swiftly to tyranny. Gower's faith in kingship, however, is not weakened. Richard is replaced in portions of the

---

60  See Rosser, 'London and Westminster'. In *La Male Regle*, Hoccleve asks: 'Wher was a gretter maister eek than y,/ Or bet aqweyntid at Westmynstre yate,/ Among the tauerneres namely,/ And Cookes whan I cam eerly or late?' (lines 177–80).
61  Anne Middleton, 'The Idea of Public Poetry in the Reign of Richard II', *Speculum* 53 (1978), pp. 94–114 (p. 95).
62  Coleman, *Medieval Readers and Writers*, p. 156.
63  Kerby-Fulton and Justice, 'Scribe D', p. 122.
64  I discuss Ricardian and Lancastrian expectations of royal address in 'Chaucer's Scogan and Scogan's Chaucer', *Studies in Philology* 96 (1999), pp. 1–21.

*Confessio* with ideas of England, and his fate is offered in the *Cronica* as a minatory example to tyrants;[65] gestures to the 'common voice' are ubiquitous in all the poetry. Nevertheless, Gower makes little effort to articulate alternative models of governance, be they popular or urban, democratic or associational. On the contrary, he offers in Book VII of the *Confessio* (if not in the poem as a whole) a *speculum principis* without a prince, and with the re-dedication he seems to be fishing about for a suitable replacement.[66] When Henry did seize the throne, Gower spent his last years recapitulating the arc of his trilingual career for the honour of Lancaster.[67] Gower was remarkable among his contemporaries for his care with and control over his manuscripts, but the evidence suggests that he exerted this influence not to broaden his reading public but rather to produce presentation copies for powerful individuals: the *Vox* for Archbishop Arundel;[68] the *Confessio* for Henry of Derby; etc.[69] Gower longed for the ear of the great.

Gower's fascination with kingship is deeply rooted in his political and ethical philosophy.[70] Though some critics have felt compelled to defend Gower from the charge of sycophancy,[71] his preoccupation with royal power is integral to his understanding of poetry and his relatively elevated conception of the role of the poet. Particularly in *Vox Clamantis*, Gower figures himself as a desert prophet, as Isaiah or Jeremiah or as his namesakes John the Baptist or John of the Apocalypse, the solitary voice in the wilderness whose lamentations go unheeded by a degenerate world. In the Prologue to the *Confessio*, he imagines himself as the more positive figure of Arion, whose harp refashions the world into harmonious concord. Arion, though, is set in apposition to one of Gower's most famous passages, the dream of Nebuchadnezzar, which is equally the story of Daniel. Gower, therefore, also imagines himself as Daniel, not just an adviser to kings but a prophet who requires a figure of imperial authority either to actualise his universal vision or to ignore it at his and the world's peril.[72]

---

[65] The *Cronica* ends, 'Explicit Cronica presentibus que futuris vigilii corde Regibus commemoranda.'

[66] Was Gower a political prophet? Critics have been divided as to whether Gower actually anticipated Henrican rule as early as 1392. Most recently, Staley has argued that the Lancastrian project predates even the 1390s, but that it was orchestrated by Gaunt with an eye to his legacy rather than by Henry seeking kingship. Gower himself, however, embraces the role of Lancastrian Merlin in the beginning of the *Cronica*: 'Libro testante, stat cronica scripta per ante' (I.9) ['With this book as witness, the chronicle was written beforehand'].

[67] The French poems known as *Cinkante Balades* are dedicated to 'noble Henri, puissant et seignural' (II.25) by 'Vostre oratour et vostre humble vassal, / Vostre Gower, q'est trestout vos soubgitz' (I.15–16). The *Cronica Tripertita* is appended to the *Vox* and reshapes the entire work as a Lancastrian document. *In Praise of Peace*, Gower's last English poem, offers advice to Henry; see Frank Grady, 'The Lancastrian Gower and the Limits of Exemplarity', *Speculum* 70 (1995), pp. 552–75.

[68] Fisher, *John Gower*, p. 100.

[69] Owners of Scribe D's *Confessios* included Henry's sons Thomas and Humphrey. See Doyle and Parkes, 'Production of Copies', p. 208.

[70] See Elizabeth Porter's treatment of 'personal kingship' in 'Gower's Ethical Microcosm and Political Macrocosm', *Gower's* Confessio Amantis: *Responses and Reassessments*, ed. A.J. Minnis (Cambridge, 1983), pp. 135–62.

[71] See Fisher, *John Gower*, pp. 133–4.

[72] See Russell A. Peck, 'John Gower and the Book of Daniel', *John Gower: Recent Readings*, ed. R.F. Yeager (Kalamazoo, 1989), pp. 159–87.

This, in Gower's time, is an audacious understanding of the poet's role, and it may paradoxically reveal the deepest effects of his urban contexts. Gower's uniquely urban condition, as a non-bureaucratic, non-aristocratic, privately employed professional, allowed him to develop a sense of the poet that was elevated in its autonomy, in its self-regard and in its ambition – but that required a strong and attentive monarch to legitimise his voice and to realise his social vision.[73]

73 I am grateful to David Benson for his advice during the preparation of this chapter.

# 3

## *John Gower and London English*

JEREMY J. SMITH

I

As his magnificent tomb in Southwark Cathedral in London demonstrates, John Gower was an important person; and this opinion is confirmed if we examine the Gower life records and what the poet tells us of himself in his verse. Gower was a courtier with legal connections, a wearer of the rayed gown and the S-clasp collar, a recipient of special grants, and a friend of important royal servants such as Geoffrey Chaucer – to such an extent that he was, with Richard II, apparently in the first audience for Chaucer's *Troilus and Criseyde*. And he was adept enough, and sufficiently cognisant of contemporary political developments, to transfer his allegiance to the 'coming man', Henry Bolingbroke. Gower was at the hub of medieval society: although (it would appear) conscious of the faults of his social group, he was undeniably, in modern parlance, an establishment figure.[1]

We might try a small thought-experiment. If Gower were a modern man, and given our knowledge of the class structure and concomitant sociolinguistic configuration of present-day England, we would have no difficulty in recreating his language, both spoken and written. A twenty-first-century Gower would write using the fixed spelling, prescribed grammar and carefully delimited lexical choices – 'standard English' – we expect of a well-educated Englishman of his class. And undoubtedly he would speak with the Received Pronunciation (RP) still so characteristic of the English legal profession, the higher ranks of the civil service, and the public (i.e. private) school- and Oxbridge-educated elite. He and a twenty-first-century Chaucer, peers within a peer-group, would sound to outsiders pretty similar.

Yet when we look at Gower's usage in its contemporary context, not as an imaginary twenty-first-century language-user, we quickly realise that not only does his language differ in certain important ways from that of his friend and contemporary Chaucer, but it also differs from much of the language found in other important writers of the period who seem to share his background and social standing. In this chapter, I propose to address the following questions: how would contemporaries have viewed the language of Gower, both spoken

---

[1] John H. Fisher, *John Gower: Moral Philosopher and Friend of Chaucer* (London, 1965), Ch. 2, *passim*.

and written? How did contemporaries react when they came to copy Gower's English? What do these reactions tell us about Gower's status? And has the study of the language of Gower anything to tell us about the evolution of that vexed phenomenon, standard English?

II

That Gower's language has a distinctive dialectal character has been known for some time. Macaulay, for instance, showed that much of Gower's spoken language, unlike Chaucer's, must have related in important respects more closely to southern than to Midland usage. Macaulay based his views on an analysis of Gower's rhymes, notably the reflexes of West Saxon *ǣ*. Whereas Chaucer's usage shows his language to descend from the Old Anglian variety of Old English, Gower's usage for several items seemed to Macaulay to descend from Old Kentish – bearing in mind that the terms 'Old Anglian' and 'Old Kentish' are essentially typological expressions, representing clusters of usages in a clinal sequence.[2]

Supporting evidence for the southern basis of Gower's usage comes (*inter alia*) from the characteristic syncopated forms of the third person present singular verb. Such syncopated forms, such as *berth* 'bears', *stant* 'stands' etc., found in the Fairfax manuscript of the *Confessio* and confirmed as Gower's own usage through metrical analysis, survived longest in the conservative grammars of the south of England. They do appear in Chaucer's verse, but are significantly less common there.[3]

Since Macaulay's time, new information about Middle English dialectology has enabled us to refine his conclusions. In 1981, Michael Samuels and I, drawing on the materials being brought together at that time for the great *Linguistic Atlas of Late Medieval English*,[4] formed the view that Gower's language was a blend of two dialect areas: Kent and Suffolk (Samuels and Smith). We based our conclusion on an analysis of the fairly idiosyncratic set of dialectal written forms found in the Fairfax and Stafford manuscripts of the *Confessio* and the Trentham manuscript of *In Praise of Peace*, all of which texts contained independently-derived material which could be regarded as Gowerian.

We found that these forms fell into two groups:

(1) a group of forms found together in Kentish texts from the fourteenth century, notably *oghne* 'own', supported by the widespread use of the syncopated third person present tense verbs, <ie>-spellings in (e.g.) *hiere* 'here' and 'hear', *whiel* 'wheel', etc.; *seluer* 'silver', *soster* 'sister', *therwhiles (that)* 'while'

(2) a group of forms co-occurring in late medieval texts from south-west Suffolk, notably *or . . . or* 'either . . . or', *bothen* 'both', *ʒoue* 'given', <-h-> in *myhte* 'could' (cf. present-day English 'might'), *hyhe* 'high', etc.

---

2  G.C. Macaulay, ed., *The English Works of John Gower*, EETS, es nos. 81 and 82 (1900–1901), Vol. I, pp. cii–civ; cf. R.M. Hogg, *A Grammar of Old English I: Phonology* (Oxford, 1992), p. 4.
3  See, for instance, M.L. Samuels, *Linguistic Evolution* (Cambridge, 1972), pp. 85–6.
4  A. McIntosh, M.L. Samuels and M. Benskin, with M. Laing and K. Williamson, *A Linguistic Atlas of Late Medieval English* (Aberdeen, 1986).

When such mixtures appear in late medieval texts, it is usual to assume two possibilities. First, they may represent some intermediate form of the language (in this case, Essex usage). Secondly, they may represent layers of scribal accretion imposed upon some earlier language, either that of the author or that of some intermediate scribe. The first possibility is made unlikely by the complete absence of such 'indexical' features from the dialect materials of intermediate counties; there is nothing like this mixture in Essex, for instance, whose dialect is well attested in the medieval materials.[5]

As for the second possibility, two opposing arguments could be raised. First, the textual evidence suggested that the language of the Fairfax, Stafford and Trentham manuscripts should be treated as a single idiolect, not as a mixture resulting from textual transmission, whereby copying scribes had blended their own forms with others deriving from exemplars.

Secondly, and more significantly, the Gowerian origins of certain forms in each group were supported by metrical evidence. Now, it has become traditional for users of the *Linguistic Atlas* to insist on its focus on the written mode. However, given that there is a necessary (if not always direct) relationship between writing and speech, since both transmit the 'same' language, it seems perverse not to recognise that some written usages point to a particular parallel spoken usage. Forms such as *or . . . or* and perhaps *bothen* in the Suffolk group, and *therwhiles that* and the syncopated verbs in the Kentish group, seem to demonstrate this. These forms must surely reflect distinctive prosodies in the spoken chain.

The implication of this argument is that Gower's own language has a 'mixed' basis, i.e. it is a 'true *Mischsprache*'. Such mixed usages are well attested amongst present-day speakers, particularly those with what sociolinguists term 'weak social ties', i.e. those who are socially mobile (either in geographical or in class terms).[6]

Such an interpretation is supported by external evidence of Gowerian associations with Kent and south-west Suffolk. The Kentish associations of Gower's family have long been known. In 1981, we cited a connection with Otford in northern Kent, an association which became traditional with Gower's early biographers in the nineteenth century. We were in error there; the Otford connections are very much less strong than we assumed. However, further work on the Kentish dialect-configuration suggests that Gower's much better-attested associations with Brabourne may be responsible for the Kentish element in his language. The Suffolk connection seems to relate to Gower's family ownership of Kentwell Manor, roughly equidistant between Bury St Edmunds, Lavenham and Clare in the south west of that county.[7]

Localising Gower's language to these two places does not, of course, mean that Gower did not, like his contemporary Chaucer, live – and thus write and speak – for much of his life in London. Rather, it means that his language was

---

5   See J. Youngson, 'Studies in the Dialect Materials of Medieval Essex', Ph.D. dissertation (Glasgow, 2002).
6   See J. Milroy, *Linguistic Variation and Change* (Oxford, 1992).
7   For details of life records, see Fisher, *John Gower*, Ch. 2, *passim*.

formed from varieties which may be typologically localised to these two places within the array of surviving Middle English texts. (I myself have lived in Scotland for almost twenty-five years, but no-one would ever mistake my language for that of a native Scot.) Although his language has a regional basis, Gower was evidently part of the linguistic community of late-fourteenth-century London. It is to this seeming paradox that we shall now turn.


# III


Late-fourteenth-century London was a remarkable place. It was the only city in Britain comparable in size to the great continental conurbations and city-states, such as Paris or Venice. But size was not the only feature which differentiated London from other English towns and cities. London was socially dynamic, swallowing up immigrants from the rest of the country and offering them opportunities to make their fortunes. This is the period of Dick Whittington, who set off to London from the countryside and ended up as Lord Mayor, as a significant wool-merchant and as a money-lender to the king. However, London was also a dangerous place, chronically riddled with disease, where the mortality rate was considerably higher than in the countryside. To move there was to gamble for high stakes: make a (comparative) fortune, or die. We know that the turnover in the population of late medieval London was huge.[8]

One source of danger, of course, came from abroad, for London was a great trading port; the Black Death arrived in London through trade with continental Europe. But, to emphasise the more positive side of this coin, London had a cosmopolitan atmosphere, with well-established communities of 'outsiders'. This atmosphere found one characteristic expression in the curious 'lading language', a macaronic mixture of English, French and Latin used as a *lingua franca* between traders;[9] but this must have been just one linguistic variety amongst many. We will return to this issue shortly.

Examination of that great repository of dialectal usages, the *Linguistic Atlas of Late Medieval English*, is, at first sight oddly, comparatively uninformative about the languages of London; putting it crudely, the *Atlas* gives us seventeen localised or localisable texts ('Sources Mapped') from sparsely inhabited Somerset, but only six texts from densely inhabited London.[10] This seeming discrepancy, however, is explicable: language, whether written or spoken, is attached to human beings, not locality; and since the turnover of humanity in London was so high, we must expect to find in the city a congeries of usages, derived from many localities. This point was strongly made by the late David Burnley in an important pioneering survey.[11] It is to these usages that we should now turn.

---

[8]  See P. Ackroyd, *London: The Biography* (London, 2000), and the sources there cited.
[9]  See V. Harding and L. Wright, eds., *London Bridge: Selected Accounts and Rentals, 1381–1538* (London, 1995).
[10]  McIntosh, et al., *Linguistic Atlas*, Vol. I, pp. 215, 236.
[11]  J.D. Burnley, *A Guide to Chaucer's Language* (London, 1983), Ch. 5.

IV

We may begin with the written mode. In a seminal article in 1963, Michael Samuels linked shifts in the population of London with his typology of 'incipient standard' written language, Types II, III and IV, whose linguistic characteristics were held to demonstrate successive waves of immigration into the capital.[12]

Type II, in the Samuels typology, is the London English of the middle of the fourteenth century, containing a mixture of East Anglian features and deriving from attested immigration to the capital from the Norfolk/Suffolk region. Good examples of Type II usage appear in the well-known Auchinleck manuscript of romances such as *Sir Orfeo*. Type III is represented by the language of the scribe of the Ellesmere and Hengwrt manuscripts, and that of the various London documents. This usage, which seems to span the turn of the fourteenth and fifteenth centuries, contains central Midland features brought into London through further waves of immigration from counties such as Bedfordshire. Type IV forms, which seem to be associated with a later wave of immigration from the Midlands, start to appear in some government documents from c. 1430. This so-called 'Chancery Standard' (perhaps more properly 'King's English') has sometimes been considered, notably by John Fisher, as part of a royal initiative in language-planning. However, Fisher's views have been comprehensively demolished by Michael Benskin in an important survey of the processes involved in late Middle English standardisation.[13]

However, it is important to emphasise that these Types did not occupy anything like the present position of standard written English. Standard written English is, in Einar Haugen's useful characterisation,[14] a fully standard language: it is selected, codified, elaborated and accepted. As far as we know, the late medieval Types were never codified officially; they were focused forms of the written language, not fixities, and admitted of a degree of variation which present-day readers and writers would find unacceptable. The Types had no status as the sole selected available usage for prestigious writing; they seem to have had particular associations with particular text-types, and were not elaborated for all kinds of written text. And (with the possible exception of Type IV) the Types were never accepted much beyond London; even within London their status was uncertain.

---

[12] M.L. Samuels, 'Some Applications of Middle English Dialectology', *English Studies* 44 (1963), pp. 81–94 (rpt. with revisions in M. Laing, ed., *Middle English Dialectology* [Aberdeen, 1988]).

[13] J.H. Fisher, 'Chancery and the Emergence of Standard Written English in the Fifteenth Century', *Speculum* 52 (1977), pp. 870–99; M. Benskin, 'Some New Perspectives on the Origins of Standard Written English', *Dialect and Standard Languages in the English, Dutch, German and Norwegian Language Areas*, eds. J.A. van Leuvensteijn and J.B. Berns (Amsterdam, 1992), pp. 71–105. Note that Samuels' Type I, which appears in many texts decocting university learning into the vernacular, notably but not exclusively Wycliffite material, is a separate matter; see M. Stenroos, 'A Variationist Approach to Middle English Dialects', *Transactions of the Philological Society* (forthcoming) for a comprehensive discussion and re-evaluation of this Type.

[14] E. Haugen, 'Dialect, Language, Nation', *American Anthropologist* 68 (1966), pp. 922–835.

This uncertainty of status is demonstrated if we look at the usage of an immigrant scribe who produced high-status volumes, in London, but who seems to have worked without much direct reference to the three Types. This is the well-known 'Scribe D', one of the most prolific copyists of his day, who was almost certainly an artisan in the 'book quarter' around St Paul's Cathedral at the beginning of the fifteenth century. Scribe D copied important texts of Chaucer, Langland, Trevisa and – above all – Gower.[15]

D's texts vary linguistically, but comparison of usage across the various traditions enables us to distinguish the scribe's 'own' input to the various linguistic mixtures found in all the manuscripts. Linguistic analysis of the complete known output of Scribe D shows him to have originated from the south-west Midlands, although his habit of transferring odd 'Gowerisms' to his copies of Chaucer's *Canterbury Tales* shows an element of plasticity in his reflection of the language of his MSS. Continual copying of Gower's *Confessio Amantis* has caused him to modify his 'own' usage, either through the adoption of Gowerian forms or, more subtly, through the selection of particular usages within his own repertoire which, coincidentally, also appear in the Gowerian system.[16]

What is interesting for our purposes is that Scribe D, whose lavishly prepared and luxuriously decorated manuscripts could have been afforded only by an elite social group, and who was clearly active in the metropolis, produced texts which differed linguistically in certain significant ways from Type III, allegedly the 'incipient standard' in London English of the time. Scribe D seems to have used not some general linguistic model – the Types – but rather a specific usage, that of Gower.

With regard to the spoken mode, we have of course no direct access to London usages of the later Middle Ages; we depend on reconstruction, and on the interpretation of writing.[17] Contemporary references to accent tend to focus on the oddity of outsiders – such as the young students in *The Reeve's Tale*, or Trevisa's notorious addition to his translation of Higden's *Polychronicon* – rather than on socially marked usages. Indeed, the northern students of *The Reeve's Tale* seem to be of a distinctly higher class than the Cambridgeshire miller they fool.[18] We have to wait until the Wakefield Second Shepherds' Play, usually dated to the first half of the fifteenth century,[19] before there is fairly clear indication that southern speech has a higher social status than that of the north. In this play, the comic sheep-stealer Mak adopts 'a Southren tothe' as part of his disguise as a king's servant.

15  A.I. Doyle and M.B. Parkes, 'The Production of Copies of the *Canterbury Tales* and *Confessio Amantis* in the Early Fifteenth Century', *Medieval Scribes, Manuscripts and Libraries: Essays Presented to N.R. Ker*, eds. M.B. Parkes and A.G. Watson (London, 1978), pp. 163–210; J.J. Smith, 'The Trinity Gower D-Scribe and his Work on Two Early *Canterbury Tales* Manuscripts', *The English of Chaucer*, eds. M.L. Samuels and J.J. Smith (Aberdeen, 1988), pp. 51–69.
16  Smith, 'Trinity Gower D-Scribe', pp. 51–69.
17  See further Smith, *An Historical Study of English* (London, 1996), Ch. 2.
18  J.R.R. Tolkien, 'Chaucer as Philologist: *The Reeve's Tale*', *Transactions of the Philological Society* (1934), pp. 1–70; J.J. Smith, 'The Great Vowel Shift in the North of England, and some Spellings in Manuscripts of Chaucer's *Reeve's Tale*', *Neuphilologische Mitteilungen* 95 (1995), pp. 433–7.
19  A.C. Cawley, *The Wakefield Pageants in the Towneley Cycle* (Manchester, 1958), p. xxxi.

Nevertheless, from our understanding of linguistic developments in comparable present-day situations, and from various indications from contemporary linguistic behaviour, it is possible to make some informed hypotheses about the likely situation with regard to the accents to be found in London. Indeed, it seems likely that interaction between accents of greater and lesser prestige lies behind the major phonological development distinguishing the Middle and Early Modern English periods, viz. the Great Vowel Shift.[20]

However, such phonological changes as the Shift are rarely simply a matter of transferring from one usage to another. The evidence suggests rather that what we have is a series of minor adjustments, driven by the perceptions of incoming persons with weak social ties who are attempting to reproduce the pronunciations of their social 'betters', and are rather uncertain as to how to do so. We will be returning to these perceptions later in this paper.

## V

Where can Gowerian usage be placed in relation to these developments? Table I presents a series of Gowerian (i.e. Fairfax manuscript) forms alongside two other sets:

(1) forms for the same items in the Ellesmere manuscript of the *Canterbury Tales*, which may be regarded as prototypical of Type III, and

(2) forms for the same items in the third hand of the Auchinleck manuscript, which Samuels cites as a prototypical example of Type II.

It will be clear from Table I that certain forms in the Fairfax manuscript which differ from those in Hengwrt/Ellesmere resemble those found in Type II texts. What does this mean?

It could be argued that Gower was simply an old-fashioned Londoner, and that the 'mixed' localisation offered by Michael Samuels and myself in 1981 was mistaken. However, within the archetypal set of forms which seem to derive from Gower's usage appear certain indexical features deriving from the Kentish and Suffolk varieties; these cannot be plausibly accommodated together (the co-occurrence of forms is important) within Type II. Nor are most of these indexical features found in Type II texts, as is indicated if a fuller comparison is made with Samuels' fuller list of prototypical forms for that Type.[21] According to the 'principle of minimising layers', the multiplication of layers of copying is to be avoided in the analysis of scribal outputs, since the more layers posited the more likely the analyst is to be mistaken. (The principle was distinguished explicitly for the first time by Benskin and Laing in 1981, but is obviously derived from Ockham's Razor.) If a set of forms can be accommodated in one layer, it should be accommodated there and not split up into subsets. In analysing Gower's usage, it is simplest to assume the presence of two (rather than three or four) layers.

So Gower's idiolect may continue to be considered a *Mischsprache*. However,

20  Smith, *Historical Study of English*, pp. 86–111.
21  Samuels, *Linguistic Evolution*, p. 167.

perhaps of greater interest for the purposes of this paper is not so much how his usage was produced, but rather how it was perceived; and here the parallel between Gowerian and Type II usage is significant. From what we know about the evolution of London English, much of Gower's usage would have been regarded by contemporaries as simply old-fashioned. His contemporaries may – must – have encountered forms from dialect areas not their own; but, not having access to a contemporary dialect atlas themselves, they would not be able to carry out the precise localisation of components which modern scholars can carry out.

When we turn to what we can reconstruct of Gower's pronunciation, a similar verdict may be given. There is little evidence in the Fairfax manuscript of written forms which reflect the characteristic speech-consonantism of medieval Kent, apart from sporadic forms such as *thong* 'thank' (beside *thonk[e]*).[22] The <z>-spellings characteristic of mid-fourteenth-century Kent as evidenced by Dan Michel's *Ayenbite of Inwyt*, do not appear. However, this may simply be an indication that the phonemic distinction between /s/-/z/ has simply disappeared by this date, even if the alveolar fricative was invariably realised as voiced, whatever the etymology or environment. The /s/-/z/ distinction is not marked in contemporary Kentish texts with much more strongly dialectal characteristics.[23]

The evidence from vocalism is a little more promising. Not much can be made of the reflexes of West Saxon /y/. The evidence is that the /e/-form, traditionally identified as a specifically Kentish phenomenon, had a wide currency throughout eastern England. Even though <e> appears in a larger number of 'West Saxon /y/-words' than in Chaucer's usage, it cannot have been a particularly marked phenomenon in Gower's language, and David Burnley showed clearly that London English had a mixture of realisations of this item.[24] Something of this mixed situation is reflected in the present-day standard English forms 'business', 'merry' and 'hill', all of which have stressed vowels reflecting West Saxon /y/.

However, more distinctive are Gower's reflexes of $\bar{æ}$. Characteristic of Old Kentish was the 'collapse' of both $\bar{æ}(1)$ and $\bar{æ}(2)$ on /e:/. Thus Old Kentish had the forms *dēd* 'deed' (with $\bar{æ}(1)$), *dēlan* 'share' (with $\bar{æ}(2)$). In Old Anglian these forms are reflected as *dēd*, *dǣlan*; in West Saxon they appear as *dǣd* and *dǣlan*. In Middle English, whatever the dialect, *ē* is reflected in /e:/, while $\bar{æ}$ is reflected in /ɛ:/. Thus the Middle English dialects descended from Old Anglian have /e:/ for '$\bar{æ}(1)$ words' and /ɛ:/ for '$\bar{æ}(2)$ words'. Dialects descended from West Saxon have /ɛ:/ for both; those descended from Old Kentish have /e:/ for both.

Of course, no contemporary would have known of this ancient distinction; historical phonologies of English did not exist in the late Middle Ages. In

---

22  See P.O.E. Gradon, *Ayenbite of Inwyt II: Introduction, Notes and Glossary* (Oxford, 1979), p. 19, n. 4.

23  J.J. Smith, 'The Letters s and z in South-Eastern Middle English', *Neuphilologische Mitteilungen* 101 (2000), pp. 403–13; S.C.H. Horobin and J.J. Smith, 'The Ordinance and Custom of St Laurence, Canterbury', *Anglia* 120 (2002), pp. 488–507.

24  Burnley, *Guide to Chaucer's Language*, p. 110.

contrast to the written material discussed above, aspects of this pronunciation would have been perceived by contemporary Londoners as 'advanced'. A mid-close rather than a mid-open pronunciation for the reflex of West Saxon $\bar{æ}$ would have been perceived as an early manifestation of the phenomenon we now term the Great Vowel Shift, which was probably already under way in northern speech and in hyperadapted varieties of English found in London.

Gower's language, therefore, though undoubtedly provincial in origin, could have been fairly easily accommodated within the London linguistic community; it would have raised no eyebrows, because Londoners encountered 'non-London' forms in speech and (if literate) in writing every day.

The accommodation of Gower's written language would have been eased by the fact that, like much southern English at the end of the fourteenth century, it was somewhat 'bleached' of distinctive dialectal characteristics. Comparison with a markedly Kentish text of about the same date, the Ordinance and Custom of St Laurence's Hospital, Canterbury, clarifies this point. Table II, which compares the realisations of selected items in Gower, the Ordinance and Custom, and the Ellesmere manuscript of Chaucer, shows that Gower's language, though retaining its dialectal basis, has been bleached of more 'grossly provincial' forms. Unlike the Ordinance and Custom, which is a rather archaic document with many linguistic forms in common with the *Ayenbite of Inwyt* copied half a century earlier, Gower's language does not contain a full set of indexically Kentish forms.

Such bleached usages are fairly widespread in late Middle English. A good example is the St John's College manuscript of Gower's *Confessio Amantis*, whose language can be localised in Herefordshire but which, when compared with that of earlier texts from that county, is much less dialectally marked.[25]

VI

There is no evidence that Gower's language would have been stigmatised in late medieval London. In the spoken mode there are indications that the 'raised' reflex of $\bar{æ}$ would have been regarded as prestigious rather than otherwise. The southern Great Vowel Shift of the fifteenth and sixteenth centuries seems to have been triggered by hyperadaptations, whereby incoming persons attempted to accommodate their phonologies to those speakers they encountered in the population they were joining. Thus (for instance) the crucial shift in the mid-vowels seems to derive from incomers attempting to reproduce slightly raised realisations which they heard from some Londoners (such as Chaucer, whose practice can be established from his rhymes), and subsequently over-shooting. Gower's raised mid-vowel in /e:/ as the reflex of West Saxon $\bar{æ}$ would have merged with such overshoots.[26]

Less hypothetically, in the written mode there is a well-attested habit of copy-

[25] See M. Black, 'Studies in the Dialect Materials of Medieval Herefordshire' (Glasgow, 1997), Ph.D. dissertation.
[26] Smith, *Historical Study of English*, pp. 86–111, and references there cited.

ists – both scribes and early printers – retaining 'Gowerisms' such as *oghne* 'own' (often slightly modified as *oughne, ougne* etc.), the syncopated verbs, and the *–ende* present participle until the beginning of the sixteenth century. By this time such forms must have seemed very eccentric. The reason for this tolerance relates to the history of standardisation of written English during the fifteenth and sixteenth centuries, which was not a straightforward process.

Research on the standardisation of written English during the late Middle Ages is still ongoing, but enough has been discovered to clarify the general process. For most of the Middle English period, English had a parochial function, and it made communicative sense to have a wide range of spelling-systems; this practice made it easier to teach reading and writing on a phonic basis. When the written mode was being used for a national function, then Latin and French were selected. However, as the use of English asserted itself for national functions during the latter part of the Middle Ages, the highly divergent spelling-systems of the earlier Middle English period began to become communicatively inconvenient. As a result, grossly provincial forms were discarded and those of wider currency were allowed to remain, producing a 'colourless' language which allowed a fair range of variation. Such colourless language seems to have arisen:

> when a writer replaces some or all of his distinctively local forms by equivalents which, although still native to the local or neighbouring dialects, are common currency over a wide area. The result is not a series of well-defined regional standards . . . but a continuum in which the local element is muted, and one type shifts almost imperceptibly into another.[27]

Thus the first phase of written standardisation seems to have been communicatively driven. The further step, to a fixed set of spellings, seems to have taken place once it became socially as well as communicatively dysfunctional to use non-standard forms at a time when a perception of 'better' or 'worse' ways of spelling was beginning to develop.

It has become usual in recent scholarship to state that this further step involved the adoption of forms associated with 'Chancery Standard', Samuels' Type IV. However, the evidence of the Gower tradition is that scribes of the *Confessio Amantis* do not seem to have had this perception of the role of 'Chancery Standard'. For them, the reference point is not an abstract Type but the language of their exemplars. An unusually high proportion of the texts of the *Confessio Amantis* can be shown to be in whole or in part *literatim* copies, i.e. letter-for-letter reproductions of exemplars, some even reproducing the peculiarities of the Fairfax manuscript itself (e.g. Harley 3869). In this peculiarity, the manuscripts of the *Confessio* are rather different from the obvious comparative benchmark, the manuscripts of the *Canterbury Tales*, where a traditional method of spelling does not seem to have emerged in the same way.[28]

Thus it could be argued that Gower's usage became, in a sense, a 'standard'

---

27  McIntosh et al., *Linguistic Atlas*, I.47.
28  Although see S.C.H. Horobin, *The Language of the Chaucer Tradition* (Cambridge, 2003).

or 'type', albeit one with a very limited function (i.e. copying Gowers), practised by a limited number of people (the Gower copyists). What gives this finding a wider interest is that the Gower tradition is not the only one to adopt a 'special' mode of spelling. Lotte Hellinga found something similar in the Nicholas Love tradition.[29] More broadly, some usages – such as Type I – seem to have been adopted for particular genres; Type I was prototypically used for decocting university learning into the vernacular, and it is thus found not only in many writings associated with the Wycliffite (and counter-Wycliffite) movement, but also in vernacular medicas.[30] In Scotland, copyists and printers of high-status poetry seem to have adopted a 'refined' Middle Scots containing curious quasi-anglicised spellings; a good example is the form *quhome* 'whom', with Scots <quh> combined with English <o>.[31] Other examples could be cited.

It seems that scribes and other copyists during the fifteenth century were seeking some authoritative reference point on which to base their usage, but a clear model to follow had not yet emerged. Indeed, this model would not emerge until the sixteenth century and the mass circulation of books consequent on the adoption of printing. Choosing Gower's usage is therefore an example of one of those non-sustainable innovations, highly characteristic of linguistic development at all levels of language conventionally distinguished (writing- and speech-systems, grammar, lexicon).[32]

Gower's *Confessio Amantis*, therefore, has a linguistic as well as a literary significance. The influence of poets on the history of the language is generally overstated; poets tend to find ('invent') the language around them rather than create things anew. But Gower does seem to have played at least a walk-on part in the story of English spelling. And his reputation as a linguistic authority survived even after people ceased to copy his strange spellings, for Ben Jonson was to use him extensively as a source of quotations in his *English Grammar*.

TABLE I

| ITEM | Ellesmere MS | Fairfax MS | Auchinleck MS (Hand 3) |
|------|--------------|------------|------------------------|
| -ING | -yng | -ende | -and (-ende, -ind) |
| DID | dide | dede | dede (dide) |
| SAW | saugh | sihe | segh(3) |
| THEY | they | þei | þai (hi, þei) |
| WILL | wol | wol | wil |
| WHILE | whil | therwhiles | (ther)while |

---

[29] Lotte Hellinga, 'Nicholas Love in Print', *Nicholas Love at Waseda*, eds. S. Oguro, R. Beadle and M. Sargent (Cambridge, 1997), pp. 143–62.
[30] See Stenroos, forthcoming.
[31] Cf. streng-Scots *quham*; for details, see A. Agutter, 'Middle Scots as a Literary Language', *The History of Scottish Literature I: Origins to 1660*, ed. R.D.S. Jack (Aberdeen, 1988), p. 17.
[32] See further Smith, *Historical Study of English*, p. 151.

## TABLE II

| ITEM | Ellesmere MS | Fairfax MS | Ordinance and Custom |
|------|--------------|------------|----------------------|
| GOOD | go(o)d(e) | good(e) | gwod |
| AFTER | after | after | efter |
| WHERE | wher(e) | wher(e) | hwer |
| SHE | sche | sche | hy |

# 4

# The Manuscripts and Illustrations of Gower's Works

DEREK PEARSALL

Previous listings of the manuscripts of Gower's writings include four that should be mentioned: those of Macaulay and Fisher, and those included in *The Index of Middle English Verse* (English poems only) and the *Manual of Writings in Middle English*.[1] For the manuscripts that were known to him and that he had inspected, Macaulay provides descriptions that are remarkably full and accurate for their day.[2] The other lists of Gower manuscripts give only brief indications of date and content and, in the case of the *Manual*, of the recent ownership and sales history of the more peripatetic manuscripts.[3] The present list is based on that prepared by the late Jeremy J. Griffiths, with the assistance of Ruth Dean, A.I. Doyle and Kate D. Harris, in December 1979, as a preparatory move in the collaborative making of a 'Descriptive Catalogue' of the manuscripts of Gower's works. The abbreviations in brackets at the end of a manuscript entry indicate the presence of the *Traitié*, the *Cronica Tripertita* and the various short Latin pieces in verse and prose that often accompany the texts of the major poems, as follows:

Ad   'Ad mundum mitto'
CT   *Cronica Tripertita*
Ex   'Explicit iste liber'
M    Minor Latin poems (sixteen Latin poems, mostly very short, occurring in various permutations)
P    *Carmen Super Multiplici Viciorum Pestilentia*

---

[1] G.C. Macaulay, ed., *The Complete Works of John Gower*, 4 vols (Oxford, 1899–1902), I.lxviii–lxix, lxxix–lxxxi; II.cxxxviii–clxviii; IV.lx–lxxi; John H. Fisher, *John Gower: Moral Philosopher and Friend of Chaucer* (New York, 1964), pp. 303–7; Carleton Brown and Rossell Hope Robbins, *The Index of Middle English Verse* (New York, 1943); with Supplement by R.H. Robbins and John L. Cutler (Lexington, 1965), No. 2662; *A Manual of the Writings in Middle English 1050–1500*, general ed. Albert E. Hartung, Vol. VII, Ch. 17: *John Gower*, by John H. Fisher, R. Wayne Hamm, Peter G. Beidler and Robert F. Yeager (New Haven, 1986), pp. 2404–9.

[2] Macaulay, *Complete Works*, describes thirty-nine of the forty-nine complete or once-complete manuscripts of the *Confessio Amantis* that are now known to survive (those not known to him were Nos. 1, 17, 20, 26, 29, 42, 45, below), and reports his knowledge of three others (Nos. 19, 30, 49). He knew all except two (Nos. 81, 82) of the manuscripts of Gower's other works. He also describes briefly or reports seven (Nos. 51, 54, 58, 59, 60, 62, 63) of the seventeen manuscripts recorded here that contain fragments of or extracts from the *Confessio*; these manuscripts, being of no use to him as an editor, interested him less.

[3] The list in the *Manual* is full and generally reliable, though not easy to use; the only additions made here are of three manuscripts containing extracts (Nos. 56, 61, 64).

Q       'Quia unusquisque' (prose colophon)
QC      'Quam cinxere' with preceding prose rubric 'Epistola super huius'
T       *Traitié*


## LIST OF MANUSCRIPTS

*Confessio Amantis*

Manuscripts are listed according to the three 'recensions' distinguished by Macaulay (II.cxxvii–cxxxviii), with Ia, Ib and Ic for manuscripts of the first recension to indicate what he more doubtfully distinguished (see below, 'The Text') as the three versions of that recension, viz. revised, intermediate and unrevised. Eight works have head-entries; manuscripts that contain more than one work and have to be repeatedly mentioned are, after their first appearance in the listing, set in italics in short form and numbered according to their first appearance.

*First recension*
1.  Cambridge, Pembroke College, MS 307 (Ic), s.xv first quarter (Ex QC Q; also Table of Contents)
2.  Cambridge, St Catherine's College, MS 7 (Ib), s.xv *med.* (7 leaves lost) (Ex QC Q)
3.  Cambridge, St John's College, MS B.12 (34) (Ia), s.xv first quarter (Ex QC Q)
4.  Cambridge, University Library, MS Dd.8.19 (Ic), s.xv *med.* (much omitted from Book V and all from VII.3684, not through loss of leaves)
5.  Cambridge, University Library, MS Mm.2.21 (Ia), s.xv first quarter
6.  Chicago, Newberry Library, Case MS 33.5 (Louis H. Silver Collection MS 3) (formerly Castle Howard, Earl of Carlisle) (Ic), s.xv *ex.* (22 leaves lost) (Ex QC Q)
7.  Glasgow University Library, Hunterian MS 7 (S.1.7) (Ib), s.xv first quarter (24 leaves lost, text supplied on added leaves)
8.  London, British Library, Additional MS 22139 (Ib), s.xv third quarter (34 leaves lost) (Ex QC Q). Added: four short poems by Chaucer
9.  London, British Library, MS Egerton 913 (Ia), s.xv first quarter, fragmentary (Prologue and I.1–1701 only)
10. London, British Library, MS Egerton 1991 (Ic), s.xv first quarter (Ex QC Q)
11. London, British Library, MS Harley 3490 (Ib), 1450–60. Also the *Speculum religiosorum* of St Edmund of Abingdon (separate quire, same hand)
12. London, British Library, MS Royal 18.C.xxii (Ic), s.xv first quarter (Ex QC Q)
13. London, British Library, MS Stowe 950 (Ib), s.xv first quarter (20 leaves lost)
14. London, College of Arms, MS Arundel 45 (LXV) (Ic), s.xv *med.* (15 leaves lost)
15. London, Society of Antiquaries, MS 134 (Ib), s.xv *med.* (7 leaves lost) (Ex QC Q). Also, in the same hand and integral with the MS, Lydgate's *Life of Our Lady* (acephalous), Hoccleve's *Regiment of Princes*, and John Walton's verse translation of Boethius (fragment)
16. Manchester, Chetham's Library, MS A.7.38 (A.6.11, wrongly, in Macaulay)

(6696) (Ia), s.xvi second quarter. An abridged text, copied from the same exemplar as Princeton Garrett (No. 30, below) (Ex QC)

17. New York, Columbia University Library, Plimpton Collection MS 265 (Ic), s.xv first quarter

18. New York, Pierpont Morgan Library, MS M125 (formerly Marquess of Hastings, then Quaritch) (Ib), s.xv first quarter (lacks leaves) (Ex QC Q)

19. New York, Pierpont Morgan Library, MS M126 (Ib), s.xv third quarter. Not known to Macaulay, except for the Frere miniatures (II.clxvi), which were reunited with the MS (purchased by Morgan in 1903) in 1926 (Ex QC Q; also an alphabetical index)

20. New York, Pierpont Morgan Library MS M690 (formerly Ravensworth Castle, Earl of Ravensworth, bought from Maggs in 1924) (Ic), s.xv first quarter

21. Oxford, Bodleian Library, MS Arch. Selden B.11 (SC 3357) (Ic), s.xv *med*. (Ex QC Q)

22. Oxford, Bodleian Library, MS Ashmole 35 (SC 6916) (Ic), s.xv first quarter (10 leaves lost)

23. Oxford, Bodleian Library, MS Bodley 693 (SC 2875) (Ic), s.xv first quarter (Ex QC Q)

24. Oxford, Bodleian Library, MS Bodley 902 (SC 27573) (Ia), s.xv first quarter (Ex QC Q)

25. Oxford, Bodleian Library, MS Laud (Misc.) 609 (SC 754) (Ic), s.xv first quarter (10 leaves lost) (Ex QC Q)

26. Oxford, Christ Church, MS 148 (I), s.xv first quarter (Ex QC Q)

27. Oxford, Corpus Christi College, MS 67 (Ic), s.xv *in*. (Ex QC Q)

28. Oxford, New College, MS 326 (Ia), s.xv third quarter

29. Philadelphia, Rosenbach Foundation, MS 1083/29 (368) (formerly Earl of Aberdeen) (Ic), s.xv *med*.

30. Princeton University, Firestone Library, Garrett MS 136 (formerly Phillipps MS 2298) (Ia), s.xv first quarter. An abridged text, copied from the same exemplar as Chetham (No. 16, above) (Ex)

31. Private Collection (formerly Mount Stuart, Rothesay, Marquess of Bute, MS I.17; Sotheby 13 June 1983, lot 10, sold to Kraus) (Ib), s.xv first quarter (18 leaves lost)

*Second recension*

32. Cambridge, Sidney Sussex College, MS 63 (Δ.4.1), s.xv second quarter (Ex QC; also *Cato's Distichs*, in English)

33. Cambridge, Trinity College, MS R.3.2 (581), s.xv first quarter (5 quires, or 40 leaves, lost at beginning) (Ex QC Q P M T)

34. London, British Library, Additional MS 12043, s.xv first quarter (21 leaves lost)

35. Nottingham, University Library, Middleton Collection, MS Mi LM 8 (formerly Wollaton Hall), s.xv first quarter (Ex QC Q P M T)

36. Oxford, Bodleian Library, MS Bodley 294 (SC 2449), s.xv first quarter (Ex QC Q P M T)

37. Princeton University, Firestone Library, Robert H. Taylor Collection, Medi-

eval MS 5 (formerly Phillipps MS 8192, then Rosenbach 369), s.xv first quarter (Ex QC Q P M T; also Table of Contents)

38. San Marino (California), Huntington Library, MS EL 26.A.17 (formerly Stafford), s.xiv *ex.* Defective (17 leaves lost): see No. 55 below (Ex QC)

*Third recension*

39. Geneva, Fondation Bodmer, MS 178 (formerly Keswick Hall, J.H. Gurney), s.xv first quarter (Ex QC P M T)

40. London, British Library, MS Harley 3869, s.xv second quarter (Ex QC Q P M T). Added, in a different hand, s.xv third quarter: (on a separate quire, at the beginning of the MS) 'Queen Margaret's Entry, 1445'; (at the end) a Latin prayer and two Latin Marian lyrics

41. London, British Library, MS Harley 7184, s.xv third quarter (52 leaves lost)

42. New Haven, Yale University, Beinecke Library, Osborn Collection, MS fa.1, s.xv first half. The Pearson fragment (see below, No. 53) is a quire detached from this MS, first identified by Jeremy Griffiths[4] (Ex QC P M T)

43. Oxford, Bodleian Library, MS Fairfax 3 (SC 3883), s.xiv *ex.* (Ex QC Q P M T)

44. Oxford, Bodleian Library, MS Hatton 51 (SC 4099), s.xvi first half. Copy of Caxton's printed edition of 1483

45. Oxford, Bodleian Library, MS Lyell 31 (formerly Clumber, bought from Sotheby 1937), s.xv *med.* (Ex)

46. Oxford, Magdalen College, MS (lat.) 213, s.xv third quarter (9 leaves lost) (Ex)

47. Oxford, New College, MS 266, s.xv first quarter (Ex QC; also Table of Contents)

48. Oxford, Wadham College, MS 13, s.xv third quarter (Ex QC T)

49. Washington, Folger Shakespeare Library, MS Sm.1 (V.b.29) (formerly Phillipps MS 8942), s.xv *med.*

*Confessio Amantis – FRAGMENTS*

50. Cambridge, Trinity College, MS Fragments Box 2 (fragment of a single leaf, recovered from a binding), s.xv second quarter

51. London, University College, MS Frag.Angl.1 (formerly Phillipps 22914) (2 bifolia), s.xv first quarter

52. Mertoun, Duke of Sutherland (single leaf), s.xv *med.* Reported in *Manual*, on the basis of information from Richard Wayne Hamm; not otherwise recorded

53. Private Collection, ex R.C. Pearson (32 Hobson Street, Cambridge), cat. 13 (1953), item 219 (a quire detached from Yale Osborn MS fa.1, see above No. 42)

54. Shrewsbury, Shrewsbury School MS (Ic) (single leaf, recovered from a binding), s.xv second quarter

55. Tokyo, Takamiya fragment (bought from Quaritch, 1999). Fragment of a leaf,

---

4   Jeremy Griffiths, 'Marginalia', *Yale University Library Gazette*, 59 (1985), pp. 174–77.

with passages from IV.2351–2520, belonging to the Huntington 'Stafford' MS (No. 38 above); first reported by Edwards and Takamiya[5]

*Confessio Amantis – EXTRACTS*[6]

56. Boston (Massachusetts), Public Library MS f.Med.94 (1521). Short extract (VII.1811–23) added in the early sixteenth century on a blank page at the end of a MS of Lydgate's *Siege of Thebes* copied by Stephen Dodesham (died c.1482) in the earlier part of his career.[7]
57. Cambridge, Gonville and Caius College, MS 176/97. A short extract included in a predominantly medical collection
58. Cambridge, University Library, MS Ee.2.15, s.xv last quarter. Fragments of two tales
59. Cambridge, University Library, MS Ff.1.6 (the 'Findern' manuscript), s.xv second half. Five extracts
60. London, British Library, MS Harley 7333, s.xv second half. Five extracts
61. Longleat House, Wiltshire (the Marquess of Bath), MS 174 (s.xv second half). Gower's account of the fifteen stars (VII.1281–1438) copied into a predominantly medical collection.[8]
62. Oxford, Balliol College, MS 354 (Richard Hill's 'commonplace book'), s.xvi first quarter. Fourteen tales, some quite long
63. Oxford, Bodleian Library, MS Rawlinson D.82 (SC 12900), s.xv second half. Long extract from Book VIII (the dismissal of Amans) in a MS originally part of a fascicular but now dismembered collection
64. Oxford, Bodleian Library, MS Rawlinson D.358 (s.xv first half), originally part of Douce 299 (21873). Latin abridgement of story of Constance (Book II) based on Latin summaries and English text.[9]
65. Oxford, Trinity College, MS D.29, s.xvi first quarter. Extracts incorporated in a prose history;[10] also Nebuchadnezzar's dream, from the Prologue
66. Tokyo, Takamiya Collection MS 32 (formerly Boies Penrose MS 6, then Delamere), 1450–60. Five tales, and also the story of Nebuchadnezzar compiled from the Prologue and Book I.

---

[5] A.S.G. Edwards and T. Takamiya, 'A New Fragment of Gower's *Confession Amantis*', *Modern Language Review* 96 (2001), pp. 931–6.
[6] The manuscripts containing extracts from the *Confessio* are exhaustively described in the unpublished thesis of Kate Harris, 'Ownership and Readership: Studies in the Provenance of the Manuscripts of Gower's *Confessio Amantis*' (University of York, 1993), pp. 27–75; see also Harris, 'John Gower's *Confessio Amantis*: The Virtues of Bad Texts', *Manuscripts and Readers in Fifteenth-Century England: The Literary Implications of Manuscript Study*, ed. Derek Pearsall (Cambridge, 1983), pp. 27–40; A.S.G. Edwards, 'Selection and Subversion in Gower's *Confessio Amantis*', *Re-Visioning Gower*, ed. R.F. Yeager (Asheville, 1998), pp. 257–67.
[7] See Priscilla Bawcutt, 'The Boston Public Library manuscript of John Lydgate's *Siege of Thebes*: its Scottish owners and inscriptions', *Medium Aevum*, 70 (2001), pp. 80–94 (pp. 89–90); Harris, 'Ownership and Readership', pp. 27–8.
[8] First reported by Kate Harris, 'The Longleat House Extracted Manuscript of Gower's *Confessio Amantis*', in *Middle English Poetry: Texts and Traditions. Essays in Honour of Derek Pearsall*, ed. A.J. Minnis (York, 2001), pp. 77–90.
[9] First reported by Harris, 'Ownership and Readership', p. 59.
[10] See Kate Harris, 'Unnoticed Extracts from Chaucer and Hoccleve: Huntington MS HM 144, Trinity College, Oxford MS D 29 and *The Canterbury Tales*', *Studies in the Age of Chaucer*, 20 (1998), pp. 167–99 (pp. 168–9); first reported in Harris 'The Virtues of Bad Texts', pp. 31–3.

Post-1600 MSS. London, British Library, Additional MS 38181 is a seventeenth-century transcript of Takamiya MS 32 (No. 66 above). The Latin notes on the fifteen stars (see No. 61 above), taken from Berthelette's edition, appear in BL MS Sloane 3847, an alchemical and necromantic collection (s.xv–xvii), and Elias Ashmole includes Gower's account of the Philosopher's Stone (IV.2457–2632), also from Berthelette, in his *Theatrum Chemicum Britannicum* (1652).[11]

## Vox Clamantis

67. Dublin, Trinity College, MS D.4.6 (214), s.xv first quarter (Q)
68. Glasgow, University Library, Hunterian MS T.2.17, c.1400 (Ad CT Q P M T)
69. Hertfordshire, Hatfield House MS (Marquess of Salisbury), s.xv second quarter
70. Lincoln, Cathedral Library, MS A.72 (235), s.xvi first quarter. *Vox* copied from Laud MS 719 (No. 76, below) (P M)
71. London, British Library, MS Cotton Tiberius A.iv, s.xiv *ex.* (Ad CT Q P M)
72. London, British Library, MS Cotton Titus A.xiii. Prologue-III.116 only. Copied from Digby MS 138 (No. 75, below) by William Lambard (s.xvi third quarter) and incorporated in a collection of chronicles and historical documents
73. London, British Library, MS Harley 6291, s.xiv *ex.* (CT Q P M)
74. Oxford, All Souls College, MS 98, s.xiv *ex.* (CT Q P M T; also unique copy of Latin verse 'Epistle to Arundel')
75. Oxford, Bodleian Library, MS Digby 138 (SC 1739), s.xv second quarter
76. Oxford, Bodleian Library, MS Laud (Misc.) 719 (SC 1061), s.xv second quarter. Book I omitted (Ad P M; also unique copy of short Latin poem 'Inter saxosum')
77. San Marino (California), Huntington Library, MS HM 150 (formerly Ecton Hall), s.xiv *ex.* (Ad P M)

## Cronica Tripertita

68. *Glasgow, University Library, Hunterian MS T.2.17 (with* Vox *and* Traitié*)*
71. *London, British Library, MS Cotton Tiberius A.IV (with* Vox*)*
73. *London, British Library, MS Harley 6291 (with* Vox*)*
74. *Oxford, All Souls College, MS 98 (with* Vox*)*
78. Oxford, Bodleian Library, MS Hatton 92 (SC 4073), s.xv first half (M)

## Mirour de l'Omme

79. Cambridge, University Library, Additional MS 3035, s.xiv *ex.*

## Traitié Pour Essampler les Amantz Marietz

33. *Cambridge, Trinity College, MS R.3.2 (581) (with* Confessio*)*

---

[11] See Harris, 'Longleat House Extracted Manuscript', pp. 89–90.

39. *Geneva, Fondation Bodmer, MS Bodmer 178 (with* Confessio*)*
7. *Glasgow, University Library, Hunterian MS T.2.17 (with* Vox *and* Cronica*)*
80. London, British Library, Additional MS 59495 (formerly Trentham Hall), s.xv *in.* (with *Cinkante Balades*, 'In Praise of Peace') (M)
81. London, British Library, MS Arundel 364. Fragment on a leaf added to a MS of Nicholas Love's *Meditationes Vitae Christi* (s.xv *med.*)
40. *London, British Library, MS Harley 3869 (with* Confessio*)*
42. *New Haven, Yale University, Beinecke Library, Osborn Collection, MS fa.1 (with* Confessio*)*
35. *Nottingham, University Library, Middleton Collection, MS Mi LM 8 (with* Confessio*)*
74. *Oxford, All Souls College, MS 98 (with* Vox *and* Cronica*)*
36. *Oxford, Bodleian Library, MS Bodley 294 (with* Confessio*)*
43. *Oxford, Bodleian Library, MS Fairfax 3 (with* Confessio*)*
48. *Oxford, Wadham College, MS 13 (with* Confessio*)*
37. *Princeton, University Library, Robert H. Taylor Collection MS (with* Confessio*)*

London, British Library, Additional MS 59496 is a transcript of No. 80 made in 1764 at the request of its owner, Granville Leveson-Gower, second Earl Gower.[12]

*Cinkante Balades*
80. *London, British Library, Additional MS 59495 (with* Traitié*)*

*'In Praise of Peace'*
80. *London, British Library, Additional MS 59495 (with* Traitié *and* Cinkante Balades*)*
82. London, British Library, MS Cotton Julius F.vii, s.xv *med.* (Latin introductory verses only)

TRANSLATIONS

83. Madrid, Biblioteca de Palacio, MS II-3088, dated 1430. Portuguese translation of the *Confessio* made by Robert Payne.[13]
84. Madrid, Escorial Library, MS g.II.19, s.xv second half. Spanish (Castilian) translation by Juan de Cuenca of the Portuguese translation of the *Confessio*.[14]
85. London, British Library, MS Stowe 951, s.xv second quarter. Quixley's English translation of the *Traitié*

---

12  See Siân Echard, 'House Arrest: Modern Archives, Medieval Manuscripts', *Journal of Medieval and Early Modern Studies* 30:2 (2000), pp. 185–210 (p. 190 and n. 23).
13  See Antonio Cortijo Ocaña, '*O Livro de Amante*: The Lost Portuguese Translation of John Gower's *Confessio Amantis* (Madrid, Biblioteca de Palacio, MS II-3088)', *Portugese Studies*, 13 (1997), pp. 1–6.
14  See Bernardo Santano Moreno, 'The Fifteenth-Century Portuguese and Castilian Translations of John Gower, *Confessio Amantis*', *Manuscripta* 35 (1991), pp. 23–34.

## The Character of the Manuscripts[15]

There is a type of manuscript of the *Confessio* which is so frequently found among the surviving copies that it can almost be characterised as 'standard'. Such a manuscript was copied during the first quarter of the fifteenth century, or just before, by a good professional London scribe. It consists of about 180–200 folio-size parchment leaves of good quality, in quires of eight with catchwords, and the text is spaciously written, almost always by one scribe only, in double columns, with forty-six lines per column. The manuscript has two miniatures and the decoration is organised according to a regular hierarchy, with vinets (full floreate borders) or demi-vinets (two- or three-sided borders), decorated initials (champs) of different sizes, pen-flourished coloured initials, and decorated or undecorated paraphs, used to mark out different elements in that hierarchy and to indicate the divisions of the text for the reader. There are no other contents in this 'standard' manuscript, apart from the Latin rubrics and poems written by Gower to accompany the *Confessio*, and also, in several cases, the *Traitié* with its Latin apparatus.

Of the forty-eight surviving manuscripts of the *Confessio*, twenty-eight date from before about 1425. Nearly all conform quite closely to this standard, and it will not be misleading to have it in mind as a 'norm' which later manuscripts will imitate or from which they will deviate. It could be called a production programme or even campaign, associated with and contributing significantly to the great expansion in the commercial production of large manuscripts of secular vernacular poetry and prose in the early decades of the fifteenth century.[16] Given the more and more prominently displayed nature of the dedication to Henry, Earl of Derby, and the energy that Gower employed in adapting the Latin apparatus of the *Confessio* to the praise of Henry (as well as in revising the *Vox Clamantis* and writing the *Cronica Tripertita*), it may be that there were political influences at work in pushing forward such a programme of production. Certainly, as we shall see later, several of these early manuscripts were made for members of the Lancastrian royal family.

The Fairfax and Huntington Stafford MSS (Nos. 43 and 38 above) are the earliest of this group of manuscripts, both copied from exemplars prepared probably under Gower's direct supervision, and providing excellent texts of the poem and excellent models of the manner in which it was to be set out. Fairfax is 343 x 235mm, Stafford 353 x 248, and these (about 13½ x 9½ inches or so, for the metrically illiterate) are a little below the average size for the group. Some are a

---

[15] The descriptions that follow draw upon first-hand knowledge or microfilm of about thirty-five MSS of Gower's works, upon Macaulay's descriptions, upon A.I. Doyle and M.B. Parkes, 'The Production of Copies of the *Canterbury Tales* and *Confessio Amantis* in the Early Fifteenth Century', *Medieval Scribes, Manuscripts and Libraries: Essays Presented to N.R. Ker*, eds. M.B. Parkes and A.G. Watson (London, 1978), pp. 163–210, and for individual MSS upon particular works cited. I am also grateful to Siân Echard, Tony Edwards, Peter Nicholson and Bob Yeager for their help with particular points.

[16] See A.S.G. Edwards and Derek Pearsall, 'The Manuscripts of the Major English Poetic Texts', *Book Production and Publishing in Britain 1375–1475*, eds. Jeremy Griffiths and Derek Pearsall (Cambridge, 1989), pp. 257–78 (pp. 257–60).

little smaller (Cambridge St John's B.12, Bodley 902, Morgan 125, Add.12043, Geneva Bodmer, New College 266) or about the same size (Cambridge University Library, hereafter CUL Mm.2.21, Royal 18.C.xxii, Stowe 950, Ashmole 35, Yale Osborn), others bigger (Egerton 1991, Bodley 693, Bute, Nottingham, Bodley 294, Princeton Taylor, Cambridge Trinity R.3.2) or much bigger, over 400mm high (Cambridge Pembroke 307, Glasgow Hunterian, Laud 609, Oxford Corpus 67). Nearly all have miniatures, usually the standard two, or have spaces for miniatures, or have had them cut out; the exceptions are Yale Osborn, Cambridge Trinity R.3.2 (which bears many marks of its chequered production career), Cambridge St John's B.12, Stowe 950 and Ashmole 35; the last four also have more modest decoration.[17]

The scribes of this group of manuscripts seem to form a close-knit group. Six of the manuscripts (Egerton 1991, Columbia Plimpton, Christ Church 148, Oxford Corpus 67, Bodley 294, Princeton Taylor) and portions of two others (Bodley 902, Cambridge Trinity R.3.2) are written in a very good, large and exceptionally regular *anglicana formata*, the hand of Scribe D of Cambridge Trinity R.3.2, one of five scribes identified in the important study by Doyle and Parkes.[18] He was active in the first two decades of the fifteenth century, and responsible also for manuscripts of three of the other large secular works of the period, the *Canterbury Tales*, *Piers Plowman* and Trevisa's Bartholomaeus translation. His is the 'classic' hand of early fifteenth-century English literary manuscripts. Closely comparable, and perhaps an associate or rival of Scribe D, is the busy full-time scrivener called Scribe Δ (Delta) by Doyle and Parkes,[19] who copied Royal 18.C.xxii of the *Confessio* as well as manuscripts of Nicholas Love's *Mirror* and Trevisa's *Polychronicon* translation. There are also other scribes of the period who can be followed from manuscript to manuscript of the *Confessio* (Laud 609, for instance, is written by the same scribe as Bodley 693), and from the *Confessio* to manuscripts of other standard works (the scribe of Cambridge Pembroke 307 copied Arundel 119 of Lydgate's *Siege of Thebes*, the scribe of Antiquaries 134 copied Harley 1758 of the *Canterbury Tales*,[20] and Scribe B of Cambridge Trinity R.3.2 copied the Hengwrt and Ellesmere MSS of the *Canterbury Tales*).

Few manuscripts of the period were written by more than one principal scribe: Bodmer has six scribes, Cambridge Trinity R.3.2 and CUL Mm.2.21 have five, Bodley 902 has three, and Add.22139 and Egerton 913 have two. A further scribe may have a walk-on part to supply an omission (as in Egerton 913) or for no evident reason (a second scribe writes three columns in Magdalen 213), and there is a second and a third revising scribe at work in Fairfax 3.[21] All manu-

---

[17] Ashmole is exceptional among early MSS in omitting all the Latin apparatus (the Latin summaries are replaced by versions in English). See Siân Echard, 'With Carmen's Help: Latin Authorities in the *Confessio Amantis*', *Studies in Philology* 95 (1998), pp. 1–40.

[18] Doyle and Parkes, 'Production of Copies', p. 177; for the addition of the Taylor MS to the Scribe D corpus, see Edwards and Pearsall, 'Manuscripts of the Major English Poetic Texts', p. 275, n. 43.

[19] Doyle and Parkes, 'Production of Copies', p. 206.

[20] I am grateful for this piece of information to Linne Mooney, who is making a study of fifteenth-century vernacular hands that can be found in more than one MS.

[21] David Anderson, *Sixty Bokes Olde and Newe*, Catalogue of the Exhibition in Philadelphia on

scripts follow the double-column format, all but one with forty-two to fifty lines per column (Cambridge St John's B.12 has thirty-nine), and at least twelve observe a strict forty-six lines per column, pricked, ruled and boxed: Cambridge Pembroke 307, CUL Mm.2.21, Glasgow Hunterian, Morgan 126, Bodley 693, Bodley 902, Cambridge Trinity R.3.2, Nottingham, Princeton Taylor, Huntington Stafford, Geneva Bodmer, and Fairfax.[22] In Trinity R.3.2 a 46–line exemplar has been copied column-for-column, with several improvisations to preserve the format where mistakes have been made by one or other of the five scribes in the ruling or copying. In CUL Mm.2.21, also copied by several scribes, column-for-column from the exemplar, similar adjustments are made by moving Latin summaries from margin to text-column. Geneva Bodmer corresponds to Fairfax column-for-column throughout, though not copied from it, demonstrating the continuing tenacity of the format among exemplars. Bodley 902 likewise corresponds column-for-column to Fairfax up to fol. 81, at which point the new scribe starts saving space by setting the Latin verse-headings in the margin; the same happens, at the same point in the text (fol. 81, at the beginning of Book V) in CUL Mm.2.21, but without change of hand. There is evidence also of column-for-column copying in Yale Osborn, and in Add.12043 a passage omitted without loss of leaf (III.1665–1848) corresponds exactly to what is supplied on an added leaf in a different hand to remedy the omission in the Stafford MS. The passage is 184 lines long, exactly four columns of forty-six lines, with summaries in the margin.

There is more variety in later manuscripts of the *Confessio*. The market for de luxe and 'economy de luxe' manuscripts was probably largely satisfied by the existing manuscripts (and their lost companions) as they passed from owner to owner and down the social chain. Some continued to be made on the 'standard' model, with illustrations (whether or not surviving), or spaces for them, and rich decoration – including Add.22139, Harley 3490 (no miniatures), Antiquaries 134, Philadelphia Rosenbach and CUL Dd.8.19 (illustration and decoration planned but never completed). There are also some that surpass in size and grandeur anything produced in the earlier part of the century, namely Cambridge St Catherine's 7 and Magdalen 213 (no miniatures) and the colossal Harley 7184 (Fig. 1), 545 x 370mm, severely mutilated, with fifty-two leaves lost, some presumably with miniatures. All these manuscripts are from the middle or third quarter of the century, when there was perhaps a renewal of production on a limited scale of *Confessio* manuscripts, some of it in the beautiful new bastard secretary hand of the 'hooked g scribe' or his lookalikes (Harley 7184, Lyell 31, Magdalen 213) and one, the lavishly illustrated Morgan 126, in the 'flamboyant

---

the occasion of the Fifth International Congress of the New Chaucer Society, 1986 (Knoxville, 1986), p. 103 finds another hand on fols 1 and 8 of the Princeton Taylor *Confessio* text and a third on fols 4–7.

22  See Edwards and Pearsall, 'Manuscripts of the Major English Poetic Texts', p. 274, n. 29. In addition, Bodley 294 and Oxford New College 266 are nearly always regularly forty-six lines. For Morgan 126, see Patricia Eberle, 'Miniatures as Evidence of Reading in a Manuscript of the *Confessio Amantis* (Pierpont Morgan MS. M. 126)', *John Gower: Recent Studies*, Medieval Institute Publications, SMC 26, ed. R.F. Yeager (Kalamazoo, 1989), pp. 311–65 (p. 318).

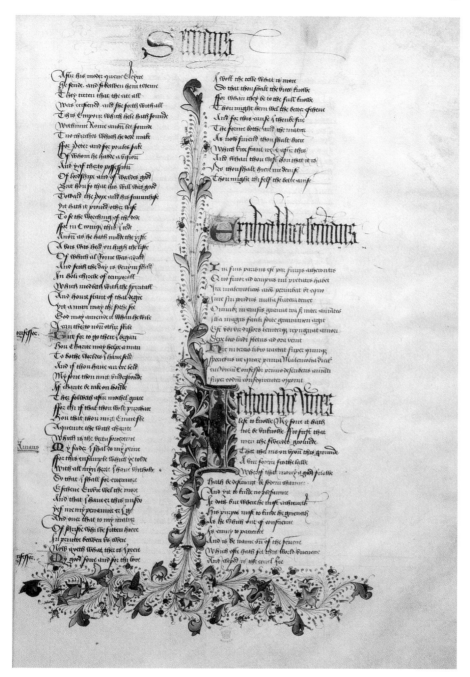

Figure 1. British Library, MS Harley 7184, fol. 45r. *Confessio Amantis*, beginning of Book III. By permission of the British Library.

spiky script' of Ricardus Franciscus.[23] None of the manuscripts of this period preserves the strict 46–line format, though there is clear evidence in Harley 3869, Harley 7184 and Magdalen 213 of ultimate derivation from Fairfax or Geneva Bodmer.

In addition to these more traditional manuscripts, there are now, almost for the first time (the only earlier instance is Ashmole 35) manuscripts written on paper (Egerton 913, College of Arms Arundel 45, Sidney Sussex 63, Wadham 13), or paper with some parchment leaves (Selden B.11), or paper with protective parchment leaves for the outsides of the quires (Harley 3869). They are mostly smaller than the old 'standard' manuscripts, about 290 x 210mm (apart from Selden B.11, which is large), with modest decoration or no decoration at all, no illustration (except for the two unfortunate miniatures in Harley 3869), and, as with many manuscripts later in the century, a much-reduced apparatus. In another break with tradition, Egerton 913 (a fragmentary MS), Harley 3869 and Wadham 13 are in single column. There is also evidence, again for almost the first time (the exception among earlier manuscripts is St John's B.12, which appears to come from the West Country), of manuscripts being produced outside the metropolis for local customers. Wadham 13, for instance, was made in Cheshire for John Dedwood, Mayor of Chester in 1468 and 1483, New College 326 in Wiltshire for Thomas Mompesson, sheriff of that county in 1478, and the Chetham MS in the 1530s by Thomas Chetham of Nuthurst in Lancashire (d. 1546), presumably for his own use. These are modest productions. By contrast, Cambridge St Catherine's 7, on the evidence of dialect and later owner-ship presumed to have been made in East Anglia, is a fine example of a tradi-tional manuscript, and Harley 3490, produced in Oxford for Sir Edmund Rede by a named Oxford scribe and known Oxford decorator, is a manuscript of the highest quality.

The nine independent manuscripts of the *Vox Clamantis* (there are also two copied from previous manuscripts) mirror those of the *Confessio* in their general character and, since at least four of them are most probably earlier than any manuscripts of the *Confessio*, perhaps provided a preliminary model, albeit on a smaller scale: the *Vox* is a much shorter poem than the *Confessio*, and the largest manuscripts are All Souls 98 (317 x 210mm) and Glasgow Hunterian T.2.17, slightly smaller, all the others being 267 x 185mm (Digby 238) or less. The five pre-1400 manuscripts of the *Vox* (Glasgow Hunterian T.2.17, Cotton Tiberius A.iv, Harley 6291, All Souls 98 and Huntington Ecton Hall) are all on good quality parchment, in quires of eight, written in single column, usually with the picture of 'Gower the Archer' (Fig. 2) and with decoration according to a regular hierarchy, more modest in Cotton Tiberius A.iv and Harley 6291. In all five manuscripts the *Vox* is written by one scribe throughout, but in all except Huntington Ecton Hall several scribes have been at work subsequently, making

---

[23] For the 'hooked g scribe', see Doyle and Parkes, 'Production of Copies', p. 201, n. 102; Edwards and Pearsall, 'Manuscripts of the Major English Poetic Texts', pp. 265, 277, nn. 74–5. Linne Mooney is in the process of sorting out the MSS attributed to the scribe. For the MSS attributed to Ricardus Franciscus, see Kathleen L. Scott, *Later Gothic Manuscripts, 1390–1490*, 2 vols (London, 1996), II.323.

Figure 2. British Library, MS Cotton Tiberius A.iv, fol. 9v. *Vox Clamantis*, frontispiece, 'Gower the Archer'. By permission of the British Library.

revisions and adding other poems such as the *Cronica Tripertita*. There is in fact a complex network of revising scribes, working independently, adding revisions of which some at least must have been in a form authorised by Gower. Two of these scribes also worked on the revisions in the Fairfax MS of the *Confessio* and on the Trentham MS of the French poems.[24] Many of the changes have to do with the adaptation of the *Vox* and its accompanying apparatus and other poems to the changing political situation, and Gower's view of it, as the *Vox*, like the *Confessio*, was made ready for appropriation by the new dynasty. The All Souls MS may be a dedication copy: uniquely, it contains a poem addressed to Thomas Arundel, Archbishop of Canterbury, the most fervent Lancastrian of them all.

The later manuscripts of the *Vox* show changes parallel to those we have seen in the *Confessio*. Laud 719 is on paper and parchment (the copy in Lincoln is on paper) and Digby 138 on paper with parchment protective leaves (the late copy in Cotton Titus A.xiii is on paper). The decoration is modest, coloured initials only (except for Hatfield, which is more lavish than any of the pre-1400 manuscripts), and the only illustration is the rough picture of 'Gower the Archer' in Laud 719.

## Illustration and Decoration

Of the manuscripts of the *Confessio* that contain pictures, the majority – and nearly all the best – come from the early phase of production. There are two 'standard' pictures, and they are so well established in the manuscript tradition that they may be presumed to have been authorised by Gower. The first picture is set, almost always in the text-column, just before Prologue 595, though sometimes rather inappropriately at the beginning of the Prologue,[25] and shows the statue that appears to King Nebuchadnezzar in his dream, with 'its head of fine gold, its breast and arms of silver, its belly and thighs of bronze, its legs of iron, its feet partly of iron and partly of clay' (Daniel 2:32–3). The dream presages the ruin of kingdoms divided and the running down of the world to decay: Gower uses the Nebuchadnezzar story in the Prologue to announce the theme of

[24]  See Macaulay, *Complete Works*, IV.lx–lxv. M.B. Parkes, 'Patterns of Scribal Activity and Revisions of the Text in Early Copies of Works by John Gower', *New Science out of Old Books: Studies in Manuscripts and Early Printed Books in Honour of A.I. Doyle*, eds. Richard Beadle and A.J. Piper (Aldershot, 1995), pp. 81–121, analyses the work of the revising scribes in fuller detail, concluding that Gower did not supervise them directly, except perhaps in Fairfax 3 (and even this is called into question in Peter Nicholson, 'Poet and Scribe in the Manuscripts of Gower's *Confessio Amantis*', *Manuscripts and Texts: Editorial Problems in Later Middle English Literature*, ed. Derek Pearsall (Cambridge, 1987), pp. 130–42 (pp. 132–7)).

[25]  See the useful table in Jeremy Griffiths, '*Confessio Amantis*: The Poem and its Pictures', Gower's *Confessio Amantis: Responses and Reassessments*, ed. A.J. Minnis (Cambridge, 1983), pp. 163–78 (p. 177), showing the placement of the miniatures. There is another table, differently organised, with information also on the Latin apparatus, in Richard K. Emmerson, 'Reading Gower in a Manuscript Culture: Latin and English in Illustrated Manuscripts of the *Confessio Amantis*', *Studies in the Age of Chaucer* 21 (1999), pp. 143–86 (pp. 184–6). Emmerson attempts to relate the positioning of apparatus and pictures to the stages of recension; Joel Fredell, 'Reading the Dream Miniature in the *Confessio Amantis*', *Medievalia et Humanistica*, n.s. 22 (1995), pp. 61–93, does the same, and also suggests political significances in the variants of the Nebuchadnezzar picture.

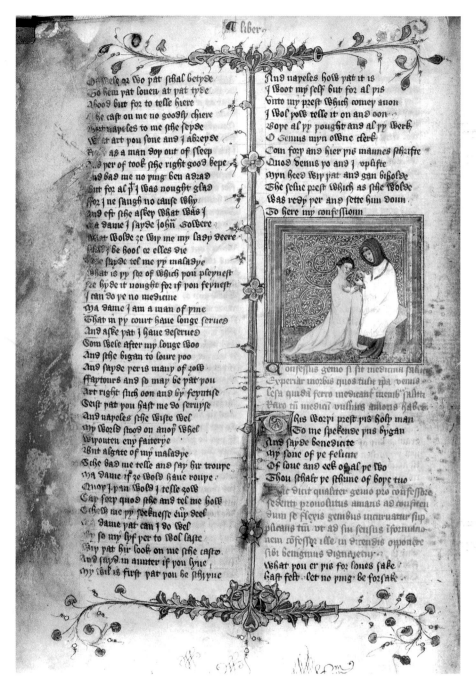

Figure 3. British Library, MS Egerton 1991, fol. 7v. *Confessio Amantis*, Confession miniature (after I.202). By permission of the British Library.

'division', which he sees as the cause of evil. The picture, which is often called 'The Image of Precious Metals', following the odd title chosen for it by Gereth Spriggs in her important early study of the Gower miniatures,[26] often shows the statue standing in front of a rocky or grassy landscape and also usually includes the king asleep in his bed. It is in many respects an idiosyncratic choice of illustration and most probably reflects Gower's own priorities and his desire to insist, through the illustration, upon the general theme of his Prologue. The second picture shows the Lover (Amans) kneeling before his Confessor (Genius), who is usually seated indoors or before a scrolled or other ornamental background (Fig. 3). The picture is set in the text-column before I.203 and sometimes shows the Confessor with a stole which, with his right hand, he is laying on the penitent's head. This is the picture which makes visually explicit the framing narrative of the poem, and it is what, on the analogy of dreamer-pictures and the pilgrim-portraits of the *Canterbury Tales*, one would expect.

These two pictures appear in many of the 'first-generation' manuscripts of the *Confessio*: Cambridge Pembroke 307, CUL Mm.2.21, Bodley 693 (the Confession picture, unusually, in an initial), Laud 609, Oxford Corpus 67, Bodley 294, Fairfax 3. In others, only one of the two is present: Egerton 1991 (spaces left for two more), Columbia Plimpton, Morgan 125, Morgan 690, Bodley 902, Huntington Stafford (which has a space left for the Confession miniature, exactly the size of the corresponding miniature in Fairfax).[27] In others, spaces are left for one or two of the standard illustrations (Bute, Nottingham, Geneva Bodmer) or leaves have been lost that almost certainly contained illustrations (Glasgow Hunterian, Add.12043). Royal 18.C.xxii has the two standard illustrations, but the Confession picture is set prematurely at the beginning of the Prologue. It may be that it was some time before the position of the miniatures became standardised, and Bodley 294, copied by the experienced Scribe D, may have played an important part in this process.[28] In the Princeton Taylor MS, as well as in the later Rosenbach MS, in addition to the standard Nebuchadnezzar picture, there is (instead of the Confession), a picture of the author, writing, set in the initial of the first English line of text on fol. 1. This is a throwback to a tradition of English text-illustration as old as Layamon. Egerton 1991 has a space probably intended for a similar picture.

Several of the manuscripts were illustrated by the finest artists working in London in the first two decades of the fifteenth century – those associated with the workshop or 'school' of Hermann Scheerre, who was active from 1405 to 1414.[29] One or two may be by Scheerre himself: many would regard the Confession miniature in Bodley 294 as one of the most beautiful examples of early fifteenth-century painting in England. It is run close by the Confession miniature

---

[26] Gereth M. Spriggs, 'Unnoticed Bodleian Manuscripts Illuminated by Herman Scheerre and his School', *Bodleian Library Record* 7:4 (1964), pp. 193–203 (p. 198).

[27] See Griffiths, '*Confessio Amantis*: The Poem and its Pictures', p. 168; Nicholson, 'Poet and Scribe', p. 141, n. 33.

[28] See Griffiths, '*Confessio Amantis*: The Poem and its Pictures', pp. 171, 174.

[29] See Spriggs, 'Unnoticed Bodleian Manuscripts', pp. 198–9, and Scott, *Later Gothic Manuscripts*, II.109–10, where, in the catalogue entry for Oxford Corpus 67, she discusses most of the illustrated Gower MSS; elsewhere (e.g. II.71, 87, 94, 106, 130, 165, 168, 186) she traces the work of the Gower-illustrators in some of the most lavish MSS of the period.

in Bodley 902, attributed by Pächt to the artist 'Johannes', perhaps a follower of John Siferwas.[30] Like Cambridge Pembroke 307, it shows the Lover as an old man with a beard, an unusual and seemingly rather inappropriate choice, since the purpose of the picture is to tell the reader at the beginning what is intended to be a poignant and salutary surprise at the end. The artist, or the supervisor who gave him his instructions, has chosen the literal truth rather than the literary subterfuge.[31]

Two manuscripts, one early (New College 266) and one later (Morgan 126), are exceptional in containing or having once contained an extensive cycle of illustrations for the *Confessio*. The former has nineteen illustrations surviving from a programme that once contained at least as many more, eleven having evidently been cut out and probably several more lost on the pages that have been cut out.[32] Morgan 126, written by the scribe Ricardus Franciscus, probably in the 1460s, has seventy-nine column miniatures (including the two 'standard' pictures) and twenty-seven smaller miniatures illustrating the signs of the zodiac and the fifteen stars in Book VII.[33] There is some similarity in layout to Oxford New College 266 – evidence of the same practical problems being solved in similar ways – but none in content. There is no information of the usual kind about the commissioning of this lavish manuscript, the first folio (where such information might be expected to be displayed) having been cut out, but Martha Driver argues from the evidence of inscriptions and arms within the miniatures and decoration that it was made for Elizabeth Woodville, queen of Edward IV.[34]

The decoration of the first-generation manuscripts is, like the miniatures, of the highest quality. The border-artists, like the miniaturists, are frequently to be associated with Scheerre, as with Bodley 693, Bodley 902, Add.12043 and Bodley 294; the decorator of Oxford Corpus 67 also worked on the 'Big Bible' (BL MS Royal I.E.ix) and the border-artist of Royal 18.C.xxii is, according to Kathleen Scott, 'one of the premier decorators of books in the first quarter of the fifteenth century'.[35] In the more expensive manuscripts, such as Bodley 693 and Bodley 902, there will be a vinet or more usually a demi-vinet at the beginning of each book, springing from a decorated initial (always that of the first line of the English text), itself extending over several lines. Demi-vinets consist of a vertical

30  Spriggs, 'Unnoticed Bodleian Manuscripts', p. 197.
31  The picture is discussed in J.A. Burrow, 'The Portrayal of Amans in *Confessio Amantis*', *Gower's Confessio Amantis: Responses and Reassessments*, ed. A.J. Minnis (Cambridge, 1983), pp. 5–24. Thomas J. Garbáty, 'A Description of the Confession Miniatures for Gower's *Confessio Amantis* with Special Reference to the Illustrator's Role as Reader and Critic', *Mediaevalia* 19 (1996), pp. 319–43, argues, more generally, that the pictures of Amans are to be understood to represent John Gower, in the long gown of his tomb effigy.
32  Macaulay, *Complete Works*, II.clxi. Braeger, in his discussion of the MS (1989), argues that pictures are provided for those tales that tell of 'conversion from sin'. See also Emmerson, in his discussion of Morgan 126: 'Reading Gower in a Manuscript Culture', pp. 178–83. The pictures in this MS are undistinguished, and the association, often reported, with the workshop of William Abell seems unlikely.
33  See Scott, *Later Gothic Manuscripts*, II.322–5 (there is a full catalogue entry for this MS); Eberle, 'Miniatures as Evidence of Reading'.
34  Martha W. Driver, 'Printing the *Confessio Amantis*: Caxton's Edition in Context', in *Re-Visioning Gower*, ed. R.F. Yeager (Asheville, 1998), pp. 269–303.
35  See Scott, *Later Gothic Manuscripts*, II.130.

stem in the left-hand margin with branches stretching out to the right at the top and bottom (where the English text begins in the left-hand column) or a central stem between the text-columns (where the English text begins in the right-hand column), with branches stretching out to the right and left at the top and bottom, or at the top only (T-shape) or bottom only (inverted T-shape). Decorated (painted) two–line or three–line initials, often in alternating pairs of colours, are used for major text-divisions ('chapters', indicated in Macaulay by a line-space) and decorated 1–line initials for minor text-divisions ('paragraphs', indicated in Macaulay by indentation), Latin verse-headings and summaries, and Latin notes and glosses. Decorated paraphs introduce speech-markers, explicits and incipits, running titles, even catchwords. In the 'economy de luxe' manuscripts such as Royal 18.C.xxii and Egerton 1991, though the demi-vinets remain (as the most potent images of the owner's taste and wealth), the hierarchy of initial decoration is more modest, with pen-flourished initials of different size and elaboration instead of champs for the different text-divisions and the Latin verse-headings and summaries, and undecorated paraphs (or nothing at all) for the shorter Latin notes and glosses and the lesser elements in the apparatus. It is as if a stationer or customer could choose from a 'sliding scale' of decorative elaborateness, in which the different elements of the *ordinatio* would be preserved in the same hierarchy.

In the later period of production, and particularly in the 1450s and 1460s, there are some manuscripts, as has been mentioned, which are richly decorated and have (or have spaces for) or once had illustrations: Cambridge St Catherine's 7, Add.22139, Harley 3490 (no pictures), Antiquaries 134, Philadelphia Rosenbach, Harley 7184, Oxford Magdalen 213 (no pictures). There is also Morgan 126, with many illustrations. But for the most part the later manuscripts tend to be plainer.

## Organisation of Apparatus

Gower provided a carefully organised Latin apparatus for the *Confessio*, with Latin summaries (almost invariably introduced by 'Hic' or 'Qualiter'), some quite long, for all the exemplary stories, and Latin glosses and notes, especially frequent in the informational sections of Books V (lines 747–1366, the pagan gods) and VII (lines 721–1438, the planets, signs of the zodiac and the stars).[36] There were also speech-markers for 'Confessor' and 'Amans'. All this material was to be set in the margin, partly so that Gower's book could borrow something of the prestige and authority attached to Latin books, which were frequently glossed in this way.[37] Such a scheme demanded large sheets of

---

[36] There has been some discussion of Gower's authorship of the Latin apparatus (references in Eberle, 'Miniatures as Evidence of Reading', p. 349, n. 22; Echard, 'With Carmen's Help', p. 4, n. 8). There is a strong presumption that it is his. For the range of terms applied to the prose 'marginalia', see Echard, pp. 12–13.

[37] See A.J. Minnis, *Medieval Theory of Authorship: Scholastic Literary Attitudes in the Later Middle Ages* (London, 1984), p. 275; Minnis, '*De Vulgari Auctoritate*: Chaucer, Gower, and the Men of Great Authority', *Chaucer and Gower: Difference, Mutuality, Exchange*, English Literary Studies,

vellum with space for wide margins, careful planning (including ideally the ruling and boxing of margins), great patience, and some degree of previous experience. In the best early manuscripts, Fairfax and Stafford, there are few signs that scribes had difficulty in following out the original plan, and the same is generally true of CUL Mm.2.21 and Bodley 902 (the two manuscripts that move the Latin verse-headings to the margin at fol. 81); of Princeton Taylor and Oxford New College 266; and, with some uncertainties and omissions, of Cambridge St John's B.12, Cambridge Sidney Sussex 63, Nottingham and Geneva Bodmer. What was involved can be seen in Bodley 902, where the Latin summaries are written in remarkably neat smaller versions of the different scribes' hands. The longer summaries (and some are very long), when they begin towards the bottom of the page, have to run out under the text-column for up to five lines; at fol. 154v there are two such summaries, and they snake out under the two columns from opposite directions, six lines deep, to meet in the middle. The new scribe who started copying at fol. 81 began by running such summaries over the next page, with a fresh paraph (fols 93–4 and 95–6), but soon reverted to the more usual practice. It was all too much for the scribe of Add.12043 (an expensively decorated MS), who was asked to move the summaries from the column, as in his exemplar, into margins that were neither wide enough nor ruled for text. From the first he had difficulty squeezing in the longer summaries that started towards the bottom of the page. He tried various expedients – running them out under the column (rather untidily), introducing the summary twelve lines above the relevant line in the English text (fol. 9r); extending the summary, after trying to scramble it in at the bottom of the page, over to the top of the next column (fol. 11r), where the limner later decorated the initial of a word in the middle of a Latin sentence. The scribe seems to have accepted defeat when he came to the story of Constance (II.587), with its many marginal summaries, and his last summary appears at II.383 (fol. 16).

The solution, and it was the one adopted by the majority of scribes (two later MSS that have the summaries in the margin, Harley 3869 and Oxford Wadham 13, are in single column), was to move the Latin summaries into the column, almost invariably in red. Here too there were problems. In copying from an exemplar with the summaries in the margin, a scribe might well take the summary into the column at the point in the English text level with the first line of the summary. This was often not the beginning of the English verse-paragraph, the appropriate place for the summary to be moved to, and the error was compounded when the decorator proceeded to ornament the initial of a line of English text, three or four or up to ten lines into the paragraph. This is a very common type of error, found for instance in Add.22139, Stowe 950, Antiquaries 134, Egerton 1991, Laud 609, and Add.12043 (where mistakes continue, after the insertion of summaries in the margin had been abandoned, indicating an exemplar with summaries in the column). Even where scribes were more careful or better supervised, for instance in Harley 3490, there were insoluble problems

ed. R.F. Yeager (Victoria, BC, 1991), pp. 36–74 (pp. 53–4). Winthrop Wetherbee, 'Latin Structure and Vernacular Space: Gower, Chaucer, and the Boethian Tradition', *Chaucer and Gower: Difference, Mutuality, Exchange*, English Literary Studies, ed. R.F. Yeager (Victoria, BC, 1991), pp. 7–35 (pp. 27–8) makes a particular comparison with glossed MSS of Ovid's *Metamorphoses*.

with short Latin glosses that related to a continuous unparagraphed English text (e.g. fols 155v, 156r), since these could not easily be introduced into the English text at any appropriate point or without attracting the irrelevant attention of the decorator. A frequently adopted compromise, which can be seen evolving in Cambridge Sidney Sussex 63, a comparatively small manuscript, was to place the summaries in the column – hopefully in the right place – but the shorter Latin notes and glosses in the margin or tacked onto the ends of the lines of English text.

There was yet another problem. If the summaries being inserted into the column were in red, as is almost invariably the case, the scribe presumably had to leave spaces and wait till the text-ink was dry before he came back to do his red-ink stint. But it was difficult to calculate how many column-lines a marginal summary would take up, and there are many examples of under-estimation. In Bodley 693 and Laud 609 (same scribe) the summaries are crammed in, with heavy abbreviation, but still often spill over onto the ends of the next two or three lines of English text (e.g. fol. 41v in Laud), while the shorter Latin notes dangle uncomfortably over the ends of three or four lines (e.g. fol. 163r in Bodley). Over-estimation is understandably rarer, but in Oxford Magdalen 213 there is often a space of a line or two between the end of a summary and the resumption of the English text. The tribulations of the scribes of the *Confessio* were manifold, and for many the speech-markers were the last straw: meticulously set out in Fairfax, they are elsewhere included sporadically, omitted for long spells, gradually left out, or, as in Oxford Corpus 67, omitted completely.[38]

Scribe and decorator often operated at some remove. There are signs of attempts by the scribe of Oxford Magdalen 213 to organise the copying so that the initial of a new book would occupy the top line or be near the top of a column and the border be less 'bottom-heavy'.[39] In later books he continues the practice of dilatation but seems to have forgotten the reason, and initials find themselves set a few lines from the bottom of the column, necessitating the inverted T-shape demi-vinets already mentioned. Scribes could often forget about the decorator and neglect to indicate the initials to be decorated; and decorators could often ignore the indications they were given. The second scribe of Bodley 902 (not Scribe D) decided at fol. 20v to set those Latin verse-headings which occurred in the left-hand column, and were encroaching upon the adjacent column, deep into the left-hand margin, with the consequence that at fol. 46v the border-artist had to open out a little box in the left-hand stem of the demi-vinet to accommodate the protruding lines. Occasionally, as in Bodley 693, Laud 609 and Bodley 294, scribes seem hesitant in the early folios about the planned decoration, as if they were waiting to receive instructions or working out a programme as they went along (in all such cases, one must understand, they might be simply copying an exemplar).

---

38  See Echard, 'With Carmen's Help', p. 16, n. 42; for a full discussion of the speech-markers in the MSS, see Echard, 'Dialogues and Monologues: Manuscript Representations of the Conversation of the *Confessio Amantis*', *Middle English Poetry: Texts and Traditions: Essays in Honour of Derek Pearsall*, ed. A.J. Minnis (York, 2001), pp. 57–75.

39  For evidence of similar attempts at page-organisation in Fairfax and Stafford, see Nicholson, 'Poet and Scribe', p. 134. See also Add.12043, fol. 32v.

*The Text of the* Confessio

Macaulay's is the only full edition of the *Confessio* based on all the available manuscripts. He chose Fairfax 3 as his copy-text, and followed it closely,[40] believing that it was prepared under Gower's direct supervision as a revised 'Lancastrian' version of the poem, perhaps in the scriptorium at the priory of St Mary Overie, where he lived, and from which he supervised the production of revised manuscripts of the *Confessio* and the *Vox*. The idea of a 'scriptorium', as put forward by Macaulay and supported by Fisher, has been in effect disposed of by Parkes,[41] and Nicholson has demonstrated that it is very unlikely that Gower had a direct role in the production of Fairfax.[42] The major revisions introduced in Fairfax – that is, the insertion of a new leaf at the beginning of the text removing the references to the 'commissioning' of the poem by Richard II and replacing them with the dedication to Henry, Earl of Derby, and the insertion of lines at the end (VIII.2938–3146), some over erasure, removing the praise of Richard (and also, probably incidentally, the praise of Chaucer) – are more probably to be seen as piecemeal alterations by scribes, introduced in the two most obviously convenient places, as Nicholson says, in order to refurbish a valuable and expensive manuscript for the new political circumstances.[43]

None of this makes any difference to the value of Macaulay's edition of the text, for no-one would dispute his choice of copy-text. Fairfax is a very good manuscript, faithful to exemplars that were close to the poet's own fair copies.[44] But Macaulay's interpretation of the revisions in Fairfax was also a key element in his attempt to organise his understanding of the whole range of manuscripts that he knew, and in this he was less successful.

Macaulay (II.cxxvii–cxxxviii) distinguishes three forms of the text, which he calls the first, second and third recensions, and which he associates with the chronological process of authorial revision. The first recension has the original form of the prologue (Prol.24*–92*) and epilogue (VIII.2941*–3114*), both with a favourable mention of Richard II; the third recension has the revised prologue (Prol.24–92), with a dedication to Henry of Lancaster more prominently displayed and Richard referred to only in passing, and the revised epilogue (VIII.2941–3172), with all mention of Richard II removed.[45] The second recension

---

40 Nicholson, 'Poet and Scribe', p. 133, counts 'some 300–400 Fairfax readings', mostly trivial, rejected by Macaulay.
41 Macaulay, *Complete Works*, II.cxxx; IV.lx; Fisher, *John Gower*, pp. 93, 101; Parkes, 'Patterns of Scribal Activity', pp. 94–5, confirming the more general view earlier expressed in Doyle and Parkes, 'Production of Copies', pp. 99–101.
42 Nicholson, 'Poet and Scribe', pp. 132–7.
43 Ibid., p. 138.
44 M.L. Samuels and J.J. Smith, 'The Language of Gower', *Neuphilologische Mitteilungen* 82 (1981), pp. 294–304 (rpt with corrections in Samuels and Smith, *The English of Chaucer and his Contemporaries* (Aberdeen, 1988)), pp. 296–7, provide a stemma, based on linguistic evidence, to demonstrate the relationships of Fairfax and Stafford, and declare them to be 'as good as autograph copies' (p. 304).
45 The *Confessio* was dedicated from the start (1392) to Henry, as the rubric at Prol.22 in some later MSS states, and as the presence of the 'Explicit iste liber' in its six-line version with dedication to Henry in seven of the sixteen first-recension MSS that still have concluding matter

is characterised by the presence of alternative versions of certain passages in Books V (1781*–92*, 6395*–6438*, 7015*–36*, 7086*–7210*) and VII (2329*–40*, 3149*–80*, 3207*–3360*), the omission of V.7701–46, and the moving of VI.665–964 to follow VI.1146. Some MSS of the second recension have or had the 'Richard II prologue', some have the 'Lancaster prologue'; all have the revised epilogue. Macaulay therefore distinguishes two forms – (a) and (b) – of the second recension, which he regards as transitional stages in revision. He also distinguishes three forms of the first recension, on the basis of variations in textual affiliation, identifying them, rather unfortunately, as (a) Revised (b) Intermediate and (c) Unrevised.

The variations in the form of the *Confessio*, especially the changes made for political reasons, clearly indicate authorial revision. But it is very doubtful whether the extant MSS will allow the recovery of detailed stages in this process of revision, if there were any. In particular, Macaulay's 'second recension' has a dubious status as a recension, while the three forms of the first recension are very imperfectly identified on the basis of what Macaulay acknowledges (II.clxx) to be a partial collation. In fact it is doubtful if the evidence of textual affiliation, even if it were exhaustively recovered (taking into account, for instance, the considerable evidence of shifts in exemplars within a single text), would ever provide support for an elaborate theory of authorial revision. The processes of manuscript production are too complex, piecemeal and random, too much governed by constraints of a technical and commercial nature, to allow a clear view of detailed aspects of an author's revising activity.[46] Macaulay's division of the copies of the poem into recensions pre-empted his analysis of textual affiliations and prejudiced much of his description of them. Nevertheless, since Macaulay's is the account of the text of the *Confessio* that has been used in all subsequent discussion and description, since the account he gives of the different forms of the text in the different groups of manuscripts (whatever the process by which they were generated) is accurate, and since a full collation of a poem of 33,444 lines surviving in forty-eight manuscripts is not going to be undertaken by anyone soon, we continue here to list the manuscripts under his 'recensions', however misleading the term, though without the sub-groupings.

The text of the *Confessio* is remarkably stable, compared with the *Canterbury Tales* or *Piers Plowman*. This stability may be attributed to various factors: the excellence of the exemplars from which all copies derive; the influence of the surrounding Latin apparatus in encouraging scribes to copy with the care they customarily exercised with Latin; the high professional quality of the first-generation copies; and the fact that such a very long poem was not likely to be often copied by amateurs. So stable is the text that scribes even found their own

makes clear. See S. Echard, 'Last Words: Latin at the End of the *Confessio Amantis*', *Interstices*, ed. Richard Firth Green and Linne Mooney (Toronto, 2004), forthcoming with valuable table of Latin addenda. The dedication to Henry involved no transfer of allegiance, or 'disillusion' with Richard (Nicholson, 'The Dedications of Gower's *Confessio Amantis*', *Mediaevalia* 10 (1988), pp. 159–80); that came later.

46 These are the arguments put forward by Nicholson in two important articles ('Gower's Revisions in the *Confessio Amantis*', *Chaucer Review* 19 (1984), pp. 123–43, and 'Poet and Scribe').

spelling habits 'constrained' – especially if they found themselves copying the text several times, like Scribe D – by the extreme regularity of the spelling-system that lay persistently before them in their exemplars.[47]

## Ownership and Readership[48]

Few manuscripts provide evidence of their original owners, though there is a significant early group associated with members of the Lancastrian royal family. Huntington Stafford has a coat of arms indicating that it was made for Henry, Earl of Derby, some time between 1393 and 1399, perhaps as a presentation copy; Oxford Christ Church 148 has a coat of arms associating it with Thomas, Duke of Clarence (d. 1421), Henry's second son; Bodley 294 has the autograph motto and *ex libris* inscription (after 1414) of Humphrey, Duke of Gloucester, Henry's fourth son;[49] and there are inscriptions in Cambridge Pembroke 307 connecting it directly with Jaquette de Luxembourg, who married John, Duke of Bedford, Henry's third son, in 1433.[50] Add to this the dedication of the *Vox Clamantis* in Oxford All Souls 98 to Archbishop Arundel, and the Lancastrian interest in Portugal (John of Gaunt's daughter Philippa married King John of Portugal in 1387) that surely prompted Robert Payne's Portuguese translation of the *Confessio*, known until recently only in the Castilian translation of Juan de Cuenca,[51] and it would seem that 'campaign' is not too strong a word to apply to the impetus given by Lancastrian patrons to the production of copies of Gower's works (though they do not seem to have minded having first recension copies).

Beyond this, the haul is disappointing. Very few manuscripts apart from those mentioned have coats of arms, with the splendid exception of Harley 3490, made for Sir Edmund Rede of Boarstall in the 1450s, which has the various arms of his family painted into the decorated borders of ten pages.[52] In Cambridge St John's B.12 a coat of arms has been cut out, and in Add.22139 arms (possibly those of the Scottish Hay family) have been imposed upon a shield previously left blank, perhaps an indication of production 'on spec' in the 1450s. Otherwise, the members of the fifteenth-century gentry who must have been the principal first owners of *Confessio* manuscripts can rarely be individually identified from ownership inscriptions. A strong case can be made that the Littleton family of

---

[47] See J.J. Smith, 'Linguistic Features of some Fifteenth-Century English Manuscripts', *Manuscripts and Readers in Fifteenth-Century England: The Literary Implications of Manuscript Study*, ed. Derek Pearsall (Cambridge, 1983), pp. 104–12 (pp. 109–10). See also Samuels and Smith, 'Language of Gower'.

[48] The thesis by Kate Harris, 'Ownership and Readership: Studies in the Provenance of the Manuscripts of Gower's *Confessio Amantis*', when published, will make available a great volume of information on both these subjects.

[49] Legible only under ultraviolet light: see Doyle and Parkes, 'Production of Copies', p. 208, n. 122.

[50] Harris, 'Virtues of Bad Texts', p. 170.

[51] For information on both translations, and important redatings, see Antonio Cortijo Ocaña, 'The Lost Portuguese Translation of John Gower's *Confessio Amantis*', and Santano Moreno, 'Translations of John Gower, *Confessio Amantis*'.

[52] For a full description, see Derek Pearsall, 'The Rede (Boarstall) Gower: British Library MS Harley 3490', *The English Medieval Book: Studies in Memory of Jeremy Griffiths*, eds. A.S.G. Edwards, Vincent Gillespie and Ralph Hanna (London, 2000), pp. 87–99.

Frankley in Worcestershire were very early connected with Antiquaries 134, and the Broughton family of Toddington in Bedfordshire with Bodley 902, while inscriptions in Cambridge Trinity R.3.2 indicate that it was in the possession of Sir Thomas Urswyck, Recorder of London 1453–71 and Chief Baron of the Exchequer 1471–79, and a well-known book-collector (he also owned a Mandeville and a *Canterbury Tales*), though it was evidently not made for him.[53]

Later in the century, manuscripts of a more modest kind were made for Thomas Mompesson of Bathampton, Sheriff of Wiltshire in 1478, with his coat of arms added (Oxford New College 326), and for John Dedwood, Mayor of Chester in 1468 and 1483 (Oxford Wadham 13). Whatever their previous owner-ship, manuscripts were now also passing to the richer London merchants: Oxford Corpus 67 was owned by the mercer Thomas Crispe (d. 1532), College of Arms Arundel 45 by the girdlers Thomas Goodenston and John Bartholomew, and Cambridge Pembroke 307 by the goldsmith Sir John Mundy.[54] The *Confessio* also enjoyed favour among members of Henry VIII's court, perhaps again as an icon of English poetic grandeur. Charles Brandon, Duke of Suffolk (d. 1545), a favourite of the king, owned Bodley 693, and the earliest recorded sixteenth-century owner of Egerton 1991 is Elizabeth Blount (Tailboys), the mistress of Henry VIII, whose son by the monarch was Henry Fitzroy, Duke of Richmond (1519–36). Large numbers of manuscripts are inscribed with the names of sixteenth-century gentry families, including the Fairfaxes (Fairfax), the Feildings (Harley 3869), the Fleetwoods (Bodley 294), the Russells and the St Johns (Bodley 902), and many more. Later in the century, Margaret Clifford, who married Henry Stanley, Lord Strange, created Earl of Derby in 1572, appears in both Royal 18.C.xxii and Cambridge University Library Mm.2.21.[55]

Owners are not necessarily readers, but there is a good deal of evidence that the *Confessio* was attentively read in the fifteenth and sixteenth centuries. Antici-pating such interest, there are, for instance, a number of Tables of Contents provided, more or less contemporary with the manuscript in which they appear, in Cambridge Pembroke 307, Oxford Magdalen 213, Princeton Taylor, and, a little later than the manuscript, in Oxford New College 326, while Morgan 126 has a full if rather useless alphabetical index of subjects.[56] The names of the sins treated in different books are helpfully indicated as running titles in Cambridge University Library Mm.2.21 and Harley 3869, and readers themselves provide many brief marginal notes of the subjects of the stories, intended as a finding-aid or reminder. Brief 'nota' marks or pointing hands indicate a particular interest in sententious statements, or in conundrums such as those proposed in the story of Apollonius (VIII.405–10) and the tale of the Three Questions (I.3099–3106). Other stories selected for particular annotation (as also for excerpting in the manu-

53  Doyle and Parkes, 'Production of Copies', p. 209.
54  Macaulay, *Complete Works*, II.cli; Harris, 'Unnoticed Extracts', p. 170.
55  See Rosemond Tuve, 'Spenserus', *Essays in English Literature from the Renaissance to the Victo-rian Age Presented to A.S.P. Woodhouse*, eds. Millar Maclure and F.W. Watt (Toronto, 1964), pp. 3–25.
56  The Magdalen and Taylor tables of contents are fully discussed in S. Echard, 'Pre-Texts: Tables of Contents and the Reading of John Gower's *Confessio Amantis*', *Medium Aevum* 66 (1997), pp. 270–87.

scripts containing extracts) include 'juicy' tales like that of Tereus (annotated, for instance, in Add.22139 and Harley 3869 and excerpted in CUL Ff.1.6 and Harley 7333), pathetic tales like that of Pyramus and Thisbe ('This ys a verye good store I saye', s.xvi, Oxford Magdalen 213, p. 110), and tales that gave opportunity for masculine asides, like the tale of Rosiphelee ('Ware yee women that yee bere non haltres', in both Harley 3869 and Oxford Magdalen 213). Some notes in Yale Osborn seem to suggest a salacious interest. There is occasional erasure of 'Pope' and systematically in the Boniface story in Royal 18.C.xxii (fol. 47), and the reference to the Lollards (V.1802) is prominently signalled (s.xvi) in Bodley 902, though there is nothing at all comparable with the engagement of post-Reformation readers with *Piers Plowman*. Generally, and from the start, readers use the *Confessio* as a bran-tub of good Ovidian narrative, and those of us who think that the *Confessio* is best read as a collection of stories and not as a programme of moral instruction will be pleased to find our mistake being made so early. But not by all: there is a seventeenth-century reader of Harley 7184 whose prolific annotations demonstrate not only an alertness to exemplary statements of general truth ('A good rule to Worke by', fol. 50v, at III.926; 'Good counsel', fol. 55v, at III.1859) but also a serious engagement with Gower the moralist, drawing inferences of his own, for instance, about the Lover's character ('This Leafe contains the demonstration of the common effects of Eager & specially singular affection', fol. 28v, at II.476).

The sixteenth century was the time when grand *Confessio* manuscripts began to be used as albums in which members of a family, over a long period, would inscribe their names, as they do in Egerton 1991. Other manuscripts began to be plundered for their miniatures and decoration, or for the usefulness of their parchment as binding material. Nearly a third of *Confessio* manuscripts bear the marks of such depredations, some of them on a large scale (as in Harley 7184 itself). Attitudes were not to change for a long time.

# 5

## *'This worthy olde writer'*:
## Pericles *and other Gowers, 1592–1640*

### HELEN COOPER

In the early 1590s, two writers turned their attention to Gower: Robert Greene and William Shakespeare. Greene did so explicitly, using Gower's reputation – the famous, or infamous, 'moral Gower' of Chaucer's description – as a means of staging a debate as to the value and function of literature. Shakespeare did so silently, by framing the most classical of all his comedies, *The Comedy of Errors*, with a romance taken from the *Confessio Amantis*: the story of Apollonius of Tyre, to which he was to return a dozen years later in *Pericles*, where he would also give Gower himself a leading role. Gower's name had remained one to cite, first of all alongside Chaucer's, then in a further coupling with Lydgate's, since early in the fifteenth century.[1] His cultural visibility was further assured by the sequence of early printings of the *Confessio*, Caxton's in 1483 and Berthelette's in 1532 and 1554; interest in the work was evidently strong enough to justify the investment in successive editions, though they did not have any obvious immediate influence on other writers. It was the decades from the 1590s down to 1640 that turned his name into one not just to cite but to conjure with, for audiences both courtly and urban. Ben Jonson has him put in an appearance, together with Chaucer, Lydgate and Spenser, to represent the best in the native English poetic tradition and so lead in the new Golden Age in his masque *The Golden Age Restor'd* of 1615.[2] John Webster cast 'the learned Gower' as one of the five 'famous Schollers and Poets of this our Kingdome' (the others being Chaucer, Lydgate, More and, for more modern times, Sir Philip Sidney), seated below his protagonist Troynovaunt, London, in his 1624 pageant for the Merchant

---

[1] A comprehensive list is given by Caroline Spurgeon in her *Five Hundred Years of Chaucer Criticism and Allusion, 1357–1900*, Chaucer Society (1914–25); for discussion, see N.W. Gilroy-Scott, 'John Gower's Reputation: Literary Allusions from the Early Fifteenth Century to the Time of *Pericles*', *Yearbook of English Studies* 1 (1971), pp. 30–47, and Derek Pearsall, 'The Gower Tradition', *Gower's* Confessio Amantis: *Responses and Reassessments*, ed. A.J. Minnis (Cambridge, 1983), pp. 179–97.

[2] C.H. Herford and Percy and Evelyn Simpson, eds., *Ben Jonson*, 11 vols (corrected edition, Oxford, 1954), VII.425. The poets speak only briefly, and in chorus or semi-chorus, so Gower is not given any lines of his own.

Taylors.[3] Although there were no further editions of the *Confessio* in the seventeenth century, and although citation of his name does not in itself prove knowledge of his work, there is abundant evidence that he continued to be both honoured and read.

Berthelette himself had insisted on the continuing value of Gower – 'this worthy olde writer', as he described him in the course of the dedicatory epistle to Henry VIII that prefaced both his editions. He endorsed the familiar view of him as moralist, quoting Chaucer's lines to 'moral Gower'. That Chaucer created the epithet on the basis of Gower's French and Latin works (it appears at the end of *Troilus and Criseyde*,[4] completed some years before Gower began work on the *Confessio*) was not a detail known, or of concern, to Berthelette or the other Renaissance authors who cited it; Gower was widely believed to be Chaucer's poetic precursor. Of equally little concern, and unmentioned by Berthelette, was Chaucer's countering attack, through the mouth of the Man of Law, on those writers (unnamed, but Gower was the only possible target) who were prepared to recount stories of incest, such as those of Canacee, or the daughter of Antiochus in the Apollonius story.[5] More unexpected is Berthelette's defence of Gower's language: unexpected, since earlier comments on Gower's rhetorical skill frequently appear as no more than an introduction to Chaucer's, and often show little actual knowledge of his work.[6] Berthelette by contrast promotes him as a continuing stylistic model for the aspiring writer, as an author 'that shal as a lanterne giue him lighte to write cunningly, and to garnishe his sentences in our vulgare tonge'. The *Confessio* is thus a work that increases both eloquence and ethics: 'It is plentifully stuffed and fournished with manifolde eloquent reasons . . . perswadynge vnto vertue.' It was the kind of advertisement that should particularly have attracted Renaissance readers (and was no doubt designed to do so), though no-one showed any immediate sign of building on the foundations Berthelette offered. When they eventually did so, Gower's example as teacher of morals and as model of the 'vulgar tonge' was divided into different works: into *Greenes Vision* of 1592, and Ben Jonson's *English Grammar*, rewritten after the fire that burnt his books in 1623 and first printed in 1640. Any idea that the homage Jonson paid to Gower in *The Golden Age Restor'd* might be merely nominal is contradicted by the fact that the *English Grammar* gives it practical and full expression, as he takes examples of English usage more often from him than from any other writer.[7] He never comments, however, on why he finds Gower so good a resource for illustrating the workings of English; and one would never have deduced that he found Gower especially attractive or intriguing were it not for a throwaway remark in his *Discoveries*, when he warns

---

3    *Monuments of Honour*, in *The Works of John Webster*, ed. F.L. Lucas, 4 vols (London, 1927), III.317–27: see pp. 319–20.
4    *Troilus* V.1856, in *The Riverside Chaucer*, general ed. Larry D. Benson (Boston, 1987).
5    *Canterbury Tales*, II.75–89.
6    See Pearsall, 'Gower Tradition', pp. 187–90.
7    Herford, et al., *Ben Jonson*, VIII.463–553; the count is done by R.F. Yeager in his study of the work, 'Ben Jonson's *English Grammar* and John Gower's Reception in the Seventeenth Century', *The Endless Knot: Essays on Old and Middle English in Honor of Marie Borroff*, ed. M. Teresa Tavormina and R.F. Yeager (Cambridge, 1995), pp. 227–39.

against giving the young too heavy a diet of reading in Gower or Chaucer, lest they fall 'too much in love with Antiquity'.[8] A dangerously seductive Gower is not a figure one expects to find, and especially not in the classicising Jonson.

For Robert Greene, indeed, writing in 1592, it was precisely Gower's un-seductiveness that made him valuable, and especially by contrast with Chaucer. *Greenes Vision* is explicitly a debate as to the value of and justification for literature, whether as entertainment or as ethics. The debate is conducted by the two authors themselves, who make a personal appearance to the dreaming Greene to tell contrasting kinds of story. It was published after Greene's death, with an added dedicatory epistle that represents the work as his final act of repentance, a 'last vision of vertue'.[9] The epistle seems somewhat over-anxious as to the work's authenticity – it notes that 'manie haue published repentaunces vnder [Greene's] name', but insists that this particular text is indeed his own. There is no good reason to doubt the accuracy of the ascription, despite the scepticism inevitably engendered by the deathbed claims of both the title page ('written at the instant of his death') and of the author himself throughout his address to his 'Gentlemen Readers', encouragingly signed 'Yours dying: Robert Greene'. It doubtless helped the marketing, and Greene was no doubt aware that that would remain the case even if he were to recover. The challenge of the work is to produce a diatribe against 'the vanitie of wanton writings' (p. 198) that will yet encourage readers to buy it. Casting the work as a dream in which Chaucer and Gower tell rival stories of mirth and morality is a neat way to resolve the problem. The debate works through the parallel of the 'wantonness' attaching to both women and literature. Their attractiveness was not in question; what was at issue was whether that attractiveness was merely a superficial disguise for something much more dangerous. The beauty of both women and literature had a propensity to go astray, and there was a long tradition of regarding the two with comparable suspicion. Both could inherently be read as possessing a surface attractiveness that doubled as a seduction towards sin.[10] Accordingly, Chaucer's heroine, 'bonnie Kate of Grantchester', does not have morality as the foremost item in her mind, though she is undoubtedly fun. Gower's heroine, Theodora (etymologically, 'gift of God'), is distrusted on account of her beauty, but her innate goodness leads the doubters back to the path of virtue.

Not the least striking thing about the work is its introduction of Gower himself, alongside Chaucer, in a manner that makes the work an interesting precursor of *Pericles*. If Gower had a reputation for being moral, and a more equivocal reputation for being a master of vernacular eloquence, he was also known as a teller of tales. Greene does not just recount the rival stories of his work: he has them told, in direct speech, by the two greatest storytellers in English. They are introduced as a pair, as 'two ancient men' with '*In diebus illis* [in those days] hung upon their garments' (pp. 208–9; the Latin alludes not only to their antiquity, but that they were 'giants on the earth', Genesis 6.4). They are

---

8   Herford, et al., *Ben Jonson*, VIII.618.
9   A.B. Grosart, ed., *Greenes Vision: The Life and Complete Works in Prose and Verse of Robert Greene* (1881–86; rpt New York, 1964), XII.201–81; quotation from p. 193.
10  See further Carolyn Dinshaw, *Chaucer's Sexual Poetics* (Madison, 1989), pp. 6–25.

then distinguished by individual descriptions, given in tetrameter couplets. The account of Gower opens:

> Large he was, his height was long;
> Broad of brest, his lims were strong;
> But couller pale, and wan his looke,
> Such haue they that plyen their booke:
> His head was gray and quaintly shorne,
> Neately was his beard worne.
> His visage graue, sterne and grim, –
> *Cato* was most like to him.
> His Bonnet was a Hat of blew,
> His sleeues straight, of that same hew;
> A surcoate of a tawnie die,
> Hung in pleights ouer his thigh.  (p. 210)

There is evidence, from *Pericles* and elsewhere, that the verse form continued to be closely associated with Gower, and any readers who were familiar with the *Confessio* would have been likely to take the form as a mark of homage to him. Greene was, however, in the habit of using tetrameters for descriptions, and similar passages occur widely in his earlier works. The fact that he includes in the *Vision* an 'ode' on classical poets in the same metre, and that he also uses it for his description of Chaucer (where the obvious alternative choice would have been the riding rhyme of the portraits of the Canterbury pilgrims), suggests that he is simply following his own earlier practice rather than imitating Gower. Such verse descriptions were apparently a known hallmark of his: it may have been the appearance of analogous descriptions in *The Cobler of Caunterburie*, an anonymous collection of partly improper tales published a couple of years earlier, that led to the accusation that he was the author, an ascription he hotly denies in the *Vision*. Greene's couplets are in any case strongly end-stopped, where Gower's are much more fluid – a contrast also frequently noted in re-lation to the choruses of *Pericles*.[11] The appearance of tetrameters in the *Vision*, therefore, does not necessarily even prove that Greene had any direct knowl-edge of Gower's work, and the story that he has Gower tell is not one of his own. His Gower, moreover, reserves his praise for those originary poets who refrained from discoursing of 'loue or hir lawes' (p. 217), a description that scarcely fits the poet of the *Confessio*.

Such factors raise the question of whether Greene was writing purely on the strength of Gower's reputation rather than familiarity with his work. The minimum requirement for the composition of the *Vision* is no more than a knowledge of that epithet 'moral Gower', and of the habitual pairing of his name with Chaucer's. There is nonetheless some counter-evidence to indicate that he did know Gower's text as well as his name. His Gower shows that he is 'moral' by telling exemplary stories, a practice that could not be deduced from the epithet alone. He is also formulated in a way that goes beyond the bare

---

[11]  E.g. by Gilroy-Scott, 'John Gower's Reputation', pp. 42, 45.

adjective to reflect more closely Berthelette's description of his 'manifold eloquent reasons . . . perswadynge vnto vertue'. Greene has him declare:

> Aristotle read not to Alexander wanton Elegies, but he instructed him in Morall precepts, and taught how to gouerne like a King, not how to court like a louer. (p. 270)

The statement is commonplace enough, but may nonetheless be an acknowledgement that the *Confessio* notably does both, its book on advice to princes being explicitly modelled on Aristotle's teaching of Alexander.[12] It may therefore not be coincidental that the Gower within the dream acts as an Aristotle, a teacher of ethics, through the medium of a protagonist with the first name of Alexander. And for all Greene's use of tetrameters elsewhere, there remains the possibility that his choice of Gower's metrical form for most of the verse contained in what is predominantly a prose treatise is deliberate, designed to match his victory over Chaucer in the debate between them.

The debate opens as a conversation, which increasingly tends towards becoming a quarrel. Chaucer starts by reassuring Greene as to the harmlessness both of his own writings and of the ascription to him of *The Cobler of Caunterburie*. Gower disagrees, with warnings against the ease with which readers may be led astray; and Chaucer responds by citing twenty aphorisms 'of the disposition of women' that warn against taking their attractiveness at face value – the same theme that is to furnish the plots of the tales that follow. Chaucer's is a story of the trick played on a jealous wheelwright by his young wife and the scholar who is pursuing her. The story is very close both to the *Miller's Tale*, though with the Reeve's (and Greene's) Cambridge substituted for the Miller's Oxford, and to the Gentleman's tale in the *Cobler* of a Cambridge student and a pretty wife.[13] Nothing more overtly sinful happens, however, than that the wife sits on the scholar's knee to eat 'a pound of Cherries'. It is described in its heading as a story 'of Iealousie', and it has no evident moral: it carries an inherent warning against women, but also against students, though as in the *Miller's Tale*, it is the gullible husband who is the character who gets his comeuppance (he is persuaded that he has been mad and suffering from delusions) and who least attracts audience sympathy. Gower's story by contrast takes a moral position from the heading forward: it is not 'of' but 'against' jealousy. It recounts how a husband, named Alexander Vandermast, casts out his virtuous wife on the strength of his unfounded suspicion of her; he tests her virtue by allowing himself to be transformed into the 'shape of a most beautiful young man' of great wealth, and going to woo her in the poor abode where she now lives. She, of course, repels his advances; he is converted to a recognition of her fidelity; and, restored to his own shape, he reinstates her to her rightful place as his wife. The narrative is conducted in large measure through assemblages of maxims on the dangers of beauty, the benefits of a good wife and so on – what its narrator

---

12  *Confessio* VII.1–53, in the edition of G.C. Macaulay, *The English Works of John Gower*, EETS, es Nos. 81 and 82 (1900–01); Genius notes that this material is at odds with the main topic of love.

13  *The Cobler of Caunterburie and Tarltons Newes out of Purgatorie*, ed. Geoffrey Creigh and Jane Belfield, Medieval and Renaissance Texts 3 (Leiden, 1987), pp. 44–61.

calls 'graue sentences' as opposed to Chaucer's 'wanton principles' (p. 270) –
which at times almost convert the story into little more than a framework for its
abundance of *sententiae*: a method that accords closely with the way Berthelette
describes the *Confessio*, with its many sayings persuading to virtue. The
dreaming Greene, called on to give a verdict between the two, declares for
Gower, and his judgement is backed by Solomon, who puts in a personal
appearance in the vision (complete with tetrameter description) to pronounce
not only Gower's superiority but that Theology, the discourse of truth unmedi-
ated by fiction, constitutes the highest wisdom of all. Greene awakes, and
declares that henceforth he will seek only after wisdom.

The husband in Gower's tale is never described as being particularly old or
ugly, but his transformation into a handsome young man clearly represents a
significant physical change. It thus recalls the transformation of the hag into a
beautiful young woman in one of the best known of Gower's stories, the *Tale of
Florent*.[14] The shape-shifting is devised for the husband by a wise old man
whom he encounters 'on a day, comming into a meadow' (p. 253) – as seemingly
casual an encounter as Florent's with his own aged and wise loathly lady. What
is described as the 'happy metamorphosis' enjoyed by the husband (p. 269)
refers, however, not to his shape-changing into a model of male beauty, but to
his change of heart towards his wife. The female metamorphosis within this tale
from rejected harlot to beloved wife happens in parallel, but without any actual
physical change in Theodora herself: it is her husband's perception of her that
changes. Whereas in the story of Florent the woman's change in appearance triggers the young man's love, here the man's beautification alters his wife's affections not one iota: she insists that she will remain true to the husband she loves
and to her own honour, and will endure what he has inflicted on her in the hope
that he will at last recognise her innocence. The man's shape-shifting has no
effect on the outcome of the story, except in so far as it serves as a catalyst for his
inward change of heart – his acceptance that his wife's inward beauty is not
compromised by her outward attractiveness – and for his own restoration to
emotional and ethical sanity. Chaucer's tale offers a wanton woman who tricks
her husband into 'reading' her as virtuous; Gower's, a virtuous woman whose
husband has to be educated out of misreading her as wanton. The plots thus
function not only to illustrate but also to conduct the parallel argument about
the imaginative fiction whose worth is the subject of the writers' quarrel and of
Greene's dream. Like women, literature may indeed be wanton; but although its
attractiveness may make it suspect, that does not in every case necessitate a
denial of its worth, its power of persuading to virtue. The responsibility may,
however, fall as much on the reader as on the writer.

---

[14] See below for a later appearance of this tale in 1640. It may also underlie John Fletcher's free
dramatisation of the loathly lady story, *Women Pleas'd* (c. 1619–23, though the play may have
existed in an earlier form), but that is more likely to be based on the Wife of Bath's version: the
final option offered to the husband, of having his wife fair and faithless or foul and true, is
Chaucer's, not Gower's (where the choice is between beauty by day or by night). The subplot
of the play is taken from *The Cobler of Caunterburie*. It is edited by Hans Walter Gabler in
Volume V of *The Dramatic Works in the Beaumont and Fletcher Canon*, general ed. Fredson
Bowers (Cambridge, 1982), pp. 441–538.

*

*Pericles* was to offer a view of Gower that intersects interestingly with *Greenes Vision*, but Shakespeare's first venture into *Confessio* material was very different. *The Comedy of Errors* was acted in 1594, as part of the Christmas festivities at Gray's Inn; whether it was a new play then, or the revival of one written closer in time to the *Vision*, is not known, though its strongly classicising dramaturgy might suggest an earlier date, when the young Shakespeare was trying to make his name in both drama and narrative poetry in ways that carried a humanist appeal. The *Comedy*, as one of the spectators noted, is closely modelled on the *Menaechmi* of Plautus; but its source play supplies neither its location nor its framing story, and for those Shakespeare turned to the story of Apollonius of Tyre. His play opens with the aged and time-changed Egeon arriving at Ephesus to seek his wife and one of his twin sons, lost at sea many years before; it ends with the reunion of parents and children, the long-lost wife being discovered, like the aged Apollonius-Pericles', serving in the city's temple of Diana. She is serving, moreover, as its abbess. Of the various versions of the Apollonius story that Shakespeare might have known, Gower's is the only one to give the lost wife such an office. Given his familiarity with the *Confessio* version of the story later in his life, the 'abbess' seems decisive for his knowledge of Gower at this date too.[15] We may therefore need to think of a Shakespeare whose imagination was sufficiently impressed by Gower's story, and not least by the wonder-inducing revelations of its ending, for it to have been working in his mind over much of his writing career, from that early comedy to the composition of *Pericles* in 1607–8. When he returned to it, he also restored its concern with fathers and daughters, replacing the Plautus-inspired twin sons with its triple sequence of such relationships.

This early reading of Gower by Shakespeare has implications for the question of the authorship of *Pericles* itself. The history of its text has been much debated – whether or not there was an earlier or different form of the play from that preserved in the quarto editions, and whether that was by Shakespeare or George Wilkins or someone else altogether[16] – but it was that first dramatist,

---

[15] *Confessio*, VIII.1849. Geoffrey Bullough accepts Gower as a source for the ending (*Narrative and Dramatic Sources of Shakespeare*, 8 vols (London; New York, 1957–75), 1.10–11, 50–4), though he does not link him with the alteration of location or the opening frame story (Egeon's account of his loss of wife and children). Laurence Twine's version of the Apollonius story, *The Patterne of Painfull Adventures*, had been printed, or perhaps reprinted, earlier in 1594; but although he, like Gower, imagines the temple on the model of a community of nuns, he describes Apollonius's wife only as one of the most reverenced among them, not as its abbess.

[16] Apart from a much-recycled assertion that the style of the first two acts in particular is unworthy of Shakespeare, and therefore must have been written by a collaborator, the evidence for Wilkins lies largely in the fact that his *Painfull Adventures*, discussed further below, contains a number of passages apparently based on blank verse speeches that do not appear in the play as printed; Bullough reconstructs them in *Narrative and Dramatic Sources*, VI.549–64. Stanley Wells and Gary Taylor restate the case for Wilkins as co-author in *William Shakespeare: A Textual Companion* (Oxford, 1987), pp. 557–8, in the face of strong opposition: F.D. Hoeninger described it as 'preposterous' ('Gower and Shakespeare's *Pericles*', *Shakespeare Quarterly* 33 (1982), pp. 461–79 (esp. p. 462)), and see also his Arden edition (*Pericles* (London, 1963), pp. lii–lxiii). The New Cambridge editors, Doreen DelVecchio and Antony Hammond, are likewise unpersuaded (*Pericles* (Cambridge, 1998), pp. 8–15).

whoever he was, who had the idea of making this explicitly Gower's play. He need not have done so; plays do not usually declare their source authors, and in any case Gower was one of two such sources, alongside the Elizabethan Laurence Twine. Gower was not so familiar a resource by this time as to make knowledge of his works commonplace; but *The Comedy of Errors* attests to Shakespeare's long-standing familiarity with him. The use of Gower as Chorus in *Pericles* strongly increases the likelihood of its having been Shakespeare himself who first had the idea of bringing the master storyteller on stage. However the text of *Pericles* evolved, its Gower would be Shakespeare's own, and the play therefore indeed, as its Cambridge editors describe it, 'the product of a single creative imagination'.[17] And if that imagination was indeed Shakespeare's, his long acquaintance with the 'Apollonius' would help to explain its extraordinary power on stage – a power that justifies the play's increasing recognition as a masterpiece.[18]

Shakespeare's return to Gower is a measure of the high value he was prepared to place on the native English traditions of poetry. He makes that the subject of the Prologue to *Pericles*, in one of his rare discussions of the theory underlying his writing (and here, of course, it is mediated through Gower himself, in his hallmark tetrameters). The issue of the worth of literature is comparable to that debated in *Greenes Vision*, though Shakespeare does not so much argue as assert it. What the play values about Gower is precisely the ability of his stories to delight:

> To sing a song of old was sung,
> From ashes, ancient Gower is come,
> Assuming man's infirmities,
> To glad your ear and please your eyes.
> It hath been sung at festivals,
> On ember-eves and holy days,
> And lords and ladies in their lives
> Have read it for restoratives.
> The purchase is to make men glorious;
> *Et bonum quo antiquius eo melius.*[19]

Pleasurableness, restorative power and antiquity ('good, in that the older, the better') together make up the virtues of the 'song' to follow. Gower, as in Greene, is represented as ancient, and his authority, as in the *Vision*'s 'in diebus illis', partly derives from that: antiquity and value are represented in the Prologue's Latin tag as equivalent. One wonders whether the Latin of the maxim was

---

[17] DelVecchio and Hammond, *Pericles*, p. 15. Compare Ruth Nevo, *Shakespeare's Other Language* (London, 1987), p. 33, who argues on thematic/psychoanalytic grounds that the text possesses 'a degree of unity bordering on the obsessive'.
[18] Wells and Taylor, *Textual Companion*, p. 559, quoted by DelVecchio and Hammond, *Pericles*, p. 15. Contrast Hoeninger's prefatory remark to his edition forty years ago: 'No one would include *Pericles* among Shakespeare's masterpieces'.
[19] Prologue 1–10; all quotations are taken from DelVecchio and Hammond's Cambridge edition. The absence of act and scene numbering from the quarto (act divisions were introduced when it was incorporated in the 1664 Folio) has the consequence of there being no consistency of numbering between editions; Stanley Wells and Gary Taylor, editors of *William Shakespeare: The Complete Works* (Oxford, 1986), number the scenes consecutively throughout the play.

included to give such a sense of antiquity, or a touch of the highbrow to counterbalance the 'ember-eves and holy days', or as a more direct tribute to the bilingual nature of the *Confessio*. In Gower's own work the Latin functions as a supplement to the text rather than being integrated into its metrical form, endorsing and enriching but not infiltrating the vernacular of the verse, but Berthelette's *mise-en-page* sets the Latin within the same column width as the verse in a way that unifies the two more closely than the marginal glossing of many of the manuscripts. The Latin here similarly asserts the value (*bonum, melius*: good and better, the basic value words) of the surrounding vernacular; and the very inclusion of this Prologue implies the existence of a debate as to the value of such old material – 'a mouldy tale', as Jonson was notoriously to refer to the play, with less sympathy for Gower's stories than he showed for his language.[20] If there had been no attack on tales of this kind, the Prologue's apologia would scarcely be necessary.

The most immediately striking feature of this opening chorus, however, dominates even over what is said; and that is that Shakespeare introduces Gower to say it. None of his other plays does anything like this. *The Two Noble Kinsmen* states in its opening chorus that the story is derived from Chaucer, but there is no question of Chaucer's speaking it himself – and it would be unthinkable that Shakespeare's other plays with well-known single-author sources, such as those based on Plutarch, should be introduced by the authority himself putting in an appearance. As in *Greenes Vision*, Gower's tale is to be mediated through Gower himself, and his continuing interventions – summarising plot transitions, conjuring up and explaining dumb shows, indulging in a little atmospheric scene-setting ('the cat with eyne of burning coal', III.i.5), marking notional act-divisions, and so on – serve as a continuous reminder that we are watching the dramatisation of a story:[21] a story told with such conviction that it acts itself out in front of our eyes, as in Peele's *Old Wives Tale*, or, for more recent examples, the television *Bagpuss* of Oliver Postgate or Anthony Minghella's *The Storyteller*. It is a method on the cusp between naivety and sophistication, primitive make-believe and modernist self-reflexiveness. The artifice that is a so-much-discussed and so evident quality of Shakespeare's last plays is at its most blatant here: an in-your-face insistence to the spectators that the play they are watching is a fiction, not so much a play within a play but a story that takes physical form. The audience is not even allowed to imagine that the stage represents real space: its function as *imagined* space is explicit. The imagination, furthermore, is in the first instance Gower's – the figure who can conjure into being the occupants of his own brain – and only secondarily that of the audience:

> Imagine Pericles arrived at Tyre,
> Welcomed and settled to his own desire.

20 *Ode to Himself*, line 29 (Herford, et al., *Ben Jonson*, VI.492).
21 DelVecchio and Hammond make the point strongly in their edition, contrasting Gower's function with that of other chorus figures (pp. 27–36). The nearest equivalent to Gower would be Barnabe Barnes' Guicchiardine, who is both the source of and the chorus to *The Devil's Charter*, but in practice his role is that of any other chorus, as presenter, not as storyteller.

His woeful queen we leave at Ephesus,
Unto Diana there a votaress.
Now to Marina bend your mind,
Whom our fast-growing scene must find
At Tarsus[.]  (IV.0.1–7)

And not only place and people but time is conjured up by the measure of Gower's numbers:

Only I carry winged time
Post on the lame feet of my rhyme,
Which never could I so convey
Unless your thoughts went on my way.  (IV.0.47–50)

The original narrative consisted largely of a sequence of stations, temporary points of rest in a series of journeys across half the Mediterranean. Gower acts to convey the audience between these stations and, with the aid of dumb shows, through and past some other resting points that do not get full dramatic representation. Journeys are notoriously hard to stage; Gower's presence means that the play does not need to rely on reports or messengers for such things, but gives performative utterance to those gaps between the scenes.

There is evidence that contemporary audiences responded not only to the story told, but to the storyteller too. The Apollonius narrative itself was a popular one in the sixteenth century, as it had been throughout the Middle Ages. It was printed as part of a larger work not only in Caxton's and Berthelette's *Confessio*, but also in Latin versions of the *Gesta Romanorum*. As an autonomous story, it was published in 1510 in a translation by Robert Copland of a French version, and Laurence Twine extracted it from the *Gesta* for retelling in *The Patterne of Painfull Adventures*, entered in the Stationers' Registers in 1576, though prints survive only from c. 1594 and 1607. It may have been the later reprint that prompted the writing of the play, since Twine is its second, silent, source alongside Gower; or it is just possible that the appearance of the play triggered the reprint. The next year, however, and certainly in response to the staging of *Pericles* – though possibly in an earlier or different form from that we now have – George Wilkins produced *The Painfull Adventures of Pericles Prince of Tyre*, which retells the story of the play with generous supplements from Twine.[22] It is not just the story of the play, however, for it includes the *telling* of the story. Wilkins insists on the title page that he is not only giving 'the true history of the play of *Pericles*' but doing so 'as it was lately presented by the worthy and ancient Poet John Gower', and a woodcut of Gower, bearing some resemblance to Greene's description of him, is included to endorse the point.[23] The emphasis is so marked as to suggest that it was intended not merely to

---

[22] For these and all other source texts, including the Apollonius story from Berthelette's *Confessio*, see Bullough, *Narrative and Dramatic Sources*, VI.349–564.

[23] Reproduced in the Oxford *Complete Works*, ed. Wells and Taylor, p. 1168, and as a frontispiece to Hoeninger's edition; the likeness is not so close as to prove direct influence from Greene. Gower's tomb effigy, in what is now Southwark Cathedral, is substantially different (reproduction in *Pericles*, ed. DelVecchio and Hammond, p. 28).

distinguish the work from the recent reprint of Twine's *Patterne*, but as an advertising ploy in its own right – something that would make browsers at a stationer's stall buy the book. This continuing interest in the telling of the story is
further indicated by the fact that Gower is not limited to the title page alone but
also functions as storyteller within the text, mediating the narrative. He is listed
as 'John Gower the Presenter' in the list of 'personages mentioned in this
Historie', a *dramatis personae* borrowed from the conventions of printed drama,
and the heading to the opening of the first chapter begins: 'Wherein Gower
describes how Antiochus surnamed the Great committed incest with his daughter'. Wilkins does not keep up the framing, but it nonetheless serves to make the
point, once again, that this is a tale told by Gower the storyteller.

Although it can be no more than hypothesis to suggest that Shakespeare had
kept Gower's story of Apollonius, and especially its ending, in the back of his
mind ever since the writing of *The Comedy of Errors*, it is the kind of speculation
to which any attempt to reconstruct Shakespeare's imaginative biography has to
appeal. He dramatises it, moreover, with a faithfulness to his source so unusual
in his work as to turn the play into an act of homage to the traditions of romance
transmitted through English.[24] '*Et bonum quo antiquius eo melius*' does not refer to
classical antiquity, but to the past of the lords and ladies who once listened to the
song that 'of old was sung'. It is unlikely that he could have known just how old
the story of Apollonius was, or how far it had travelled before it reached the
*Confessio*; but he does know it is older than Gower, as that first chorus makes
clear, and his treatment is designed to reinforce that sense of its antiquity. The
few changes that he makes to Gower's development of the story almost all serve
to add to its medieval qualities. The games at Pentapolis whose nature Gower
avoids specifying become a tilt between knights in armour, with Thaisa,
'beauty's child' (II.ii.6), set where she can best admire their exploits. The elaboration of the brothel scenes turns them into a dramatic equivalent of the lives of
those virgin saints, notably St Agnes (whose story was still included in Foxe's
*Book of Martyrs*), whose persecutions included a similar degradation, and from
which they likewise emerged unscathed. If Shakespeare's representation of
fierce virginity is hagiographic, his representation of chaste desire is deeply in
keeping with the traditions of English romance. In all versions of the story, the
Thaisa figure takes the initiative in choosing Apollonius-Pericles for her
husband;[25] given the widespread belief that female as well as male orgasm was
necessary for conception, the begetting of their daughter on their wedding
night, also found universally, encodes the lovers' mutual desire. Such frank narrative approval of female desire had largely been lost in European romance
outside the Anglo-Norman and English traditions, but it survives generously in
Shakespeare, and in *Pericles* he takes it one step further than the original
romance had ever done. When the old and time-ravaged Pericles, still with his

---

[24]  Bullough indicates the precise borrowings from Twine and Gower, but the basic story remains
so similar through all its versions that most of the play does not need to be an either/or choice
between them.

[25]  For an account of the story in all its versions, see Elizabeth Archibald, *Apollonius of Tyre: Medieval and Renaissance Themes and Variations* (Cambridge, 1991).

hair uncut (V.iii.69–70), presents himself at the temple of Diana and tells his story, he is visually unrecognisable; but Thaisa tests his identity, uniquely in the history of romance, by whether she feels desire for him:

> If he be none of mine,
> My sanctity will to my sense bend no
> Licentious ear, but curb it spite of seeing.  (V.iii.26–8)

It is an inspired development from her exclamation in the *Confessio* when she sees her husband, 'That whilom he and I were on' (VIII.1861), but it is a development deeply in keeping with Gower's long exploration of the nature of 'kynde love', and with Shakespeare's of the desiring woman.

Just one alteration to the *Confessio* serves Shakespeare's own agenda, and that is the excision of the Thaisa figure's mother: in *Pericles*, the triple sequence of fathers and daughters is uninterrupted by any other parent. The change serves the dramatic and narrative economy of the story, but it also focuses the narrative on the same relationship that dominates his other late plays. The opening incest and riddle invite oedipal readings of *Pericles* that turn it into a dramatic psychoanalysis of the protagonist,[26] and the omission of Thaisa's mother strengthens the sense of Pericles encountering a series of doubles. Illuminating as such readings are, however, they also distract from the breadth of the concern with the nature of love and desire, both heterosexual and parental, which fuels both Gower's and Shakespeare's treatments of the story, and which is focused through the women as well as the men. Love, for Gower, can take both life-enhancing and injurious or wicked forms. That is one reason why Greene can so easily metamorphose the debate over literary value into the analogous debate on the nature of women's virtue and beauty. If the Prologue of *Pericles* functions as the defence in an implicit debate about the value of old writings, the action of the play embodies the parallel debate about women and love. It does so, moreover, through the same story, of Antiochus' daughter, that Chaucer had used to call into question his earlier description of Gower as 'moral'. Shakespeare fashions his play to make her into a kind of demonic shadow of its ensuing action. Its sequence of female characters is designed to demonstrate, first the separation between beauty and virtue, then their unity. Antiochus' daughter is 'so buxom, blithe, and full of face, / As heaven had lent her all his grace' (Prol. 23–4), but her incest with her father renders her a 'glorious casket stored with ill' (I.i.78). Thaisa is at once beautiful and desiring, but the man she desires is the man she wants to marry: the focused desire that constitutes marital chastity. Her father, moreover, is delighted to grant his daughter the fulfilment of her desire in the arms of another man. She is recovered from the sea after her apparent death in a casket stored both with riches and with the beauty and virtue of her own self, the grace that heaven has indeed lent her. In her case, there is no division between outward attractiveness and inward virtue, any more than there is in the case of Theodora. Marina finds herself in the most vicious of settings, the brothel where her virginity is put up

---

[26]  See for instance Nevo, *Shakespeare's Other Language*, pp. 33–61.

for sale at a premium price, but she shames its clients with her goodness: here, the casket is foul, but she contradicts the corollary that she is therefore 'a creature of sale' (IV.v.73) just as firmly as Antiochus daughter's sin denies the glory of her own enclosing beauty. Her discovery of her father gives him new life in a beneficent re-enactment of the love of father and daughter that had instigated the action, in a scene that exorcises her (and his) demonic double. Gower sums up the moral in the Epilogue:

> In Antiochus and his daughter you have heard
> Of monstrous lust, the due and just reward;
> In Pericles, his queen and daughter seen,
> Although assailed with fortune fierce and keen,
> Virtue preserved from fell destruction's blast,
> Led on by heaven, and crowned with joy at last. (lines 1–6)

The trite moralism of it is scarcely adequate to the play,[27] but it is very much in line with the early seventeenth-century notion of 'moral Gower'. It pairs up too with the opening apologia for the 'song of old', told before wit reached its present stage of ripeness, but which can bring both pleasure and healthfulness (even Freudian healthfulness): the play too can be read 'for restoratives'.

An epilogue to the idea that Gower's tales might act as restorative finds its most curious expression in a cheap quarto pamphlet produced in 1640, designed to appeal to the popular appetite for stories of monsters and prodigies. Entitled *A Certain Relation of the Hog-faced Gentlewoman, called Tannakin Skinker*, it tells the story of a girl from a city on the Rhine who was born with a hog's face, and was incapable either of speaking or of eating other than out of a trough. It would seem an unlikely place to look for evidence of the *Nachleben* of one of the greatest of the Middle English poets; but the anonymous author not only offers the last five pages of his pamphlet to tell a story out of the *Confessio*, but uses it as a substitute climax for the main story. The girl's parents are advised that the only hope of a cure for their daughter is to find a gentleman who is prepared to marry her. They offer a dowry of forty thousand pounds, and display her with her face covered. 'I should but lose my selfe in writing', declares the anonymous author,

> and tyre the Reader turning over many Voluminous leaves of paper, to shew you here many severall men and of sundry conditions, came in a kinde of jealousie one of another, to purchase this masse or magazine of money: every one ambitious after the portion, but not one amongst them amorous of the person, whose countenance was so far from seeming lovely to them, that it appeared altogether lothsome, and so I will leave her in this exigent, to acquaint you with a short story, that the carriage of the one, may make the other appeare more probable, they being of like affinity. My Author is *Iohn Gower*, and thus it hapned.
>   A noble and warlike Knight, Cousin to the Emperour *Claudius*, of a spirit

---

[27] For the contrast between the author Gower and the Gower of the play, see further Stephen J. Lynch, 'The Authority of Gower in Shakespeare's *Pericles*', *Mediaevalia* 16 (1993 for 1990), pp. 361–78.

undaunted, and honour unquestioned, named *Florentius*, as hee rid upon an adventure [. . .][28]

Tannakin's is a story without a conclusion: she is still living, either in the Low Countries or in London, still besieged by eager but ultimately unwilling suitors, and the happy ending of the loathly lady whom Florent marries and who is subsequently de-enchanted back to her natural beauty takes the place of any happy ending that the main narrative might or might not eventually reach.

The rather thin story line of the whole pamphlet is expanded to fill the nine pages that precede the story of Florent by an abundance of analogous prodigies, from classical omens of speaking dogs and mountains in combat, through monstrous births – Siamese twins, a baby with cloven feet, the future Richard III – to the ability of witches from Circe forwards to transform shapes. One such witch, we are told, confessed to causing Tannakin's hideous deformity by cursing her pregnant mother, and was duly executed for that and other crimes, though she left no hint as to how the girl might be restored to a natural shape. It is at that point that Gower's story is inserted, to turn its analogous account of an enchantment into a means of suggesting a resolution for Tannakin. 'Know', the newly transformed lady tells Florent,

> I am the Kings daughter of Sicily, who by a wicked and sorcerous step-dame was thus inchanted, never to returne to my pristine shape, till I was first married, and after had received such power [of being granted her own freedom of choice] from my Husband.

The story seems to promise the possibility of a comparable happy ending for Tannakin, but the author is careful not to go beyond setting the two accounts side by side. Readers who want a happy ending may reassure themselves from Gower's tale, but the text gives them no explicit encouragement. The juxtaposition of the two narratives may suggest a metaphorical relationship between them, but in practice it remains metonymic, with no transformation of one story by means of the other.

Although the *Certain Relation* is a late addition to the early modern reception of Gower, it can be read as emblematic of that reception. It gives in small compass all the characteristics that marked how readers had responded to, and writers imitated, the *Confessio* over the previous decades. The most obvious is how explicitly the debt to Gower is declared. He may not be introduced in person into the pamphlet, but it is made very clear that the authority for the ending is his. That authority, moreover, is specifically that of the storyteller; to everyone except the Ben Jonson of the *English Grammar*, the Stuart Gower, like the Elizabethan, is a teller of tales.[29] His stories, furthermore, are not just a repos-

[28] The quotation comes from sig. B2v of the variant edition published in the same year as the first edition: see *STC* 22627.5.

[29] One other quality of Gower is taken up in the mid-seventeenth century by Elias Ashmole, who uses him as a source for alchemical knowledge in his *Theatrum Chemicum Britannicum* of 1652: see Kate Harris, 'The Longleat House Extracted Manuscript of Gower's *Confessio Amantis*', *Middle English Poetry: Texts and Traditions: Essays in Honour of Derek Pearsall*, ed. A.J. Minnis (York, 2001), pp. 87–90.

itory of material for reading, but for rewriting; and they constitute a corpus in a distinctive verse form. In the *Tannakin* pamphlet, this acknowledgement takes the form of an eleven-line quotation from the description of the loathly lady, given in the 'olde English' of his 'author' and beginning:

> She was the loathest wight
> That ever man cast on his Eye:
> Her Nose baas, her Brows hye.[30]

The pamphlet might seem too unsophisticated to extend its concerns to those that Greene and Shakespeare show for the value of literature to its readers, and for Gower's example within that debate; but even those are reflected in its 'Florent'. In *Greenes Vision*, Kate's husband is misled into misinterpretation, but Theodora carries no double meanings, and her husband's misreading is his own fault, not inherent in her. Shakespeare takes from Gower one woman who is the subject of a riddle which, truly read, encodes her beauty as corruption; another woman who writes a frank declaration of her own sexual preference, identifying the man she intends to marry; and a third whose beauty can be rightly read only as chastity, and so a text that persuades men to virtue. The loathly lady in the pamphlet's tale of Florent, newly turned beautiful, assures her husband that her overt meaning is her true one – 'Sir, I am indeed no other than I now seeme unto you'; yet he still has to choose how she is to appear to himself and to others. His remitting the choice to her frees her to match her surface appearance with her 'pristine self':

> At which, how incredible his joy was, I leave to the opinion of the understanding Reader, who I hope will easily conceive what affinity this story may have with the former.

The sceptical or literal-minded reader might reasonably respond to this last clause, 'Not much'; but it is nonetheless intriguing, given the long association of Gower with the debate over the effects of literature on its readers, that the tale here should be remitted to them. Tannakin's own chances of beautification do not lie in the main narrative, but on whether the reader of John Gower's *Tale of Florent* allows her disenchantment – an act that is at the same time one of reading, and one of a willed imaginative magic.

---

[30] The lines correspond to I.1676–86 (I.1676–8 quoted) in Macaulay's edition; they are found on fol. xvii of Berthelette's 1554 edition of the *Confessio*. The *Tannakin* author modernises the spelling, in the process turning 'lockes hore' into 'looks hore' (if it is not simply a misprint).

# 6

## *Gower in Print*

### SIÂN ECHARD

In Paper, many a Poet now suruiues
Or else their lines had perish'd with their liues.
Old Chancer, Gower, and Sir Thomas More,
Sir Philip Sidney who the Lawrell wore,
Spencer, and Shakespeare did in Art excell,
Sir Eward Dyer, Greene, Nash, Daniel,
Siluester, Beaumont, Sir Iohn Harington,
Forgetfulnesse their workes would ouer run,
But that in Paper they immortally
Doe liue in spight of Death, and cannot dye.[1]

John Taylor's *Praise of Hemp-Seed* (1630) expresses a confidence in paper which, by the nineteenth century, John Gower might have had cause to question. Around 1508, William Dunbar wrote in his *Goldyn Targe* in praise of 'reverend Chaucere, rose of rethoris all', and 'morall Gower and Ludgate laureate'.[2] Gower still gets a mention in Taylor's poem, unlike the third member of Dunbar's medieval triumvirate, but even as *The Praise of Hemp-Seed* links Gower with Chaucer, the later print history of the two poets clearly illustrates Gower's demotion from the Chaucerian heights. This print history travels in tandem with the reception history outlined in the introduction to this volume, illustrating the extent to which paper has not, in fact, been Gower's friend.

The first printing of Gower's *Confessio Amantis* was by William Caxton in 1483. Caxton seems to have known of Gower's work as early as 1480,[3] and Norman Blake wonders whether the delay in printing, and the striking brevity of Caxton's preface, might be evidence of a lack of interest in Gower on the printer's part.[4] But Caxton does package his *Confessio* carefully, in this case by

---

1   John Taylor, *The Praise of Hemp-Seed*, in *All the Workes of Iohn Taylor the Water-Poet. Beeing Sixty and three in Number* (London, 1630), lines 859–68.
2   William Dunbar, *The Goldyn Targe*, in *The Poems of William Dunbar*, ed. James Kinsley (Oxford, 1979), lines 253, 262.
3   For a full summary of Gower's early print history, see N.F. Blake, 'Early Printed Editions of *Confessio Amantis*', *Mediaevalia* 16 (1993), pp. 289–306. Blake argues that there are verbal echoes of Gower in Caxton's 1480 translation of Ovid's *Metamorphoses*, p. 291.
4   Blake, 'Early Printed Editions', p. 291.

means of a long table of contents.[5] The table runs to twelve double-columned pages, in which quite detailed entries point a reader directly to the narratives contained within the *Confessio*'s frame. The table thus facilitates the treatment of the *Confessio* as a compendium of stories. Caxton's brief preface reinforces that understanding: he writes that the book was 'maad and compyled by Johan Gower'. The language of compilation is followed by an emphasis on the table as a key to the stories in the book: 'and by cause there been comprysed therin dyuers hystoryes and fables towchynge euery matere/ I haue ordeyned a table here folowynge of al suche hystoryes and fables where and in what book and leef they stande'.[6] Caxton's table may reflect the publisher's awareness of his audience's disjunctive reading practice, whether of Gower's *Confessio* or of longer works by other writers as well.[7]

Caxton's Gower is printed in one blackletter font throughout, in double columns of forty-six lines (a layout which echoes a common manuscript design for the *Confessio*). Space is left for initials of six or seven lines at the head of books, and for smaller initials within the books. There are gaps at the outset and at the opening of some of the books, perhaps for woodcuts which never materialised.[8] One manuscript of the *Confessio*, Hatton 51, was itself copied (rather badly) from this edition: the copy includes Caxton's table.

Gower next appeared in print in the edition by Thomas Berthelette, then printer to Henry VIII, in 1532. As Tim William Machan points out, by this time Chaucer had been reprinted several times, from the 1490s on.[9] While Gower may have had to wait rather longer than Chaucer to appear in print again, the results were in many ways worth the delay. Berthelette used Caxton's edition,[10] but he added some missing passages and expanded considerably on the prefatory matter, writing an extensive introduction which praised Gower's language and the moral value of the stories contained in the *Confessio*. He also made some additions and changes to Caxton's table of contents, changes which subtly reorient a reader's perception of the text. He tends, for example, to include entries for the parts of the *Confessio* that are focused more on information than on narrative – the signs of the zodiac in Book VII are one instance. A reader of Berthelette's edition might see the *Confessio* as a kind of encyclopaedia, as well

5   This table was one of the reasons that G.C. Macaulay believed Caxton to have had MS Magdalen 213 in his possession and to have based his edition on this and two other manuscripts. Blake, however, points out that Magdalen 213 shows none of the marks one would expect from a copy-text, and argues instead that Caxton used a single, third-recension manuscript: 'Caxton's Copytext of Gower's *Confessio Amantis*', *Anglia* 85 (1967), pp. 282–93. For a fuller discussion of tables of contents to the *Confessio*, see my 'Pretexts: Tables of Contents and the Reading of John Gower's *Confessio Amantis*', *Medium Aevum* 66 (1997), pp. 270–87.
6   *This Book is Intituled Confessio Amantis*, ed. William Caxton (London, 1483), sig. iir.
7   See Joyce Coleman, 'Lay Readers and Hard Latin: How Gower May Have Intended the *Confessio Amantis* to Be Read', *Studies in the Age of Chaucer* 24 (2002), pp. 209–35, for a recent discussion of this issue.
8   Blake, 'Early Printed Editions', p. 295.
9   Tim William Machan, 'Thomas Berthelette and Gower's *Confessio*', *Studies in the Age of Chaucer* 18 (1996), pp. 143–66 (p. 143): Machan lists Pynson, Julian Notary and de Worde in the 1490s; Pynson again in 1526; and Thynne in 1532.
10  He seems to have had a manuscript copy to refer to as well; Macaulay suggested a copy resembling Bodley 294, G.C. Macaulay, *The English Works of John Gower*, EETS, es nos. 81 and 82 (London, 1900–1901), I.clxix.

as the story compendium Caxton suggests it to be. This impression is furthered by the design of Berthelette's book. He prints the *Confessio* in two columns of forty-eight lines, continuing Caxton's double-column format, but unlike Caxton, he uses type to distinguish between the different parts of the text. He uses a blackletter font for the English text; a smaller blackletter font for the Latin glosses; and yet a third font, a small Roman, for the Latin verses. Thus Berthelette's edition clearly marks out for a reader the different parts (and languages) of the *Confessio*, and in so doing, it *emphasises* the poem's Latin apparatus. Several critics have argued that the effect of this particular treatment is to suggest visually that Gower is a compiler and not a poet in the same way as, for example, Chaucer might be. Blake points out that Chaucer looked very different from Gower in both Caxton and Berthelette,[11] and Machan argues that in Berthelette's design, Gower 'as *commentator* speaks before the stories in order to guide readers' responses to them'.[12]

Berthelette reprinted his Gower in 1554 and after that, Gower has to wait until 1810 to see print again. The beauty of Berthelette's book may, over the centuries, have become a handicap. Derek Pearsall has argued that the availability of Berthelette's good text helped to keep Gower's reputation alive,[13] but as Machan points out, the format of Berthelette's Gower – a humanist format Joseph Dane has christened 'monumental' – would have looked increasingly antiquated as time went by.[14] Early nineteenth-century readers were still reading what was, after all, a sixteenth-century book, both in appearance and in its editorial treatment of the text. And whether or not people were actually reading Gower is an open question. If Berthelette's *Confessio* at first ensured a modest surge of interest in the poet, it is nevertheless the case that references to Gower, especially from the seventeenth century on, seem most concerned with the poet's political affiliations and with the nature of his relationship with Chaucer.[15] There are exceptions, of course. Gower is, as R.F. Yeager demonstrates, the most quoted writer in Ben Jonson's *English Grammar*, a fact Yeager traces in part to Berthelette's praise of Gower's use of the vernacular in his preface.[16] This survival is nevertheless perhaps as mixed a blessing as the tag 'moral Gower'. Another mixed blessing is suggested by Taylor's reflection of the common tendency to link Chaucer and Gower.

Gower's position in the line of descent of English poets, by the seventeenth century expressed as the Gower-Chaucer pairing, is a forced marriage whose tenacity has been explored by many commentators on Gower's reputation. In its

---

[11] Blake, 'Early Printed Editions', p. 296.

[12] Machan, 'Thomas Berthelette', p. 156.

[13] Derek Pearsall, 'The Gower Tradition', *Gower's* Confessio Amantis: *Responses and Reassessments*, ed. Alastair J. Minnis (Cambridge, 1983), pp. 179–97 (p. 190).

[14] Machan, 'Thomas Berthelette', pp. 162–63; Joseph A. Dane, *Who is Buried in Chaucer's Tomb?: Studies in the Reception of Chaucer's Book* (East Lansing, MI, 1998), pp. 67–9.

[15] These concerns are nearly always to the detriment of Gower, as the two main forms of the *Confessio*'s Prologue come to be seen as evidence that the poet was a turncoat. See the introduction to this volume for further details.

[16] R.F. Yeager, 'Ben Jonson's *English Grammar* and John Gower's Reception in the Seventeenth Century', *The Endless Knot: Essays on Old and Middle English in Honor of Marie Borroff*, eds. M. Teresa Tavormina and R.F. Yeager (Cambridge, 1995), pp. 227–39 (pp. 231, 232–3).

original, the link did not construct a decidedly inferior Gower, but by the end of
the eighteenth century even a defence of Gower such as one finds in Thomas
Warton's *History of English Poetry* moves rapidly into the familiar pattern of
negative comparison. In the Introduction to this collection, I used the example of
Warton's praise for Gower's learning:

> when books began to grow fashionable, and the reputation of learning conferred
> the highest honour, poets became ambitious of being thought scholars; and sacri-
> ficed their native powers of invention to the ostentation of displaying an exten-
> sive course of reading, and to the pride of profound erudition. . . . Chaucer is an
> exception to this observation: whose original feelings were too strong to be sup-
> pressed by books, and whose learning was overbalanced by genius.[17]

Gower's learning has become a mark of his *lack* of poetry: in an age which cultivated 'natural sensibility', Gower is, by this account, simply not sensitive
enough. Berthelette had praised Gower for the very learning which is here deni-
grated, and I have already discussed how the printer uses the table of contents
he created for his edition to characterise the *Confessio* as a sort of encyclopaedia.
Warton's comments make it clear how that characterisation, persisting by means
of the physical presence of the sixteenth-century book into a new and very
different cultural context, could contribute to the construction of Gower as
not-poet, producing instead that hyphenated 'Gower-Chaucer's-contemporary'
who is still with us today.

Warton's assessment set the tone for the next hundred years, and one need
not look far in the nineteenth century to find books whose pages, by their very
design, confirm these views of Gower and his role in the English literary tradition. It is hardly surprising, then, that one of Gower's two appearances in 1810
linked him overwhelmingly, textually and visually, with Chaucer. The title page
of the Reverend Henry Todd's *Illustrations of the Lives and Writings of Gower and
Chaucer* [Fig. 1] presents the reader with the famous Ellesmere portrait of the
pilgrim Chaucer; the pilgrim's finger points at the title of Todd's work. In
keeping with this emphatic presence, there is far more of Chaucer than of Gower
in the *Illustrations*. The Gower material includes Gower's will and a deed
bearing the signature of a 'John Gower'; an account of some of the manuscripts
of Chaucer and Gower; the Preface from Berthelette's edition; the *Tale of the
Caskets* from Book V of the *Confessio* and a few lines on the role of the eye in the
lover's plight from Book VI – these two extracts total some 180 lines of the
*Confessio*. Some of Gower's *Balades* are reproduced in the manuscript descriptions.[18] The rest of the book (about two-thirds the total length) is given over to
Chaucer and to material related to Chaucer. Todd implicitly recognises the effect

---

17  Thomas Warton, *The History of English Poetry from the Close of the Eleventh to the Commencement
    of the Eighteenth Century*, Vol. II (London, 1778), pp. 1–2, 31.
18  Earlier printings of some of Gower's French may be found in Warton's history, which
    contains four of the *Balades* in the 'Emendations and Additions' to Vol. II, and in the single
    poem included in George Ellis's *Specimens of the Early English Poets, to which is prefixed an
    historical sketch of the rise and progress of the English Poetry and Language; in three volumes*
    (London, 1801): 'Pour comparer le joli mois de Mai', I.170–1. The first edition of the *Specimens*
    was 1790; the 1801 edition represents a considerable expansion.

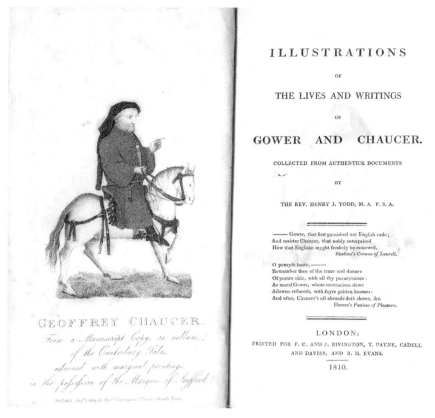

ILLUSTRATIONS

OF

THE LIVES AND WRITINGS

OF

GOWER AND CHAUCER.

COLLECTED FROM AUTHENTICK DOCUMENTS

BY

THE REV. HENRY J. TODD, M. A. F. S. A.

——— Gower, that first garnished our English rude;
And maister Chaucer, that nobly enterprised
How that Englishe myght freshely be ennewed.
                          Skelton's *Crowne of Laurell.*

O pensyfe harte, ———
Remember thee of the trace and daunce
Of poetes olde, with all thy purseyaunce :
As moral Gower, whose sentencious dewe
Adowne reflareth, with fayre golden beames :
And after, Chaucer's all abroade doth shewe, &c.
                          Hawes's *Pastime of Pleasure.*

LONDON:
PRINTED FOR F. C. AND J. RIVINGTON, T. PAYNE, CADELL
AND DAVIES, AND R. H. EVANS.

1810.

GEOFFREY CHAUCER.
*From a Manuscript Copy, on vellum,*
*of the Canterbury Tales,*
*adorned with marginal paintings,*
*in the possession of the Marquis of Stafford.*

Figure 1. The title page of the Reverend Henry Todd's *Illustrations of the Lives and Writings of Gower and Chaucer* (1810).

of presentation on reception when he makes it clear that he has not placed Gower first in the collection as a result of the poets' relative merits:

> no one will suppose me influenced by any other motive than that of attention to chronological propriety. He was born before Chaucer. Authors, both historical and poetical, in the century after the decease of these poets, usually coupling their names and describing their accomplishments, place Gower before Chaucer; not intending (for I cannot think so badly of their taste as to suppose that they preferred Gower to Chaucer,) any precedence in respect to *talents*, but merely the accustomed tribute due to *seniority*.[19]

Chaucer belongs on the title-page; ancient Gower's freak of chronological precedence is less significant than Chaucer's enduring appeal.

Todd was best known as an editor for his editions of Milton (1801) and Spenser (1805). His proximity to various manuscript collections throughout his

---

[19]  Henry Todd, *Illustrations of the Lives and Writings of Gower and Chaucer collected from authentick documents* (London, 1810), pp. xxvi–xxvii.

ecclesiastical career led to his position as keeper of the manuscripts at Lambeth Palace, and his published descriptions of some of these manuscripts. His obvious lack of enthusiasm for Gower might make his decision to publish his *Illustrations* seem rather peculiar, but there were in fact very pragmatic reasons for Todd's choice. The *Illustrations* are dedicated to George Granville Leveson-Gower, Marquis of Stafford, described by Todd as 'the friend of Literature and the head of the illustrious House of Gower'.[20] Todd's concentration on Gower's will, his reproduction of a deed signed by John Gower of 'Stitenham', his assertion that Gower was well-born – these all stem from Todd's acceptance of 'the proud tradition in the Marquis of Stafford's family',[21] the (erroneous) tracing of John Gower's ancestry to the Gowers of Stittenham in Yorkshire.[22] Todd's *Illustrations* may well have included Gower simply because that inclusion flattered an important aristocratic family.

The brief extracts from the *Confessio* in Todd's *Illustrations* are completely detached from their Latin framing: verses, glosses and speaker markers are absent. In this practice Todd is no different from the producers of medieval manuscript anthologies who also, with only a few exceptions, excised Gower's stories from their frames, both English and Latin: the tables of contents in the early printed editions facilitated a similar reading practice. Yet Todd's omission of Gower's Latin is ominous in light of later developments, for I will argue that nineteenth-century book design, even when it gave space on the page to the Latin frame, set up visual associations which later encouraged the complete discarding of that frame.

In some ways, Todd's is simply a book uncertain of its purpose or its audience: to dwell on the imbalance in its pages between Chaucer and Gower would seem to put unreasonable weight on slim foundations. But the book does participate in an important moment in the development of the English canon and the solidification of Gower's place in that canon: the series which were to become so important in shaping the general reading public are foreshadowed fitfully in Todd, and completely in 1810's other contribution to Gower's nineteenth-century presence, in volume two of Alexander Chalmers' *Works of the English Poets, from Chaucer to Cowper*. While the serialisation of the English literary tradition is a phenomenon which takes off most clearly towards the end of the nineteenth century, Chalmers shows that the impulse to organise and guide reading was in place early in the century.

Like Todd, Chalmers begins with a life of Gower: he wrote this one himself, drawing heavily on Warton and on Ellis's *Specimens of the Early English Poets*. And like Todd, Chalmers is quite clear as to the relative importance of Chaucer and Gower: 'as an English poet Gower was far inferior to his great contemporary'.[23] Chalmers was not particularly sanguine about the appeal of that 'great

---

[20] Ibid., dedication.
[21] Ibid., p. xxi.
[22] Sir Harris Nicolas's 'John Gower the Poet', *Retrospective Review*, second series 2 (1828), pp. 103–17, was a scathing indictment of Todd's neglect of armorial and other kinds of evidence in the advancing of the connection, and concludes categorically that the tradition 'has been founded upon error'(p. 117).
[23] Alexander Chalmers, *The Works of the English Poets, from Chaucer to Cowper; including the Series*

contemporary' either, remarking that 'it is not probable that [Chaucer] can ever be restored to popularity'.[24] Yet if Chalmers did not see himself as producing 'popular' Chaucer or Gower, he did bring them both into a new century. For Gower the movement is particularly decisive, bringing the *Confessio* forward more than 250 years – into the cramped pages and type of a typical early-nineteenth-century book. Gower's appearance here is as one part of a series, and all poets in the series receive similar treatment: Gower looks exactly like Chaucer. Far more distinctive is Reinhold Pauli's 1857 edition of the *Confessio*, the first truly new edition of the *Confessio* since Berthelette's, and the first with any claims to be considered a scholarly edition in the evolving understanding of the word.

The anthologies and serials which are so much a part of the nineteenth century make one kind of contribution to the study of medieval literature; another is made by the burgeoning projects of editing and recovery. After 1810, Gower was available to readers with a nineteenth-century 'look', but the text was still one which had been established according to the editorial principles of the sixteenth century. The title page of Reinhold Pauli's 1857 edition suggests Gower's true coming-of-age: this text markets itself as one 'edited and collated with the best manuscripts'.[25] Series such as Chalmers' usually rested on the editorial work of others, and for Gower that necessitated relying on Berthelette. But the preparation of new scholarly editions was proceeding apace: original editing of Chaucer, for example, was well under way by mid century. It is not unexpected, then, that it should occur to someone to edit Gower according to nineteenth-century principles. What is unexpected is that Reinhold Pauli should have decided to do so.

Pauli was a well-published German scholar of English history, whose works ranged from lives of Alfred the Great and Cromwell to general histories of England. While much of Pauli's output was in German, his books on English history were translated into English and were quite popular – the life of Alfred, in particular, went into many editions. He does seem to have had a particular interest in medieval and early modern England, but until the edition of the *Confessio* this interest manifested itself mainly in discursive history. He was not, in other words, a specialist in the editing of literary texts.

Pauli's 'Introductory Essay' includes a lengthy discussion of the available documents for establishing Gower's family, the nature of the relationship with Chaucer, and his political allegiances; while these are matters which would clearly appeal to an historian, they are standard in introductions to Gower and indeed to other medieval writers in this period. Pauli's assessment of the manuscript evidence does seem a bit cavalier, however: 'The text of a work like the Confessio Amantis does not require the same scrupulous attention to every existing MS. as that of an ancient classical author. Everybody who examines the MSS. of Gower will soon be satisfied that the principal differences are merely of

*Edited with Prefaces, Biographical and Critical, by Dr. Samuel Johnson: and The Most Approved Translations*, Vol. II (London, 1810), p. iii.
24  Chalmers, *Works of the English Poets*, I.xv.
25  Reinhold Pauli, *Confessio Amantis of John Gower: Edited and Collated with the Best Manuscripts by Dr. Reinhold Pauli*, 3 vols (London, 1857), title page.

an orthographical nature.'[26] But it is quite clear that Pauli did not himself make any kind of careful assessment of the manuscripts at all. He makes general statements which are simply untrue about the manuscripts he claims to draw on, and G.C. Macaulay, Gower's Oxford editor at the end of the century, all but accuses him of lying when he claims to have collated 'the best manuscripts': 'It is almost impossible that this full collation can really have been made, for by it nearly all Berthelette's errors might have been corrected, whereas we find them as a matter of fact on every page of Pauli's edition.'[27] Pauli certainly did not proceed in a way likely to meet with the approval of a specialist in literary editing, but he did exercise judgement, correcting errors in Berthelette with some regularity. And while one might not approve of exaggerated claims on a title page, it is true that they were not uncommon – several mid-century popular editions of Chaucer made similar, and similarly unfounded, claims. The Pauli-Macaulay conflict has in part to do with the conventions and procedures common in differing fields of endeavour; but because Pauli's was the only complete nineteenth-century edition of Gower until Macaulay's at the turn of the century, its flaws as an edition are magnified. It is, however, a lovely book.

The Pauli Gower was printed by the Chiswick Press, at this time under the guidance of Charles Whittingham the Younger.[28] Histories of typography are full of despairing comment about the prevailing ugliness of early nineteenth-century English book design, and the Chiswick Press is often written of as a shining exception. In 1857, the Press was still a small operation using hand-presses, and while it did a good bit of job-work and ordinary printing – Whittingham the Elder, for example, printed Chalmers – it is remembered for the presentation-style books it printed. In partnership with the publisher William Pickering, who also had a large antiquarian bookselling business, Whittingham had revived the use of the old-face roman types of the eighteenth century, epitomised by William Caslon's roman types, instead of the so-called 'modern-face' types which prevailed for most printing at the time. The Pauli Gower is printed in a Caslon-style old face [Fig. 2]. From 1844, the Chiswick Press frequently used this type for this sort of book, and this is the point of interest here. The Press had a huge inventory of type, only about an eighth of which was old face.[29] Caslon old face appears in books it printed for bibliophilic societies,[30] in its famous prayer books and in other small runs of fine work, but most of the Press's ordinary work, as well as some of its fine printing, was done in modern face. After its reintroduction by Chiswick, Caslon type was preferred at first chiefly by printers of religious or 'moral' books, such as the Anglo-

---

[26] Pauli, *Confessio Amantis of John Gower*, p. xliv.

[27] Macaulay, *English Works*, I.clxix–clxx.

[28] The imprint was first used by Charles Whittingham the Elder (1767–1840). Charles Whittingham the Younger (1795–1876) became his uncle's partner in 1824 and gained control of the Press in 1840. He met the publisher William Pickering (1796–1854) in 1829. On the death of Charles Whittingham the Younger, the Chiswick Press was acquired by the publisher George Bell of Bell and Daldy. The Pauli Gower was printed for Bell.

[29] Janet Ing, 'A London Shop of the 1850s: The Chiswick Press', *Papers of the Bibliographical Society of America* 80:2 (1986), pp. 153–78 (p. 161).

[30] Whittingham did work for the English Historical Society, the Arundel Society, the Philobiblon Society; Ing, 'London Shop,' p. 158.

# Prologus.

*Torpor hebes senfus, fcola parva labor minimufque*    I.
  *Caufant, quo minimus ipfe minora canam,*
*Qua tamen Eugifti lingua canit infula Bruti*
  *Anglica carmen te metra juvante loquar.*
*Offibus ergo carens qui conterit offa loquelis*
  *Abfit et interpres ftet procul oro malus.*

F hem, that writen us to-fore,
   The bokes dwelle, and we ther-
     fore
   Ben taught of that was writen
  tho.
Forthy good is, that we alfo
In oure time amonge us here
Do write of newe fome matere
Enfampled of the olde wife,
So that it might in fuche a wife,
Whan we be dede and elles where,
Beleve to the worldes ere
In time comend after this.
But for men fain, and fothe it is,
That who that al of wifdom writ
It dulleth ofte a mannes wit

B

Figure 2. The opening of the Prologue in Reinhold Pauli's *Confessio Amantis* (1857), printed by Chiswick.

Catholic printer Joseph Masters.[31] In 1532, Berthelette's preface had stressed Gower's morality, and Berthelette's design for the *Confessio* is one which would have suggested the moral or the 'worthy' to a sixteenth-century audience. In 1857, Caslon face carried similar connotations and represented a consciously backward look. It remained rare until picked up towards the end of the century by William Morris, a man with his own antiquarian projects and his own interest in beautiful books. It is not surprising, then, that the 1858 review essay in the *British Quarterly Review* occasioned by the publication of Pauli's Gower should remark on 'a style of typography which, we think, must gratify the most enthusiastic admirer of the venerable old poet'.[32]

This 'style of typography' included a range of ornaments and typefaces, from the Gothic-inspired decorated type of the title, in black and red, to the head ornaments to book pages, and the four- to six-line woodblock capitals. The effect sought is one of age and rarity, without any attempt to suggest manuscript facsimile.[33] But like blackletter facsimile, Caslon is not particularly easy to read in large doses. This difficulty may not have been perceived as a drawback, however. From the late 1840s, gift books frequently used Caslon types, and A.F. Johnson's remarks on the relative status in the 1850s of Caslon and modern face seem to echo Gower's whole manuscript and print history: 'The ordinary publishers as yet certainly did not believe that the old faces were more legible. They were all right for books which might or might not be read, but they were not going to use them for sensible reading matter.'[34] The Chiswick Press Gower is intended to be collected but not, it seems, read. One can find Chaucer similarly 'packaged' throughout the century, most famously in the Kelmscott Press *Canterbury Tales* of 1896. But while the Kelmscott Chaucer is undoubtedly an art book, in many ways less readable than the Chiswick Gower, the important point is that it was *not* the only available representation of Chaucer's text. The Aldine Chaucer produced by Chiswick for Whittingham [Fig. 3], for example and in contrast to the Pauli Gower, presents a 'sensible' Chaucer in modern face, part of an inexpensive, portable, popular series which sold far more copies than the Chiswick Press's more obscure bibliophilic printings.

Pauli's text, despite his claim to have re-edited the poem, does not present Gower with the standard accoutrements of a scholarly edition. Apart from his 'below the line' printing of the alternate opening and second-recension passages in the poem, there is nothing on the pages of the work itself to tell the reader how the text was arrived at or where emendation occurs. Italic type – used in other Victorian books, including the second edition of the Aldine Chaucer, to signal emendation or varying attestation – in Pauli's Gower is used for the Latin verses, while the Latin prose and the speaker markers are printed in a smaller

---

[31] A.F. Johnson, *Type Designs: Their History and Development*, third edn (Norwich, 1966), p. 81.

[32] 'John Gower and his Works', *The British Quarterly Review*, no. 53, Jan. 1 (1858), p. 5.

[33] There were many medieval works reprinted in the nineteenth century in blackletter type, in an attempt to suggest facsimile: many of the volumes printed for the Roxburghe Club fall into this category.

[34] Johnson, *Type Designs*, pp. 82–3.

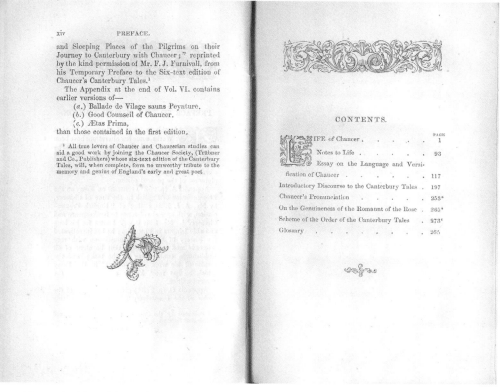

Figure 3. The Aldine Chaucer, second edition (1866), printed by Chiswick.

version of the same old-face type. As Berthelette used roman for the Latin verses, so the Chiswick Press uses italic.

Italic had been an independent typeface, especially popular in Italian books of the sixteenth century: the Venetian printer who invented it, Aldus Manutius, used it to save space, and it was not uncommon for small Italian books of the period to be printed entirely in italic. Given Whittingham and Pickering's interest in historical book design, it is not surprising that the Chiswick Press would use an old-face italic along with its old-face romans. But while we still use italic type to distinguish foreign languages, and sometimes to give *added* emphasis, I would argue that expectations about the reading of italics have shifted – a shift suggested in part by the common nineteenth-century tendency to use italics to indicate either editorial emendation or the expansion of scribal abbreviation. Such italics say, 'this has to do with editing' – and perhaps, tacitly, 'and not with reading'. What happens, then, when Latin is italicised in nineteenth- (and twentieth) century editions of a bilingual poem? Perhaps throughout his history, few readers have actually been reading Gower's Latin. But there is a difference in effect between the text-sized red Latin in two-thirds of the Gower manuscripts, and the small italic font in Pauli. One could argue that italics produce extra emphasis – certainly they produce a *different* emphasis, but that emphasis needs to be weighed against the smaller size, and against other associations readers might have with the script. In the Chiswick Press Gower, the italics are part of a visually pleasing design, but they may also be one of several design features which subtly affect (or reinforce) how we read Gower; assuring us, for example, that it is acceptable to skim or skip the Latin.

Consider the presentation of the opening of the book. *Confessio* manuscripts use miniatures, capitals and dialogue markers to move a reader as carefully as Gower did into the framing of the poem. In Pauli's version, the title 'Confessio Amantis' appears, entirely in upper case, before the opening of Book I (and not the Prologue), and Book I itself begins with a six-line capital, the only six-line capital in the three volumes [Fig. 4]. The Prologue, in this design, has become preliminary; the poem called the *Confessio Amantis* begins with Book I. By contrast, the second edition of the Aldine Chaucer reserves its largest capital for the opening of the General Prologue. *The Canterbury Tales* is seen in this design to start with its framing prologue; the *Confessio Amantis* starts *after* the Prologue. Gower as not-Chaucer, in other words; Gower's frame is expendable, Chaucer's integral. The implications of these design decisions were doubtless neither foreseen nor consciously understood, but at the end of this chapter I will suggest ways in which these decisions have had lasting effects on how we read, and teach, Gower.

Whatever its subsequent reputation, Pauli's Gower did indeed represent a step forward for the poet's image. The 1858 essay in the *British Quarterly Review* quoted above, for example, took the occasion of this publication[35] to review Gower's biography and works in a much more sympathetic tone than had Todd or Chalmers. But Gower remains a relic of the past, and the appearance of the Pauli Gower does nothing to dispel that impression. The review essay both accomplishes the writer's goal of bringing Gower to the attention of the English nation again, and simultaneously assures that nation that it need not actually read Gower. The writer's closing remarks 'place' the Pauli edition as clearly as does that edition's design: 'as a curious relic of thought and feelings nearly five centuries ago, and as the first English poem which claimed the notice of the fair and noble, we rejoice that it [the *Confessio*] has been published at length *in a style that does justice* [my emphasis] to the once popular writer'.[36]

The Pauli Gower, then, is rather like Harley 7184, the manuscript on which it is based – a beautiful book which it is difficult to imagine anyone actually reading. It did, however, stand as the first serious attempt to restore the poet and his text to public notice, and it formed the basis for the next attempt to do the same. It is significant that this next attempt – the appearance of the *Confessio* as one of the volumes in Henry Morley's Carisbrooke Library – excerpted Gower, and it is significant too that, while Morley's avowed intention was to popularise the *Confessio*, he nevertheless did so in a series which was not, unlike some of his other work, aiming at the cheapest possible production.

For the *Dictionary of National Biography*, Henry Morley's main contribution to

---

[35] It refers as well to the Roxburghe Club printings of the *Balades* in 1818 and the *Vox Clamantis* in 1850.

[36] 'The Works of John Gower,' p. 36.

## CONFESSIO AMANTIS.

### Incipit Liber Primus.

*Naturatus amor nature legibus orbem*
  *Subdit et unanimes concitat eſſe feras.*
*Huius enim mundi princeps amor eſſe videtur,*
  *Cuius eget dives pauper et omnis opes.*
*Sunt in agone pares amor et fortunaque, cecas*
  *Plebis ad inſidias vertit uterque rotas.*
*Eſt amor egra ſalus, vexata quies, pius error,*
  *Bellica pax, vulnus dulce, ſuave malum.*

I.

MAY nought ſtrecche up to
the heven
Min hond ne ſetten al in even
This world, whiche ever is
in balaunce,       [ſaunce
It ſtant nought in my ſuffi‐
So great thinges to compaſſe.
But I mote lette it over paſſe
And treaten upon other thinges,
Forthy the ſtile of my writinges
Fro this day forth I thenke chaunge
And ſpeake of thinge is nought ſo ſtrange,

Poſtquam in prologo
tractatum hactenus
exiſtit, qualiter hodi‐
erne condicionis divi‐
ſio charitatis dilectio‐
nem ſuperavit, inten‐
dit auctor ad preſens
ſuum libellum, cuius
nomen Confeſſio A‐
mantis nuncupatur,
componere de illo
amore, a quo non ſo‐
lum humanum genus,
ſed et cuncta ani‐
mancia naturaliter
ſubjiciuntur. Et quia
nonnulli amantes ul‐
tra quam expedit de‐
ſiderii paſſionibus cre‐
bro ſtimulantur, ma‐
teria libri per totum

Figure 4. The opening of *Book I* in the Pauli *Confessio*.

English literary scholarship (despite professorships at University College and Queen's College London) was 'as a populariser of literature'.[37] The hundreds of volumes which came out under his editorship in various series are a formidable witness to his efforts in this respect, including sixty-three volumes of 'Morley's Universal Library', 214 in 'Cassell's National Library', and his oft-reprinted *First Sketch of English Literature*. The Gower volume appeared in the Carisbrooke Library, published by Routledge and intended to offer 'reprints of less familiar English classics'.[38] In a series like Chalmers', Gower appears in a chronological arrangement (volume one was devoted to Chaucer, and volume two also includes Skelton, Surrey, Wyat, Gascoigne and Turbervile). In anthologies devoted to lesser-known poets, Gower appears with other unfamiliar medieval authors – Ellis's first volume in his revised edition, for example, ran from Robert of Gloucester to Stephen Hawes. In Morley's Carisbrooke series, on the other hand, Gower rubs shoulders with John Stow, Daniel Defoe, Ben Jonson, Niccolo Machiavelli, John Milton, Torquato Tasso, Jonathan Swift and Edward Gibbon, among others. The series context for this representation of Gower, then, is confused and confusing, although it does seem clear before one even opens the covers that Gower is here presented, just as in the *Review* article, as a worthy but curious relic of the literary tradition. 'Worthy' in a literal sense – in his advertisement for the Carisbrooke Library, Morley draws a contrast between the 'sixty-three cheap shilling volumes' of his Universal Library, and the new series:

> In the 'Carisbrooke Library' there will be no small type. The volumes will be larger; each of about four hundred and fifty pages. They will be handsome library volumes, printed with clear type upon good paper, at the price of half-a-crown.[39]

Once again, Gower appears in a book with some (admittedly middlebrow) pretensions to beauty.

Yet there are significant differences between Pauli's and Morley's editions, one of which is immediately clear from the opening of the *Confessio*. The page lives up to Morley's billing: it is well printed, in double columns of clear type; a decorated Gothic face is used for titles and section changes. Smaller type reproduces alternate versions at the foot of the page; difficult words are glossed on the page [Fig. 5]. But unlike Pauli's text, this one omits the Latin verses and glosses. Morley's comments on his own editorial method are restricted to the assertion that he has restored Gower's metre: 'I believe, however, that the reader here has Gower's song more nearly than in any former edition given as he sang it himself, nothing modernised, but rather with a few words carried back to their original form for the recovery of the right rhythm of a line.'[40] Nowhere is there any indication that the *Confessio* has a Latin frame. It is perhaps no accident that Morley demotes Gower's Latin title to a subtitle; in his edition, Gower wrote *Tales of the Seven Deadly Sins*.

---

37  *Dictionary of National Biography*, Vol. XIII (London, 1921–22), p. 976.
38  Ibid., pp. 975–6.
39  Henry Morley, *Tales of the Seven Deadly Sins being the Confessio Amantis of John Gower* (London, 1889), p. iv.
40  Ibid., p. xi.

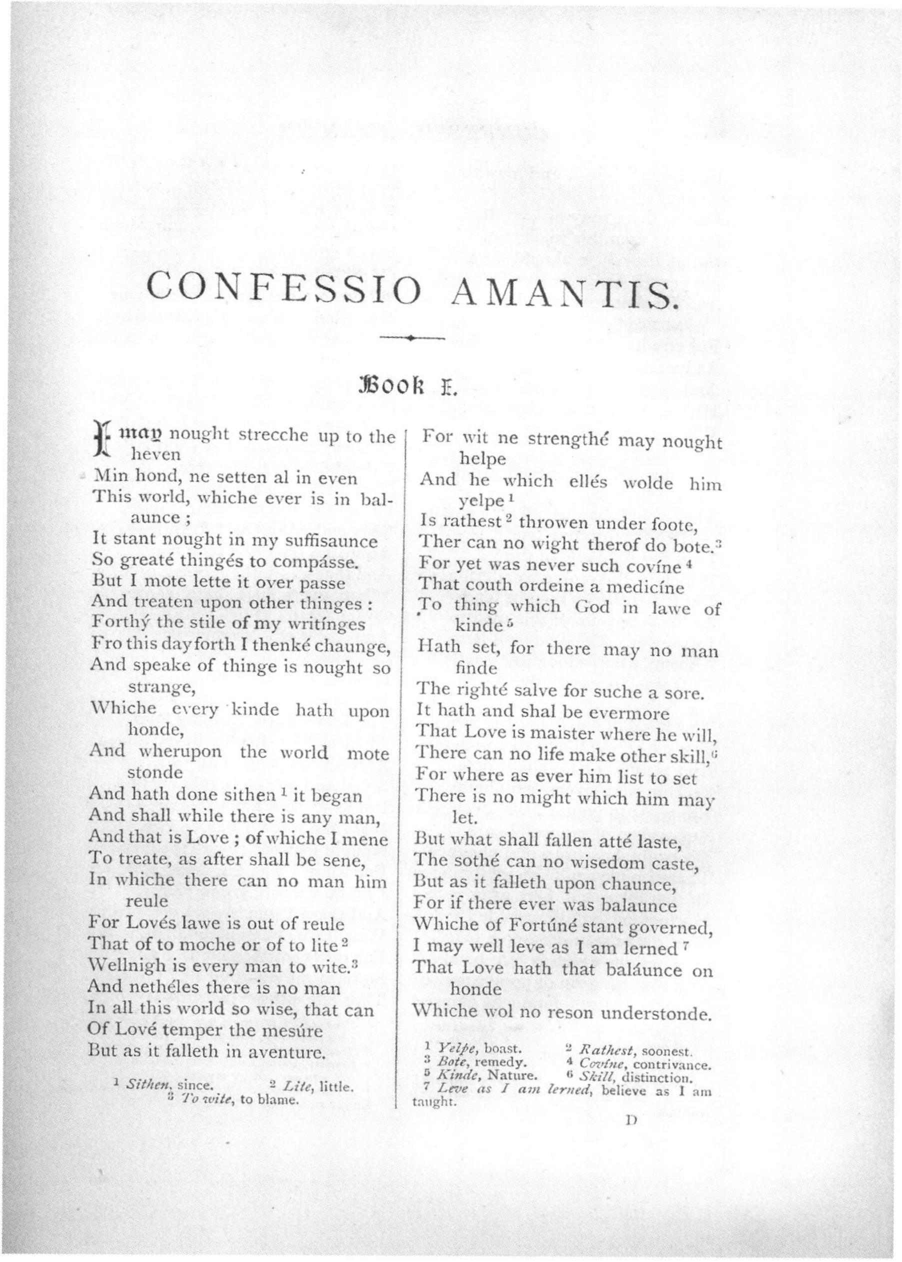

# CONFESSIO AMANTIS.

## 𝕭oo𝕶 𝕴.

It may nought strecche up to the heven
Min hond, ne setten al in even
This world, whiche ever is in bal-
aunce ;
It stant nought in my suffisaunce
So greaté thingés to compásse.
But I mote lette it over passe
And treaten upon other thinges :
Forthý the stile of my writínges
Fro this day forth I thenké chaunge,
And speake of thinge is nought so
strange,
Whiche every kinde hath upon
honde,
And wherupon the world mote
stonde
And hath done sithen [1] it began
And shall while there is any man,
And that is Love ; of whiche I mene
To treate, as after shall be sene,
In whiche there can no man him
reule
For Lovés lawe is out of reule
That of to moche or of to lite [2]
Wellnigh is every man to wite.[3]
And nethéles there is no man
In all this world so wise, that can
Of Lové temper the mesúre
But as it falleth in aventure.

[1] *Sithen*, since.   [2] *Lite*, little.
[3] *To wite*, to blame.

For wit ne strengthé may nought
helpe
And he which ellés wolde him
yelpe [1]
Is rathest [2] throwen under foote,
Ther can no wight therof do bote.[3]
For yet was never such covíne [4]
That couth ordeine a medicíne
To thing which God in lawe of
kinde [5]
Hath set, for there may no man
finde
The righté salve for suche a sore.
It hath and shal be evermore
That Love is maister where he will,
There can no life make other skill,[6]
For where as ever him list to set
There is no might which him may
let.
But what shall fallen atté laste,
The sothé can no wisedom caste,
But as it falleth upon chaunce,
For if there ever was balaunce
Whiche of Fortúné stant governed,
I may well leve as I am lerned [7]
That Love hath that baláunce on
honde
Whiche wol no reson understonde.

[1] *Yelpe*, boast.   [2] *Rathest*, soonest.
[3] *Bote*, remedy.   [4] *Covíne*, contrivance.
[5] *Kinde*, Nature.   [6] *Skill*, distinction.
[7] *Leve as I am lerned*, believe as I am
taught.

D

Figure 5. The opening of *Book I* in Richard Morley, *Tales of the Seven Deadly Sins* (1889).

Morley makes various interventions to render Gower's text more accessible. He provides a table of contents which uses the sins as a framework. As in the Pauli Gower, typography suggests that the Prologue is preliminary to this framework: Morley's table uses Gothic display type for the book division headings but not for the Prologue. The headings for the stories are in English, and brief source notes are provided (in italics). The *Confessio* is presented, then, as a collection of stories based on past models. It is also in the table that Morley tells his readers that he has (agreeing with Chaucer) omitted the tale of Canace, in which 'Gower against his own habitual good sense has by some aberration of mind here made his Confessor tolerant of incest'.[41] As in the tables in Caxton and Berthelette discussed above, Morley's table is part of the packaging of the *Confessio* for his audience, and it is striking that this table is the most clearly laid out and hierarchised part of the book. Five different levels of type, a numbering system and ample white space all make this a most accessible reference tool, and the more one used such a tool, the more one would absorb its constructing of the text to which it is the key. The table is perhaps conceived of as replacing the Latin, but the Latin verses and the dialogue markers are gone too, and this wholesale, silent excision of the Latin frame significantly reorients the *Confessio*.

Morley writes that his text is meant 'to be popular and yet not modernised', and that his corrections to the text should appeal to 'the student as well as to the general reader'.[42] His appealing pages, keyed to a table of contents, certainly suggest a reading audience. Yet the reader and the student are here presented with much less Gower than would be found in Pauli, and, more strikingly, there is no reference to what has been omitted.[43] Pauli and his printer had perhaps no intention of exiling Gower's Latin entirely by presenting it in a small Caslon italic, but Morley may be evidence that the effect of that design could indeed be to encourage a tendency to overlook the Latin frame without even a reference to it, let alone an apology. The situation will become more striking in the twentieth-century excerpted editions, books which offer us yet another social context – the classroom and the marketplace of academic publishing. But before moving into that world, I wish to consider the only 'real' scholarly edition of the *Confessio*, by G.C. Macaulay.

In addition to the editions of the *Confessio* discussed thus far, there had been a few print copies of Gower's other works, in this case exclusively in the nineteenth century. The Roxburghe Club, a bibliophilic society made up of a combination of aristocrats and gentlemen-scholars,[44] contributed two such books. The first was *Balades and Other Poems by John Gower*,[45] based on the only surviving manuscript of the *Cinkante Balades*, the Trentham MS, then in the possession of

[41] Ibid., p. xxiv.
[42] Ibid., p. xii.
[43] Macaulay seems highly suspicious of Morley's procedures with respect to the English text as well: 'The editor professes to omit iii. 142–338, and a few lines here and there in other places. The omissions, however, are much more extensive than this seems to imply.' *English Works*, p. clxx.
[44] See David Matthews, *The Making of Middle English, 1765–1910* (Minneapolis, 1999); the chapter 'Turtle Soup and Texts' discusses the Roxburghe Club and other literary societies.
[45] All the other poems from the Trentham MS were included, except for the English poem *In Praise of Peace*.

George Granville Leveson-Gower, Earl Gower and later second Duke of Suther-land, who edited it for the club in 1818. This book was printed in Gothic type and attempted to mimic the original manuscript, reproducing the circular gaps produced by earlier damage. Gower the earl believed himself a descendant of Gower the poet, and the Roxburghe printing included photographic reproduc-tions of the various signatures and inscriptions on the manuscript – elements which linked the manuscript to royalty and to the noble Gowers.[46] The other Roxburghe printing of Gower's work was an 1850 edition of the *Vox Clamantis*, contributed by H.O. (Henry Octavius) Coxe, then sub-librarian (and later head librarian) of the Bodleian Library. Coxe's edition was printed in ordinary type and favoured classical spellings of the medieval Latin.

Roxburghe Club books were printed exclusively for club members and were not widely circulated. Their obscurity is reflected in the Reverend George Gilfillan's apparent unawareness of their existence when he remarks, in 1860, that: 'The "Confessio Amantis" is the only work of Gower's which is printed and in English. The rest are still slumbering in MS.; and even although the "Vox Clamantis" should put in a sleepy plea for the resurrection of print, on the whole we are disposed to say, better for all parties that it and the rest should slumber on.'[47] Gilfillan might also be excused for being unaware of the printings of some of the Latin poems in Thomas Wright's *Political Poems and Songs relating to English history, composed during the period from the accession of Edw. III. to that of Ric. III.*, *Rolls Series* xiv (London, 1859).[48] And in any case it remains true to say, as the century drew to a close, that there had been neither a true scholarly edition of the *Confessio*, nor a collected edition of all of Gower's works.[49] G.C. Macaulay solved that with his *Complete Works of John Gower*, published from 1899–1902 by Oxford's Clarendon Press. Macaulay's remains the only scholarly edition of the *Confessio* to this day.

Macaulay published Gower's works in four volumes. The first presented the French works while the fourth was taken up with the Latin texts, but Macaulay is clear from the start that the edition of the *Confessio*, which occupies volumes two and three, was the main goal: 'I submitted to the Delegates of the University Press a proposal to edit the *Confessio Amantis*, and this proposal they accepted on the condition that I would undertake to edit also the other works, chiefly in French and Latin, of the same author. . . . To this condition I assented with some

---

[46] This printing was the basis for Edmund Stengel's *John Gower's Minnesang und Ehezuchtbüchlein: LXXII Anglonormannische Balladen, aus Anlass der Vermählung seines Lieben Freundes und Collegen Wilhelm Vietor neu hrsg. von Edmund Stengel* (Marburg, 1886). As Stengel had no access to the Trentham MS, his edition consisted of the *Balades* and the *Traitié Pour Essampler les Amantz Marietz*.

[47] Rev. G. Gilfillan, *Specimens with Memoirs of the Less-Known British Poets. With an Introductory Essay . . . In Three Vols*, Vol. I (Edinburgh, 1860), pp. 4–5.

[48] Wright included the *Carmen super multiplici viciorum pestilencia*, 'De lucis scrutinio', 'O deus immense', etc., and the *Cronica Tripertita*.

[49] A few more editions of works related to Gower deserve mention here. These include Henry Noble McCracken's 'Quixley's Ballades Royal (?1402)', in the *Yorkshire Archaeological Journal* xx (1908), pp. 33–50, an edition of a fifteenth-century translation of the *Traitié*; and Adolf Birch-Hirschfeld's edition of the Spanish translation of the *Confessio*: *Confision del Amante por Joan Goer. Spanische Übersetzung von John Gowers Confessio Amantis aus dem Vermächtnes von Hermann Knust nach der Handschrift im Escorial* (Leipzig, 1909).

hesitation, which was due partly to my feeling that the English text was the only one really needed' (I.v–vi). Macaulay provided a thorough survey of all the Gower manuscripts then known, though there were some he managed to see only briefly, and others which have since been discovered. He provided a 'Life of Gower' in his fourth volume, and each volume included an account of the manuscripts, an outline of editorial procedure and extensive textual notes. His dislike of his material is sometimes clear; the description of the form of the *Mirour de l'Omme* begins: 'The poem (if it may be called so)' (I.xliii), and he calls Gower's practice in the *Vox* 'schoolboy plagiarism' in a work whose style is 'nearly as bad as it can be' (IV.xxxii, xxxiii). Even the *Confessio* is to some extent damned with faint praise; Macaulay writes of Gower that: 'His narrative is a clear, if shallow, stream, rippling pleasantly over the stones and unbroken either by dams or cataracts. . . . There is no doubt that this gift of clear and interesting narrative was the merit which most appealed to the popular taste, the wholesome appetite for stories being at that time not too well catered for, and that the plainness of the style was an advantage rather than a drawback' (II.xii).

In keeping with the emphasis in the rest of this essay, it is useful to consider the appearance Gower takes on Macaulay's pages – particularly because Macaulay has now represented Gower for over a century. While there are excerpted editions, and a new teaching edition of the *Confessio* based on Macaulay is now appearing, Macaulay's remains at the time of writing the only scholarly edition of Gower's works, and so it is his face, either in the late nineteenth-century printing or in the similarly-appearing EETS reprints of *The English Works of John Gower*, that is presented to most modern readers.

Macaulay's edition maintains the use of smaller typefaces for the Latin, roman for the summaries and italic for the verses. This is not a pretty book; it is clearly a scholarly edition, with apparatus at the foot of the page. Like Pauli, Macaulay places the Latin summaries in the margins; his inclusion of his own English marginal notes actually displaces the marginal commentaries from the English textual divisions to which they correspond. The manuscripts with marginal commentary tend to be quite careful about where the glosses start; Macaulay's attempts to facilitate his readers' access to the text has the perhaps unintended consequence of allowing the editorial apparatus to dominate the edited text, particularly in the case of his most striking intervention or innovation. It was Macaulay who bequeathed to us the practice of talking about the three recensions of the *Confessio*, and Macaulay who decided that the third recension, as represented by his base text, the Fairfax manuscript, was Gower's last and therefore most important word on the form of his poem. This decision travels in tandem with the layout, which prints significant variations from the other recensions at the foot of the page, below a line and with asterisked line numbers. Once again, it is the fact that Gower has not been re-edited since which makes this practice, entirely acceptable in Macaulay's day, somewhat problematic – in an age when we recognise different versions of, say, *Piers Plowman* as independent poems, the *Confessio*'s richer textual possibilities remain untapped.

But one reason Macaulay's edition has not been replaced may simply be that it is so good. He has a quite cheerful disregard for recording every variation in spelling, but his collations are very thorough, his descriptions and notes often quite exhaustive, and his text entirely readable. Nevertheless, some of Macaulay's apparently sensible choices have had long-lasting consequences. The most significant, to my mind, have to do with language. First, the decision to group the poems by language means that a reader is given a false impression of the manuscript contexts for these works: the works in the Trentham MS, for example, are divided among the three parts of the *Works*. Thus the poem to Henry IV, *In Praise of Peace*, which survives only in the mixed-language Trentham MS, is moved to the end of the volumes containing the *Confessio* – which is all very well until one considers the theory that the trilingual Trentham MS may well have been put together around 1400 specifically to showcase Gower's skills while honouring Henry IV's coronation. That is, the Trentham MS has particular political and linguistic themes which become muted in Macaulay's rearrangement of its contents.

Macaulay does represent the *Confessio* as bilingual, keeping all of the Latin apparatus of the English poem – an apparatus which, it will be recalled, the popularising Morley had excised. Macaulay's contrasting practice can be read as an elite, rather than a popular, gesture: there are no translations and few linguistic notes throughout the four-volume *Works*. Macaulay evidently assumed that anyone reading Gower would also (or should also) be able to read Latin and French. Whether the audience for Gower became less academic, or whether the academic audience became less likely to possess the linguistic skills Macaulay took for granted, is unclear. What is clear is that the next wave of print Gowers addressed the challenge posed by Gower's trilinguality, though in very different ways. A reader can now access complete translations of the Latin works and of the *Mirour*.[50] But the bilingual nature of the *Confessio* has been addressed, until very recently, quite differently. Rather than providing translations of Gower's Latin, the twentieth-century student editions tended to return to Morley's practice, by removing most of it.

Excerpts and abridgements of the *Confessio* gradually came to be the standard presentation of Gower's work. Some of these were highly idiosyncratic and barely circulated. One such is the story of Lucius and the statue, from Book V of the *Confessio*, which appeared under the title *Of False Allegations* in 1913. Charles Clinch Bubb, of the Clerk's Press, Cleveland, Ohio, produced thirty-two copies of this attractive booklet, printed in Caxton type – an echo, perhaps, of the bibliophilic appeal of the Pauli Gower. But most of Gower's twentieth-century presence speaks to his emergence into the schoolroom, as a number of texts aimed at a student audience appeared. A brief collection of excerpts from Gower was published in the Cambridge Plain Texts series in 1927, based on Pauli's text. J.A.W. Bennett's wider range of choices for the 1968 Clarendon Medieval and Tudor series also included brief excerpts from Gower's Latin and French work. This collection was based on Macaulay's edition. Another brief sampling

---

[50] Eric W. Stockton, *The Major Latin Works of John Gower* (Seattle, 1962); the Latin verses to the *Confessio* are translated in Siân Echard and Claire Fanger, *The Latin Verses in the* Confessio Amantis: *An Annotated Translation* (East Lansing, MI, 1991); William Burton Wilson and Nancy Wilson Van Baak, *Mirour de l'Omme* (East Lansing, MI, 1992).

appeared in a 1983 excerpted edition by Carole Weinberg.[51] These three editions share a striking feature: each starts with Book I. There is no framing Prologue, and no Latin, gloss or verse, at all.[52] And while most of the English verse of the Prologue does appear in Terence Tiller's 1963 translation for Penguin, he too, in addition to excerpting the English text, has entirely omitted the Latin: 'The poem has been cut by me to about one-third of its original length. Excised passages are always summarized in prose, and their precise extent indicated, with two general exceptions: I have ignored the Latin marginal glosses, and the Latin verse summaries.'[53]

In the Introduction to his excerpted edition, Bennett directs his readers to the Prologue which he has omitted (recommending that they consult Macaulay's edition), and points out as well, quite rightly, that the process of excerpting Gower began in the fifteenth century. There is indeed nothing new in excerpting Gower (or even in removing the Latin from the *Confessio* – there are a few manuscripts which do exactly that). But because the print history is thin, it means that one impulse, the excerpting one, can take over the poet's whole posterity. Chaucer was frequently excerpted, but he has also continued to be available in whatever format any given age regarded as a 'full' edition. Chaucer's format, as well as his text, is continually revised. Gower continues to wear the workaday EETS face, so his readers are offered a choice between the undeniably 'old' appearance of Macaulay, or the clean look of the modern excerpted editions – editions which are, however, misleading about the framing of the poem. But there are two positive signs about Gower's future in print in the twenty-first century. The first is the reworking of what has been the most popular classroom edition, Russell Peck's excerpted text, based on Macaulay and published first in 1968. In its first guise this edition had very little Latin, and while it included parts of the Prologue, it too tended to emphasise the stories. The new edition is a complete text, including all the Latin – and by providing translations of that Latin, it makes it possible for a student to appreciate the relations between the parts of the text. It is also a pleasant text to read, with a clear font and few editorial interventions on the page itself. The Latin glosses, in keeping with much of Gower's later print history, have been sidelined – here by appearing in the notes at the end of the volume, a practice signalled in the text itself by pointing hands – but they *are* included. The second positive development is a conference which took place in London in July 2003, to explore the possibility of a new – perhaps a hypertext – scholarly edition of Gower.

The appearance of the text on the page, in script and print, has always been governed, partly or wholly, by financial considerations. Increasing separation of the procedures involved in making the book, as early printers gave way to type founders, compositors, publishers, printers, designers, editors, and so on, makes

---

51  Carole Weinberg, ed., *Selected Poetry: John Gower* (Manchester, 1983).
52  A peculiar exception to this rule is Gower's appearance in *The Works of the British Poets*, ed. Ezekiel Sanford, Vol. I (Philadelphia, 1819). Professing a distaste for Gower's recounting of old stories (see the introduction to this volume), the editor presents the reader with only one narrative excerpt (the story of Florent), choosing instead to reproduce some of Genius's definitions of the sins.
53  Terence Tiller, ed. and trans., *Confessio Amantis [The Lover's Shrift]* (Harmondsworth, Middlesex, 1963), p. 14.

it almost impossible to speak of, say, 'Bennett's Gower' in the same way that we can speak of Berthelette's Gower. But Gower's printing history shows that decisions motivated by aesthetic or financial considerations can have lasting implications for reading. In *Bibliography and the Sociology of Texts*, D.F. McKenzie writes: 'Every society rewrites its past, every reader rewrites its texts, and, if they have any continuing life at all, at some point every printer redesigns them.'[54] When an author is as rarely printed as Gower, the redesigns do not happen and the text is not, in this sense, rewritten. At the end of the Ricardian version of the *Confessio*, Venus bids Gower greet Chaucer in particular, as her special poet; in all versions, she gives Gower a set of beads and tells him to pray. Venus seems to have continued to favour Chaucer. Gower is still praying – perhaps for a new edition of his work.

[54] D.F. McKenzie, *Bibliography and the Sociology of Texts* (London, 1986), p. 16.

# 7

## *John Gower's French*

Gower's known French writings consist of a small number of prose examples (see 'Prose', below) and three unique poetical 'works' – the lengthy and variously titled *Mirour de l'Omme*, and two balade collections, the so-called *Cinkante Balades* and the *Traitié Pour Essampler les Amantz Marietz* – a prodigious *oeuvre* amounting to nearly 35,000 lines in several styles and meters. Gower is thus assuredly the most prolific English practitioner of French poetry in the fourteenth century; but more importantly, at its best the quality of this verse is such that, had we nothing else of Gower's, either in English or Latin, his extant French work would, alone, earn him a place among the notable poets of his age.

That Gower considered his French poetry significant to his achievement is readily apparent in many quarters, from his tomb (where the *Mirour de l'Omme*, under its later Latin title, *Speculum Meditantis*, supported his other two major poems, the *Confessio Amantis* and the *Vox Clamantis*, as the first of the three books lying pillow-like beneath the head of Gower's effigy)[1] to the ways in which the two balade sequences were reproduced and disseminated – the *Traitié* attached to manuscripts of Gower's major poems, the *Cinkante Balades* as the centerpiece in what may have been a manuscript intended for Henry IV. Although it has sometimes been speculated that Gower's French poetry is his earliest, giving way, as his talent matured, to Latin and English, there would seem to be no more truth to this than to the assumption of early critics that Chaucer's work progressed through 'French' and 'Italian' periods on its way to his 'English' triumph. There is, however, no way to establish an unequivocal chronology for the French poems, as none contains an allusion to topical events, or other notations of the kind, sufficient to date them precisely, or even in relation to Gower's other works. The reality seems to be that Gower composed in French throughout his life, a fact that Macaulay recognized regarding the *Traitié* at least, by remarking that its eighteen pieces may have been written to celebrate Gower's marriage to Agnes Groundolf in 1398, when he would have been nearly seventy years old.

As for influence, there is some possibility that Spenser and Milton may both have known the *Mirour de l'Omme*: Spenser's depiction of the parade of Sins in

---

[1]  The order on the tomb now differs, reading, from top to bottom, *Vox Clamantis*, *Speculum Meditantis*, and *Confessio Amantis*. See the essay by Hines, Cohen and Roffey in this collection, for discussion of the original order, as attested by various antiquaries.

Book I of the *Faerie Queene* bears resemblance to Gower's, and Gower's account of the engendering of Death upon Sin by Satan is a close analogue to Milton's in *Paradise Lost*. Compared to that of the *Confessio Amantis*, or even the Latin poems, however, the readership of Gower's French poetry seems never to have been large. Possibly Gower himself sensed this, while continuing to compose in French for reasons of his own, or with particular patrons in mind. The existence today of both the *Cinkante Balades* and the *Mirour de l'Omme* in single copies (and the adoption of the Latin *Speculum Meditantis* for the latter's title on the tomb) ought perhaps to be seen as indicative: certainly evidence exists to argue that when Gower conceived the notion, he had means to proliferate copies of whatever works, under whatever name, he chose. The likelihood, in any case, is that the body of Gower's French poetry fell victim to historical forces larger than its literary merits. The clear direction of letters in England – briefly interrupted during Henry IV's usurpation – had been composition in English, to the exclusion of French, a process much advanced with the blessing of Richard II and carried out as a matter of crown policy under Henry V. Death in 1408 prevented Gower from observing the process to completion, but undoubtedly there was enough 'writing on the wall' during his later years for him to read the trend, at least for lengthy pieces like the *Mirour*, if not for sequential balades like the *Traitié*, for which, judging at least by the manuscript record, he continued – whether paradoxically or stubbornly – to assume an audience. But just how close was the change to come is registered by the awkward translation of the *Traitié* into English by a Yorkshireman, perhaps one John Quixley, in 1402.

To an appreciable degree, the nature of Gower's French would itself have hastened its antiquation. As Macaulay observed, by way of explaining his preference for 'Anglo-Norman' to designate Gower's language: 'It must be remembered that [his was] not a dialect popularly spoken and with a true organic development, but a courtly and literary form of speech, confined to the more educated class of society.'[2] In short, Gower's French was exceptional from the start. Insular in a sociological as well as a geographic way, it bore some resemblance to the French he undoubtedly spoke with fluency, but nonetheless could only have been notably 'elevated' in its literariness. This, no doubt, must have been an early advantage: for, despite what Macaulay has called the 'Englishness' of Gower's metrics – that is, especially its dependence upon stress rather than syllabic count, as on the continent – Gower's work in French has an uniquely polished 'voice', as well as the linguistic elasticity to admit theological argument and devotional avowal, both sacred and profane. This would have marked it as artful, and the desirable work of a talented hand – but it also guaranteed itself an eventual obsolescence with the turning of the times.

---

[2]   G.C. Macaulay, *The Complete Works of John Gower* (Oxford, 1899–1902), IV.xi, n. 1.

## *The* Mirour de l'Omme

Gower's major poem in French is the *Mirour de l'Omme*, or *Speculum Hominis* – either title having been initially in use, depending apparently only upon the language of the statement at hand. At some point, perhaps shortly before his death, Gower elected to change the name to *Speculum Meditantis*, and it is this which appears along the spine of the lowest of the three books beneath the head of Gower's effigy on his tomb. The sole copy of the *Mirour* is Cambridge University Library Additional MS 3035, purchased in 1891 by the university librarian at a public sale. The manuscript is described by Macaulay, who identified it as Gower's hitherto 'lost' third book, as follows:

> Written on parchment, size of leaves about 12' x 7¾', in eighths with catchwords; writing of the latter half of the 14$^{th}$ century, in double column of forty-eight lines to the column; initial letter of each stanza coloured blue or red, and larger illuminated letters at the beginning of the chief divisions, combined with some ornamentation on the left side of the column, and in one case, f. 58v., also at the top of the page. One leaf is pasted down to the binding at the beginning and contains the title and table of contents. After this four leaves have been cut out, containing the beginning of the poem, and seven more in other parts of the book. There are also some leaves lost at the end. . . . The manuscript is written in one hand throughout, with the exception of the Table of Contents, and the writing is clear, with but few contractions. In a few cases . . . corrections have been made over erasure. The correctness of the text which the MS presents is shown by the very small number of cases in which either metre or sense suggests emendation. Apart from the division of words, only about thirty corrections have been made in the present edition throughout the whole poem of nearly thirty thousand lines, and most of these are very trifling. I have little doubt that this copy was written under the direction of the author.

Punctuation in the manuscript, as Macaulay also notes, 'where it exists, is of a very uncertain character'.[3]

As we have it, the *Mirour* consists of 29,945 octosyllabic lines in what amounts to iambic meter – essentially the same form used in the *Confessio Amantis*. Unlike the couplets of the *Confessio*, however, the *Mirour* rhymes in stanzas of twelve lines: *aabaabbbabba*. It is a pattern the *Mirour* shares with (among others) Hélinant de Froidmont's *Vers de la Mort*, a widely known twelfth-century poem of similar length and high moral purpose. Probably, since Gower names Hélinant and the *Vers de la Mort* in the *Mirour*, both were in his mind as he wrote. Because the MS Camb. Univ. Add. 3035 scribe was a very regular worker, managing just under sixteen stanzas per page, it is possible to guess that up to the end of the manuscript as we know it approximately two thousand lines are lacking, including fifty to sixty stanzas at the beginning and the rest on leaves lost irregularly throughout – that is, at lines 5879–6069; 19,122–314; 19,506–890; 21,977–9; 22,359–743, by Macaulay's numbering, which

---

3  Macaulay, *Complete Works*, IV.lxxix–lxxxi.

counts the lines that he determined to be lost on the missing leaves. An unknown number of leaves has also gone missing at the end. If, however, the table of contents is a true guide to the original, what has been preserved breaks off but another half-dozen leaves or so short of Gower's conclusion. We can therefore estimate the finished length of the *Mirour* to have been close to 34,000 lines.

The *Mirour de l'Omme* is, then, a vast undertaking – but given the scope of Gower's purpose, a space much shorter could scarcely have accommodated it. His plan is palpably Miltonic and, indeed, no Englishman's poem until *Paradise Lost* seems comparably ambitious. Like Milton, Gower's major theme is man's salvation – and no less than Milton, Gower understood that to mean the salvation of a rational being, one for whom logical argument, if framed effectively, stood the best chance of being persuasive. Thus Gower too begins his story, which he divides into ten sections of unequal length, at the beginning, with the fall of Lucifer from grace – a rebellion productive of Sin, upon whom the Devil incestuously begets Death. Sin and Death busy themselves in turn, creating seven daughters: Pride, Envy, Ire, Sloth, Avarice, Gluttony and Lechery. Sin and her daughters are sent first, to recruit the World to their side (a task none too difficult) and then, along with the Devil himself and aided by the messenger Temptation, to win over Man, both to their cause, and to his doom. Man's Flesh finds Temptation irresistible, but his Soul recoils, and calls for help from Reason and Fear. Temptation soon overpowers Reason, but Fear shows Flesh the hideous figure of Death, who has been hidden by Sin and the Devil. A frightened Flesh listens then to Conscience, who has wrested Reason away from Temptation. Reason reconciles Flesh and Soul, and the Devil turns to Sin for another plan (lines 1–756). The World proposes the need for reinforcements, which to provide he marries all seven of the Vices, Sin's daughters, each of whom subsequently gives birth to five daughters of her own. These daughters are all aspects of their mothers (e.g. the five daughters of Pride are Hypocrisy, Arrogance, Vain-glory, Boasting, and Disobedience), and are carefully described (lines 757–9720). The collective force of Sin, her daughters and granddaughters, along with the World, are too much for Man, and he gives himself over into their control. Reason and Conscience do not give up, however, and appeal to God for help. God sends the seven Virtues (Humility, Charity, Patience, Prowess, Generosity, Measure and Chastity) as brides for Reason who, with each of them, has five daughters. All match the daughters of the Vices and the World: Humility, the Virtue opposing Pride, has for example the daughters Devotion, Fear, Discretion, Modesty and Obedience (lines 9721–18,372).

Thus, says Gower, the battle-lines were drawn long ago, but to see the outcome it is necessary to look at contemporary life. What follows (lines 18,373–26,521) is an extensive examination of the corruption of the Three Estates of society – Church (from Pope to parish priests, and the mendicant and monastic orders), State (rulers, knights and nobles, the judiciary) and Workers (merchants, manufacturers, laborers). Everyone is tainted, and all seek to blame either the times or the World for their wickedness. Seeking truth, the poet asks the World for the source of all this evil – and systematically eliminates the four elements, the stars and planets, the plants, animals and birds, all of which merely behave according to natural law. Only Man himself, a microcosm of the world at large, made in God's image and gifted with Reason, can bring about all of the disorder that everywhere abounds. For order again to reign in creation, Man must repent and stop his sinning (lines 26,521–27,120).

But this is not so easy, as the poet himself acknowledges by confessing, in the persona of 'l'omme pecchour', the depth of his own sin, and the despair he feels – the great mercy of Christ notwithstanding – at the thought of addressing his appeal to God, since he is so very undeserving. Only one being could have sufficient compassion to hear his prayer, and then to intercede on his, or any man's, behalf with God – Mary, the Holy Virgin and the Mother of Jesus. This is so because of her humanity – and in characteristic fashion Gower sets out to explain the Virgin's unique salvific power to the rational reader by starting at the beginning (lines 27,121–27,480). What follows is an account of the Virgin's conception and birth, her childhood, marriage and the birth of Jesus, her Seven Joys, an adumbrated Life of Christ (including his circumcision, purification, baptism, selected miracles, crucifixion, and resurrection), the Sorrows of the Virgin, her life with St John, her death, burial and ultimate apotheosis in the Assumption.

Having justified his faith, the poet (still speaking as 'l'omme pecchour') offers up prayers, first to Christ and the Virgin together, asking that they recall the pains they too suffered while imprisoned in the flesh, and that they forgive him (and other poor fleshly creatures by extension) and lead him to the joy they now experience in heaven. Next he turns to praise the Virgin alone, starting by reciting her many honorific names, and explaining their origins and the aspects of her special compassion which they reveal (lines 27,481–29,904). As the final leaves of the manuscript are lost at this point, we can assume that a good portion of what followed was praise of the Virgin, but Gower's precise conclusion cannot be known.

Even incomplete, the *Mirour de l'Omme* is an extraordinarily ambitious poem – not easy, either to read or always to appreciate, and demanding in ways which for the most part have yet to be encountered. The 'problem' is its Frenchness: had Gower chosen to write in English, the difficulties of the *Mirour* would have been addressed long ago. But the *Mirour* is, simply, a major poem by one of the four most important English poets of the last quarter of the fourteenth century. Even the fact of its being in French is significant testimony of a kind to the state of letters in England at the time – and Gower's reasons for his choice of language are worth pursuing.

What makes the *Mirour* unique are the magnitude of its vision and the creative eclecticism with which Gower approached his sources in order to achieve it. Critical appreciations have, in the past, attempted to categorise the *Mirour* too narrowly, as an unusual, but still identifiable, example of one pre-existing form or another. Strong arguments have thus been made that the *Mirour* should be classified as a penitential poem, a descendant of Pennafort and Peraldus, and heavily dependent upon the *Miroir du Monde*; others, that it ought to be considered a 'poem of complaint' – an essentially hortatory amalgam (and a modern one, at that) of various elements, usually including identification of man's sinful state as the cause of the world's misery, descriptions of the Seven

Sins, and criticism of the Three Estates which, in their current corruption, exhibit a fall from a Golden Age.

Were it not for the Life of the Virgin and the poet's prayer to her, which form the concluding section, the *Mirour* might fit any of these well enough. But therein lies the problem: no medieval genre exists which embraces so many elements. The *Mirour* is, quite simply, *sui generis*. And in fact, by combining the generic strengths of his sources – allegory from *psychomachiae* and the Sins traditions, microcosmic Man and *memento mori* from moral philosophy, social critique from estates satire, and (most importantly, perhaps) the promise of compassionate rescue offered to 'l'omme pecchour' by the Virgin's reassuringly human biography – Gower was attempting to create what amounts to a new kind of poem. Little wonder he wanted future generations who viewed his tomb to remember him for the achievement.

That said, it may be worth considering why only one copy of the *Mirour* remains. Although there is no possibility of answering the question with certainty, it is valuable to ask nonetheless, since it necessarily raises the important issue of why the *Mirour* (and by extension Gower's other French work) was written in French at all. Here undoubtedly the matter of composition date plays a part. While obviously not Gower's first poetic endeavour (what writer's first-ever work is a 30,000–plus-line attempt in twelve-line stanzas to reform the world through rational argument?), the *Mirour* is just as clearly the earliest of the three major poems, and a product primarily of the reign of Edward III. That Gower had effectively set the poem aside before 1381 may be inferred from the fact that it contains no reference to the Peasants' Rising of that year; that he had done so somewhat earlier, before Edward's death in 1377, may be guessed as well from a similar absence of references to Richard II.

But the more profound question, and by far the more interesting one, is not when the *Mirour* was finished, but rather when it was *begun*. The conditions dominant at the time of its beginning would have governed Gower's decision to write his poem in French, and in that language, despite changes around him, to carry it through to the end. If, as is generally assumed, Gower was born in 1330, to commence a large poem like the *Mirour* in 1360 would not be unimaginable for reasons of youth and inexperience; nor would it have been out of step – linguistically, at any rate – with the national focus. French was the customary language of discourse in the court of Edward III, and there all eyes had been firmly fixed on France for thirty years. With King John a captive in England since the victory of the Black Prince at Poitiers in 1356, there may not have seemed a moment more auspicious for the durability of French poetry for an English audience.

That Gower was wrong is obvious in hindsight – but the *terminus a quo* of the *Mirour* is worth considering nonetheless, since it may suggest several things about the poem, both internal and external. Internally, it can help guide our understanding of both the politics and the closely related poetics of the *Mirour*. Externally, a point of origin in the (what must have been) heady early 1360s helps explain the primary puzzle about the single manuscript.

But to look at the politics first. In the *Mirour*, Gower exchanges a certain simplistic patriotism – unquestioning support of the French war and Edward

III's leadership, belief in the right behavior of secular and ecclesiastical authorities – for an increasingly supra-national moral universalism. In the course of a decade or more of writing (the *Mirour* wasn't built in a day) times changed, souring Gower's view of the world's leaders and their lives. Papal division, Edward III's faltering war policies and oppressive taxation – of the church especially – and the royal dotage under the thumb of Alice Perrers: all are topical passages that, apparently, were added late. As his criticism of its leaders grew more particular and acute, Gower's solution – to turn away from the world toward the Virgin, for compassion and salvation as public institutions founder – is prototypical of his own political theory, and of his age.

But the political is less than half the story. The turn toward the Virgin is the culmination of an elaborate poetic strategy, as well – for the *Mirour* is much more a poem about poetic antecedents and the relation of language to right living than it is about politics, either secular or religious. Because it had such hegemony over the poetic idiom he chose to use, the courtly world initiated by the *Roman de la Rose* seldom seems far from Gower's mind. This is as true of Gower's early work, including the *Mirour*, as it is of the *Confessio Amantis*. Nothing is truly borrowed from the *Roman* into the *Mirour*, but its allegory stands conspicuously behind significant characters from the *Mirour*, like Reson, Paour and Foldelit. Because the *Mirour* is written in French, the pressure is that much stronger.

The audience Gower apparently intends to address in the *Mirour* also seems intended to recall the *Roman de la Rose*. 'Escoulte cea, chascun amant', he says in the first line of the poem as we have it, not 'chascun homme', where appropriately we could expect it, in a work that is a meticulous catalogue of every human virtue and vice, and not a 'love' poem at all. Very shortly we see what Gower is up to, of course. 'Amant' in the *Mirour* subsumes anyone who takes delight in the things of this world ('Quanq'en son coer souhaideroit/ Du siecle, pour soy deliter', lines 26–7). It is thus against 'l'amour seculer' (line 31) in general that Gower will harangue, and he means by it any love directed elsewhere than toward God.

The structure of the *Mirour* reveals how central to Gower's poetic imagination were the language and rituals of love. The body of the poem with its diverse antecedents – penitential literature, Prudentian *psychomachia*, estates satire and complaint, biblical narrative – is developed within an 'envelope' of amorous address: first, as we have seen, to the audience as 'chascun amant' and then, throughout the concluding sections, to the Virgin presented as a *donna* in the manner of lyric, in the voice of 'l'omme pecchour'. The frame of the *Mirour* is thus of a piece with its primary metaphors, marriage and generation. By comparison with the two marriages (of the World with the Sins and Reason with the Virtues) and the subsequent naming of the progeny, the combat between the good and evil forces receives perfunctory attention. Now, this seems strange, for it is this battle which provides the *raison d'être* for all the unions. By rights, it ought to be cataclysmic, but instead the actual battle shrinks steadily in importance as it recedes before its elaborate preparations.

There is in this puzzling recession a key to Gower's treatment of courtly language in the *Mirour*, and to the poem's structure. Essentially the *Mirour* is about desire, good and bad. The moral encyclopaedism of the poem, the naming and describing of virtues and vices, is an apparatus necessary because desire is omnipresent in such vast variety in human affairs that it must be adumbrated to be discussed. This enumerative process is the real 'battle' in the *Mirour*, as it is in all didactic literature: the struggle to identify right and wrong, and then to cast what we know of these things into words.

Thus the *Mirour* is, like the *Roman de la Rose* (and the *Divine Comedy*, for that matter), also about language, which Gower (and Dante, following Augustine) would have thought resembled desire in its origin and movement. In the *Mirour*, Gower offers us two kinds of evidence that he also connected language and desire in this way. There is the courtly 'envelope' of the poem's beginning and end. This trains attention on desire by speaking of it as we do most often: using the language of amorous discourse, in which 'desire' itself has an immediate sexual register. And Gower's treatment of his narrator-figure represents proof of another kind. Although he claims to be afflicted by all seven of the sins ('Ce sont les sept, tresbien le sai,/ Qui sont les chiefs de ma folie', *MO* lines 27,369–70), he names but one serious offence – the composition ('fesoie') and performance ('chantant') of poetry, of 'fols ditz d'amours' (*MO* line 27,340). The suggestion is that wrongful desire, expressed in wrongful language, was the origin of the poet/narrator's plight. Consequently, the narrator realises that, for him, salvation can come only by reversing this sin – by turning, that is, his mortal *carole* into 'un chancon cordial', a truer 'song of the heart' (*MO* line 27,351).

That this song turns out to be a long prayer to the Virgin, addressed as a courtly lady, should not surprise us. It constitutes a lyrical solution to a problem the poet/narrator presents consistently in lyrical terms. Nor should we find it strange that Gower elected so to conclude the *Mirour*. For prayer (as Augustine and Dante knew well) uniquely resolves the dilemmas of desire and language – courtly and otherwise – by properly directing both toward satisfaction in the Word of God. Thus Gower's conclusion draws together the multivalent concerns of the *Mirour*. At once a poet's closure well suited to his narrator and himself, it is also theologically sound.

And it was also, in certain important ways, out of date. In 1360 or thereabouts, when Gower started work on the *Mirour*, the English court was never more French. It was filled with noble Frenchmen and their accompanying retinues – the forty hostages (including the king's brother Philippe, Duke of Orleans, and the younger princes John of Berry and Louis of Anjou) exchanged for the return of King John to France to raise his ransom. The result of this influx was essentially the conversion of the English court into a French one: French music, French dances, French fashions in all things, from clothes to poetry. It was this court culture which undoubtedly prompted Gower to compose the *Mirour* in French, and also – because the influence of the *Roman de la Rose* remained strong – to conceive the larger structure of his poem in reaction. Indeed, even the cross-current of English writing still potent and functioning – in the popular literature of the likes of Laurence Minot and, more importantly, in the clerical efforts of Ranulph Higden, Richard of Bury and Bradwardine (all precisely the kind of reading Gower demonstrably knew) – provided, in its strident accusations of French nobility for cowardice and immorality, a further prompt to Gower to use the culture of French courtly writing against itself. But Edward's latter years saw a transformation, and ultimately an end, to the hegemony of France, both in England and for Gower himself. Had the Black Prince survived to reign, perhaps he would have appreciated a copy of the *Mirour,* and others of his court as well. As it was, English court tastes during Richard II's minority were unfocussed, and those of Richard himself, as he grew into power, were less and less French. In effect, the years after 1377 left the *Mirour* linguistically without an audience, out of step politically, and poetically without a clear target. In such a climate, Gower had little reason to prepare many copies of the *Mirour de l'Omme.*

## *The* Cinkante Balades

The *Cinkante Balades* exists in only one known copy, the Trentham MS, now London, British Library, Additional MS 59495. The manuscript measures 6¼' x 9¼' and contains forty-one leaves of parchment, two being blank at both beginning and end. Each page is ruled for thirty-five lines; the verse is copied single-column. There is no ornamentation except a colored letter at the beginning of each stanza. The hand is uniform throughout, with the exception of a second hand for two brief Latin passages; both hands are late fourteenth or early fifteenth century. There is a note by Sir Thomas Fairfax, who owned the manuscript in the seventeenth century, to the effect that Gower himself presented the book to Henry IV. While this seems unlikely – the manuscript is plain, unlike most royal presentation copies – its contents were clearly chosen with the king in mind. Thus in addition to the *Cinkante Balades* (which occupy fol. 12v to fol. 33) the Trentham MS contains 'To King Henry IV, In Praise of Peace', 'Rex celi deus', two balades in French addressing the king, along with various brief Latin pieces of which Henry IV is also the subject, and the *Traitié Pour Essampler les Amantz Marietz.*

The title *Cinkante Balades* is something of a misnomer, since the collection actually contains fifty-four balades altogether, including the dedicatory poems to Henry IV, fifty-one balades of love (there are two poems numbered 'IIII'), one unnumbered balade at the end, honouring the Virgin, and a final seven lines, also unnumbered, addressed to 'gentile Engleterre', that may have been intended as an envoy directed at the entire collection. Half of the balades are in seven-line stanzas, all rhyming *ab ab bcc* with an envoy in *bc bc,* save three, which rhyme *ab ab baa* with an envoy *ba ba;* the other half are eight-line stanzas, all but seven rhyming *ab ab bc bc* with *bc bc* envoy. The seven exceptions all rhyme *ab ab ba ba,* with an envoy *ba ba.* All but two of the poems are standard balade form – that is, three stanzas with identical rhymes, and an envoy. The exception are IX, which has five stanzas and an envoy, and XXXII, which lacks an envoy.

Warton, who rediscovered the Trentham MS and plucked the *Cinkante Balades* out of centuries of obscurity, thought them Gower's earliest work, c. 1350 – and he praised them highly, for their treatment of 'the passion of love with . . . delicacy of sentiment and elegance of composition'.[4] Macaulay, while sharing

---

4   Thomas Warton, *A History of English Poetry,* Vol. II, London, 1778, no page number (the

Warton's assessment of the quality of the poetry, argued for a later date of composition, either contemporary with, or following, the coronation of Henry IV. Apart from those poems specifically acknowledging Henry's kingship, however, there is no evidence to connect any of the balades to any specific point in Gower's life, and perhaps in their collected form they represent the completion of a long-term project pursued piece-by-piece over time, in the manner followed by Petrarch in writing the *Canzoniere*.

If so, the *Cinkante Balades* resembles the *Canzoniere* in more than one way for, like Petrarch, Gower assembles the story of a love affair out of the individual poems. The *Cinkante Balades* has a narrative unity, even a chronology, traceable through references to feast days and seasonal changes over the course of two or three years. Essentially its outcome is announced in the first five poems which Gower, in a prose aside, identifies as for those lovers whose wooing leads to 'droite mariage'. The balades to follow are to describe, another prose passage explains, the universal condition of lovers afflicted by 'la fortune d'amour'. This they do, primarily in the voice of the male lover, who variously praises his lady's good points and laments her aloofness, while also including from time to time comments on the scandalous tongues of society: at one point, the lover removes himself from his lady's presence, having heard that her reputation is suffering from his devotion; then later, upon being told that she feels herself deserted and is angry, he writes in apology and explanation for his departure. We hear from the lady also: balades XLI–XLIV and XLVI are in a feminine voice, addressing the lover of the sequence and male lovers generally. The concluding balades offer advice harking back to the first four poems. They define honourable love, and advocate that the only satisfactory kind is 'Amour [that] s'acorde a nature et reson'. Structurally, they provide a comfortable passage into the final balade, in praise of the Virgin.

Such a brief description does no justice to the skill of individual balades, but it may suffice to indicate the unique character of the *Cinkante Balades*: nothing similar exists by the hand of an English poet. If Gower had not elected to write them in French, the course of lyric poetry in England might well have changed. In any event, the nation would not have had to wait for *Astrophil and Stella* to see a successful lyric sequence built around a narrative. But Gower may well have had his reasons for choosing French. His models were French – possibly Machaut's *Voir Dit*, various pieces by Deschamps and Grandson, and undoubtedly the *Joli Buisson de Jonece* of Froissart. This is clear because Gower poetic's included the technique of *cento* – that is, purposely incorporating lines from known poems by (in this case) his French contemporaries into the *Cinkante Balades* verbatim, but now with fresh meanings, given the different context.

For this there may be many reasons. It is possible, for example, that Gower simply liked the lines he borrowed from the French poets; or, because they are almost always very good lines, and memorable, perhaps he built his own poems around them to capitalise on their cachet. But it is also possible that Gower's intent was similar to his treatment of the *Roman de la Rose* in the *Mirour* – that is,

remarks, and the printing of four of the *Balades*, are in the "Emendations and Additions" at the back of the volume.

an attempt to turn the strength of a tradition against itself by exposing what Gower believed to be its essential immorality, and it to reclaim it for legitimate lovers everywhere. This has been suggested – and the 'discourse' (if we consider each of the balades to be a separate speech-act, both male and female) of the *Cinkante Balades* would seem to carry us in that direction, as Gower maneuvers his reader from the first five balades dedicated to conjugal love through the history and 'conversation' of his lovers (where the *cento* lines are to be found) to the conclusion of the sequence, first in the didactic, theoretical balades concerned with the 'rationality' of true love to (finally) the supra-rational love due the Virgin, whose model as a seldom-requited, loyal lover exceeds all human examples touted by the tradition of the courtly lyric. No Jason, no Aeneas, no Lancelot (and certainly no Guinevere) ever loved like the Mother of God.

And that was, apparently, Gower's point – one he hoped to emphasise with a version of *cento*. Three balades especially are built around lines lifted from well-known lyrics of Machaut, Deschamps and Grandson. Two of these are poems in the lady's voice – XLIII and XLIIII. The other is Balade XXV, in the voice of the male poet. Balade XLIII is the third of three in which the Lady describes and condemns false lovers. It is a tough-minded, straightforward poem, and acts as a kind of summation to XLI and XLII, both of which are on the same subject. In Balade XLIII the Lady states very directly that most men's protestations of love – whether they be the great heroes of literature or in her own experience – are as 'common as the highway' ('comun plus qe la halte voie'), and intended only to trick women into bed. In Balade XLIIII, however, the Lady turns to address her faithful poet – he whose forty lyrics we (and presumably she also) have read, and who has remained true over the course of years. In it, she rewards his faithfulness with her pledge of love. The juxtaposition of the two poems emphasises the contrast between empty words (however 'poetical' and skillfully expressed) and deeds – in short, the difference between the standard 'lines' of the amorous lyric tradition which Gower, in the persona of the Lady, weaves into her poems (in the fiction, it is almost as if she has read/heard them so many times that she has them by heart) and the poet/lover's legitimate care and concern for her, his beloved.

Balade XXV amply prepares a stage for the Lady's bravura. In it, Gower's male poet writes to explain why he is absenting himself from the Lady: false 'jangle' and conspiracy ('fals jangle et le tresfals conspir') aroused by his visits to her are damaging her reputation. Giving up these visits is the only course a gentleman can take under such conditions, 'Because he who loves well forgets his love but late' ('Car qui bien aime ses amours tard oblie'). In one of the most significant lines of the sequence, the poet/lover says that he sends his heart in place of himself ('En lieu de moi mon coer a vous envoie').

The line – indeed, all of Balade XXV generally – helps bring into focus how carefully Gower plotted the structure of the *Cinkante Balades* to create a unified work. The poem occupies the exact center of the sequence, and represents a turning-point of several kinds, but precisely how isn't fully revealed until Balade XLIIII, when the Lady pledges herself to the poet/lover. Significantly, her words of commitment echo the lover's own line from Balade XXV: 'Vous m'avetz vostre corps et coer donné/ Qe jeo resçoive et prens a grant leesce' ('You have given me your body and heart,/ Which I receive and take with great delight').

By returning our attention to Balade XXV in this way, Gower achieves several goals simultaneously. As it does for the sequence, Balade XXV represents a turning-point in the poet/lover's suit. Relinquishing access to his Lady for her better good, despite what it may cost him in tears, transforms his balade-standard pledges of the earlier poems into selfless action, and himself from a literary cliché to a man to be loved. It is the moment when the balance shifts, so that the latter half of the sequence can lead to Gower's moral conclusion – the honest union of two honest lovers who have, by their acts of devotion, extracted themselves from the amoral verbiage of *amour courtois*.

Of course the poet/lover does not know that will happen when he resigns himself to give her up – it would be a hollow trick if he did – and like him, we as Gower's readers do not know, when we read Balade XXV, how it will lodge in the mind and heart of the Lady. But it does – specifically because for her he has proven himself trustworthy ('certain de vo promesse'), as one who will turn what he says into deeds. And specifically also, because the Lady now is transformed along with her poet/lover from a literary device, a disembodied voice, to someone we can imagine with a life, a mind and a heart. Her testimony that she has read the poems of the poet/lover we have just been reading ourselves, and kept them close enough to quote back to him his own lines in paraphrase, is a fictive act of recall that brings verisimilitude to the lovers' correspondence, and a necessary measure of reality to them both.

Thus the movement of XXV to XLIIII is the movement of the whole sequence. That we should see the lovers progressing steadily from empty fictional voices of a thoroughly traditional kind to beings capable of moral choices and a credible affection is crucial to understanding the *Cinkante Balades*. Gower's sequence is designed to illustrate the way promise should be turned into action, words into deeds. Love between a man and a woman should lead to marriage, always Gower's most powerful image of promise successfully transformed into fact.

## *The* Traitié Pour Essampler les Amantz Marietz

The *Cinkante Balades* share much with Gower's other collection of balades, known as the *Traitié Pour Essampler les Amantz Marietz*. The title is a modern one, given by G.C. Macaulay, who derived it from a version of the heading in seven of the ten manuscripts he knew – those, that is, in which the *Traitié* is joined to the *Confessio Amantis*: 'Puisqu'il ad dit ci devant En Englois par voie d'essample la sotie de cellui qui par amours aime par especial, dirra ore apres en François a tout le monde en general *un traitié selonc les auctours pour essampler les amantz marietz*, au fin q'ils la foi de lour seintes espousailes pourront par fine loialté guarder, et al honour de dieu salvement tenir.' ('Having described in English the foolishness of one who loved greatly for the sake of love, [the poet] will now relate hereafter in French, to all the world generally, a treatise according to the authorities, to teach married lovers by example so that they will be able to preserve the promise of their sacred marriage vows with absolute loyalty, and truly to maintain honour to God.')[5] From all indications, the *Traitié* was Gower's most popular – and perhaps favourite – French work. Unlike the *Mirour* and the *Cinkante Balades*, of which only a single copy exists, there are thirteen known manuscripts containing the *Traitié*.[6] Nine of these also include the *Confessio Amantis*; two others also include the *Vox Clamantis*. Only in the Trentham MS does the *Traitié* appear without one of the long narrative poems. Although there is no known copy of the *Traitie* alone, it seems clear that it was conceived independently: in Oxford, Bodleian Library MS Fairfax 3; Oxford, All Souls College 98; and Glasgow, Hunterian MS T.2.17, the *Traitié* is appended to the *Confessio* and the *Vox* respectively, but in a different hand, which suggests that it was added later and so implies its existence as a separate work.

The *Traitié* consists of eighteen balades, each of three stanzas of seven lines, rhyming *ab ab bcc*. Unlike the poems of the *Cinkante Balades*, none of the pieces in the *Traitié* has an envoy. Each of the balades in the *Traitié* has at least one, sometimes several, explications of plot and/or meaning in Latin prose placed in the adjoining margin. From Latin verses appended at the end of all undamaged copies of the *Traitié* ('Hinc vetus amorum Gower sub spe meritorum/ Ordine sponsorum tutus adhibo thorum'), it would seem that Gower wrote the poems comprising it in or about 1397, his own marriage to Agnes Groundolf taking place in 1398.

Like the *Cinkante Balades*, the *Traitié* has as its primary theme the problem of how to accommodate human love and divine law. It is important to note that Gower – despite his close, long-term associations with the priory at St Mary Overie and his obviously deep reading in the Bible and in moral and theological works – was not prejudiced against acts of the body; rather, his view seems to have been (not unlike the Wife of Bath's in this one regard at least) that the body, being created by God, was to be honoured by appropriate use of all of its functions. Sexual relations were therefore more than merely allowed – they were part of God's plan for men and women, provided of course that they were carried out within the bounds of a sanctified marriage. Like the *Cinkante Balades*, the *Traitié* takes aim at the poetic tradition of *amour courtois*, and employs characters – Lancelot, Tristan, Gawain – from the romance tradition to exemplify false lovers.

But in many important ways, the *Traitié* is not like the *Cinkante Balades* – it is a very different piece of work altogether. As its description explains, the eighteen balades are to be understood as a 'treatise', that is, as an argument. There is no narrative fiction, no voices of Lady and poet/lover here, to personify and suggest behaviour. In this the *Traitié* resembles more Gower's Latin work, where he states his case directly, albeit in verse. There is, therefore, a structure in the *Traitié*, but it is rhetorical, not 'poetic': it is intended to persuade, not to allegorise or move through metaphor. The progress, as in a good speech, begins with the general, moves to the specific, and returns again to conclude with the general,

---

[5]   John Gower, *Traitié*, in *Complete Works*, IV.379.
[6]   For a complete list, see Derek Pearsall's essay in this collection.

restated and supported by the offered examples. Thus the first five balades of the *Traitié* establish the major themes: marriage, its purposes, and the destruction caused by adultery. The following ten balades offer examples of out-of-wedlock sex, adulterous and merely unsanctified 'free love' between unmarried partners. In the final three balades, Gower reiterates the general principles laid down in the first five, and draws conclusions extendable to society as a whole.

Primary among these is the idea of vengeance, which permeates all of the balades. Although the agents carrying it out are most often human (e.g. Tereus and Jason are punished by the murder of their children by, respectively, Progne and Medea), Gower leaves no question that the ultimate source of all retribution is divine outrage. 'God will avenge broken wedlock' ('Freinte espousaile dieux le vengera') is the refrain of balade VIII, and it applies universally. This allows Gower to draw larger conclusions. Not only are individual sinners punished, but whole societies are as well, if they harbor them, or condone their actions, tacitly or otherwise. Hence Troy falls for defending the adulterous Helen and Paris; King David is humbled and the power of the Jews curtailed because of adultery.

There are also similarities between the *Traitié* and the *Confessio Amantis*, with which it is most often connected. Formally, there is the use in both the *Confessio* and the *Traitié* of explanatory notes in Latin. In both cases, the attempt (not always achieved) seems to be to present a direct explication in prose of what the verse is saying at a particular point. In many ways this purpose is better served in the *Traitié* than in the *Confessio*, perhaps because the point of the balades is easier to summarise than the ambient English narrative. More specifically, all of Gower's examples – the likes of Nectanabus, Jason, Tarquin, Mundus, Rosamund, Elmege, Ulysses, David, Lancelot – in the *Traitié* are also found in the *Confessio*. Necessarily, the demands of balade form require simplification, and so the *Traitié* versions seem narratively thin beside their English counterparts; but the shorter French versions are often more pungent, and reward comparison with those of the *Confessio*.

*Prose*

The prose passages in Latin and in French, which appear variously in manuscripts of Gower's work, have over time incited some debate regarding their origin – i.e. whether they are of scribal composition, or Gower's own words. The debate, for those wishing to carry it on, cannot be resolved for every case; but, since the interpolation of prose passages in whatever language is a significant characteristic of manuscripts containing Gower's poetry (as it is not for, say, Chaucer's), it is probably worth treating the prose passages, and the technique of including them, as authorial.

The French prose found in manuscripts of Gower's poetry is of two types: what might be called explanatory instances, and structural ones, although the distinction is more for purposes of discussion than exact. Of the first, the *Mirour de l'Omme* contains the most examples, beginning with the table of contents (which, because it is in a different hand from the rest of the *Mirour*, may or may not be Gower's), and appearing throughout the poem to preview coming action and to focus attention on how it should be understood. These are explanatory, in that they serve variously as summaries, but always as guides in the vast, some-times amorphous-seeming *Mirour*, reminding the reader that there does exist a controlling hand. The second type – 'structural' prose – appears between works, and is conceptually related not to the works themselves but rather to the prog-ress of the manuscript. That is, while they do often suggest what works are to mean, their primary purpose is to explain why the works appear in the partic-ular place in the manuscript at hand. They are therefore bridges of a certain kind, and they bear a different kind of testimony about Gower's artistic sensibil-ities – about his larger concerns for the reception of his works by readers – than do the 'explanatory' passages within the poems themselves.

The value of both types of prose, however, is the same. Both present us with the best proof of Gower's poetic ideal of the primacy of clear argumentative content. To put it simply, he does not want to take chances with readers missing his point. Whether he achieved this end is a matter of debate, perhaps, but in terms of what, taken as a whole, the existence of the French prose has to tell us, the debate is of lesser significance. What should be noticed is that such an ideal classifies Gower among those writers for whom the medium – ultimately – is less important than the message. Nor is this the same as saying (as has been said) that he is merely sermonic or hortatory. Gower is both, in places, but neither covers the entire ground. Neither category provides for his imaginative capacity, for example. But the French prose (and the Latin also, in precisely the same way), by offering evidence of Gower the poet standing outside his fictions, crafting their venues as well as their images, presents us with a different view of his way of imagining poetry itself – what it was for in the world, why he would have spent so many labored hours (obviously) devoted to producing line after line of French, Latin and English, how he sustained his moralist/reformer's urgency, year after year.

The French prose also, it should not go without noting, is lucid, well-appointed work. Compared to contemporary prose-writing in English (including Chaucer's), as well as to French written by Englishmen in the late fourteenth century (particularly French constructed by lawyers, or those with legal training, as it is thought Gower was), Gower's French passages possess an almost anachronistic directness and clarity. They have the matter-of-fact voice often admired in the English prose of Walter Hilton and Nicholas Love, but otherwise rarely found in prose written by contemporary Englishmen in their native vernacular. On some in his primary audience, very many of whom were bourgeois Englishmen speaking French as an alternate, if not a second, language, the tenor of Gower's French prose may have left a measurable impres-sion worth taking into account for its possible contribution to the growth of prose-writing generally (English included) in England at the end of the four-teenth century.

# 8

## *The Latin Works:*
## *Politics, Lament and Praise*

A.G. RIGG AND EDWARD S. MOORE

During his lifetime, Gower's contemporaries seem to have considered his three major works – the English *Confessio Amantis*, the French *Mirour de l'Omme* (*Speculum Meditantis*), and the Latin *Vox Clamantis* – to be of equal worth. In the centuries since his death, however, Gower's reputation has rested principally on his major English work, the *Confessio Amantis*, which soon outstripped the other works in popularity.[1] Consequently, prior to the twentieth century, Gower was held in highest esteem as an English poet and a teller of tales, considered second only to Chaucer (albeit a distant second). Throughout the nineteenth century, critical interest focused on the *Confessio*, largely to the exclusion of the *Mirour* and the *Vox*. In the twentieth century, scholars of English became more interested in Langland and the Gawain poet than in Gower, although recent decades have witnessed a revival of interest in Gower's English writing. His Latin and French works, however, remain as neglected as ever.

Living at the end of the fourteenth century, Gower could not have foreseen this eventuality. During Gower's lifetime, English was not a privileged language, even in England. A writer wishing for fame and literary immortality was in a somewhat precarious situation linguistically. The educated classes put three different languages to common use – English, French, and Latin. Seeking to communicate to as wide an audience as possible, and thereby to secure present as well as future success, an author was obliged to choose one of those languages. Such a predicament had not faced Gower's literary forebears.

---

[1] Early praise of Gower often mentions his three works together. For example, an anonymous philosopher sent Gower a short poem comparing Gower's trilogy to Virgil's *Aeneid*, *Bucolics* and *Georgics* (*The Complete Works of John Gower*, ed. G.C. Macaulay, Vol. IV [Oxford, 1899–1902], p. 361). Additionally, Gower's tomb at St Saviour's church depicts him reclining with his three major works serving as a pillow (Macaulay, *Complete Works*, pp. xix–xxv). Gower certainly perpetuated this conception of his works as a trilogy. In the colophons that appear in the manuscripts of the *Vox* and the *Confessio*, Gower describes his three major works, gives equal weight to each, and identifies their general purpose to be the same – education. In manuscripts prepared after Henry's accession, Gower also refers to the *Mirour* as the *Speculum Meditantis*, rather than *Speculum Hominis* as previously, so that the titles of all three works had a similar ring. See John H. Fisher, *John Gower: Moral Philosopher and Friend of Chaucer* (New York, 1964), pp. 88–90 and pp. 311–12. There is one extant manuscript of the *Mirour* and eleven of the *Vox*. In contrast, almost fifty manuscripts of the *Confessio* survive, and it was also one of the first major English works to be copied and circulated abroad.

Certainly, the 'three crowns of Italy' – Dante, Petrarch and Boccaccio – made much of their need to choose between two languages, Latin and their native Italian, but they did not have three choices.

Although with hindsight we can see the eventual triumph of English in the century following his death, to Gower English would have held no particular promise as the future medium for literary expression. English was a language very much in flux. Considering the linguistic differences between the Gawain poet and Gower, one can easily imagine the difficulties posed by dialect variation and the anxiety such variation would create for an author seeking to maximise his audience. Further, English remained socially and intellectually inferior to French and Latin, despite the fact that the use of English for literary purposes was increasing during Gower's lifetime. At the same time that Gower was composing the *Confessio Amantis* and the *Vox Clamantis*, Chaucer produced *Troilus and Criseyde* and versions of William Langland's *Piers Plowman* were already in circulation, but in no way could English compete with the literary heritage of French and Latin. Middle English literature as yet had nothing to rival, for instance, the thirteenth-century *Roman de la Rose*, which remained extremely popular and exerted a tremendous influence on later English writers. Froissart, Gower's nearly exact contemporary, chose French for his *Chroniques*.

French, the socially superior of the two vernaculars in England, began its decline in the mid fourteenth century. Witness Trevisa's complaint in 1385 that children 'now leave French and construe and learn in English' and that 'they know no more French than their left heel'.[2] French, previously the dominant language in parliament and the law courts, had given way to English as the official language in 1362. By the end of the century, English had become the dominant language for legal proceedings. One can cite many reasons for this decline in the use of French, chief among them the Black Death of 1348 and the consequent rise in the English-speaking middle class, as well as the effect of the Hundred Years War on English attitudes towards all things French. Nonetheless, French enjoyed a literary heritage that English could not rival and it remained a powerful literary presence.

Of the three languages, Latin appeared to be the most likely vehicle for literary immortality. While English had not yet come into its own and French was losing ground, Latin remained secure as the language of serious endeavor in all areas. In Gower's time, as in the centuries before and after, Latin remained the principal language for scientific, philosophical, theological and administrative affairs. Furthermore, English and French could not possibly match Latin's literary heritage. For centuries, whether one was writing epic or lyric poetry, drama, satire or hymns, Latin was the obvious choice. The reasons for this are clear. Unlike works in the vernacular, Latin works were not restricted to a particular geographic locality. An Italian could read and address a Latin work of English origin with little or no difficulty. Furthermore, unlike English or French writers, Latin writers could draw on over 1400 years of intertextual allusion known to all educated readers; from classical texts, the Vulgate Bible, the liturgy, philosophy,

---

2  John Trevisa, *Policronica*, in *Polychronicon Ranulphi Higden, . . .*, ed. C. Babington and J.R. Lumby, 9 vols (London, 1865–86), Chapter 59.

theology, science, and law, they could weave a multitextured and allusive language. Thus Latin was a language unconstrained by time or geography. It was a truly international language.

Consequently, Latin authors appear to have conceived of their work as being self-evidently literary; there was no need for an apology for language or methodology. In contrast, Gower provides such an apology at the second Prologue of the English *Confessio Amantis*:

> And for that fewe men endite
> In oure englissh, I thenke make
> A bok for Engelondes sake    (lines 22–4)[3]

Further, an author composing a poem in Latin was generally recognised as being engaged in a work of a higher caliber. By virtue of its language alone, a work could associate and interact with the most respected works of the Western literary tradition, through the use of tropes and intertextual references. It was natural and expected for a Latin writer of any time and place to use traditions common to the literature. For instance, for centuries – from Virgil to Henry of Huntingdon – it had been commonplace for Latin authors to invoke their Muse at the beginning of a major work.[4] It was this old tradition that Gower and Chaucer imitated in their English works, and which later critics construed to be stylistically original. Similarly, Gower's *Confessio* is often considered the most original of his works, while his *Vox Clamantis* has been criticised as unimaginative for its extensive use of Ovid and other writers. Such criticism overlooks the fact that Gower was acting in a well-established tradition of intertextual allusion and, yes, often blatant borrowing that extended back to include even Ovid himself. That the *Confessio* is not equally full of allusions and borrowings is testimony to the lack of an extensive English literary tradition, rather than to any fault in the *Vox Clamantis*.

It is true that by the last quarter of the fourteenth century, Latin had lost some of its previously absolute control over the literary production of England. The thirteenth century had witnessed a wealth of Anglo-Latin writers, including most notably Henry of Avranches, Michael of Cornwall, Walter of Wimborne, John Howden and John Pecham. Prior to Gower, the fourteenth century saw a decline in the number of Anglo-Latin writers and in the quality of their work.[5] It was only in the area of political satire that fourteenth-century Anglo-Latin writers continued to excel. Despite the decline in England, given the extensive Latin literary tradition and the continued production of major Latin works

---

3  All citations of John Gower's work are drawn from Macaulay, *The Complete Works of John Gower*.

4  For discussion of the Muses in Western European literature, see Ernst Robert Curtius, *European Literature and the Latin Middle Ages*, trans. Willard R. Trask (Princeton, 1953), pp. 228–46.

5  Richard Ledred's Latin hymns (adapted to be sung to secular tunes), the alliterative prose of Richard Rolle and the works of the 'classicising friars' – Trivet, Waleys, Ridewall, Holcot and Lathbury – while in many ways unique and learned, were not remarkably creative. For further discussion of these authors, see A.G. Rigg, *A History of Anglo-Latin Literature 1066–1422* (Cambridge, 1992).

beyond England, no writer could possibly imagine that Latin was on the wane. Nonetheless, some English writers chose to hedge their bets.

Many English writers wrote in more than one language. Simon du Freine wrote poems in both French and Latin at the beginning of the thirteenth century. John Howden wrote his lyric-epic *Philomena* in Latin and later translated it into French as the *Roosignos*. William Herbert, a fourteenth-century Fransciscan, composed sermons in Latin but also translated Latin hymns into English. Richard Rolle is best known for his alliterative Latin prose, though he also wrote religious lyrics and pastoral advice in English. Richard Maidstone, the author of a Latin poem celebrating the entry of Richard II into London in 1392, probably also composed a verse translation of the Seven Penitential Psalms in English. Gower, however, with impressive industry, chose to write a major work in each of the three languages – the *Mirour de l'Omme* (*Speculum Meditantis*) in French, the *Vox Clamantis* in Latin, and the *Confessio Amantis* in English. Gower is the only medieval English writer known to have written in all three languages; he was also the last major medieval English writer to compose in Latin as well as French.

Gower was a prolific writer, and his Latin works were no exception. The *Vox Clamantis* consists of over ten thousand lines of unrhymed elegiac couplets. Appended to the *Vox* in four out of the ten extant manuscripts is the *Cronica Tripertita*, a versified chronicle in Leonines depicting Richard's reign and downfall.[6] Though not an independent Latin work, each section of the *Confessio Amantis* is prefaced with a short Latin poem in unrhymed elegiacs, to which the English text acts as an elaborate commentary. Gower also wrote numerous short poems in Latin. The *Carmen super multiplici viciorum pestilencia*, composed in the twentieth year of Richard's reign (1396–97) and written in unrhymed elegiacs mixed with single-sound Leonines, addresses the sin of Lollardy and, to a lesser extent, the sins of pride, lust and avarice. 'De lucis scrutinio' is a short poem in Leonines on the faults of the various estates, beginning with the papal schism of 1378–1417. Written toward the end of Gower's career, when his eyesight was failing, the poem frequently uses imagery of darkness and lightness. Around the time of Richard's deposition, Gower composed 'O deus immense', also in Leonines, which reviews the responsibilities of kings and Richard's shortcomings. Toward the end of his life, Gower also composed a number of poems in honour of Henry IV: 'Rex celi, deus', 'H. aquile pullus', and 'O recolende, bone', among others.

Here we will focus on the first book of the *Vox Clamantis* and the *Cronica Tripertita*, arguably Gower's most impressive works in Latin. Book I of the *Vox*, first called the *Visio* by Wickert, differs decidedly in tone and purpose from the

---

6   'Leonine' verse first became popular in the twelfth century and consisted of rhymed hexameters or elegiac couplets, most often using one of three different rhyme schemes. 'Single-sound Leonines' (*unisoni*) rhymed the syllable before the strong caesura with the last syllable of the line. 'Collateral Leonines' (*collaterales*) rhymed the strong caesuras of the first and second verse and, separately, the last syllables of each verse. 'Cruciform Leonines' (*cruciferi*) rhymed the caesura of the first line with the final syllable of the second and vice versa. For those unfamiliar with medieval Latin metres, a useful summary can be found in the *Dictionary of the Middle Ages*, ed. Joseph R. Strayer (New York, 1982–89). With regard to Anglo-Latin in particular, see Rigg, *A History*, pp. 313–29.

rest of the *Vox* and must rightly be considered a separate work.[7] Books II–VII
comprise an estates satire similar to the *Mirour* on fairly common themes: the
avarice of church officials and the destructive power of temporal possessions
(the image of the 'pregnant purse' is used, familiar from Walter of Wimborne's
*De mundi vanitate*); the gluttony and luxury of the various religious orders; the
flight of justice (described by John Garland in his *Epithalamium beate virginis*); the
effect of women upon men and their vices (owing much to Ovid's *Ars amatoria*);
the decline of the world as represented by the statue of Nebuchadnezzar's
dream; and a review of the Seven Deadly Sins. The *Visio* contains 2150 lines on
the Peasants' Revolt and must have been written soon after the actual Revolt of
1381. The progression of events in the poem is modeled on the historical event,
beginning with the peasants' march on London and ending with the death of
Wat Tyler. However, Gower recounts these events in the form of a personal
nightmare. The effect is frighteningly realistic; among numerous other medieval
dream-visions, a more convincing representation of a nightmare cannot be
found.

In a fashion common to vernacular dream-visions, the poem begins with a
proverb:

> Scripture veteris capiunt exempla futuri,
> > Nam dabit experta res magis esse fidem.  (I, Prol. 1–2)

> [Of ancient book those yet to come take heed,
> > For thing experienced commands belief.]

After a discussion of the validity of dreams, Gower informs us of his name
through a cryptogram:

> Primos sume pedes Godefridi desque Iohanni,
> > Principiumque sui Wallia iungat eis:
> Ter caput amittens det cetera membra, que tali
> > Carmine compositi nominis ordo patet.  (I, Prol. 21–5)

> [Take Godfrey's first two feet; give these to JOHN,
> > And let the start of Wales be added next.
> Then headless (t)ER supplies the rest, and so
> > The compound name is clear from this short verse.]

The author then laments his lack of suitable eloquence and invokes the aid of
John, the author of the Book of Revelations, 'whose name he [Gower] bears'.
There follows a description of a pleasant summer day in June 1381. At the end of
the day the poet returns home. Inexplicably anxious, he passes a troubled, sleepless night until, at dawn, he falls asleep and begins to dream.

The rest of Book I may be divided into four sections that connect to each other
following the logic of the dream-vision. In the first section (lines 165–1358), the
dreamer finds himself picking flowers in a field. It is Tuesday, the day of Mars,

---

7   Maria Wickert, *Studien zu John Gower* (Cologne, 1953). Regarding the dating of Book I and
    Books II–VII of the *Vox*, different versions of the *Confessio* and the *Vox*, and Gower's changing
    political views, see Fisher, *John Gower*, pp. 99–109.

the day of war. He sees beastly mobs of peasants transformed by God's curse into domestic or wild animals, according to their characters. Some become asses, some cows, pigs or dogs, others cats, foxes, birds or frogs. A leader steps out from among them, a Jay (cryptically alluded to as Wat Tyler). John Ball appears as well; the animals regard him as a prophet. The Jay incites the animals to attack London, sack the Savoy, murder the archbishop and riot in the streets. With the reintroduction of the subjective 'I', the second section begins (lines 1359–1592). The dreamer describes his personal fears, which drive him from the city to hide in the woods. He believes that nowhere is safe, and he evades danger by cloaking himself in grass and leaves; if he could, he would have crawled beneath the bark of a tree for safety and shelter. He begins to waste away with grief and anxiety, and even the voice of Wisdom is no comfort. In what seems to be either lucid dreaming or slippage between the voice of the author and the speaker, the dreamer laments his 'cruel sleep' ('crudeles somni', line 1565).

The third section (lines 1593–1940) begins with the dreamer's seeing a ship that the author identifies as the Tower of London. The dreamer boards the ship to find himself in the company of terrified nobles. The ship nearly founders in a storm and is assailed by Scylla's wrath, but God hears the passengers' prayers, calms the waters, and saves the ship. Neptune, however, demands a sacrifice, so Mayor William (Walworth) zealously kills the Jay (Wat Tyler) and brings peace to the ship and the ocean. In the fourth section (lines 1941–2058), the ship lands on the Island of Brutus – Britain – a country given to brutality. Here the dreamer finds himself suddenly alone, whereupon he hears a voice commanding him to write down his vision. He awakes, and his previous anxiety is replaced by a new concern for the literary task ahead of him. The poet is not yet at rest, but is faced with the equally fearful task of documenting the events of his 'wakeful sleep':

> Dum mea mens memor est, scribens memoranda notabit
>   In specie sompni, que vigilando quasi
> Concepi pavidus, nec dum tamen inde quietus
>   Persto, set absconso singula corde fero.  (I.2135–38)

> [While mind recalls, it will record what's worth
>   Report: what I conceived awake, in fear,
> In form of dream. I don't yet rest in peace
>   But bear each thing within my hidden heart.]

Gower's own final literary task, the last major poem he composed, was the *Cronica Tripertita*, which dates from shortly after the accession of Henry IV in 1399. Written in Leonines, the *Cronica*'s three parts describe the Merciless Parliament of 1387 and Richard's fall from power; Richard's revenge in 1397 (the so-called Revenge Parliament); and his final loss of the throne in 1399 and the accession of Henry IV. The work's title suggests a straightforward, unbiased account of these turbulent events; the *Cronica*, however, is anything but that. Gower indicates as much at the beginning of the poem, referring to Part I (Richard's fall) as 'the work of man' (*opus humanum*), Part II (Richard's revenge) as 'the work of hell' (*opus inferni*) and Part III (Richard's final undoing) as 'the work of Christ' (*opus in Christo*).

The events of Richard's reign are organised, edited and altered to fit into this neat, anachronistically dramatic structure. In Part I, Richard is described as hard-hearted, power-hungry and at the mercy of his advisers, chief among them Robert de Vere (called the 'Boar', from Latin *verris*, 'boar'). Filled with avarice and urged on by unsound advice, Richard moves to seize the goods of the 'Bear', the 'Horse', and the 'Swan' (the Earl of Warwick, the Earl of Arundel, and the Earl of Gloucester, respectively). However, with the help of God, these three force King Richard to submit, and they purge the kingdom by eliminating the king's supporters. In Part II, Richard deceives the three appellants by feigning peace. The king then seizes the appellants; the Revenge Parliament executes the faithful Earl of Arundel and sends the Earl of Warwick into exile. The kind-hearted Swan is trampled down and murdered in secret, smothered in his bed. Lastly, the king exiles the innocent Archbishop Arundel. Part III recounts the ruin of King Richard. Desirous only of destroying the kingdom – as Gower tells it – King Richard devises charters to ensure his power and exiles the Duke of Lancaster and his son, the future King Henry IV, seizing their property. Henry, who becomes Duke of Lancaster upon the death of his father, returns and with popular support executes the king's supporters and secures the submission of the cowardly Richard, who later dies in prison, 'destroyed by Christ' (Part III, line 451).

At the time Gower first wrote the *Confessio Amantis* and the *Vox Clamantis*, he was an ardent supporter of King Richard II, as can be seen in the first version of the *Confessio* and the address to the king in Book VI of the *Vox*. However, some-time during the 1390s his political stance changed, as did his text of the *Confessio*.[8] By the time of Henry's accession and the composition of the *Cronica*, Gower clearly counted himself a great supporter of King Henry and was expressly hostile to the late King Richard. In the *Cronica*, Gower's deviations from or alterations of historical fact are numerous and clearly intentional. He fails to mention that John of Gaunt, Duke of Lancaster, led the eight appellants of the Revenge Parliament in 1397, which also included John of Gaunt's son, the future Henry IV. No doubt Gower did not want to depict his hero as collabo-rating with the enemy. Recounting the punishments meted out at the Revenge Parliament, Gower describes the exiling of the Archbishop Arundel last, though it in fact occurred earlier. This was done for dramatic effect. By having Richard punish the archbishop last, whom he portrays as a man who simply 'spread peace and checked the deadly sword' (II.262), Gower makes Richard appear all the more wrathful. In Part III, he presents Henry's exile as yet another rash, avaricious act of the king, and neglects to mention the duel between the Earl of Derby (Henry) and the Earl of Norfolk that occasioned the exile of both. More-over, aside from the initial date of 1387, Gower provides no dates for the events described. This gave him *carte blanche* to select and arrange historical events as best fits his theme. The final result: the *Cronica* is the first and perhaps most overt piece of Lancastrian propaganda.

Few scholars have paid much attention to Gower's Latin works, and those

---

[8]  Regarding the different versions of the *Confessio* and the *Vox*, and Gower's changing political views, see Fisher, *John Gower*, pp. 99–127.

who have done so have often held a rather low opinion of his accomplishments. In comparison with vernacular medieval writers, Chaucer foremost among them, Gower holds less appeal for a modern reader. As opposed to Chaucer's short, witty, character-rich narratives, Gower's Latin works offer a moralising summary of social ills, all told at tremendous length. The narratives found in Gower's Latin works are only those that history has afforded. Furthermore, Gower's extensive use of Ovid and medieval Latin poets in the *Vox Clamantis* has been met with consternation by critics unfamiliar with the practices of medieval Latin writers. Indeed, in order justly to assess Gower's worth and his significance as an Anglo-Latin poet, it is necessary to consider his work in light of the Anglo-Latin tradition and in relation to his Anglo-Latin contemporaries.

While Anglo-Latin literature has a long and varied history, Anglo-Latin literature from the reign of Richard II is rather limited. The principal works include short, lyric poems (all written around 1382) concerning Lollards and the Peasants' Revolt ('Heu quanta desolatio', 'Praesta Jhesu', and 'Prodolor accrevit'); Thomas Barry's poem concerning the English defeat at the battle of Otterburn in 1388, written for the most part in variously rhymed hexameters; Richard Maidstone's Latin poem in unrhymed elegiac couplets celebrating Richard II's entry into London in 1392; the *Chronicon metricum ecclesiae Eboracensis*, written in elegiacs and hexameters and composed between 1388 and 1396; and the last segment of the *Metrical History of the Kings of England*, begun sometime after 1400 and written in unrhymed elegiac couplets.Let us first consider meter. Between approximately 1240 and 1367, Anglo-Latin writers most often wrote in rhymed hexameters (mainly Leonines) or rhythmical stanzas. Gower himself often composed in Leonines, most notably in the *Cronica Tripertita*, as well as the 'De lucis scrutinio' and 'Est amor', among others. However, this period ended in 1367 with Walter of Peterborough's use of unrhymed elegiacs in his poem on the battle of Najèra. Prior to Walter of Peterborough, Henry of Avranches in the early thirteenth century had been the last to use unrhymed verse, and Walter's usage heralded a resurgence in the use of classical metre during the Ricardian period. In his poem on the battle of Otterburn, Thomas Barry used the unrhymed lyric metre of Boethius's *De Consolatione Philosophiae* Book I, metrum 2, in addition to rhymed hexameters. In the *Vox* and the *Visio*, Gower himself was the first to write in unrhymed elegiac couplets since Henry of Avranches. Richard Maidstone later followed Gower's lead in a poem for Richard II in 1392. Of course, Gower's use of this meter was not innovative, but rather just the opposite; it signaled a return to classical and earlier medieval practice. Gower's beloved Ovid, as well as the medieval poets Nigel Wireker and Peter Riga, and Anglo-Latin poets such as Alexander Neckam and Alexander Ashby, all wrote in this meter. Occasionally, Gower wrote in a mix of meters, such as in the *Carmen super multiplici viciorum pestilencia*, composed in unrhymed elegiacs mixed with single-sound Leonines.

When we consider the material about which these poets wrote, we notice that they have much in common. Gower's Latin works, like those of his contemporaries, all concern political history in some fashion or another. For centuries, political satire had been a popular genre among Latin writers in England as well as on the continent. The works of continental writers such as Walter of Châtillon,

Bernard of Cluny, John of Hauville and the anonymous *Apocalypsis Goliae* remained quite popular and continued to be copied throughout the fourteenth century. In England, works such as Nigel Wireker's *Speculum stultorum* maintained and developed the genre further still. Historically, political satires ranged from the general lament of the shortcomings of the various estates to discussion of particular events such as the murder of Becket, the reigns of Richard I and John, and the Wars of the Barons. The fourteenth century saw an increased interest in political matters and a corresponding increase in the popularity of the satirical genre. This increase owed much to the political and social upheavals of that turbulent century, the Black Death and subsequent fluctuation in social hierarchies, the papal schisms, and the Hundred Years War. In England, the reign of Edward III witnessed a surge in impassioned, partisan, political poetry. Between 1346 and 1347, the 'Anonymous of Calais' produced several poems that take a harsh stance against the French and the Scottish in connection with the Hundred Years War (specifically the battles of Halidon Hill, Sluys, Crecy, and Neville's Cross). Shortly thereafter, 'John of Bridlington' (whose actual name is unknown) wrote another satirical poem in the form of a prophecy about the French and Scottish wars. Later (1362–64), the Augustinian John Ergom added a prose commentary to the poem, exploring the implications of John's cryptic language. In 1367 Walter of Peterborough, traveling in Spain with the Black Prince and John of Gaunt (whom he claimed as his patron), wrote the poem on the Battle of Najèra. Additionally, numerous satirical poems appeared in connection with the universities, especially Oxford, and the conflict between the secular clergy and the friars. Those poems include Richard Tryvytlam's 'De laude universitatis Oxonie' as well as the anonymous 'Quis dabit meo capiti', 'De superstitione phariseorum' and 'De astantibus crucifixo', among others. Lollardy also gave rise to numerous invectives between 1375 and 1382. Thus Gower, in writing political satire, was acting within a well-established popular tradition. His work represents a similar breadth of concern and political passion, from the universal satire of the *Vox* Books II–VII to his specific accounts of the Peasants' Revolt (*Visio*) and Richard's reign (*Cronica*).

Surveying the popularity of historical and political topics among fourteenth-century Anglo-Latin writers, we notice a new trend – the heraldic use of Latin poetry for public and political ends. The 'Anonymous of Calais' offers his account of the Hundred Years War from the siege at Calais; Walter of Peterborough travels in Spain, giving accounts of the battles there; Richard Maidstone offers a detailed, almost certainly first-hand account of Richard II's entry into London. Perhaps as a result of his wealth, Gower does not appear to have engaged in such first-hand reporting. Nonetheless, Gower's observations of the Peasants' Revolt and his anxiety ring true in the same immediate, personal and passionate way. The *Cronica* reads like the 'official' spin given after a recent coup or nationally tragic event. In general, it is notable that both the English *Confessio* and the French *Mirour*, while certainly concerned with political matters, differ in tone and methodology from Gower's Latin works. The *Confessio* is cast in the form of a personal confession, while the *Mirour* takes the form of a personal contemplation. In contrast, Gower's Latin works are declarative and decidedly more public.

Within this context, Gower and his contemporaries present their historical and political material in a variety of ways. At one end of the spectrum, we have works such as the last segment of the *Metrical History of the Kings of England*, an abbreviated, unembellished history of English kings from Edward I to Richard II. The *Chronicon metricum* offers a similar, relatively unadorned history of the Church of York, confined to those events that relate to York Minster and the spread of Christianity in the north. Richard Maidstone's poem, while certainly more vivid than the two aforementioned poems, owes its vividness to the events described – the pageantry of Richard II's entrance – rather than to the poet's own efforts at artistic presentation. The events themselves provide the entertainment.

Gower seems to have had too strong a personality to have composed merely historical works. Much of his *oeuvre*, however, falls into a second category of historical-political writing. While not 'historical' in a modern sense, many works used history as a means of addressing the attitudes and values of their times and thereby sought to bring the reader into agreement with their views. The 'Praesta Jhesu' mentions the Donation of Constantine only to make a point about the importance of traditional Catholic theology in matters of state. 'Heu quanta desolatio' refers to the Council of London in 1382, as well as to other events taking place at the same time, but casts them in a harshly anti-fraternal light; there is no doubt about the poet's sympathies. 'Prohdolor accrevit' is a lament for the Peasants' Revolt and especially for Kent, rather than an objective history of the events themselves. In this same fashion, Gower's *Vox Clamantis*, Books II–VII, as well as the shorter *Carmen super multiplici viciorum pestilencia* and 'De lucis scrutinio' are politically motivated works that attempt to persuade the reader through the analysis of contemporary society and the review of historical events.

However, there is a much smaller, third category, in which we must place the *Visio* and the *Cronica*. Both these works represent a thorough re-creation of historical events, reordered and recombined so as to fulfill the poet's own artistic vision and political purpose. Only Thomas Barry's poem on the battle of Otterburn shows a similar creative aptitude for weaving the threads of history into the fabric of literature.[9] In the *Visio*, Gower manipulates recent history, casting reality in the form of a dream, in order to provide a personal and horrific vision of the historical event. In the *Cronica*, Gower makes free with historical chronology and the events themselves in order to show Richard II in the worst light and to glorify the Lancastrian cause.

We can account for much in Gower's Latin works by considering the Latin tradition within which he was writing. With regard to Middle English literature, it has been observed that Ricardian writers bore a certain awareness of themselves as authors, and that this self-awareness gave rise to an increasingly personal quality in the literature of the Ricardian period.[10] Ricardian authors

9   On Thomas Barry, see A.G. Rigg, 'Anglo-Latin in the Ricardian Age', *Essays on Ricardian Literature in Honour of John A. Burrow*, eds A.J. Minnis et al. (Oxford, 1997), pp. 123–141 (pp. 136–7).
10  John Burrow, *Ricardian Poetry: Chaucer, Gower, Langland and the Gawain Poet* (London, 1971), passim, and *Medieval Writers and Their Work: Middle English Literature and its Background 1100–1500* (Oxford, 1982), pp. 40–6.

often depicted themselves as players in their own productions. While this was perhaps an innovation in Middle English literature, it had much precedence in Anglo-Latin literature. Adam of Barking, for instance, describes how the Virgin Mary introduced him to God in order that He might direct the author's writing. In the *Epithalamium beate virginis*, Faith places a pen in John Garland's hand when he is about to describe the birth of the Virgin. Similarly, at the beginning of the *Marie carmina*, Walter of Wimborne invokes the aid of the Virgin and tells how she places a pen in his hand. More strikingly, Walter depicts himself as being present throughout Christ's life. He is the donkey that bears the holy family safely away from Herod; he implores the young Christ to leave the wise men in the temple and return to his family; he attempts to outbid Judas; he imagines himself slaying the carpenter who made the cross as well as the smith who fashioned the axe that made the cross. Gower's *Visio* certainly fits well within the tradition of self-referential fiction. The third and fourth sections, in which he first attempts to hide, then joins the other nobles in a bid to escape the raging peasants, are especially representative of this Anglo-Latin practice.

In the *Visio* several topoi from vernacular literature are evident. There is, of course, the interest shown in the validity of dreams and the cryptic allusion to the author's name. The name reference is reminiscent of Langland's line in *Piers Plowman*: 'I have lyved in lond,' quod I, 'my name is Long Wille' (B-Text, *Passus* XV, line 152).[11] The description of the pleasant day at the beginning of the poem represents the common topos of the *locus amoenus*. Such a description is familiar from numerous dream-visions and serves to set the scene for the main event. In Latin dream-visions (*Apocalypsis Goliae, Phyllis and Flora, Debate between Wine and Water*) this introductory portion is kept rather short. In English dream-visions, such as those of Chaucer, this introductory passage is much longer and more involved. Gower writes a long introduction; however, he alters the familiar dream-vision formula in a few key ways. First, because he is setting the scene for no ordinary dream, but rather a nightmare, Gower's *locus amoenus* is meant to stand in harsh contrast to the horrors of his vision. Second, in most dream-visions the imaginary event itself bears only an abstract relationship to reality. The land of dream is a far-off place, and the author is usually only a passive observer, recording the events revealed to him. Gower writes the reverse. In the *Visio*, the poet's dream is in fact reality and the frame itself is fiction. Gower proclaims:

> O vigiles sompni, per quos michi visio nulla
> > Sompniferi generis set vigilantis erat! (I, Prol. 2141–2)

> [O wakeful sleeps, in which none of my sights
> > Were seen in sleep, but while I was awake!]

Furthermore, Gower very much participates in the action and is an equal victim of the violence. He attempts to flee into the woods and to join the other nobles in the Tower. Gower blurs the distinction between the vision and the frame; when the poet awakes from his dream, he is still shaken and thanks the Lord for

---

[11]  William Langland, *The Vision of Piers Plowman*, ed. A.V.C. Schmidt (London, 1978).

rescuing him – whether from the dream or from the reality makes little difference. The fears kindled in the dream correspond neatly with the poet's waking
anxiety over the present political situation.

Given the attention scholars have paid to Gower's English work, it is a shame
that so little attention has been paid to his Latin work. Some scholars have examined Gower's Latin as used in conjunction with the *Confessio*, but this is principally motivated by their interest in the English text.[12] Of course, the great barrier
to further study of Gower's Latin is, simply, that it is Latin. His language is difficult, often inherently obscure, sometimes even impenetrable. Although a few
recent studies have given cause for optimism, there has been an almost patho-
logical inability among scholars to deal with Gower's Latin.[13] However, the
need for such endeavor and the rewards found therein are immense. An
intriguing mixture of the old and new, Gower's Latin works embody many
aspects of Anglo-Latin literature, while displaying considerable innovation.
Gower was arguably the most significant Anglo-Latin poet of the fourteenth
century, in addition to being one of the most important writers in the English
language and the last major medieval English author to write in French. His
work offers scholars an unparalleled opportunity to assess the use of each of the
three languages of the period. His trilingualism is not only an essential aspect of
his identity, it also represents a valuable resource for the literary historian.
Reading Gower offers a keen insight into the literary and linguistic situation in
England at the close of the fourteenth century.

---

12  See, for instance, Derek Pearsall, 'Gower's Latin in the *Confessio Amantis*', *Latin and Vernacular:
Studies in Late-Medieval Texts and Manuscripts*, ed. Alastair J. Minnis (Cambridge, 1989),
pp. 13–25; Robert Yeager, 'English, Latin, and the Text as "Other": The Page as Sign in the
Work of John Gower', *Text* 3 (1987), pp. 251–67; ' "Oure englisshe" and Everyone's Latin: The
*Fasciculus Morum* and Gower's *Confessio Amantis*', *South Atlantic Review* 46 (1981), pp. 41–53;
and Siân Echard and Claire Fanger, *The Latin Verses in the* Confessio Amantis: *An Annotated
Translation* (East Lansing, Michigan, 1991).

13  No translation of Gower's Latin was available until Eric W. Stockton (*The Major Latin Works of
John Gower*, Seattle) provided one in 1962. At a time when there was extremely little work
being done on Gower (and still less on his Latin works), Stockton's translation represented a
worthwhile and much-needed contribution to Gower studies. Nonetheless, it contains many
errors of translation, some of which are quite egregious: e.g. 'Sunday' (*Major Latin Works*,
p. 320) for 'sola dies' (*Cronica*, Part III, line 300). As an additional example, the translations of
Frederick Locke, which Russell Peck includes in his edition of the *Confessio Amantis* (Toronto,
1980), are often incorrect. For example, Locke translates 'Ossibus ergo carens que conterit ossa
loquelis/ absit, et interpres stet procul oro malus' (Prologue) with 'It has not, therefore, been
my intention to cover over with pretty words a lack of inner substance in my verses; and may
a vicious expounder of them never discover the gold that lies hidden there' (*Confessio*, p. 494).
As Derek Pearsall has observed, 'Locke seems to have got almost everything wrong that
could be got wrong in these lines' ('Gower's Latin', p. 17). Thankfully, the work of Siân Echard
and Claire Fanger, *The Latin Verses in the* Confessio Amantis: *An Annotated Translation*, marks
an exception to this trend and gives cause for optimism.

# 9

## Confessio Amantis *and the French Tradition*

ARDIS BUTTERFIELD[1]

*Confessio Amantis* has a punning title. Translated as 'The Lover's Confession' or equally 'The Confession of the Lover' it can mean either a confession made by the lover, or one made about the lover. Even before we begin reading, then, we might be led to wonder whether the confession will be direct or indirect, in the first person or the third person, within the lover's control or at the lover's expense. Thinking about the nature of confession provides a further sense of potential ambiguity. The lover (whether directly or indirectly) could be making a simple admission that he is a lover (this is what being a lover is like); on the other hand (more enticingly) he might be about to express something shameful or scandalous about being a lover. Confusingly, perhaps, confession can mean self-affirmation, as well as self-accusation. Augustine, in his *Confessions*, plays on both possibilities by presenting himself as one who confesses God, that is, who testifies to the glorious nature of God, and as one who has sinned and is testifying to his own corruption. Confession can thus be directed outward and inward at the same time. It turns on a precarious relationship between revelation and concealment.

By choosing to call his work a confession, Gower exposes it to these ambiguities. He makes it a work about self-revelation and self-concealment, of affirmation and shame. In doing so, he uses confession as a means of exploring the self. I will be arguing in this essay that this makes his *Confessio* part of the central tradition of later medieval French writing. Writers such as Guillaume de Lorris and Jean de Meun, joint authors of the great thirteenth-century love narrative *Le Roman de la Rose*, and the fourteenth-century poets Guillaume de Machaut and Jean Froissart, are preoccupied by a desire to investigate the relationship between writing and the self, the kind of access a writer has to truth, and how the art of fiction both enables and inhibits this access. In all these writers, the figure of the lover acts as one of the main ways for them to represent the art of writing: the lover generates the poetry, and indeed is often represented as a poet. Observing what kind of relationship exists in a work between the Lover and the author-figure proves to be a way of gaining vital insight into medieval notions of fictionality, and into how a medieval writer perceives himself and his role. To

---

[1]   I am grateful to John Burrow and to the following members of my undergraduate seminar group on Gower for their comments on a draft of this essay: Candice Brackpool, Rachel Chapman, Priya Patel and Lytton Smith.

investigate these questions, this essay will focus on two main areas, each stimulated by the title of Gower's work: confession (*Confessio*) and the lover (*Amans*).
In a final section, the essay will consider what happens when the lover, as a
model for the author, is shown by French poets and by Gower to be subject to
change, age and decay.

## Confessio

The question of whether the lover is making his own confession or being
exposed by a third party suggests that the process of confession is fraught with
risk. The practice of confession is central to the Catholic church (both in the
medieval period and now). In one definition it is 'the sinner's sacramental
self-accusation through shame for what he has done, which through the keys of
the church makes satisfaction for his sins, and binds him to perform the penance
imposed on him'.[2] Each person, as a member of the church, is obliged to confess
his or her sins to a priest in order to express sorrow and contrition for his or her
actions, receive notice of the penance he or she must do as a punishment, and
obtain forgiveness and healing. It is a shared experience, between the one who
confesses and the one who receives the confession, yet this makes the process
not more but less comfortable.

There is some subtle discussion of this in Thomas Aquinas, the formidable
thirteenth-century philosopher and theologian. Commenting on Augustine's
proposition that 'Confession lays bare the hidden disease by the hope of pardon'
(148), Aquinas fastens on the metaphor of the 'hidden' being laid 'bare'.[3] He
rightly points out that this is only a partial description. For one thing, this
hidden disease (sin) 'is sometimes manifest'.[4] The role of confession in that case
is not necessarily a matter of exposure, but rather of identification and punishment. Moreover, according to canon law, once a confession is made it becomes
strictly secret: 'sin which is confessed is placed under the seal of confession.
Therefore sin is not laid bare in confession, but closed up.'[5] Aquinas finishes the
point, however, by quoting Gregory who, like Augustine, says that 'confession is
the uncovering of sins, and the opening of the wound'.[6] This debate is important
because it shows Aquinas weighing up two different perspectives on confession,
that of the sinner and the priest. Augustine and Gregory emphasise the exposure

---

2   St Thomas Aquinas, *Summa Theologiae*, 3a, supplement, q7, a1; trans. by Fathers of the English
    Dominican Province (London, 1917), pp. 148–50 (p. 149). [Confessio est sacramentalis
    delinquentis accusatio, ex erubescentia et per claves Ecclesiae satisfactoria, obligans ad
    peragendam poenitentiam iniunctam. Leonine text, ed. Rubeis, Billuart and Faucher (Rome,
    1948), p. 658.] On the theory and practice of confession in the later Middle Ages, see
    T.N. Trentler, *Sin and Confession on the Eve of the Reformation* (Princeton, 1977).
3   [Videtur quod Augustinus inconvenienter confessionem definiat dicens: Confessio est per
    quam morbus latens spe veniae aperitur. Ibid.].
4   [Sed peccatum aliquando est apertum. Ibid.].
5   [Sed peccatum quod quis confitetur, sub sigillo confessionis ponitur. Ergo non aperitur in
    confessione peccatum, sed magis clauditur. Ibid.].
6   [Gregorius enim dicit quod confessio est peccatorum detectio et ruptio vulneris. Ibid.] For the
    original citation, see Gregory, *Homilia* xl, *Homiliae in Evangelia*, ed. Raymond Etaix, CC 141,
    394 (Turnhout, 1999).

of the inward self; Aquinas puts this in the context of the public purpose of confession. The result is that he shows how the form of confession both traps and liberates the speaker and listener in different directions. From both points of view, confession is at once private, and utterly revealing. The sinner must tell all to the priest, yet the act of telling binds the priest to lifelong secrecy. The priest's position of power in exacting this secret knowledge is thus never publicly realisable. From the sinner's perspective, he makes himself vulnerable in order to be empowered. In revealing himself, the sinner is also changing himself. He does not merely uncover his sin, he releases himself from it. In Gregory's tortuous phrase, he is opening up a wound, yet also sealing it in. The very process of painful exposure is the cure. Hidden depths are transformed through confession into the smooth surface of theological satisfaction.

Gower sets up the device of the confession near the beginning and again at the end of his huge eight-book work. Coming after the book-length Prologue, Book I (after a further short introduction) begins like a typical French love narrative, with the narrator walking in a wood in the month of May. He finds a green clearing ('a swote grene pleine', line 113)[7] and begins to lament, throwing himself repeatedly onto the ground in a trance-like state of despair. Awaking out of his 'peine', he appeals to Cupid and Venus for help. Cupid glowers at him and turns away angrily, but as he leaves throws a fiery dart into his heart. Venus remains, but her look is also far from kindly. She insists that if he wants help then he must first make a confession to her priest, Genius. The narrator looks up, finds Genius standing there, falls on his knees and begins. This triggers the larger-scale structure of the work: Genius asks him questions first about the sins of Seeing and Hearing, and then about the Seven Deadly Sins, illustrating them with a vast conglomeration of stories, anecdotes and *exempla*.[8]

In some ways, this opening gambit in Book I is a plain enough narrative. Yet it also has some unexpected moments. The first of these is Venus's response: she does not ask him straightaway why he is suffering. Instead her first words are an abruptly direct question: ' "What art thou, Sone?" ' (line 154). He starts, as if he had been woken from sleep, and she repeats the question. Even before the formal confession begins, the identity of the narrator is thus questioned, almost harshly. He replies self-effacingly, and also evasively:

> And eft sheo asketh, what was I:
> I seide, 'A caitiff that lith hiere' (lines 160–1)

It is a strange question. She asks not 'who' but 'what' he is, a question which penetrates rather further into the void of the self.[9] His reaction seems to confirm

---

7   All references to the *Confessio Amantis* are taken from G.C. Macaulay, ed., *The English Works of John Gower*, 2 vols, EETS, es nos. 81 and 82 (London, 1900–1901).
8   On confession as a structuring device in Book I, see Peter Nicholson, 'The "Confession" in Gower's *Confessio Amantis*', *Studia Neophilologica*, 58 (1986), pp. 193–204.
9   It is interesting to note in this context the variants reported by Macaulay for this line (161): 'Ma dame I sayde Iohn Gower' (MSS Egerton 1991 and Bodley 294), which pre-echo, as it were, Book VIII, line 2312. I am grateful to John Burrow for alerting me to them. There is not space to comment more fully, except to say that this scribal reading draws attention to the many verbal parallels between Books I and VIII, some of which are discussed below.

that her question is disturbing; yet this, too, is presented puzzlingly. We did not realise the narrator was asleep. He had fallen into the usual complainer's swoon, but had already surfaced from that when he prayed to Venus. Gower's syntax is delicate, ambiguous and unsettling:

> 'What art thou, Sone?' and I abreide
> Riht as a man doth out of slep  (lines 154–5)

Strictly speaking, it is only a metaphor: he starts in the same way as a man does when he has just woken. But its retrospective force makes one wonder at the question's effect: it appears to have jolted him into a new level of consciousness.

I have spent some time on this passage because, as I shall later describe, it draws heavily on strategies central to French love narratives: in many of these, there is constant play on the borderlines between different kinds of consciousness, dreaming, waking, swooning, dying. Gower similarly, in presenting a narrator caught up in confusion, conveys his state of mind as a sequence of shifts from one kind of consciousness to another. He passes dizzyingly from swoon to (metaphorical) sleep, through madness, illness and blindness. But this is more than a cleverly constructed portrayal of psychological disorientation. Gower makes the disorientation depend on a question about identity: the narrator appears to be about to learn a new truth about himself, one which can only be perceived if he submits to the procedures of confession.

The great compilation of stories that follows, if we take this framing love narrative seriously, functions to extend and develop the narrator's education in himself. For many readers, the sheer number and exuberant telling of these stories gives them a far broader meaning; indeed Macaulay, the work's first modern editor, voices the still common view that the framework of the confession and the myriad narratives within it are pulling in opposite directions.[10] For him, the frame is almost embarrassingly irrelevant to the bulk of the work. Since 1900, the date of Macaulay's edition, there have been some powerful arguments in support of the overall coherence of the work.[11] The persistent problem, as many perceive it, is that these arguments themselves diverge amongst those who see penance as dominant, and those who do not. The theme of penance and the theme of love are felt to be incompatible. One recent critic has gone so far as to say that 'readings of the *Confessio Amantis*, if not the poem itself, are governed by what appears to be a binary law: the poem is primarily about courtly love *or* penitence'.[12] It cannot be about both. My argument, in so far as it touches on the work as a whole, is that closer attention to the many-layered structures of the French tradition gives us a better understanding of the kind of contemporary vernacular context within which Gower was working, and hence more reasons for appreciating his choices of material. In particular, there is a broader range of means in French writing for investigating the self than is often taken into

---

[10]  Macaulay, *English Works*, I. xix.

[11]  Notably, R.F. Yeager, *John Gower's Poetic: The Search for a New Arion* (Cambridge, 1990) and Kurt Olsson, *John Gower and the Structure of Conversion: A Reading of the* Confessio Amantis (Cambridge, 1992).

[12]  Elizabeth Scala, *Absent Narratives, Manuscript Textuality, and Literary Structure in Late Medieval England* (New York; Basingstoke, 2002), p. 137.

account by modern readers of Gower, and this turns out to make the language of confession and the language of love less incompatible than they may seem.

Once we arrive at the last book, we find that Gower makes the end of the love narrative a close sequel to the beginning. Having posed several questions in the first book, he re-opens them and takes us through many further twists and turns before the work closes. Here I will be concentrating on the celebrated passage where Venus hands Amans her mirror:

> Er I out of mi trance aros,
> Venus, which hield a boiste clos,
> And wolde noght I scholde deie,
> Tok out mor cold than eny keie
> An oignement, and in such point
> Sche hath my wounded herte enoignt,
> My temples and my Reins also.
> And forth withal sche tok me tho
> A wonder Mirour forto holde,
> In which sche bad me to beholde
> And taken hiede of that I syhe;
> Wherinne anon myn hertes yhe
> I caste, and sih my colour fade,
> Myn yhen dymme and al unglade,
> Mi chiekes thinne, and al my face
> With Elde I myhte se deface,
> So riveled and so wo besein,
> That ther was nothing full ne plein,
> I syh also myn heres hore. (lines 2813–31)

As in Book I, the narrator (Amans) passes through many different states of consciousness. The first shock comes when Venus tells him with unsparing severity: 'Remembre wel hou thou art old' (line 2439). Amans takes the injunction badly: like a blazing fire that has been put out with water, he suddenly feels cold, his 'dedly' face becomes 'pale and fade' through sorrow, and he swoons. Lying on the ground, 'ne fully quik ne fully ded', he sees 'in avisioun' a laughing company of young lovers pass by, followed in turn by a more sedate and sober group of elderly lovers. With charming concern the old men, and even some of the young ones, appeal to Venus to take pity on him. Still lying there swooning on the grass he finds himself surrounded by a thick crowd of lovers, most of them elderly, all arguing hotly about his case. They are interrupted by Cupid who, groping about blindly on the grass, finds the lover's body and pulls out the fiery dart that he had originally plunged into his heart. Retracing the narrative of Book I, Cupid vanishes along with the rest of the lovers, but Venus remains. Just as she initiated the process of confession by asking him what he was, she now initiates the process of healing. With an ointment 'colder than a key' she soothes his wounded body. In place of a searching question, she now gives him a mirror. It is only with this new vision of his own face that Amans finally, and paradoxically, relinquishes his identity. In a beautifully crafted sequence of lines, he draws his life back into his memory, and compares it to the seasons of the year. His mind full of such thoughts, he is jolted once again out of his swoon ('I was out of mi swoune affraied' [line 2859]) and brought back to reason, sobriety and wholeness. When Venus comes at last with a smile to her old question (rephrased as 'what is love'), he cannot even answer. He has been so transformed that he cannot recognise what the question might mean.

The scene is a subtle mixture of religious and erotic elements. It draws remarkably closely on the metaphors used by Augustine and Gregory to describe the process of confession. The layered states of mental apprehension – swoons, visions, revelations – through which Amans views the successive stages of the narrative correspond to Augustine's sense of the hiddenness of the sinner's condition. Venus gradually lays bare, with ghastly and all too vivid accuracy, the wrinkles and white hairs on the lover's face: he only comes to see them clearly by being taken through a whole series of representations of the truth, some more blunt than others. Gregory's image of the sealed wound is also reflected in the scene – the lover's wound is no sooner exposed than it is healed and closed up, to the extent that it has gone for ever:

> So ferr it was out of mi thoght,
> Right as it hadde nevere be. (lines 2876–7)

Yet although it is possible to trace the lineaments of confession quite directly through this part of the narrative, in other respects it is imbued with images from the *Roman de la Rose*. These are themselves, of course, saturated with religious references. Thus Venus's ointment has two kinds of counterpart in the *Rose*: in Guillaume de Lorris's narrative the lover is shot with not one but five arrows, and the fifth, Biau Semblant (Fair Seeming), comes with its own remedy. Dipped in precious ointment, the excruciating pain of this arrow is simultaneously soothed; it is a source of pain and sweetness at the same time. More lasting relief is promised by the God of Love who says he will give him a sweet ointment to heal his wounds if he proves himself loyal. The passing mention in Gower of a key recalls the keys of the church held by the priest as confessor;[13] in the *Rose*, the God of Love uses a gold key to lock the lover's heart in order to seal his possession of it.

The double strand of allusion here points to Gower's easy and unforced assimilation of the language of identity in French writing with the language of the confessional. He achieves this partly because the assimilation has already been made by Guillaume de Lorris and Jean de Meun. As many have noted, the last sections of Jean's part of the *Rose* include a long confession by Nature.[14]

This confession contains an extended discourse on mirrors. The comparison with Gower's use of a mirror is illuminating. In Gower's hands, the mirror becomes an unmasking device. This is a brilliant and complex manoeuvre. At first sight, it simply shows the truth: Amans has the face of an old man. Yet this apparently simple truth acts to disclose a much more obscure process of repre-

---

[13] See p. 166, n. 2 above.
[14] *Le Roman de la Rose*, ed. F. Lecoy, CFMA, 3 vols (Paris, 1965–70), II.10,308–384, trans. F. Horgan (Oxford; New York, 1994), pp. 159–60. This passage refers back to Lecoy, I.2221–566; Horgan, pp. 34–40.

sentation. It concerns the supposed connection between Amans and the author. A Latin gloss near the beginning of Book I tells us that the author is now going to feign to be a lover (*fingens se auctor esse Amantem*).[15] Yet when the lover looks in the mirror after the confession is past he finds that he is a lover no longer. The face he sees is more ambiguous than it seems, because it does not reflect back Amans, it reflects back the author. More than this, it was not just that the author was pretending to be a lover, but that the lover was also pretending to be a lover.[16] The image comes as a shock because it does not conform to the image Amans seemed to have of himself. Thus, although the mirror appears to be a simple reflecting surface, in fact it offers a view of self-concealing depths.

The most famous mirror image in the *Rose* occurs near the beginning of Guillaume's narrative, when the lover finds the spring of Narcissus. I will be commenting on that more fully shortly. However, here I want to consider part of Nature's speech at the other end of the double work, towards the end of Jean's narrative. Its placement at this part of the narrative is no accident, but part of Jean's elaborate system of parallels to and amplifications of Guillaume's text.[17] In other words, it mirrors the Narcissus story. Where the Narcissus story reverberates within the romance as pure myth and narrative action, Nature's discussion of mirrors is almost comically different in its elaborate yet informal scientific discursiveness. She talks for several pages on the science of optics: the principles and properties of mirrors, the different kinds of mirror images, and the variety of optical and psychological responses people make to what they see. In this way it functions as a commentary on the earlier use of a mirror in the same text; similarly, we can read it as a way of interpreting Gower's mirror image.

Perhaps the main source of interest in relation to Gower concerns Nature's insistence on the multiple projections of a mirror. Her lecture first explains that not only are there many types of mirror, but also that they produce many special effects. Bulky objects can appear tiny, near objects appear distant; some mirrors can even set objects alight if the sun's rays are adjusted to pass through them at a certain angle. Her next point is more revealing:

---

[15] The gloss occurs at line 59 in full as follows: 'Hic quasi in persona aliorum, quos amor alligat, fingens se auctor esse Amantem, varias eorum passiones variis huius libri distinccionibus per singula scribere proponit' [From here on the author, feigning himself to be a Lover, as if in the person of those others whom Love constrains, intends to write about their various passions one by one in the various sections of this book]. Trans. J.A. Burrow, 'The Portrayal of Amans in *Confessio Amantis*', Gower's Confessio Amantis: *Responses and Reassessments*, ed. A.J. Minnis (Cambridge, 1983), pp. 5–24 (p. 13).

[16] See Burrow's classic account, 'The Portrayal of Amans', and also Olsson, *John Gower and the Structure of Conversion*, Ch. 4. For further discussion of the connections between manuscript representations of authorship in Gower and in French writers, see Ardis Butterfield, 'Articulating the Author: Gower and the French Vernacular Codex', *The Yearbook of English Studies*, Volume 33 (2003), Special Number: *Medieval and Early Modern Miscellanies and Anthologies*, ed. Phillipa Hardman, pp. 80–96.

[17] The most famous example of Jean's mirroring (in the sense of echoing) of Guillaume's text occurs at the mid-point of the poem (discussed below). For more examples, see lines 18,357–74, and the discussion in Sarah Kay, *The Romance of the Rose* (London, 1995), pp. 17–18, 65–70. Jean gives the whole work the title 'le Miroër aus Amoreus' (Lecoy, II.10,621); ['mirror of lovers'] (Horgan, p. 163).

Et d'une an font il pluseurs nestre
Cil qui des mirouers sunt mestre;
Et font .III. euz en une teste,
S'il ont a ce la fourme preste  (III.18,147–50)

[Those who are expert in the use of mirrors can produce several
images from just one; if they have set up the image properly, they can
put four eyes in one head  (Horgan, p. 280).]

By clever use of the right reflective medium and the positioning of the mirrors,
these experts can create tricks and illusions. The observer can see the opposite of
what is there, or a double, or a distortion. This often leads to people making wild
deductions about the nature of visions and revelations. Jean de Meun, through
these comments, cannot resist – in a typical move – undermining the very form
of his own work. Like the experts in optics he has artfully created in his mirrored
narrative a doubled, even distorted image of Guillaume's text, and provided
material for wild fantasy and speculation. Gower, too, though with apparently
simpler means, uses a mirror to create an image that distorts as it clarifies, that
unveils as well as merely reflects, that produces 'several images from just one'.[18]

### Amans

If confession structures the *Confessio Amantis*, then it is the figure of Amans that
dominates it. In this next part of the essay I am going to set Amans in the context
of the lover-figures that dominate medieval French love narratives: *Le Roman de
la Rose*; Guillaume de Machaut's *Le Remede de Fortune* (*The Consolation of Fortune*)
and *La Fonteinne Amoureuse* (*The Fountain of Love*); and two works by Jean
Froissart, *La Prison Amoureuse* (*The Prison of Love*) and *Le Joli Buisson de Jonece* (*The
Pretty Shrub of Youth*). It may be helpful to give some outline of these works, their
authors and their connections. The *Roman de la Rose*, as I have already implied,
was of special importance and influence in the late medieval period. It was more
widely read throughout Europe than any other secular narrative, and stimulated
dozens of writers to recreate, re-invent and rework it in their own fashion. It was
begun by Guillaume de Lorris in the 1230s; after around three thousand lines his
narrative breaks off and is continued by Jean de Meun, so he tells us, forty years
after Guillaume's death. It is thus not a single but a double work, in two very
different parts: the first a decorous, richly visual and visionary portrayal of love,
the second a huge, chaotic, fiercely intellectual continuation, variously comic,
obscene, didactic and ironic.[19]

---

[18] Compare the use of an image to remind the lover of his absent lady in Machaut's *Voir Dit*
(discussed below, p. 179), a device imitated, in turn, by Froissart in *L'Espinette Amoureuse*, ed.
A. Fourrier (Paris, 1972), lines 2412–3057.
[19] For introductions to the *Rose*, see Kay, *The Romance of the Rose*; William Calin, *The French
Tradition and the Literature of Medieval England* (Toronto, 1994); and the still classic accounts by
C.S. Lewis, *The Allegory of Love* (Oxford, 1936), Ch.3; and C. Muscatine, *Chaucer and the French
Tradition* (Berkeley, 1957). See also David F. Hult, *Self-Fulfilling Prophecies: Readership and
Authority in the First* Roman de la Rose (Cambridge, 1986).

Machaut and Froissart are the two most important French writers of the four-teenth century. Machaut (1300–77), widely admired by his contemporaries as the greatest living poet and composer of the period, was a master of love poetry in both lyric and narrative genres; Froissart (c.1337–1404) had a double career, first as a writer of artful love poetry (like Machaut, both narrative and lyric) and then as a historian with his great prose work, the *Chroniques*. An exact contemporary of Chaucer, Froissart spent some six years in the English court of Edward III and his queen, Philippa; although the evidence is only circumstantial, he is likely to have known both Chaucer and Gower in person.[20]

Gower's Amans is usually thought to have more in common with Machaut's and especially Froissart's lover (L'Amant) than with the Amant of Guillaume de Lorris or Jean de Meun. On the level of characterisation this is certainly true. Machaut's L'Amant tends to be self-deprecating, with touches of faintly comic idiocy.[21] In fact, his usual mode is extreme despondency. He spends much of his time in the *Remede de Fortune* shaking, trembling and shuddering in response to glances from his lady, with an emotion he cannot express. What prevents such descriptions from being merely bittersweet is Machaut's deft insertion of phrases, sometimes single words, that seem to undercut the seriousness of his condition:

> Mais la teste encline comme ours
> Recevoie son doulz vouloir,
> Fust de joye, fust de douloir,
> Humblement comme amis parfais
> Et loyaus par dis et par fais. (*Remede de Fortune*, lines 396–400)

> [But with head hung like a bear, I accepted her sweet biddings, whether for joy or for sorrow, meekly like a perfect lover, loyal in word and deed.]

His touch is so delicate that one cannot always be sure of it: here it is the comparison of L'Amant, often presented as something of a coward, with a subdued bear that strikes a note of comedy, together with the implied ascription of such feelings as loyalty, humility, joy and woe to a cumbersome animal.

Amans in Gower has similar moments of uneasy comparison, such as his reply to Genius's question about whether he is ever disobedient:

> Mi fader, ye schul wel believe,
> The yonge whelp which is affaited
> Hath noght his Maister betre awaited,
> To couche, whan he seith 'Go lowe,'
> That I, anon as I may knowe
> Mi ladi will, ne bowe more. (lines 1258–63)

[20] On Machaut and Froissart, see Calin, *French Tradition* and J. Wimsatt, *Chaucer and the French Love Poets* (Chapel Hill, 1968) and *Chaucer and his French Contemporaries: Natural Music in the Fourteenth Century* (Toronto, 1991).
[21] For further discussion, see also Burrow, 'The Portrayal of Amans'.

Not a bear this time, but an eager puppy, Amans pictures himself unflatteringly as crouching low on the ground in servile anticipation of his lady's command.

Where Gower's Amans is more like Froissart's L'Amant is in the occasional lengthier description of his own behaviour. Machaut tends to concentrate on the fine gradations of misery that L'Amant is experiencing; Froissart gives detailed accounts of his attempts in social circumstances to attract his lady's attention, cast glances at her, or watch her in company with other people. In one episode, in *L'Espinette Amoureuse*, Froissart describes how he watched her once through the chink of a window, and saw her dancing with friends, but he dared not enter (lines 3219–23). Later that evening he cannot stop thinking about what happened, and despises himself for holding back. He orders himself sternly to sleep, but of course he gets little rest (line 3245). With equally prurient inhibition, Gower's Amans, confessing his 'stealth' as a lover, admits to lying awake on long cold nights and going to the window to gaze at his lady's room. He wishes he could transform himself and steal under her bedclothes; but after getting very cold, he realises he is accomplishing nothing and creeps back to bed (V.6653–96).

In such respects, Gower's Amans is recognisably based on the same model of lover as Froissart's or Machaut's. Within the framework of the confession, Amans becomes a stylised, gently characterised and stable figure, that of the low-achieving lover. Yet Gower's technique of placing Amans within several further framing devices serves to destabilise him. As we have seen, once the last book is reached a complex process of unveiling takes place. The primary model here is Jean de Meun, and his slippery, rebarbative figurations of the lover.

In trying to grasp Jean's machinations, we need to appreciate that they have a double aspect. They include both what he is doing with the figure of the lover in his own terms, and what he is doing in the wake of Guillaume de Lorris. Indeed, it could be argued that Jean's work is so intensively reactive it makes little sense to think of it as separable from Guillaume's: in other words, although it is often remarked of the two *Romans de la Rose* that Guillaume's text is subsumed and overtaken by Jean's, my point is rather that Jean's is consumed by his efforts to define himself in relation to Guillaume. The most famously destabilising moment in the *Rose* occurs in Jean's version, at a point roughly halfway through the 'whole' work or the two versions joined end to end. The dreamer has just been conversing with the God of Love. He has managed to kiss the rosebud, but Jealousy has retaliated by building a formidably strong fortress around the rose garden and imprisoning Fair Welcome in a tower in the middle. The God arrives to assess the situation. Casting himself in the role of confessor, he announces that instead of a *confiteor* (a formal term for a prayer of confession) the dreamer must recite all the commandments of love. The dreamer accomplishes this: in pleased response, the God decides to call a parliament of his barons to prepare for a siege on the castle.

Here, at the midpoint, the narrative seems to pause temporarily. The God appears discomfited. The great love poets of the past – Tibullus, Catullus and Ovid – are all dead and rotting: Guillaume de Lorris is here instead, and he is in difficulty and danger, deprived of Fair Welcome, dying with grief and without enough wisdom to find a solution. However, he must begin a romance before he dies, the last lines of which are quoted. Jean de Meun will complete it using the following opening lines (these are also quoted): he is not yet born, but the God prophesies that his birth will take place after Guillaume's death. This very strange passage breaks several narrative rules with giddying impunity. From being the generalised Amant, the dreamer/narrator is suddenly named as a 'real' poet: Guillaume de Lorris. Without warning, the fiction of the lover is decoded as the author. At the same time, we are told both that he is already dead and that he will write a romance, whose ending we have already read without realising it. The new author is likewise named, yet he remains a fiction since he has not even been born, although he has already started finishing this romance.

There are several parallels with the *Confessio Amantis*. The naming of L'Amant as Guillaume de Lorris corresponds to the naming of Amans as John Gower: in both poems, this is the first time the lover has been identified. In both poems this is placed within a confessional setting, and one which triggers a deliberate unravelling of the poetic procedures of the work. Both poets cast doubt on fictionality while also giving their fictions unusual imaginative reach: Jean de Meun breaks and distorts the barrier between the 'real' author and the literal narrator; Gower, likewise, shows Amans to be a construct that has more than one literal level. They thus present a complex model of the lover, one whose apparently clear outlines are obscured by their careful disruptions of his role as a narrator.

We can see then that to say Jean de Meun's presentation of the lover is central to French writing involves appreciating that it is characterised by irony and instability. This is just as true of other parts of the *Rose* where, as many have commented, the use of allegory is inconsistent enough to make it impossible to read on a single level. Machaut and Froissart straighten out this allegorical profusion to produce lover-figures that have far greater social definition and hence can be appreciated more easily and directly. However, they take on the destabilising tendencies of Jean's narrative in other ways, notably in terms of formal structure. Their love narratives place the lover and his utterances in a wide variety of formal enclosures that complicate his role.[22] For example, in Machaut's *Remede de Fortune*, L'Amant is depicted through a series of nine inset lyrics as well as through the narrative: *lai, complainte, chanson roial, baladelle, ballade, prière, virelai/chanson baladée*, refrain and *rondeau*.[23] Late exponents of a tradition that extends back to the early thirteenth century, Machaut and Froissart layer different forms of love language in intricate sequences interleaving narrative and lyric. In the case of Machaut's *Voir Dit* and Froissart's *La Prison Amoureuse*, letters and prose commentaries are also woven in, creating further levels of self-consciousness about the process of articulating love.[24]

---

[22] Keith Busby, 'Froissart's Poetic Prison: Enclosure as Image and Structure in the Narrative Poetry', *Froissart Across the Genres*, ed. Donald Maddox and Sara Sturm-Maddox (Gainesville, 1998), pp. 81–100.

[23] Seven of these are provided with music: that is, all except the *prière* and the refrain. See Guillaume de Machaut, *Le Jugement du Roy de Behaigne and Remede de Fortune*, ed. and trans. J.I. Wimsatt and W.W. Kibler (Athens, GA, 1988), music ed. Rebecca A. Baltzer.

[24] Guillaume de Machaut, *Le Livre dou Voir Dit/The Book of the True Poem*, ed. D. Leech-Wilkinson, trans. R. Barton Palmer (New York; London, 1998); *La Prison Amoureuse (The Prison of Love)*,

The presentation of the lover in these thirteenth- and fourteenth-century French narratives is thus more than a matter of characterisation. Perhaps most significantly we see that the lover acts as a mask (Latin: *persona*) for the poet. As in the *Rose*, we can observe the author using the lover figure partly as a means of articulating his role, partly as a means of concealing it. It is in this context that I want now to consider the most famous story of a mirror: that of Narcissus. This story, taken from the version in Ovid's *Metamorphoses*, is retold by Guillaume de Lorris near the start of the *Rose*. Guillaume takes the myth and gives it new life in his dream vision. As he is strolling through the beautiful garden, the narrator suddenly discovers the very spring where Narcissus drank. Having cruelly rejected the love of Echo, a nymph, Narcissus is made by the gods to suffer the same fate by falling in love with his own reflection. Unable to satisfy his love, he pines away and dies. In Guillaume's narrative, the dreamer not only stumbles across the myth, but finds himself re-enacting it: there's the very spring, and there's the place where Narcissus looked – what will happen if he does the same? At first, the dreamer is afraid to go near, but then he bends over and through the lucent, gushing water sees two brilliant crystals. Just as one can stand in front of a mirror and see the reflection, so these crystals reveal the entire garden to the dreamer. He is astonished at the beauty of the sight and by the enormity of what he has done: this is the perilous mirror in which Narcissus gazed at himself and then died. Anyone who also looks at himself in the same spring will not escape being ensnared by love.

Narcissus becomes a figure for how the dreamer falls in love. His story carries implications of sterility and frustration, and also deception: Narcissus sees himself but fails to recognise himself. As I have suggested, Jean makes the device of the mirror a focal point for the structure of the whole work. Reinforcing this, alongside the discussion of mirrors at the end of his version, Jean puts in the story of Pygmalion, taken again from Ovid. This story is an anti-type to the story of frustration told by the Narcissus myth. In Pygmalion, a sculptor creates a beautiful image of a woman. Through the miraculous transforming power of his love she becomes a real woman. The Pygmalion story thus functions as a mirror image of the story of Narcissus.[25]

Gower, like Machaut and Froissart, also tells these two stories as part of his own work on love.[26] Narcissus comes, as in the *Rose*, near the beginning in Book I (lines 2275–2358); Pygmalion occurs in Book IV (lines 371–436) at a place that it is tempting to describe as the midpoint of the work as a whole. Gower's readings of the stories, though not identical to those of Guillaume and Jean, confirm them as type and anti-type: Narcissus is a story of shame, of an appro-

---

ed. and trans. Laurence de Looze (New York, 1994). For a convenient collection of translated extracts from the love narratives of Machaut and Froissart, see B.A. Windeatt, trans., *Chaucer's Dream Poetry: Sources and Analogues* (Cambridge, 1982).

25  For further discussion, see Sylvia Huot, *From Song to Book: The Poetics of Writing in Old French Lyric and Lyrical Narrative Poetry* (Ithaca; London, 1987), pp. 96–9.

26  On the Narcissus and Pygmalion stories in Machaut, see Huot, *From Song to Book*, pp. 296–7; on Froissart's and Gower's use of Narcissus, see respectively Huot, pp. 308–9 and Yeager, *John Gower's Poetic*, pp. 133–5; and finally, on Gower's use of Pygmalion, see Olsson, *John Gower and the Structure of Conversion*, pp. 136–7.

priate punishment for someone who rejected love; Pygmalion by contrast shows the result of being faithful in love (he marries his living statue and they produce a male child). It is a story of self-delusion rewarded. They function as two versions of the lover's self-presentation that parallel the two modes of confession we encountered at the beginning of the essay: one a model of shame and the other of affirmation.

Both stories explore how the lover might be a figure for the author. Each presents it as a tricky process of doubling that in one version can lead to death and sterility, and in the other to marriage and regeneration. Throughout the thirteenth and fourteenth centuries French authors engaged in a process of playing off the figure of L'Amant against the figure of the author in ways that are both self-revealing and self-accusing. The archetypal example of this, as we have seen, is Jean de Meun; his bold assertion of authorship is undercut by his revelation that he is a mere continuator of a work whose author has now died. Authorship is a fiction, he seems to say – or rather, authors are created by fictions. Jean needs Guillaume's name to create his own identity: without Guillaume, Jean would not exist – at least as an author. Some modern readers have argued that Guillaume is a fiction created by Jean (the name Guillaume de Lorris is not known from any other context). The confusing playfulness with which Jean links his own identity as author with that of Guillaume makes it hard to trust him in any direction.

Whether or not the lover is to be identified as the author, Jean adds the further complication of claiming that the author can only be identified through another author's fiction of being a lover. This is a central device in the love narratives of Machaut and Froissart, and has many sophisticated formulations. For example, Machaut's *La Fonteinne Amoureuse* has his sleepless love-sick poet/narrator listen through the walls of his room to his patron reciting a *complainte*.[27] The next morning, when his patron asks him to compose something for him, the narrator presents him with a copy of his own *complainte*. Here the patron is double-crossed by having his fiction of being an author revealed by the narrator posing as a lover. Machaut's *Voir Dit* is a further instance. The story is of the elderly poet receiving a love letter from a young female admirer, Toute Belle. She has fallen in love with him through reading his love poetry, and sends him some of hers. Machaut's prowess as a poet is thus identified through a female poet's presentation of herself as in love. In Froissart's *La Prison Amoureuse*, the device is taken one stage further by the author's friend, who sends him a prose commentary on his love affair and the lyrics he composes as part of it. Since this commentary is incorporated into the overall narrative, Froissart's narrator is identified as a poet by a figure that he invents to identify him as such. Genius plays a similar role in the *Confessio*. As Rita Copeland has argued, the figure of Genius acts to split the authorial presence in the poem so that the act of commentary and interpretation is included within it. Genius is the interlocutor of the author and at the same time an internalised projection of him: 'this allows

---

[27] *Guillaume de Machaut: The Fountain of Love (La Fonteinne Amoureuse) and Two Other Love Vision Poems*, ed. and trans. R. Barton Palmer (New York; London, 1993).

the author to co-opt the role of exegete for his own text'.[28] This is an example of Gower drawing from French practice in two directions: he takes the figure of Genius from Jean de Meun's *Roman de la Rose* (Meun in turn derived it from Alain de Lille's *De Planctu Naturae*) and re-appropriates it using an interpretative logic from Froissart.[29]

Gower's trick at the end of the *Confessio* makes play with similar strategies. Amans is revealed as the author by Venus, a figure the author has invented to unveil him. Yet it could be said that, by looking in a mirror, he identifies himself: like Narcissus he sees himself without recognising himself. Taking this one stage further, we are shown the spectacle of the author identifying the lover as the author, yet without recognising his own agency. Gower makes another connection that is latent in the *Rose*, but becomes a more explicit part of the fourteenth-century tradition: he combines the use of a mirror with the device of naming.[30] Triggered by the doubling antics of Guillaume and Jean, subsequent authors develop the concept of authorial identity by playing on further doublings. For Machaut and for Froissart, toying with a poetic persona called Guillaume and Jean, respectively, must have been an irresistible form of allusion to Guillaume de Lorris and Jean de Meun. Froissart, in particular, whose narratives are closely modelled on Machaut's and are also dominated by forms of enclosure, rather like Chinese boxes, seems to see the process of establishing himself as an author as part of a long line of mirrored reflections: from Guillaume to Jean, from Jean to Guillaume, and from Guillaume to Jean. As yet another Jean (John), Gower stands in the same line, an author born from a French literary trope that defined the birth of the author as fissured and fictional.

## The Lover in Old Age

The moment when Amans sees his faded face at the end of the *Confessio* is one of the most brilliantly memorable portrayals in medieval writing of the shock of old age. Amans was always old, but it is only now that he is prepared to see it. There are many vivid descriptions of the ageing body, such as Chaucer's close-up on the flap of skin on old January's neck in *The Merchant's Tale* as he sits up in bed next to his new young bride. But Gower's is marked out by his presen-

---

[28] Rita Copeland, *Rhetoric, Hermeneutics, and Translation in the Middle Ages: Academic Traditions and Vernacular Texts* (Cambridge, 1991), p. 205.

[29] The figure of Genius in Gower's *Confessio* has received a great deal of comment. See, for example, George D. Economou, 'The Character of Genius in Alain de Lille, Jean de Meun and John Gower', and Denise N. Baker, 'The Priesthood of Genius: A Study of the Medieval Tradition', both collected in *Gower's Confessio Amantis: A Critical Anthology*, ed. Peter Nicholson (Cambridge, 1991), pp. 109–16 and pp. 143–57 respectively. The relationship between Gower and Alain's conception of Genius is extensively explored in James Simpson, *Sciences and the Self in Medieval Poetry* (Cambridge, 1995), pp. 148–97.

[30] Compare Hoccleve's use of a mirror in his *Complaint*: see J.A. Burrow, ed., *Thomas Hoccleve's Complaint and Dialogue*, EETS, os no. 313 (Oxford, 1999), lines 155–68. For further discussion of medieval naming in an English context, see Anne Middleton, 'William Langland's "Kynde Name": Authorial Signature and Social Identity in late Fourteenth-Century England', *Literary Practice and Social Change in Britain 1380–1530*, ed. Lee Patterson (Berkeley; Los Angeles, 1990), pp. 15–82.

tation of age as a matter of self-perception and, in a way which speaks to readers in our culture just as much as his, of self-delusion. In the last part of this essay I want to discuss the French context for this depiction.

The most important precedents are Machaut's *Voir Dit* and Froissart's *Le Joli Buisson de Jonece*. It is worth emphasising to begin with that both these works are highly exploratory and unusual. The *Voir Dit*, in particular, has excited considerable controversy over its status as a work of 'truth': purporting to be autobiographical, it takes the form of a large collection of lyrics and prose letters exchanged between the elderly poet and a young girl, and compiled within a love narrative describing their composition. Opinion is divided over whether the work records an actual relationship between the poet and a younger female contemporary, or whether it is an elaborate fiction designed to imitate such a relationship with ingenious accuracy. At the heart of the *Voir Dit* there is thus a doubt about the veracity of the author that has been created by the author's very attempts to be as credible as he can. Machaut refuses to let go of the story's credibility, even to the very end. It finishes with him accusing Toute Belle of disloyalty. In a kind of inversion of the Pygmalion story, Guillaume has an image made of Toute Belle that he uses to gaze on, dream of and talk to while they are physically separated.[31] He dreams that the image appears dressed in green, the colour of betrayal; this causes a rift between them. Finally, they re-affirm their love and promise to meet, but the work ends in hope rather than fact – the kind of hope that contains within it a powerfully suppressed sense of incipient failure.

*Le Joli Buisson* ends with a more emphatic pronouncement of failure.[32] Unlike other *dits*, Froissart begins the work by describing a love affair that is already over. In direct imitation of the beginning of Machaut's *Voir Dit*, he casts himself as an ageing poet unable to compose because it is so long since he was last in love. Regretting the passing of youth, he finds in a chest a ten-year-old portrait of his lady. This suddenly rejuvenates him, and he has a dream in which the portrait comes to life in the form of his lady as she was ten years ago. He excitedly starts composing lyrics once more; his lady is polite but unimpressed. Jolted out of his dream when someone pushes him, he realises that this attempt to re-live his memories is futile and undignified for someone of his age. He resolves to turn his thoughts away from carnal desires and finishes by composing a *lai* to the Virgin.[33]

On the face of it, Gower's *Confessio* has more affinities with *Le Joli Buisson* than it does with the *Voir Dit*. Froissart and Gower present lovers whose sense of age prompts them to repudiate love: Machaut's L'Amant persists in his fantasies right to the end. Yet the relationship between these three authors and their works is more intertwined than that summary allows. Machaut is the first of the

---

[31] *Le Livre dou Voir Dit/The Book of the True Poem*, ed. Leech-Wilkinson and Palmer, p. 455, and, for discussion, Huot, *From Song to Book*, p. 285 n. 8. See also n. 18 above.

[32] *Le Joli Buisson de Jonece*, ed. A. Fourrier, TLF 222 (Geneva, 1975), lines 5156–end (pp. 228–39).

[33] An important early precedent for this *volte face* occurs in Gautier de Coinci, *Les Miracles de Nostre Dame*, ed. V.F. Koenig, TLF, 4 vols (Geneva and Paris, 1955–70). Gautier rejects the composing of secular songs in favour of those composed for the Virgin; for discussion, see Ardis Butterfield, *Poetry and Music in Medieval France from Jean Renart to Guillaume de Machaut* (Cambridge, 2002), ch. 6, pp. 103–15.

three to subject the model of the lover to the ravages of age and decay. It is a calculated and daring risk since it pushes the analogy between lover and author to new limits. If Jean presents the birth of the author, Machaut explores his transformation through the unforgiving passage of time. The problem is that if authors gain increased fame with age, lovers acquire more shameful reputations: few character-types are more widely scorned throughout literary history than the *senex amans*. Machaut attempts the difficult trick of keeping the model of the lover intact with the onset of age and fame; Froissart and then Gower allow it to fail and fade.

Gower, however, does more than merely follow Froissart here. By framing his narrative so elaborately he makes the final de-masking of Amans a kind of double bluff. The author turns out not to be as distinct from the lover as he might have hoped: both are old men, and both have indulged in forgivable fantasies. To return to Aquinas:

> Punishment is exacted in consideration of the remedy, either as regards the one who sinned, or as regards others: and thus sometimes a greater punishment is enjoined for a lesser sin: either because one man's sin is more difficult to resist than another's (thus a heavier punishment is imposed on a young man for fornication than on an old man, though the former's sin be less grievous).
>
> (3a, Supplement, 9.8, a.7)[34]

For an old man to fornicate is more grievous than it is for a young man, but the punishment is lighter: this seems to capture exactly the mood of shame balanced against relief that we find at the end of the *Confessio*.

Gower's artful subjection of the lover to confession gives him the perfect means to refine and reformulate his role as author. The work is a confession of authorship as well as a confession about authorship. The subtleties of French figurations of the author as a lover find further momentum in Gower's handling of the precarious distinction between Amans and Auctor. Working within the central tradition of French writers on love, his name linked with theirs, Gower finds similar inspiration in the topic of love. It becomes for him, as for them, a way of examining the art of fiction, and hence the multiple art of confessing the self.

---

[34] Trans. op. cit. [Secundo, quantum ad remedium vel illius qui peccavit, vel aliorum. Et sic quandoque pro minori peccato iniungitur maior poena. Vel quia peccato unius difficilius potest resisti quam peccato alterius: sicut iuveni imponitur pro fornicatione maior poena quam seni, quamvis minus peccet. Op. cit. p. 668.]

# 10

## *Classical and Boethian Tradition in the* Confessio Amantis

WINTHROP WETHERBEE

> Naturatus amor nature legibus orbem
> Subdit, et unanimes concitat esse feras.
> (*Confessio Amantis* I.i.1–2)

This chapter is largely a commentary on the first two lines – really the first two words – of Book I of the *Confessio Amantis*. The lines describe the power of love in universal life, and the words, which give that love a name, are *Naturatus amor*. This phrase is evidently Gower's own coinage, and like so much in the Latin apparatus of the *Confessio*, it conveys a sense of scholastic authority which is belied by close scrutiny.[1] Is it love in the service of nature, the power that sustains the natural order? Or is it love reduced to the state of nature, a force that bonds humankind to its lower, bestial self? The problem is not clarified by the phrases that follow. *Amor* subjects all creatures to (or by means of) 'the laws of nature', but do these laws bring wild things into unanimity, or do they compel peaceful beings to grow wild? The syntax of the final phrase is fundamentally ambiguous.

These ambiguities provide a focal point for considering the role played by the Latin tradition in Gower's ostensibly straightforward didactic project. The deliberate difficulty of his Latin is a way of incorporating into his poem fundamental questions about the authoritative role of the Latin tradition in forming his literary culture,[2] and these which imply larger questions about the relation of

---

1 No source has been discovered for the phrase. J.H. Fisher, *John Gower: Moral Philosopher and Friend of Chaucer* (New York, 1964), p. 193, suggests a connection with '*naturatus nature*, nature "in being" ', and '*natura naturans*, nature "becoming" '. For Russell Peck, *Kingship and Common Profit in Gower's* Confessio Amantis (Carbondale, IL, 1978), p. 27, *naturatus amor* is the 'sexual drive'.

2 Derek Pearsall, 'Gower's Latin in the *Confessio Amantis*', in *Latin and Vernacular: Studies in Late Medieval Texts and Manuscripts*, ed. A.J. Minnis (Cambridge, 1989), pp. 13–25, gives a rather contradictory view of the relation of Latin and vernacular. On the one hand, Gower's Latin is a stabilising frame for his 'slippery, elusive, fluid' English (p. 18); Pearsall quotes Walter J. Ong, *Orality and Literacy: The Technologizing of the Word* (London, 1982), p. 114, on Latin's power to insulate meaning from the emotionality of the vernacular (p. 20). But Pearsall also cites passages in which it is the Latin that is elusive – more obscure, 'violent' and 'hectically coloured' than the corresponding English (pp. 18–19). Robert F. Yeager, 'English, Latin, and the Text as "Other": the Page as Sign in the Work of John Gower', *Text* 3 (1987), pp. 259–64, distinguishes usefully among the different Latin 'voices' of the *Confessio* and that of the

human life and history to the natural order. Behind this questioning lies Gower's astute reading of the literary tradition that informs the *Confessio*, a tradition which descends, via Alain de Lille and Bernardus Silvestris, from the *De Consolatione Philosophiae* of Boethius, and enters vernacular poetry with the *Roman de la Rose*.

Recognising Gower's debt to this Boethian tradition is essential to understanding the poetics of the *Confessio Amantis*. The *Consolation* was of course a rich source of conventional wisdom, a brilliant distillation of the cosmology of Plato and the ethical teachings of a range of ancient thinkers. To it Gower owes his instinctive sense of a providential universe of hierarchically ordered powers, unified and sustained by the binding force of love; his conception of Fortune; and his formulations of a number of classic questions about the human condition. But he is also responsive to the human element in the *Consolation*, the consistency with which its philosophical affirmations are punctuated by existential doubt. And one of the most significant features of the Boethian tradition as he interpreted it is a constant questioning of its own authority. This tendency, strong but subdued in Boethius and Alain of Lille, emerges with overwhelming force in the *Roman de la Rose*. As Jean de Meun, by confronting the lover-hero of the delicate allegory of Guillaume de Lorris with *Raison* and a host of more worldly partisans of love, first exposes the isolated and artificial nature of Guillaume's courtly construct, and finally destroys it, so the questions of Gower's priest-confessor Genius gradually unveil the futility and self-delusion of Amans, his inability to engage the sexual and social realities of love directly. In both poems, exemplary stories and extended passages of scientific and historical discourse set the love-theme in a perspective which finally comes to include the providential purpose behind the order of nature. But for both the attempt to apprehend the workings of providence from the perspective of the human subject involved in the world is itself a central issue. They present a world which has suffered a fundamental dislocation; for which the Golden Age, when love and virtue together were 'sett above', is long since past; and in which the elements of human love are fragmented and at odds.

In the Boethian tradition the attempt to apprehend the relation of human life to a larger order is mediated by authority figures: Boethius's Philosophy; Alain's goddess Nature; the Reason, Nature and Genius of Jean's portion of the *Rose*. Gower's priestly Genius, seeking to adapt his teaching to the condition of a human subject whose confusion about his worldly situation poses a serious obstacle to the teacher, is carrying forward a dialogue which is in the direct tradition of the *Consolation*. But Gower's complex perspective on the relationship of this tradition to his vernacular text is revealed in the very format of his pages. The English text of the *Confessio* is framed by Latin marginal glosses, which summarise and often moralise the individual tales, and its principal divisions are marked by Latin head-verses which summarise the psychological and

English text, but does not attempt to define their relations. Joyce Coleman, 'Lay Readers and Hard Latin: How Gower May Have Intended the *Confessio Amantis* To Be Read', *Studies in the Age of Chaucer* 24 (2002), pp. 209–35, offers an interesting theory of how the import of Gower's Latin might have been conveyed to a cultivated but non-Latinate audience.

moral themes of the poem. The inclusion of the Latin materials is sometimes treated as if it were an end in itself, Gower's way of advertising his poem as sufficiently substantial and learned to be worthy of learned exposition. In fact the relationship among these different elements is complex, and the interplay between vernacular text and Latin apparatus becomes in many respects a substitute for the traditional Boethian dialogue. The marginalia oscillate between the poles of authoritative commentary, which places Gower's narratives in a historical and religious economy, and a dogged, schoolmasterly moralism, pompous and at times ludicrously irrelevant in its attempts to engage the subtleties of the vernacular text.[3] The disembodied voice of the head-verses frequently exposes the limitations of the glossator with gnomic pronouncements on love, virtue and vice, whose calculated ambiguity points up the complexities of Gower's treatment of human love.

Set in balance with the vernacular dialogue and its repertory of tales, the Latin apparatus defines Gower's debt to a tradition which affects both his treatment of philosophical and psychological themes, and his sense of his role as poet. For an ongoing dialogue between poetry and the conventions that determine its role in medieval thought and pedagogy is an important element of the tradition. What begins in Boethius as a challenge to the hermeneutics of late neo-Platonism becomes a critique of mythography and the allegorical interpretative tradition in the work of Alain de Lille. This in turn prepares the way for the assertiveness of a Jean de Meun or Dante in claiming something like traditional *auctoritas* for poetry in the vernacular. Gower's elaborate framing of the text of the *Confessio* makes explicit and central the confrontation between the traditional authority of Latin and a vernacular with its own claims to meaning. Between them the uneven perspective of the glosses and the ambiguous sententiousness of the head-verses express the difficulty of invoking the authority of the Latin pedagogical tradition as a control on the vernacular text, and so collaborate in Gower's assertion of his status as a vernacular author. The effect is a distancing of traditional *auctoritas* which, if less flamboyant, is as decisive and innovative as Chaucer's. But before considering how Gower's Latin superstructure inscribes into his poem the history of the Boethian tradition with which he aligns his work, it will be useful to review the tradition itself, highlighting those elements which were most important for Gower.

Boethius's *Consolation* may seem an odd work to identify as inaugurating a revisionist tradition in medieval poetics. It is usually seen as solidly grounded in the tradition of late-antique Latin educational writing, a narrative of intellectual and spiritual evolution closely aligned with the view of literature expounded by critics like Macrobius, for whom the mythos of mental pilgrimage constitutes the latent content of virtually all classic literature. But the *Consolation* is a more truly dialogic work than its neo-Platonic models, one which both invokes and deliberately challenges their idealism. The Prisoner's sense of wrong and his need to attain a rational perspective on his situation conflict. Throughout the

---

3   On the complex status of Gower's Latin glosses, see Siân Echard, 'With Carmen's Help: Latin Authorities in the *Confessio Amantis*', *Studies in Philology* 95 (1998), pp. 1–40, esp. pp. 6–7, 12–14.

early books the delineation of nature, providence and cosmic law is pervaded by ambiguities and contradictory formulations, and we are continually aware of the tension between the relentless movement of Philosophy's argument and the doubts of her all-too-human interlocutor, whose view of the natural order is clouded by a sense of his powerlessness in the face of Fortune and the forces of nature.

Nature and the laws of nature, Boethius suggests, bear a fundamentally ambiguous relation to human behavior, considered from an existential perspective. On the one hand the *machina mundi* is a paradigm of order and continuity which humanity must seek to comprehend: by so doing we participate in the divine wisdom and become as gods (*Cons.* III, p. 10). On the other hand this cosmic machine is fuelled by an irresistible *amor*, the catalyst of those drives and appetites whereby humanity sustains and perpetuates its existence; as such it imposes a kind of cosmic determinism that exploits our natural 'intention' toward self-preservation in order to bind us to the cycle of nature (*Cons.* III, p. 11). How far our reading of the *Consolation* as a whole should be influenced by these hints of determinism is beyond the scope of this essay, but the anxiety and doubt to which they give rise are an important part of the effect of the dialogue. Boethius's response to the Plotinian ideal of human perfectibility that structures Philosophy's argument is darkened by a lurking awareness of something like original sin, and in the major works that constitute the Boethian tradition the history of man's relations with nature become an important consideration.

It is precisely the dialogic aspect of the *Consolation* that most strongly influenced the first major medieval imitation of Boethius, the *De Planctu Naturae* or *Complaint of Nature* of Alain de Lille. The problem posed by the ambiguous power of Boethius's *natura potens* is the very theme of the *Complaint*, a dialogue between the poet and the goddess Nature which centers on the problems of communication between them. Alain's Nature is very much the cosmic legislator of the *Consolation*, but she is also a would-be teacher. She asks of humankind what Philosophy had asked of Boethius: on the one hand, a return to that primordial dignity which consists in a full understanding of the nature of things; on the other, active participation in the natural continuum defined by her laws. And the twofold challenge gives rise to similar contradictions. Humanity in its fallen condition is psychologically unable to both 'possess' Nature, in the sense of embracing and comprehending her cosmic significance, and simultaneously fulfill its self-preservative and procreative role in the natural economy.

Nature's role in the dialogue of the *Complaint* is largely an attempt to re-indoctrinate the poet with a proper sense of the place of human art and sexuality in the cosmic scheme, but she is forced to acknowledge that humanity's dislocated state involves more than willfulness, and exceeds her power to control. The admission takes the form of an undermining of the theory of poetic language which is an essential part of Nature's appeal. Noting her use of the language of myth in condemning human behavior, the poet asks why humanity alone should be condemned, since mythology shows the gods to have committed similar excesses. Nature responds that such stories about the gods, where not simply scurrilous, are mere *fabulae*, an elegant overlay that veils deeper, philosophical meanings. But as the dialogue proceeds she is forced to acknowledge that these surface fables are at least as true to the nature of things as any inner meaning they may harbor. In spite of herself she reveals the sorry story of her betrayal at the hands of Venus and Cupid, and it becomes clear that natural desire itself, and the language of myth in which she seeks to represent it, are pervaded by contradiction, their once sacred purpose compromised by a long history of intrigue, betrayal and violence.

To deal with the impasse thus defined, Nature summons her 'priest', Genius, the cosmic principle that ensures the orderly union of form and matter, and, in human nature, the orientative principle of procreative sexuality. Genius concludes the *Complaint* by excommunicating from Nature's 'Church' all who refuse to obey her sexual laws. This is clearly an unsatisfying resolution, and it is significant that Genius's action ends the dialogue: the discord between Nature and humanity, it is suggested, cannot be resolved by natural or rational means. This recalls the final silencing of Boethius's Prisoner, early in Book V of the *Consolation*, after he has vented his frustration at the uncertainty of his freedom of will within a scheme governed by divine providence. But the problem in the *Complaint* is complicated, as Nature's mythic discourse obliquely acknowledges, by history. To introduce Genius, an essentially subliminal principle, is to acknowledge that the 'unnatural' element in human life is not just a failure of rational knowledge or moral will, but a chronic condition of the human psyche in its present state. Nature and the cosmic harmony for which she stands can still inspire awe, but they constitute an impossible standard for the corrupted sensibility of fallen humanity. Nature and humankind, Nature and that 'Genius' who figures humanity's vestigial capacity for renewal, can communicate only across the barrier of the Fall.

An aura of vestigial idealism surrounds the reunion of Genius and Nature. There is a sense in which their communion transcends the traditional cosmological formulation of their relations, and the mythological disasters which have corrupted those relations. In the presence of the goddess, Genius senses the 'first beginnings' of a renewal of the lost joys of Paradise, and Nature, in response to his impassioned greeting, bestows her 'grace' upon him. The gestures of both figures suggest the appeal and the fulfillment of the desire embodied in troubadour lyric; Alain seems to invoke *fin amors* to suggest a register of feeling and value that defies categorization in terms of traditional Latinate *auctoritas*, but confirms the vestigial survival in humankind of a capacity for religious idealism. The hypothetical rapport of priest and goddess shows Alain tentatively assigning to the aesthetic of courtly poetry a role corresponding to that formerly played by the now discredited aesthetic of the neo-Platonist tradition.

The intrusion of 'courtly love' into the domain of Latinate authority is carried still further in *Le Roman de la Rose*, which strongly invokes the Boethian tradition but makes plain the impossibility of any real dialogue between that tradition and the courtly sensibility of the poem's lover-narrator. Guillaume de Lorris begins by portentously citing Macrobius, but never provides an authoritative basis for a moral-spiritual reading of the Lover's experience. Yet the vision of love that informs the Lover's quest clearly has its archetypal, Edenic aspect. The experience that claims him through his encounter with the fountain of Narcissus is radically preconditioned by his fascination with his own adolescent awareness of desire, and is in that sense Narcissistic, yet it is also the means through which he is first drawn to attach his feelings to something outside himself, and in that sense it transcends Narcissism.

In Jean de Meun's continuation the sexual telos of Guillaume's tentative quest becomes dominant, and the resurgence of a 'naturalistic' view of desire is marked by a reversion to a Latin tradition that is recognizably 'Boethian'. The courtly tone and structure of Guillaume's vision are disrupted, and the narrative is recast on the model of the dialogues of Boethius and Alain. Jean begins by subjecting Guillaume's Amant to the discourse of Reason, who plays the role of Philosophy and attempts to dissuade him from his fruitless love-quest, but offends him by her use of the myth of Jupiter's castration of Saturn to explain the peculiar relation of human love to the natural economy. Reason's defence echoes the Nature of the *Complaint*, arguing that the myth of Saturn's castration must be read allegorically, as one of those *integumenz* that conceal philosophical truth.[4] But the Lover cannot understand her 'Latin';[5] he is blind to allegory and incapable of a stable, 'natural' relation to language. His dilemma constitutes Jean's critique of the courtly aesthetic, its liability to reduction to mere euphemism and decoration. Jean's Lover is neither fish nor fowl: Nature and courtliness are at odds in him, leaving him cut off both from the ideal world to which the 'Latin' of the *poeta platonicus* gives access and from the natural continuum of desire and procreation which the myth of Saturn in its historical aspect announces.

In the ensuing narrative the God of Love assumes the ascendancy, finally drawing Nature and Genius themselves into the action. Genius's preaching of Nature's 'gospel of procreation' to the 'barons' of the God of Love precipitates the battle that ends with the impregnation of the Rose. Genius claims the authority of Nature, but he preaches in vestments provided by Cupid and Venus, and his audience are the forces of unregenerate desire; the net effect of his sermon is a wholly subliminal appeal to sexual appetite. His message, moreover, is that procreation at the bidding of Nature is the sole means to the attainment of the joys of Paradise – a doctrine that confirms Genius's role as a vestige of the primal dignity of unfallen humankind, but remains oblivious to the historical causes of humanity's present disordered state.

In Jean's development of the *Rose* the love-cult of courtly poetry and the cosmic idealism of the Latin tradition become terms in a broader dialectic, subject to the law of a 'nature' lost the power of direct appeal exerted by Alain's goddess, and which has reassumed some of the dark complexity of the Boethian *natura potens*. In the *Confessio Amantis* this dialectic is given a new prominence, and the withdrawal of Nature is balanced by the greatly expanded role of Genius, who emerges here for the first time to engage in direct dialogue with a human lover. The very presence of Genius is a sign that the natural continuum of the Boethian universe is operative in human love, but his emergence into the courtly world means that his authority is mediated in new and significantly complicating ways.

---

4   *Le Roman de la Rose*, 3 vols, ed. Felix Lecoy (Paris, 1965–70), lines 7051–7150.
5   Ibid., line 5810.

The essential dialectic of the *Confessio* is expressed in the Latin couplets which introduce the main theme of the Prologue, the decline of human life from an earlier state of harmony:

> Tempus preteritum presens fortuna beatum
> Linquit, et antiquas vertit in orbe vias.
> Progenuit veterem concors dileccio pacem,
> Dum facies hominis nuncia mentis erat:
> Legibus unicolor tunc temporis aura refulsit,
> Iusticie plane tuncque fuere vie.
> Nuncque latens odium vultum depingit amoris,
> Paceque sub ficta tempus ad arma tegit.
> Instar et ex variis mutabile Cameliontis
> Lex gerit, et regnis sunt noua iura nouis:
> Climata quae fuerant solidissima sicque per orbem
> Soluuntur, nec eo centra quietis habent.  (Prol. ii)

> [The fortune of the present day has forsaken the blessed life of the past, and diverted the world from its ancient course. Harmonious love produced peace in days of old, when a man's face declared the state of his mind. In that time the wholly 'golden' character of life shone forth in laws, then the paths of justice were easy to follow.
> Now lurking hatred presents a loving face, and in a feigned state of peace the world makes ready for war. The law in its inconsistency behaves like the ever-changing Chameleon, and for new kingdoms there are new kinds of law. And so throughout the world boundaries that had seemed wholly firm are dissolved; things no longer possesses a centred stability.]

The phrase 'antiquas vertit in orbe vias' in the first couplet is hardly translatable, and virtually obliterates any distinction between the 'orb' of the world and Fortune's wheel.[6] The lines that follow recall lyrics in Boethius's *Consolation* that contrast the Golden Age with the violence and treachery of the modern world, and, more broadly, the stable concord of the universe at large with the instability of human life. The emphasis is seemingly on the failure of human institutions, but the passage ends by declaring that the once firmly fixed 'climata' of the world itself have been unmoored, and now lack a stable center – language which suggests, without fully articulating, a link between cosmic disorder and human folly. As the Prologue moves forward, the uncertain relation of human and cosmic life becomes a recurring theme. In an extended review of the estates of society, the volatility of the 'comune' is compared to the violence of elemental forces in a state of imbalance:

---

[6]  The phrase might also be rendered: 'alters the ancient paths [e.g. the 'plane vie' of justice, line 6] in the world', or perhaps 'alters the ancient course of things by turning them on her wheel'. The ambiguity of 'orbis', noted by Macaulay in line 11, seems equally present in line 2.
   Here and throughout I have provided my own translations of Gower's Latin verse in order to highlight its ambiguities, but I have found very helpful the complete rendering of the head-verses by Siân Echard and Claire Fanger, *The Latin Verses in the* Confessio Amantis: *An Annotated Translation* (East Lansing, MI, 1991).

Si caput extollat et lex sua frena relaxet,
Vt sibi velle iubet, Tigridis instar habet.
Ignis, aqua dominans duo sunt pietate carentes,
Ira tamen plebis est violenta magis. (Prol. iv. 3–6)

[If [the commons] rears its head, and the law relaxes its hold on the
reins, the people's will dictates for itself, and becomes like a wild
beast. Fire or water, grown too powerful, is wholly without mercy, but
the rage of the commons is more violent still.]

The language once again suggests that the problem of social violence is
grounded in a larger complex of forces. Both Fortune and the chronic instability
of the world are firmly linked to the unstable behaviour of man, 'Which of his
propre governance/ Fortuneth al the worldes chance' (lines 583–4); yet the
world, too, 'of his propre kynde/ Was evere untrewe' (lines 535–6). The use of
'propre' (Latin *proprium, propria*) links the two couplets, and conveys a
disturbing suggestion that instability is in fact 'proper' to human nature in an
absolute sense,[7] while the coined verb 'fortuneth', used here to characterise the
unruliness of humanity, shows the vernacular blurring the complex perspective
of the Latin in the process of assimilating its concepts.

The Latin verses that introduce the final section of the Prologue sum up the
ambiguous relationship of man to the world and its evolution:

Sicut ymago viri variantur tempora mundi
Statque nichil firmum preter amare deum. (Prol. vi. 5–6)

[Like an image of man are the times of the world as they change;
nothing remains constant but the need to love God.]

The problem of ceaseless change is traced to man's loss of his original lordship
over creation, but then, by a sudden shift, change and 'division' are presented as
imposed on man by his natural condition:

The which, for his complexioun
Is mad upon divisioun
Of cold, of hot, of moist, of drye,
He mot be verray kynde dye  (Prol. 975–8)

For a moment, the relations of man and cosmos are seemingly reversed: man's
divided state, rather than disrupting nature, appears determined by nature.
Gower's perspective recalls that of Alain de Lille, or Alain's great predecessor
Bernardus Silvestris, whose *Cosmographia* concludes by contrasting the wasting
of human life to the perpetual self-sufficiency of the universe at large:

Influit ipsa sibi mundi natura superstes,
Permanet et fluxu pascitur usque suo:
. . .
Longe disparibus causis mutandus in horas,

---

7    Gower is consistent in using this adjective to denote the natural character, office or attribute of
     things. Cp. Prol. 954, II.439, IV.2536, etc.

Effluit occiduo corpore totus homo.
Sic sibi deficiens, peregrinis indiget escis,
Sudat in hoc vitam, denichilatque dies.[8]

[The nature of the universe outlives itself, for it flows back into itself,
and so survives and is nourished by its very flowing away.
      . . . But man, ever liable to affliction by forces far less harmonious,
passes wholly out of existence with the failure of his body. Unable to
sustain himself, and wanting nourishment from without, he exhausts
his life, and a day reduces him to nothing.]

The irresolution of the Prologue as a whole, its failure to provide a coherent
view of the place of man in the natural economy, is essential to Gower's project,
and the ambiguities of his Latin convey his concern with the fundamental
Boethian problem of human freedom. B.L. Jefferson long ago remarked that
Chaucer never expresses a complete acceptance of Boethian doctrine on free will
or the existence of evil, though he often discusses these questions and invariably
cites the *Consolation* in doing so. In refusing to adopt a definite position he is at
odds with Dante and Jean de Meun, as well as the Nun's Priest's Augustine and
Bradwardine.[9] Gower's Prologue expresses a similar reluctance in a similarly
Boethian spirit.

   The shift to the love-theme of the *Confessio* proper is clearly marked in the
opening Latin verses of Book I:

> Naturatus amor nature legibus orbem
> Subdit, et unanimes concitat esse feras.
> Huius enim mundi Princeps amor esse uidetur,
> Cuius eget diues, pauper et omnis ope.
> Sunt in agone pares amor et fortuna, que cecas
> Plebis ad insidias uertit uterque rotas.
> Est amor egra salus, uexata quies, pius error,
> Bellica pax, uulnus dulce, suaue malum. (1. i)

> [Love bound to nature subjects the world to the laws of nature, and
> drives those who live in concord to become wild [or compels wild
> beings to accord with one another]. For love may be seen to be the
> ruler of this world, of whose aid rich, poor and all alike stand in need.
> Love and fortune act in the same way [or 'compete on equal terms'?
> 'are equivalent in the conflicts they create'?], and both turn blind
> wheels to entrap mankind. Love is sickness in health, a troubled
> repose, a virtuous straying from virtue, a warlike peace, a desirable
> pain, a pleasant evil.]

Nature's laws control the world, for better or worse, but her regent is Amor, and
our response to the 'goddess' is subject to his complex mediation.[10] All things

---

[8]   Bernardus Silvestris, *Cosmographia* II.14.171–8; ed. Peter Dronke (Leiden, 1978), pp. 154–5.
[9]   B.L. Jefferson, *Chaucer and the Consolation of Philosophy of Boethius* (Princeton, 1917; rpt. New
      York, 1965), pp. 79–80.
[10]  Gower's reference to *amor* as *princeps* is significant. Boethius assigns this title only to God, and
      Gower's displacement of it reflects his ontological perspective.

depend on love, as the second couplet declares, but the third effectively identifies love with Fortune, and the concluding oxymora echo Alain's Nature and
Jean de Meun's Reason, whose endlessly paradoxical definitions of *cupido-amors*
define as well the limits of their authority. The opening lines of the English text
reflect on the unknowability of this all-controlling power. We cannot know the
implications of our desires 'til that the chance falle' (lines 52–6), and we can
never trace these desires with certainty to the benevolent power that is their ultimate source.

    We now learn that love has seized the poet himself. He prays to Venus, and
greets her appearance with quasi-Marian idolatry; she is 'mannes hele' (line
133), the 'Source and Welle/ Of wel or wo' (lines 148–9). But the Latin verses
which bracket this episode provide an ominous chorus, defining Venus's power
in terms of entrapment and disease (I.ii.7, I.iii.2), and in the event her treatment
of the Lover is brusque and cold.

    The impasse between Venus and Amans is largely a failure of communication
between the Latin and vernacular traditions. Venus's role brings the psychological concerns of Boethius's Philosophy and Alain's Nature to bear on human
nature in its sexual aspect, but her appeal is inseparable from and fundamentally conditioned by *cupido*, the agent of *naturatus amor*, with the implications of
treachery and violence that lurk in the Latin head-verses. Amans, for his part, is
the prisoner of courtly convention, and his vernacular language, like his courtly
sensibility, cannot acknowledge directly the sexual aspect of Venus's appeal or
recognise the disordering effects of *cupido* for what they are.

    It is significant that Genius, whose relation to human nature had hitherto
been wholly subliminal, emerges here for the first time to engage in direct
dialogue with the lover-hero of the poem, and that he appears at the beginning
of the poem, rather than at its climax as in the *Complaint* and the *Rose*. The
starting point of the penitential dialogue is also the point at which the conventions of vernacular love-poetry take control of the poem's action. Gower's
Genius cannot be simply identified with the overarching authority of the Latin
tradition. The priestly figure who had anathematised sodomy in the name of
Alain's Nature, and preached unstinting procreation to the barons of Jean's God
of Love, retains a sense of the larger purpose of sexuality and the lost integrity of
unfallen human nature, but he also participates fully in the impulses and aspirations of the vernacular tradition of courtly love. He is less a spokesman than a
mediator – a mediator, moreover, whose own perception of the standards of
'kinde' and 'resoun' which he holds up to Amans preserves unresolved the
ambiguous perspective of the Boethian tradition. Boethius's balancing of philosophical authority and existential uncertainty has evolved into an opposition
between Latin and vernacular worlds of meaning; Genius participates in both
worlds, but he can provide no authoritative basis for reconciling the conflicting
claims of Nature and courtly idealism. Genius's difficulty in addressing the situation of Amans, in one aspect a version of the crisis that had confronted Nature
and Reason in Gower's sources, is also a measure of the difficulty of bringing the
resources of the Latin tradition to bear on the more radically vernacularised
world of the *Confessio*. His first *exemplum*, a version of the legend of Acteon
(lines 333–78), provides a good example of the problems he faces.

Genius's ostensible purpose in this story is to exemplify the liability of the senses to sinful temptation. Thus where Ovid's only indication that Acteon has actually seen Diana bathing is the passive participle *visae*, used of Diana herself (*Met.* III.185), Genius focuses directly on the fatal gaze:

> Bot he his yhe awey ne swerveth
> Fro hire, which was naked al[.] (lines 366–7)

The head-verses to this section of the poem assert the inability of any person tainted by sin to prevent pernicious influences from reaching the mind through the portals of the senses (I.iv.1–2); they proclaim a moral climate in which the contamination of innocence has always already taken place, where the haplessness of fallen man provides the *donnée* of the narrative. The marginal gloss suggests that Acteon *chose* not to avert his eyes, but rather gazed 'attentively' (*diligencius*) at the goddess, thus provoking her wrath. But the two non-committal lines just quoted leave his motivation obscure, and Gower seems to be at pains to purge his tale of overt moral suggestion. For the Theban landscape of Ovid's story, where the earth is 'infected' by the blood of countless slaughtered animals, he substitutes a forest filled with flowers and the song of birds. The moment in the story when Ovid is recalled most directly is simultaneously a quiet assertion of Gower's independence vis-à-vis the moralising emphasis of the Latin frame. Ovid had prefaced his story with hints of the metamorphosis to come, 'the forehead endowed with alien horns' and 'dogs sated with a master's blood'. Gower, too, begins with 'Houndes' and 'grete Hornes', but here they have no history. The hounds are still at their master's command, and Ovid's *cornua*, the mark of Acteon's hapless bestialisation, have become hunting horns, an emblem of the pursuits of noble youth.

These small transformations constitute a vernacular counterbalance to the inevitable metamorphosis. They adapt the story to a purpose that is wholly Gower's, and assert the autonomy of his vernacular fictional world. But Gower's distancing of his vernacular narrative from the encroaching authority of the marginalia is also a means of renewing contact with Ovid himself, who had declared openly that his version of the tale had no moral, and questioned Diana's harsh treatment of Acteon. A conventional moral reading is still present on the page, but the obliviousness of Genius's vernacular narrative to moralization emphasises the extent to which this viewpoint has been relegated, literally and thematically, to the margin. The clear implication that moralisation is an inappropriate response to the story is precisely responsive to Ovid's censure of the wrath of Diana.

It is Ovidian, too, in a broader sense which provides further evidence of Gower's sensitivity to the implications of his Latin apparatus. The *Metamorphoses* descended from antiquity unaccompanied by commentary, and posed a unique challenge when they resurfaced in the schools of the later Middle Ages. The glossing of the text became a project of segmentation, reducing each separate tale to an *exemplum* conveying its own bit of doctrine, as though the cumulative force of Ovid's serial narrative were too overwhelming to be faced directly. The format of the *Confessio* is similar to that of a manuscript of the *Metamorphoses*. The many Ovidian codices where the text is framed by marginal *allegoriae*, and each legend is introduced by the corresponding couplets from the *Integumenta Ovidii* of John of Garland, anticipate the tension among text, head-verses and gloss, so important to the meaning of the *Confessio*.[11]

The relationship, at once intimate and skewed, of Gower's Acteon narrative to its source is typical of his dealings with classical poetry in the *Confessio*. The same kind of quasi-parodic close reading is evident in the tale of Perseus and Medusa, which follows (lines 389–435). The ostensible point in this story is in the 'wisdom and prouesse', symbolised by the shield of Pallas and the sword of Mercury, which enable Perseus to slay the Gorgon (lines 429–35). But Gower intrudes this conventional moral into a narrative which closely imitates Ovid's artfully perfunctory telling of the story. Ovid's Perseus, who tells the story himself, is more adventurer than hero. His disjointed narrative ends anticlimactically when he discovers Medusa asleep, and dispatches her with minimal reliance on his divine weapons (*Met*. IV.777–85). Whatever value we might read into his victory is further diminished when he appropriates her fatal power for himself, and uses it to massive and random effect in the grotesquely un-Homeric battle which erupts at his wedding (*Met*. V.177–249).

Gower was alert to the incongruities in Ovid's treatment of Perseus, and in combining a faithful imitation of Ovid's narrative with the elements of a mythographic interpretation he invites us to see a parallel between Perseus's 'heroism' and the moralising purpose to which Genius subjects it. Labeling Perseus's arms as moral symbols is an interpretative act as arbitrary as the bestowal of the arms themselves. So used, the tools of moralisation are as efficient and as meaningless as the petrifying power of Medusa in the hands of Perseus, subjecting human experience to their effect in a wholly coercive way. Gower's narrative, which exhibits the form of heroic action without the substance, is finally an image of how moralization can perform its task, yet wholly fail to realise the essence of a human situation.

These early Ovidian tales are isolated, part of a critique of moralising allegory which provides a sort of prolegomenon to the larger project of the *Confessio*. An important part of this larger project is a critique of chivalry, and it is within this framework that most of Gower's appropriations of the classical story must be read. A convenient starting point is the speech in which – in the midst of a book bristling with tales of seduction and abandonment, love disrupted by war and heroic purpose undermined by love – Genius offers a bracing, almost jaunty affirmation of active knighthood as the basis of harmonious relations between men and women:

---

11  See John of Garland, *Integumenta Ovidii*, ed. Fausto Ghisalberti (Messina, 1933), pp. 5–10; C.A. Robson, 'Dante's Use in the *Divina Commedia* of the Medieval Allegories of Ovid', in *Centenary Essays on Dante by Members of the Oxford Dante Society* (Oxford, 1965), pp. 5–18. The layout of Gower's manuscripts is discussed by Siân Echard, 'With Carmen's Help', pp. 9–10; see also her 'Glossing Gower: In Latin, in English, and *in absentia*: The Case of Bodleian Ashmole 35', in *Re-visioning Gower*, ed. R.F. Yeager (Asheville, NC, 1998), pp. 237–56. Richard Emmerson, 'Reading Gower in a Manuscript Culture: Latin and English in Illustrated Manuscripts of the *Confessio Amantis*', *Studies in the Age of Chaucer* 21 (1999), pp. 143–86, notes the various ways in which manuscripts present Gower's Latin (pp. 155–64), and the radically contrasting emphasis on Latin or English in different manuscripts (pp. 175–8).

> Lo, now, mi Sone, as I have told,
> Thou miht wel se, who that is bold
> And dar travaile and undertake
> The cause of love, he schal be take
> The rathere unto loves grace;
> For comunliche in worthi place
> The wommen loven worthinesse
> Of manhode and of gentilesse,
> For the gentils ben most desired. (lines 2191–9)

The occasion for this little homily is a series of *exempla* which make aggressive behaviour a model of right conduct – the sin being addressed in this book is Sloth – and a means to success in love. The series ends with Aeneas. Had he not used his might to defeat Turnus, he would not have won Lavinia:

> But for he hath him overronne
> And gete his pris, he gat hire love. (lines 2188–9)

The language of this couplet suggests that the connection between aggression and amatory success is less direct than Genius implies. Between Aeneas's defeat of Turnus and his winning of Lavinia intervenes all that Genius's exemplum omits, the entire Vergilian action implied by 'overronne' and 'pris'. The former – an odd choice to describe victory in single combat – hints at the larger issue of the conquest and occupation of Italy; we may also see Aeneas as having 'over-run', in the attested sense of 'transgressed', the limits of self-control at the moment of savage madness in which he runs Turnus through. 'Pris' often means 'renown', but here suggests the concrete 'prize' that provokes Aeneas's terrible wrath, the sword-belt of Pallas which Turnus wears as a trophy.

In ignoring the political significance of Aeneas's defeat of Turnus and reducing Lavinia's 'love' to a function of chivalric success, a secondary 'pris', the story is typical of Gower's narratives of chivalry.[12] Throughout the *Confessio*, knighthood is placed in an uncertain, often hostile relation to social order and the institutions of government; the world-historical role of the great 'knights' of classical legend is underplayed in favor of an emphasis on the violent pursuit of individual glory and, secondarily, love.

Gower's version of Chiron's education of Achilles 'upon the forme of knyhtes lawe' (IV.1963–2019) presents violent chivalry in embryo. Each day, when Achilles returns from the hunt, Chiron inspects his weapons for the trace of blood that will confirm that he has killed – or at least wounded – his prey (lines 1998–2004). Genius asserts that the fearlessness Achilles acquired by this means served him well in the 'grete nede' (line 2012), but there lurks about the episode the aura of a primitive sexual rite, and this suggestion becomes stronger when Genius ends with an emblematic maxim:

---

[12] Political implications are stressed in the Latin gloss that accompanies these lines: 'Nota pro eo quod Eneas Regem Turnum in bello deuicit, non solum amorem Lavine, set et regnum Ytalie sibi subiugatum obtinuit'.

> That the corage of hardiesce
> Is of knythode the prouesce (lines 2015–16)

and then disconcertingly adds that this 'prowess':

> is to love sufficant
> Aboven al the remenant
> That unto loves court pursue.  (lines 2017–19)

We may well ask whether the 'great need' that Achilles' training is designed to meet is finally martial or sexual. But, as if in compensation, Genius later tells the tale of Thetis's attempt to forestall Achilles' recruitment for the Trojan war by concealing him among the daughters of King Lichomedes (V.2961–3218). Achilles adapts to life as a girl with remarkable ease. Gower's source, the *Achilleid* of Statius, makes much of the awkward, pseudo-feminine posturings of the brawny adolescent, and his Achilles anticipates the sexual opportunities that concealment will provide.[13] Gower's Achilles is both graceful and innocent. Even Ulysses cannot spot him dancing with the king's daughters, and his sexual union with Deidamia conveys no suggestion of the rape frankly described by Statius. It results, not from the promptings of chivalric 'hardiesce', but from a mutual innocent 'stirring', wholly free of the tensions and constraints chivalric culture would normally have imposed.

But the story's real point is in the power with which the conditioning effect of Achilles' earlier training in 'knythode' reasserts itself when Ulysses shows him arms and armour. He is instantly drawn back to the male world, as if transposed to a different genre. Deidamia is at once relegated to the past, betrayed by knighthood itself, as emblematised in the arms that induce Achilles to abandon her.

The defining frame for Gower's critique of chivalry is a sustained opposition between two spheres of activity which may be called the world of chivalry and the world of Rome. Rome is mainly a vaguely defined ideal in the *Confessio*, but is clearly associated with wise government – witness the parade of emperors and other exemplary figures from Roman political history whose aphorisms and disciplined behaviour punctuate Book VII – and stable institutions. It is not a perfect world: the two most prominent Roman tales deal with abuses of hallowed Roman institutions, the Donation of Constantine and the usurpation of the papacy by Boniface VIII. But both narratives affirm fundamental principles in the process of showing the dangers that menace them, and, in relation to the world at large – whether the pagan world of Demetreus and Perseus or the early Christian world of Constantine and Constance – Rome is both identified with justice and, broadly speaking, opposed to chivalry. The seducer Mundus is the only Roman expressly identified with 'chivalry' in the *Confessio* (I.782–5). Constantine, whose conversion is the climax of Book II, is a former knight, but

---

13  Statius, *Achilleis* I.560–618. With Achilles' private smile as he prepares to take part in secret feminine rituals (line 595), cp. Gower's Achilles' smiling 'upon himself' at the spectacle he presents in female disguise (lines 3011–12). With his colour, 'betwen the whyt and red', in Gower (lines 3016–18), cp. his flush on first beholding Deidamia in Statius (I.304–6).

has been forced by leprosy to cease 'riding forth', and has laid aside his arms once and for all, before Gower's tale of him begins (II.3194–5).

By contrast, the world of chivalry is amorphous, unified only by the preoccupations and besetting whims of knighthood as defined by the many tales that deal, almost always indirectly, with Troy. It is largely the world of Benoît de Ste Maure, and Gower is clearly responsive to the distinguishing features of the *Roman de Troie*. His view, like Benoît's, encompasses pre-Homeric legend, the judgement of Paris and the career of Jason, and extends forward to the post-Homeric fortunes of Ulysses and the House of Atreus. But Gower's version of Benoît's Troy world is far more subject to the *ambages* of romance, an uncentred world of ceaseless, random movement. Both the Rome world and the Troy world are to some extent historicised, but Gower ignores the historical relation of the two cities. Aeneas is named several times in the *Confessio*, but nothing is said of his Vergilian mission and its contribution to the foundation of Rome.[14] Rome has an evolving relation to the development of the Church and the defining of its relation to secular power, whereas the Troy narratives often show their chivalric heroes resisting or repudiating such development. Several explicitly set chivalry in an adversary relation to the emerging institutions of civil law and parliamentary government.[15]

Even on its own terms, the Troy world is emphatically not an epic world. Gower radically downplays the decisive events of epic history that center on Troy itself, and his individual heroes exhibit little trace of Homeric or Vergilian dignity. Hector, prominent in Gower's account of Paris's ravishing of Helen and its background, appears in his warrior aspect only as the object of the love of Penthesilea (IV.2139–41, V.2547–51), and the fleeting glimpses we are given of Achilles and Agamemnon at Troy center on their relations with women (II.2452–5, IV.1693–1701, V.7591–6). Ulysses' epic role is viewed through a haze of chivalric fantasy: Penelope, after sending a letter full of arch hints about the importunities of the suitors who surround her, is rather unexpectedly rewarded at war's end with the prompt return of her anxious husband. The outwitter of Circe and Calypso is reduced to a sort of Troilus, overwhelmed by imaginings of love betrayed, and his homeward journey is a speedboat ride, an odyssey ten lines long (IV.224–33).

I have argued elsewhere that in reading Chaucer, and particularly in *Troilus and Criseyde*, the world of classical legend is presented to us in two forms.[16] One is the medieval romance version of that world which Chaucer derived from Boccaccio, Benoît and other medieval sources. The other is the more 'authentic'

---

[14] The point of Gower's tale of Aeneas and Dido (IV.77–142), corroborated by the accompanying Latin gloss, is Aeneas's 'lachesse' in failing to return from Italy to Carthage.

[15] In Gower's tale of Orestes (III.1885–2195) the Athenian parliament convened to judge Orestes' murder of his mother is interrupted by Menestheus, who asserts Orestes' innocence, challenges anyone who denies it to single combat, and goes on to make a number of false charges against Clytemnestra. In the two Trojan parliament scenes in the tale of Paris and Helen (V.7195–7585), caution and diplomacy are overwhelmed by enthusiasm for Paris's 'campaign' to steal Helen.

[16] Winthrop Wetherbee, *Chaucer and the Poets: An Essay on 'Troilus and Criseyde'* (Ithaca, N.Y., 1984), pp. 21–9; 'Romance and Epic in Chaucer's Knight's Tale', *Exemplaria* 2 (1990), pp. 303–28.

classical world of Vergil, Ovid, and Statius – present only through the medium of allusion, but offering a kind of authoritative commentary on the limitations of the world view of Chaucer's medievalised romance characters by setting it in the perspective of the more complex, tragic vision of history and human experience their poetry provides.

Gower's literary program is far less ambitious than Chaucer's, but for him, too, the calculated naiveté, thematic and historical, of romance sets off the dangers of chivalric individualism, the concatenated violence and instability with which knightly restlessness affected fourteenth-century society at all levels. Like the parliamentary government and enlightened diplomacy which surface in the final episode of the 'Knight's Tale', Gower's Rome-world, and his more tentatively drawn Athens, exist as a standard by which the excesses of chivalry may be judged. But the opposition remains unresolved, and the tension between the essentially private interests of chivalry and the public concerns of newer governmental institutions remains a serious issue. In this fundamental respect the finished *Confessio Amantis*, like the fragmentary *Canterbury Tales*, is very much a work in progress.

The Latin tradition provides the essential context for Gower's social critique. Against the background it provides, we can recognize the *Confessio Amantis* in one of its most important aspects, as a new, composite version of the *roman d'antiquité*. The erratic scholarly voice of the marginal glosses complements, and at times exposes, the wavering historical perspective of Gower's 'epic' narratives, setting the fortunes of his chivalric adventurers and the plight of his hapless courtly lover-hero in relation to the harsher, Ovidian and Vergilian versions of history and politics, while the dense, highly allusive head-verses link them to the bewildering complex of natural forces that is the Boethian universe. Skeptical of its own authority, the Latin tradition is thus normative for Gower, a stable framework for his questioning of the values of his own world.[17]

---

17  Portions of this chapter are adapted from two previously published essays of mine: 'Genius and Interpretation in the *Confessio Amantis*', in *Magister Regis: Studies in Honor of Robert Earl Kaske*, ed. Arthur Groos (New York, 1986), pp. 241–60; 'Latin Structure and Vernacular Space: Chaucer, Gower and the Boethian Tradition', in *Chaucer and Gower: Difference, Mutuality, Exchange*, ed. R.F. Yeager (Victoria, BC, 1991), pp. 7–35.

# 11

## *Gender and Sexuality in* Confessio Amantis

### DIANE WATT

John Gower's *Confessio Amantis* is a poem focused on men and deeply concerned with the masculine ideal.[1] The framing narrative is dominated by the homosocial relationship between the confessor, Genius, and the penitent, Amans; the female beloved remains absent, elusive. The famous discussion of politics and ethics in Book VII directly addresses the subject of good governance on the part of the prince and the man. In this conduct book for rulers and for common men, virtues such as truth, largesse, justice, pity and chastity are conceived in masculine terms. The corresponding vices are implicitly linked to effeminacy. In the case of chastity's opposite partner, lust, the connection is made explicit (e.g. at VII.4252–6). Yet Gower cannot and does not ignore women. Venus has her place alongside Cupid in the frame, and heroines and anti-heroines such as Lucrece, Virginia, Constance, Helen of Troy, Procne, Philomela, Medea and Clytemnestra all figure within the exemplary narratives. These introduce us to a range of different types of femininity, from silent modesty and submissiveness to monstrous promiscuity, murder and witchcraft. In the analysis of gender in *Confessio* I offer here, I concentrate on stories which centre on women and femininity, not because I consider men and masculinity to be irrelevant or less important,[2] but because I believe that the complexity of Gower's representation of the feminine throws into relief certain aspects of his stated concern with issues of ethics and personal responsibility. Critics have, however, emphasised the need to consider gender alongside sexuality, heterosexual and homosexual.[3] Recently, Karma Lochrie has responded to what she considers to be the problematic over-emphasis on sexuality at the expense of gender.[4] Ostensibly, of course, *Confessio Amantis* is not *about* men or women, masculinity or femininity, but about love, its virtues and vices, fulfilment and frustrations. As a poem about love, it can give the contemporary reader insights into medieval constructions of sex, from the exalted state of marriage (VII.4215–37) to the depravity of acts against nature, sacrilege, incest, rape, adultery, seduction and fornication.[5] The present essay, which concentrates on the much-discussed 'Tale of Canace and Machaire', the

1  All references to *Confessio Amantis* are to *The English Works of John Gower*, ed. G.C. Macaulay, EETS, es nos. 81 and 82 (London, 1900–1901), Vols I–II, by book and line number.
2  See Allen J. Frantzen, 'When Women Aren't Enough', *Speculum* 68 (1993), pp. 445–71.
3  See especially Nancy F. Partner, 'No Sex, No Gender', *Speculum* 68 (1993), pp. 419–43.
4  Karma Lochrie, *Covert Operations: The Medieval Uses of Secrecy* (Philadelphia, 1999), p. 226.
5  This sub-classification of *lust* is from St Thomas Aquinas, *Temperance* [2a2ae], q. 154, a. 12 in

less well-known 'Tale of Iphis and Ianthe', and the hitherto-overlooked 'Tale of Calistona', will be loosely structured according to the categories of incest, unnatural vice (specifically sodomy), rape and seduction. Karma Lochrie has argued that Gower, in line with other writers of his day, depicts sexual perversion as essentially feminine.[6] In many ways this claim seems plausible: in medieval theology, Eve was, after all, held responsible for the Fall, and in contemporary scientific thinking, womankind was associated with the flesh, the senses, and the emotions. As Lochrie points out, in verses which were widely cited in the Middle Ages, St Paul seemed to blame women before men for succumbing to 'unnatural' affections (Romans I.26–7).[7] Moreover, within the *Confessio* itself, Venus is depicted as a contradictory figure who, at least in part, stands for the immanence and instability of corrupt and corrupting sexual desire.[8] Nevertheless, I hope to show that Gower's representation of gender and sexuality is not so straightforwardly anti-feminist as Lochrie suggests. In this chapter I will specifically examine the issue of culpability: are women responsible for sexual sin, or powerless victims of male desire, or both, or neither?

*Incest: Accountability in the 'Tale of Canace and Machaire'*

Incest is central to *Confessio Amantis*.[9] In the framing narrative, Amans confesses to Genius, the priest of Venus, and to her son Cupid, and the incestuous relationship between these two deities is outlined, and – bizarrely – condemned by their servant Genius in his account of world religions and the pantheon of the pagan gods in Book V.1382–1446. The culmination of the penitential scheme of the work, structured according to the Seven Deadly Sins, is postponed by the analysis of good government and self-conduct in the penultimate book. It is further disrupted with the synecdochic substitution of 'Incest' for 'Lust' as the subject of the final volume, which centres on the 'Tale of Apollonius of Tyre', the longest narrative in the entire poem. Of the many incest narratives in the collection, the one to have received the most attention, especially in the last century, is the 'Tale of Canace and Machaire' (III.143–336), a fairly free retelling of Ovid's *Heroides* (XI).[10] Two principal issues have divided responses to this story. One is the ques-

*Summa Theologiae*, Vol. XLIII, ed. and trans. Thomas Gilby (London, 1964–76); the list declines according to order of gravity.

6   Lochrie, *Covert Operations*, pp. 177–227; esp. pp. 205–27.

7   Ibid., p. 181.

8   Ibid., pp. 209–11; see also Theresa Tinkle, *Medieval Venuses and Cupids: Sexuality, Hermeneutics, and English Poetry* (Stanford, California, 1996), pp. 178–97, esp. p. 190.

9   See Georgiana Donavin, *Incest Narratives and the Structure of Gower's Confessio Amantis* (Victoria, BC, 1993).

10  Ovid, *Heroides and Amores*, ed. and trans. Grant Showerman, rev. G.P. Goold, Loeb Classical Library (London, 1977); see A.C. Spearing, 'Canace and Machaire,' *Mediaevalia* 16 (1993), pp. 211–21. It should be noted that Genius does not follow the *accessus* tradition, which asserted that Ovid related the story of Canace and her brother under the heading of 'mad passion': C. David Benson, 'Incest and Moral Poetry in Gower's *Confessio Amantis*', *The Chaucer Review* 19 (1984), pp. 100–9 (p. 105). This is consistent with his rejection elsewhere of the allegorical interpretations found in the *Ovide Moralizé* of tales such as Iphis and Ianthe, or Calistona.

tion of whether or not Gower – or his mouthpiece Genius – is sympathetic in his portrayal of incest.[11] The other related issue concerns Genius's account of the role of nature in human sexuality: is it coherent or incoherent?[12] However, in an excellent article on reading and ethics in the *Confessio*, Elizabeth Allen proposes that the 'Tale of Canace' is concerned not with distinguishing between what is 'natural' or 'unnatural', but with questions of accountability; she argues that Gower's tales 'ultimately place the responsibility for moral behaviour not on nature but on the human will'.[13] Here I will develop further Allen's suggestion in order to examine the impact of gender on the distribution of responsibility and blame.

The third book of *Confessio Amantis* is concerned with Wrath. For the ease of confession, Genius follows his usual practice of dividing this mortal sin into sub-categories: melancholy, 'cheste' or contention, hate, 'contek' or strife, and homicide. The 'Tale of Canace and Machaire' appears as the first exemplary narrative embedded within this sequence. In brief, it tells of a sister and a brother, the children of a king, who are brought up together and eventually have sex. Inevitably, Canace becomes pregnant, and her brother Machaire takes flight. When their father discovers what has happened, he is overcome with rage. He has Canace kill herself, and her child is abandoned in the wilderness, to be eaten by animals. In relating this sorry story, Genius's ostensible focus is on the figure of patriarchal authority, King Eolus, who is driven by 'his sodein Malencolie/ To do so gret a felonie' (III.335–6). Genius introduces the narrative by agreeing to instruct Amans, so that he may learn: 'What mischief that this vice stereth,/ Which in his Anger noght forbereth,/ Wherof that after him forthenketh/ Whan he is sobre and that he thenketh/ Upon the folie of his dede' (III.137–41). Yet Genius's tale does not fully live up to his promise: while we may witness the horrible consequences of Eolus's violent temper, there is no evidence that the king repents his rash acts of vengeance against his daughter and grandchild. Genius has, moreover, some difficulty in making his narrative consistent. First, he has to go to some considerable lengths to make the guilt of Eolus stand out. Genius criticises Eolus for being 'strange' to love (III.213). The father's anger is depicted as immoderate, frenzied, and contrary to reason (III.210 and 245). It is also directed solely at the daughter rather than the daughter and the son. The effect of this is to suggest that Eolus is less offended by the nature of the crime than concerned that he has lost control of his daughter's sexuality. Indeed, he seems to be implicated in the sin of his children: the 'melancholy' that lies behind his wrath implies some sort of love-longing.[14] Furthermore, as we will

---

[11] For an overview of critical responses up to the early 1980s, see Benson, 'Incest and Moral Poetry', pp. 100–2.

[12] Lochrie states that 'one of the most blatant problems with Genius's taxonomy of sins against love is his contradictory account of the natural world that claims love as one of its operations': *Covert Operations*, p. 207. See also Hugh White, *Nature, Sex, and Goodness in a Medieval Literary Tradition* (Oxford, 2000), pp. 174–219.

[13] Elizabeth Allen, 'Chaucer Answers Gower: Constance and the Trouble with Reading', *English Literary History* 63 (1997), pp. 627–55 (p. 632).

[14] María Bullón-Fernández, *Fathers and Daughters in Gower's* Confessio Amantis: *Authority, Family, State, and Writing* (Cambridge, 2000), pp. 160–1.

see, his own loss of reason parallels that of his children. It seems that, in psychoanalytical terms, Eolus has repressed his own guilty desire for his daughter, only for it to resurface in the ire which he directs at her and her child.

At the same time as he establishes Eolus's culpability, Genius vindicates the sinful relationship between Canace and Machaire. We are told that the siblings are in effect driven by instinct into each other's arms:

> While thei be yonge, of comun wone
> In chambre thei togedre wone,
> And as thei scholden pleide hem ofte,
> Til thei be growen up alofte
> Into the youthe of lusti age,
> Whan kinde assaileth the corage
> With love and doth him forto bowe,
> That he no reson can allowe,
> Bot halt the lawes of nature:
> For whom that love hath under cure,
> As he is blind himself, riht so
> He makth his client blind also.  (III.149–60)

Some six lines later, this argument is reiterated:

> And so it fell hem ate laste,
> That this Machaire with Canace
> Whan thei were in a prive place,
> Cupide bad hem ferst to kisse,
> And after sche which is Maistresse
> In kinde and techeth every lif
> Withoute lawe positif,
> Of which sche takth nomaner charge,
> But kepth hire lawes al at large,
> Nature, tok hem into lore
> And tawt hem so, that overmore
> Sche hath hem in such wise daunted,
> That thei were, as who seith, enchaunted.  (VIII.166–78)

The inclusion of the personifications, Nature, kinde, and love, alongside Cupid contributes to our sense that the two lovers are subject to external forces beyond their control. In suggesting that incest can be driven by instinct, Genius follows Thomist definitions, which imply that although incest is to be condemned as a form of unchastity, it is not necessarily contrary to nature.[15] Indeed, as Gower goes on to explain in Book VIII of the *Confessio*, sibling incest was believed to have been sanctioned by God until the time of Abraham: 'Forthi that time it was no Sinne/ The Soster for to take hire brother,/ Whan that ther was of choise non other' (VIII.68–70). Retrospectively, these lines may help explain Genius's efforts to absolve Canace and Machaire. In his account of their affair, Genius emphasises the youthfulness of the two lovers (and cf. III.227), and their isola-

---

[15] Aquinas, *Temperance*, q. 154, a. 9.

tion. They are, in a sense, in their own First Age, and thus apparently exempt from ecclesiastical moral prohibition (the 'lawe positif' of III.172, which in Thomist thought is contrasted with natural law).[16] It seems that there is no one to teach the children right from wrong.[17] They are also lacking choice: alone together in their chamber, they have no companions, and there is no other outlet for their emerging sexuality. To underscore the innocence of Canace and Machaire, Genius chooses to conclude his tale with a further extended discussion of the evil consequences of melancholy. He warns Amans that he should restrain his anger against those who love and find themselves compelled to follow the dictates of Nature (III.337–60), and adds another *exemplum* – the 'Tale of Tiresias' (III.361–80) – to back up this argument.

Genius's debt to Ovid is visible in the retelling of this tale in *Confessio Amantis*. In *Heroides*, the entire story is narrated in epistolary form, and the point of view is solely that of the letter writer, Canace. The first half of the narrative is concerned with her growing passion for her brother, the second concentrates on her suffering and grief. This perspective is partially preserved in Gower's version: one fifth of the way into the story, Machaire disappears from sight, allowing the conflict between father and daughter to dominate the remainder. Canace is the only character granted direct speech (she begs for the king's mercy at III.225–31), and – in an implicit acknowledgement of the form of the source story – she expresses her despair in a letter to her brother before her forced suicide (III.279–305). The theme of uncontrollable fury, the main stated concern of Genius's tale, is present in Ovid: Aeolus is god of the winds, but cannot rule his own anger (*Heroides*, XI.11–16). In Ovid, Canace also describes her father's savage cruelty at length (*Heroides*, XI.73–100). Yet Ovid's version differs from Genius's in that it does not offer any extenuation of the incestuous relationship, and consequently Ovid's Aeolus appears justified in punishing it with severity.

Genius's sensitive portrayal of Canace is consistent with his innovative defence of Canace and Machaire. However, discordant elements are introduced into Gower's version of the tale, which point to a harsher judgement of the two lovers than the one stated. While Genius may suggest that the siblings are ignorant of moral law, the very fact that they hide their relationship betrays some knowledge of sin and error. The narrator tells us that like the bird lured into the net by bait, the couple saw 'no peril' (III.185; the phrase is repeated by Canace at III.229). But as soon as they realise that their affair is about to be exposed, both reveal their awareness of guilt: Canace by trying to hide, Machaire by fleeing. Canace and Machaire are not innocent; they simply choose not to think about the consequences of their actions until it is too late. Canace subsequently acknowledges to her father that she has acted wrongly (III.227). Paradoxically, the 'Tale of Tiresias', related by Genius in order to reinforce his contention that it is a mistake to interfere with the course of nature, actually undermines it.[18] In

---

16 Donavin, *Incest Narratives*, pp. 35–6; and see, especially, Kurt Olsson, 'Natural Law and John Gower's *Confessio Amantis*', *Medievalia et Humanistica* n.s. 11 (1982), pp. 229–61.

17 In Ovid, Canace has a nurse in whom she confides, and with whom she colludes (*Heroides*, XI.33–72).

18 See James Simpson, *Sciences and the Self in Medieval Poetry: Alan of Lille's Anticlaudianus and John Gower's Confessio Amantis* (Cambridge, 1995), pp. 176–7.

Genius's version, Tiresias is punished by the gods for lashing out in anger and killing a pair of copulating snakes: 'for he hath destourbed kinde/ And was so to nature unkinde' (III.373–4). Genius defends Canace and Machaire by claiming that reason has been overcome by instinct and desire at the same time as he admits that humankind is set apart from the animals: 'Wherof thou miht be reson wite,/ More is a man than suche a beste' (III.382–3). Later, in Book VII, Genius argues for the supremacy of reason, which should always control the will and lust:

> For god the lawes hath assissed
> Als wel to reson as to kinde,
> Bot he the bestes wolde binde
> Only to lawes of nature,
> Bot to the mannes creature
> God yaf him reson forth withal,
> Wherof that he nature schal
> Upon the causes modefie,
> That he schal do no lecherie,
> And yit he schal his lustes have.  (VII.5372–81)

Canace and Machaire are like their father in that they show no reason (III.156), nor do they demonstrate insight (III.181) or intelligent thought (III.187–8). In other words, they behave like brute beasts.[19] Incest may be natural, but it is also, in Genius's own terms, a vice (III.388). As Winthrop Wetherbee puts it, in his portrayal of Canace and Machaire, Genius depicts the abomination of 'a moral void'.[20]

Despite hints that Machaire initiated the affair (III.163–5), responsibility for the incestuous relationship is, at the start of the story, shared evenly between sister and brother. However, the distribution of blame clearly shifts in the course of the narrative. It is, after all, Canace and her child who receive the full force of the father's wrath, while the brother escapes punishment. Gower integrates allegorical dimensions into this story. The story as Genius tells it has resonances of the expulsion of Adam and Eve; indeed, there is a telling allusion to the 'falle' of Canace and Machaire at III.180.[21] This can be seen in the famous description of Canace's suicide:

> The pomel of the swerd to grounde
> Sche sette, and with the point a wounde
> Thurghout hire herte anon sche made,
> And forth with that al pale and fade
> Sche fell doun ded fro ther sche stod.
> The child lay bathende in hire blod
> Out rolled fro the moder barm,

---

19  Benson, 'Incest and Moral Poetry', p. 104.
20  Winthrop Wetherbee, 'Constance and the World in Chaucer and Gower', *John Gower: Recent Readings*, ed. R.F. Yeager (Kalamazoo, Michigan, 1989), pp. 65–93 (p. 67).
21  See Benson, 'Incest and Moral Poetry', p. 103.

And for the blod was hot and warm,
He basketh him aboute thrinne. (III.307–15)

For many critics, this passage simply reinforces the argument that Genius's (and Gower's) compassion actually lies with Canace. According to Rosemary Woolf, for example, 'it is she who is seen primarily as the pathetic and helpless victim of her father's fury'.[22] Nevertheless, the child bathing in its mother's blood is a complex image not only of innocence, but also of original sin.[23] While the immediately preceding portrait of the mother embracing the child in her bosom may remind us of visual images of the Virgin and Christ-child, the baby wallowing in the gore flowing from its mother's corpse is a horrific reversal and parody of the pietà. The child is stained with the crimes of its mother. Eolus, like the vengeful God of the Old Testament, will punish it for the iniquity it has inherited. Genius depicts Canace as an Eve-figure, whose suffering body bears witness to her transgressions; Machaire is an Adam, exiled from his first home. Yet if the 'Tale of Canace and Machaire' is in part an allegory of the Fall, it is a revisionist one. The leading figures remain individuals, not abstractions. Unlike the Eve and Adam of medieval exegesis, there is no suggestion in this Tale either that Canace represents the flesh, or that Machaire stands for the higher faculty of reason. Nor does Canace stand accused of leading Machaire into sin. The child has to suffer next to its mother for the sin of incest jointly committed by its parents, but the injustice of this and the inequity of the distribution of punishment between sister and brother is made manifest.

## Sins against Nature: The Vindication of Iphis

Wrath and disturbing the course of nature are represented by Genius in the tales of Canace and Tiresias as sins against nature. But what of unnatural vices such as bestiality or self-abuse (masturbation)? Neither of these sins is discussed in *Confessio Amantis*. Nor does Genius relate any tales of sodomy between men. This is particularly surprising, given his namesake's explicit and condemnatory treatment of the subject of sodomy in *Le Roman de la Rose* and Alain de Lille's *De Planctu Naturae*,[24] and given the number of tales (eight in total) concerned with the subject of homosexuality in Ovid's *Metamorphoses*.[25] There could be a number of reasons for this omission.[26] To cite just one, it is possible that Gower

---

22 Rosemary Woolf, 'Moral Chaucer and Kindly Gower', *J.R.R. Tolkien, Scholar and Storyteller: Essays in Memoriam*, ed. Mary Salu and Robert T. Farrell (Ithaca, 1979), pp. 221–45 (p. 227).
23 See Thomas J. Hatton, 'John Gower's Use of Ovid in Book III of the *Confessio Amantis*', *Mediaevalia* 13 (1987), pp. 257–74 (p. 264). Donavin describes this as a scene in which 'the perverted product of an incestuous union revels in the results of violence': *Incest Narratives*, p. 38.
24 See, for example, Elizabeth B. Keiser, *Courtly Desire and Medieval Homophobia: The Legitimation of Sexual Pleasure in Cleanness and its Contexts* (London, 1997), esp. pp. 71–92, 113–33.
25 Reference is to Ovid, *Metamorphoses*, ed. and trans. Frank Justus Miller, Loeb Classical Library (London, 1916), Vols I–II. The complete list appears in Mark D. Jordan, *The Invention of Sodomy in Christian Theology* (Chicago, 1997) p. 81, n. 70.
26 See Diane Watt, 'Sins of Omission: Transgressive Genders, Subversive Sexualities and Confessional Silences in John Gower's *Confessio Amantis*', *Exemplaria* 13 (2001), pp. 529–51.

felt that it would be inappropriate to introduce the subject in a narrative centred on a confession. Chaucer's Parson referred to sodomy as 'thilke abhomynable synne, of which that no man unnethe oghte speke ne write' (X (I).909).[27] Priests were warned to avoid the topic, or approach it only indirectly, for fear that it might inspire inappropriate lust in confessor and/or penitent.[28] It is perfectly appropriate, given his role, that Genius should not mention it. Genius does, however, relate a story taken from Ovid's *Metamorphoses* (IX.666–797) which is concerned with *female* same-sex desire: the 'Tale of Iphis and Ianthe' (IV.451–505). This brief narrative tells of Iphis, a girl brought up as a boy, who, having been betrothed to another girl, Ianthe, is subsequently and miraculously transformed into a man. One of Genius's main innovations in his rendering is to make it clear that a sexual relationship develops between the two young women *before* the conflict surrounding Iphis's sex is resolved. If one were to follow Aquinas, who defined sodomy as intercourse 'with a person of the same sex, male with male, female with female', the relationship would be regarded as abhorrent.[29] Genius does not appear to see it in such a light. Even in Ovid, Iphis laments at length that her love cannot be fulfilled because it is monstrous, contrary to nature, and more insane than bestiality (*Metamorphoses*, IX.726–63). Gower's protagonist has no such concerns, and Genius represents her, and her partner, as exempt from blame.

There are a number of rather striking parallels between the 'Tale of Canace and Machaire' and the 'Tale of Iphis and Ianthe'. In both narratives the central focus is on the triangular relationship between a king and two children, and at its heart lies the father-daughter relationship. In the 'Tale of Iphis and Ianthe', King Ligdus initiates the crisis by announcing that if his pregnant wife bears a daughter rather than a son, the baby will not be allowed to live. Like Eolus, Ligdus seems given to savage and unreasonable bouts of temper: he speaks to his queen 'upon a strif' (IV.451), and, in a deviation from the source, Genius offers no motive for his cruel resolution to kill his own child.[30] Although Ligdus drops out of the narrative after the opening lines, the threat of his anger and viciousness underlies the subsequent events: if Iphis's biological sex is discovered he/she will certainly die. But the similarities between Eolus and Ligdus may be even stronger than this suggests. The legend of Iphis and Ianthe seems to have inspired other legends of cross-dressing and/or transsexual heroines and female same-sex desire in the Middle Ages.[31] One such narrative is *La Chanson d'Yde et Olive*, a continuation, in verse, of the epic poem *Huon de Bordeaux*.[32] In this story and a number of others, there emerges a clear link

---

[27]  Reference is to *The Riverside Chaucer*, ed. Larry D. Benson (Boston, 1987).

[28]  Pierre J. Payer, 'Sex and Confession in the Thirteenth Century', *Sex in the Middle Ages: A Book of Essays*, ed. Joyce E. Salisbury (New York, 1991), pp. 126–42 (p. 127).

[29]  Aquinas, *Temperance*, q. 154, a. 11.

[30]  In Ovid, Ligdus – who is portrayed, not as a king, but as a staunch and virtuous freeman – does not want to be shackled with a weak girl-child (*Metamorphoses*, IX.669–79).

[31]  See Diane Watt, 'Behaving Like a Man: Incest, Lesbian Desire, and Gender Play in *Yde et Olive* and its Adaptations', *Comparative Literature* 100 (1998), pp. 265–85.

[32]  *Esclarmonde, Clarisse et Florent, Yde et Olive: Drei Fortsetzungen der Chanson von Huon de Bordeaux*, ed. Max Schweigel (Marburg, 1889), pp. 152–62.

between incest, transvestism, and woman-woman love. It is the father's incestuous desire for his daughter, combined with his tyrannical insistence that
nothing and nobody will stand in his way, which drives the young woman into
disguising herself as a man. The flight from the father's advances and threats
leads the woman-passing-as-a-man into a series of adventures which culminate
in her/his marriage to another woman. This marriage is depicted as a sexual
relationship, and paralleled with and contrasted to the earlier one between
father-daughter. In such narratives, female same-sex desire is figured as a form
of incest (which Donavin terms 'the narcissistic sexual pursuit');[33] both are
examples of like desiring like. If father-daughter incest threatens the patriarchal
order because is goes against the laws of exogamy, female same-sex desire is
challenging because it is non-reproductive, and thus threatens to disrupt
patrilineage. Within such narratives is a hidden message, similar to that implicit
in the 'Tale of Canace and Machaire': incest breeds incest.

Returning to the 'Tale of Iphis and Ianthe', the incest threat is veiled, and the
fury of the king circumscribed. This may be largely because in this narrative
(unlike the 'Tale of Canace and Machaire') there is a maternal presence. It is as a
result of the collusion of the queen, Thelacuse, with the goddess, Isis, that
Ligdus is deceived and Iphis's life saved.[34] As with the 'Tale of Canace and
Machaire', Genius here shows considerable compassion for the plight of Iphis
and Ianthe. Once again Genius emphasises the youthfulness of the two lovers:
Iphis is engaged to Ianthe when s/he reaches the age of ten – in other words, in
the eyes of canon law, s/he is still a child and below the age of marriage
(IV.475–6; thirteen in Metamorphoses, IX.714).[35] The proximity of the two lovers
is also emphasised: 'and ofte abedde/ These children leien, sche and sche,/
Whiche of on age bothe be' (IV.478–80). For some years they remain together as
playfellows (VII.481–2), until – as in the case of Canace and Machaire – the
combined and externalised forces of Nature and Cupid intervene. The former
makes them sexually active, if not sexually aware: 'Nature . . ./ Constreigneth
hem, so that thei use / Thing which to hem was al unknowe' (IV.484–7). The
latter takes pity on them because, confusingly, 'love hateth nothing more / Than
thing which stant ayein the lore / Of that nature in kinde hath sett' (IV.493–5),
and transforms Iphis into a man. Genius goes on to emphasise that it is only as a
man that Iphis can enjoy 'kinde love' (IV.502) and a life 'Which was to kinde non
offence' (IV.505). A number of critics have commented on the contradictions in
Genius's narrative. Genius effectively tells us that Iphis and Ianthe are led by

---

33  Donavin, *Incest Narratives*, p. 50.
34  In Ovid, the role of the two is even greater: first, Iphis appears to Telethusa in a dream, and
    then later, in response to Telethusa's prayer, she performs the miracle of Iphis's transforma-
    tion (*Metamorphoses*, IX.684–701 and 770–84); a nurse is also involved in the deception (*Meta-
    morphoses*, IX.706–7).
35  Woolf, 'Moral Chaucer,' p. 225 and n. 8. Iphis is also below the age of criminal responsibility:
    Shulamith Shahar, *Childhood in the Middle Ages*, trans. Chaya Galai (London, 1992), pp. 24–6.
    Carolyn Dinshaw points out that according to John Mirk's *Instructions for Parish Priests*, chil-
    dren over the age of seven, possibly even those of the same sex, should be prohibited from
    sleeping together in order to avoid the possibility of fornication: *Getting Medieval: Sexualities
    and Communities, Pre- and Post-modern* (London, 1999), pp. 10–11.

Nature into a sexual relationship which is itself contrary to natural law.[36] There seems no solution to this problem. Genius doesn't concern himself with it, and concludes optimistically:

> And thus to take an evidence,
> It semeth love is welwillende
> To hem that ben continuende
> With besy herte to poursuie
> Thing which that is to love due.  (IV.506–10)

Genius draws a moral from the story which is compatible with those he extracted from the Tales of Canace and Machaire and of Tiresias. If it is wrong to disturb the course of nature, no matter how perverse (incest) or revolting (copulating snakes) it might seem, then it is right to further it, even if to do so is to encourage 'unnatural' desires.

What then of the allocation of blame in the 'Tale of Iphis and Ianthe'? In this narrative, Genius shows only compassion for the predicaments in which first Thelacuse and then Iphis and Ianthe find themselves. Only the behaviour of Ligdus is open to reproach, although Genius does not speak out openly against him. In a tale such as Gower's of Iphis and Ianthe – where the disruptive potential of female same-sex desire is largely that it undermines patrilineage – when that threat is dissipated, female same-sex desire loses its significance and disappears from view.[37] Yet Iphis is not merely exempt from blame, s/he is actually offered as a *positive* role model to Amans. Genius prefaces the narrative by promising to tell a Tale which reveals that 'The god of love is favorable/ To hem that ben of love stable' (IV.443–4). He concludes it by stating that he has illustrated that it is 'grete besinesse' (IV.513) rather than Sloth which achieves the goal of love. Such moralising begs the question of how not only female same-sex desire, but also sex transformation can go uncondemned by Genius. We might, after all, remember that in the 'Tale of Tiresias', Genius represents the mutation of man into a woman as unnatural:

> And for he hath destourbed kinde
> And was so to nature unkinde,
> Unkindeliche he was transformed,
> That he which erst a man was formed
> Into a womman was forschape.  (III.373–7)

Gower here actually changes his source material (Ovid does not describe the

---

[36] See Woolf, who argues that 'Gower has obscured the moral issue': 'Moral Chaucer', p. 225; Lochrie agrees, *Covert Operations*, pp. 214–16; as does Dinshaw, *Getting Medieval*, p. 11; and White, *Nature, Sex, and Goodness*, pp. 192–4. For an attempt to resolve the contradictions, see R.F. Yeager, 'Learning to Read in Tongues: Writing Poetry for a Trilingual Culture', *Chaucer and Gower: Difference, Mutuality, Exchange*, ed. R.F. Yeager (Victoria, BC, 1991), pp. 120–6.

[37] For the argument that what we would now think of as lesbian activities do not count in medieval culture, see Ruth Gilbert, 'Boys will be . . . What? Gender, Sexuality and Childhood in *Floire et Blancheflor* and *Floris et Lyriope*', *Exemplaria* 9:1 (1997), pp. 31–62 (p. 45).

metamorphosis in these terms).[38] The reproach is his innovation. Why then does Genius not deplore Iphis's sex-change in similar terms? Do we have here a further example of the confusion over what is natural and what is unnatural? My argument is that we do not, in this instance. According to certain medieval theories of medicine, the one-sex model, the transformation from female to male was not in itself contrary to nature.[39] Indeed, because women were perceived to be inferior to men, such a transformation from female to male could only be seen as an improvement, a change from an imperfect state to a perfect one; it could bestow on the woman a potency she would otherwise lack. Iphis suffers no punishment for cross-dressing; quite the opposite, as she is rewarded for her perseverance and strength of character. If, according to Lochrie, Genius defines Sloth as 'the abdication of masculinity', then by demonstrating 'besiness' Iphis is laying claim to the virtues of manhood.[40] Lochrie is surely wrong to dismiss Iphis as a 'caricature' of the masculine ideal, a mere imitation of virility and patriarchal power.[41] What is striking about Genius's stance is that he does not exclude women from masculinity, but rather allows the masculine woman to exist as a positive exemplary model and distinct gender category.[42]

### Rape or Seduction? The Allocation of Blame in the 'Tale of Calistona'

A key area of conflict in questions of sex and accountability is that of rape. Arguments over who is responsible for the forced violation of a woman – aggressor or victim – continue to be waged in the twenty-first century. Claire Fanger has offered the potentially radical argument that in Gower's writings, 'rape is never the woman's fault'.[43] Certainly, there are a number of rape narratives in the *Confessio*, including the Tales of Tereus (who raped Philomela) and Arrons (who raped Lucrece), which condemn the men outright. But how sustainable is Fanger's position? After the 'Tale of Acteon' (discussed below), the second most oft-recounted story involving Diana is that of Calistona. Gower's treatment of this legend in Book V of the *Confessio* (lines 6225–6337) is highly original; he translates and transforms his sources. (The story is told by Ovid, Apollodorus, Hyginus, and Euripedes; Calistona, or more commonly Calisto or Callisto, is not named by Ovid in *Metamorphoses*, II.409–530.)[44] Genius includes the 'Tale of Calistona' under the heading of 'Robbery', because it ostensibly describes Jupiter's theft of Calistona's virginity ('thilke good/ Which every womman that is

[38] See Hatton, 'Use of Ovid', pp. 264–5.
[39] Thomas Laqueur, *Making Sex: Body and Gender from the Greeks to Freud* (Cambridge, MA, 1990), pp. 134–42; but see also Joan Cadden, *The Meanings of Sex Difference in the Middle Ages: Medicine, Science and Culture* (Cambridge, 1993), esp. p. 3.
[40] Lochrie, *Covert Operations*, p. 212.
[41] Ibid., p. 216.
[42] For a recent study of the politics of this issue in relation to modern culture, see Judith Halberstam, *Female Masculinity* (London, 1998).
[43] Claire Fanger, 'Magic and the Metaphysics of Gender in Gower's *Tale of Circe and Ulysses*', *Re-Visioning Gower*, ed. R.F. Yeager (Asheville, NC, 1998), pp. 203–20 (p. 218).
[44] *Confessio Amantis*, ed. Macaulay, Vol. II, p. 506, n. 6225ff; Valerie Traub, 'The Perversion of "Lesbian" Desire', *History Workshop Journal* 41 (1996), pp. 19–49 (p. 27).

good/ Desireth forte kepe and holde': V.6345–7). Yet, typically, the narrative offers no simple correlation between moral and *exemplum*. In Gower's version, Jupiter may commit the crime, but the woman, Calistona, is the one who is castigated and punished. The fact that Calistona is held responsible by Genius for her own expulsion from Diana's chaste troop seems to undermine the argument that Genius does not scapegoat women for the crimes of men. However, as we will see, Gower adapts his sources, so that Calistona is no longer the victim of rape, but of her own lack of self-control, and therefore 'merits' her punishment as an individual who has sinned.

Genius begins the tale in typical romance fashion by telling us of Calistona's parentage: 'King Lichaon upon his wif/ A dowhter hadde, a goodly lif,/ A clene Maide of worthi fame,/ Calistona whos rihte name/ Was cleped' (V.6225–9). He goes on to relate how many suitors approached Calistona, but were unable to win her love because she had 'no lust therinne' (V.6232) and resolved to remain a virgin and to join Diana's troop.[45] Genius tells us, in other words, that Calistona removes herself from the marriage market by making what amounts to a religious oath. This notion is picked up on later in the narrative, when the angry goddess Juno (incensed by the fact that Calistona has had sex with her faithless husband Jupiter) castigates her as an 'ungoodlich ypocrite' (V.6293) in the name of Calistona's own father, who 'Schal noght be glad, whan he it wot/ Of that his dowhter was so hot,/ That sche hath broke hire chaste avou' (V.6299–301). Genius – or Juno – thus figures Calistona's loss as an affront to patriarchy: by breaking her covenant, Calistona has offended against her father's right to dispose of his own daughter, his right to marry her to the most appropriate comer. In Ovid, in contrast, the only reference to Calistona's father occurs when Juno rants against Jupiter's incorrigible behaviour, claiming that he might as well take Lycaon as a father-in-law and be done with it (*Metamorphoses*, II.523–6). Lycaon has of course already been turned into a wolf in the *Metamorphoses*, following his own defiance of Jupiter (*Metamorphoses*, I.237), and is thus presumably beyond caring about the fate of his daughter. The emphasis in Genius's tale on Calistona's father is important because it has the effect of making her crime seem the greater (it is a crime against patriarchy) and Calistona the more deserving of punishment.

In a further change to the Ovidian original (in which it is the other nymphs rather than their captain who notice that Diana's former favourite is pregnant), Diana is a knowing and a vengeful goddess, who 'in a ragerie' (V.6258), that is in 'sport' but surely also, in this context, with connotations of 'fury',[46] forces Calistona to bathe naked in her sight. Having exposed Calistona's sin, Genius's Diana exclaims: ' "Awey, thou foule beste,/ For thin astat is noght honeste/ This chaste water forto touche;/ For thou hast take such a touche,/ Which nevere mai ben hol ayein" ' (V.6275–79). These lines anticipate Calistona's subsequent punishment, when she is transformed into a bear by a jealous Juno, suggesting perhaps that the events which follow are down to Diana as much as to Jupiter's

---

[45] Cf. the account of Diana's rejection of marriage at V.1259–69.

[46] MED s.v. 'ragerie' a: 'sprightliness, gaiety, mirth; also, a fit of playfulness, spirit of frolic'; but cf. 'ragen' 1: 'To be furious, have a fit of insanity'.

beleaguered wife. In fact, Calistona's subsequent fate echoes that of Acteon, when she narrowly escapes being killed by her own son, out hunting in the woods. Thus, in the narrative itself if not the moral, Genius focuses on the guilt of the woman; Jupiter in the meantime is let off the hook.

To understand why Genius does this we have to look at two other significant changes Gower makes to the Ovidian tale. First of all, Gower actually removes the rape from the narrative. Ovid, in *Metamorphoses*, II.425, describes how Jupiter disguises himself as Diana in order to get close to her beloved follower. This enables him to take Calistona by force, despite her resistance (which Ovid tellingly emphasises: *Metamorphoses*, II.434–7). Genius, in contrast, simply states that Jupiter took her 'maidenhode' by means of his 'queintise' or cunning (V.6246 and 6249).[47] In Gower's tale itself, there is little to suggest that Jupiter actually forced Calistona to have sex with him: rape is translated into seduction.[48] The final change Gower makes to this story follows on from the first in so far as, by removing the account of the rape, there is no need to mention Jupiter's cross-dressing. Superficially, it might seem that Gower is 'straightening out' this narrative by removing the kisses which Calistona willingly exchanges with the figure she takes to be 'Diana', in other words, by removing the homoerotic references. But this is too simple an explanation. In Gower's tale, allusion is made to the 'spring of freisshe welles' (V.6239) in which Diana and her nymphs desport themselves. Such wells or grottos can simultaneously be read as symbolic of chastity and also, paradoxically, as symbolic of female eroticism: the motion of water recalls masturbation, while the playful activity of this troop of nubile young women is suggestive of same-sex female desire.[49] Writing about the sensuality of Renaissance depictions of Diana bathing with her nymphs, Patricia Simons observes that 'the very sensual anarchism or slipperiness of the visual image may encourage "deviant" and "perverse" possibilities we have not yet allowed ourselves to see'.[50] This comment is applicable to narrative representations in the earlier period, and Gower's tale can be seen to maintain some of the sensual elements found in the original story. Calistona's metamorphosis is the focal point of the illustrations to this story in the illuminated manuscripts of the *Confessio*. Oxford, New College MS 266, for example, emphasises Calistona's

---

[47] There may be a subtle allusion here to Jupiter's passing as a woman in the source narratives. For the sexual connotations of the noun 'queynte', see *The Wife of Bath's Prologue*, III(D).332 and 444.

[48] The Latin commentary to the tale at V.6227 is less equivocal than the English narrative: we are told of Jupiter 'virginis castitatem subtili furto surripiens' (snatching the virgin's chastity by secret theft).

[49] See Bettina Mathes, 'From Nymph to Nymphomania: "Linear Perspectives" on Female Sexuality', *The Arts of Seventeenth-Century Science: Representations of Natural Knowledge in European and North American Culture*, ed. Claire Jowitt and Diane Watt (Aldershot, 2002), pp. 179–83.

[50] Patricia Simons, 'Lesbian (In)visibility in Italian Renaissance Culture: Diana and Other Cases of *donna con donna*', *Journal of Homosexuality* 27 (1994), pp. 81–122 (p. 110). As Traub explains, 'the ideology of chastity rendered same-gender female eroticism between conventionally "feminine" women [such as Diana and her nymphs] as culturally insignificant': 'The Perversion of "Lesbian" Desire', p. 25. See also Christine Downing, *Myths and Mysteries of Same-Sex Love* (New York, 1989), pp. 184–98.

exclusion, by representing her after her transformation into a bear.[51] The bear is positioned in the foreground, watching (enviously?) as five naked nymphs in the stream attempt, not entirely successfully, to shield their breasts and pubic area from view. Our gaze is aligned with that of the bear, and we are drawn into the eroticism of the scene by the perspective granted us and by the voyeurism of the situation.

What then is the effect of the omission of Jupiter's cross-dressing, if not to edit out any allusion to same-sex desire? In the story as we have it, Calistona indulges in heterosexual rather than same-sex sexual relations. To place this narrative in perspective, we have to recall Gower's compassionate treatment of the 'Tale of Iphis and Ianthe', in which two girls do sleep together. It may be that Calistona is condemned here, not only because she is not represented as a victim of rape, but also because *as the story is told* she cannot claim she has been tricked into thinking she is with another woman (Diana). Gower's version of this tale encourages the reader to think that, because Calistona is neither raped nor even, it seems, deceived, she may have desired Jupiter; in other words, that she has simply been seduced. Ultimately, then, in Gower's version, it is Calistona who has broken her vow and it is she, not Jupiter, who is guilty of theft because she robbed herself of her maidenhead. That is why Diana as well as Juno makes sure that she is punished. The moral seems to come down to a statement about self-control and accountability. In Gower's version Calistona is made to take the blame, not for Jupiter's actions, but for a deed for which she herself is ultimately culpable.

### Gower's Sexual Poetics?

The title of the final section of my essay refers, of course, to Carolyn Dinshaw's book, *Chaucer's Sexual Poetics*.[52] In this key feminist study of the late 1980s, Dinshaw locates her analysis of Chaucer's construction of gender and sexuality within the broader context of an explication of the gendering of literary activity. According to medieval literary theory, the text is feminine, to be written and interpreted by a masculine (and usually male) author or reader. What I *do not* want to do here is to ask whether Gower's treatment of gender and sexuality is the same as or different to Chaucer's. For too long, Gower has lived in the shadow of his now more famous contemporary, and has suffered from the comparison.[53] Nevertheless, it is important to acknowledge that, especially in the last decade, critics have suggested that Gower, like Chaucer, sees a connection between gender and poetics, and manipulates tales of feminine experience and suffering to describe his own creative processes. Of the tales discussed in this chapter, the only one to have been subject to such a reading is that of Canace

---

51  Oxford, New College, MS 266, fol. 124r; cf. New York, Pierpont Morgan, MS M126, fol. 126r. The illustration in the latter manuscript shows Calistona as a bear being shot at by her son.
52  Carolyn Dinshaw, *Chaucer's Sexual Poetics* (Madison, Wisconsin, 1989).
53  For a fascinating analysis of the gender politics behind the critical construct of the rivalry between Chaucer and Gower, see Carolyn Dinshaw, 'Rivalry, Rape and Manhood: Chaucer and Gower', *Chaucer and Gower*, ed. R.F. Yeager, pp. 130–52.

and Machaire. Bullón-Fernández, for example, argues that the narrative is a metaphor for the curtailing of literary creativity.[54] Developing this idea further, we might suggest that sexual relationships also function in Gower's writing to articulate the writer's own language politics. The *Confessio Amantis* was Gower's first major English poem; previously he had composed his poetry in the élite languages of Latin and Anglo-Norman. His decision to write in his 'mother tongue', rather than in the languages of patriarchy, the idioms of church, state, and court, may have caused him no little anxiety. His decision to compile a collection of narratives drawn from sources which included the Bible as well as classical texts would have intensified this. At times Gower seems to draw our attention to the problems inherent in the process of translation; a process that is often figured in hierarchical and sometimes in gendered terms.[55] The conflict between Gower's authoritative and masculine sources and the vernacular, feminine rendering, which is mirrored in the tensions between the exemplary narratives and their respective morals, and between the Latin commentaries and the corresponding Middle-English text, is manifest throughout the poem. The image of incest which is at the heart of the *Confessio Amantis* may even be taken to represent the creative but potentially risky process of translation, which threatens to break social taboos and religious prohibitions, and which may, ultimately, result in chaos.

However, the main point I want to make here is that the construction of gender and sexuality is important in its own right. The conflict between the sexes does not have to be read metaphorically as an exploration of other issues, be they literary, political or religious.[56] Going against the tide of recent gender criticism, I would like to suggest that when a writer like Gower writes about women or men, about homosexual or heterosexual desires, or about transvestism or transsexuality, he (or she) is not necessarily discussing something else. Marjorie Garber has famously argued that we should not look through, but *at* the transvestite – but surely the same applies to all genders and sexualities?[57] For example, it is important in the narratives discussed above to look at the women *as women*. Gower's main concern in the *Confessio Amantis* is how people live their lives, how they conduct themselves in public and in private, but gender, sexuality and ethics are interconnected issues. Just as they cannot be separated or discussed in isolation, so we should not always or automatically ascribe some sort of further signification to discussions of gender and sexuality.

Up to now I have looked principally at narratives centred on women, and so to conclude – and to draw together my arguments in this essay – I wish to

---

[54] Bullón-Fernández, *Fathers and Daughters*, pp. 167–172. Canace's death represents not only Eolus's assertion of his control over Canace's body, but also his desire to terminate a narrative (the story of Canace) over which he has lost authorial control. According to this reading the tale also points towards the limitations of the discourses of courtly love and of patriarchy more generally.

[55] Alexandra Barrett, ed., *Women's Writing in Middle English* (London, 1992), p. 13.

[56] Bullón-Fernández's main concern is in fact the ways in which Gower utilises the father-daughter dyad to describe relations between a king and his subject: *Fathers and Daughters*. Lochrie agrees that in Gower 'gender ideology secures a range of social, political and theological ideals': *Covert Operations*, pp. 224–5.

[57] Marjorie Garber, *Vested Interests: Cross-Dressing and Cultural Anxiety* (London, 1992), p. 9.

examine a sequence of short *exempla* in which the focus is mainly on men. In
*Confessio Amantis*, Book I.333–529, Genius relates the tales of Acteon, Medusa,
the Serpent, and the Sirens. In so doing, he moves seamlessly from describing
the justified if extreme vengeance wreaked by the beautiful, chaste goddess
Diana, to the motiveless man-hating malignity of the snake-like one-eyed
Gorgons, who are deformed as well as unnatural. He follows these accounts
with the seductive evil of the Sirens, who, although fish from the waist down,
are 'Of body bothe and of visage/ Lik unto wommen of yong age' (I.487–8).
Having Genius relate these stories in this way, Gower appears to follow anti-
-feminist tradition in depicting the female (and this includes Diana, judging
from the company she keeps in this section) as Venus-like; dangerously alluring,
malevolent, and monstrous.[58] However, it is all too easy to miss the fact that
Genius includes one other tale in the midst of this sequence: the positive
example of the serpent, Aspidis. Aspidis protects himself from the enchantment
of men, who try to charm him in order to steal the carbuncle embedded in his
forehead, by stopping one ear with his tail, and pressing the other to the ground.
Here, in a curiously homoerotic twist, it is the would-be (male) thieves who are
potentially seductive and destructive, while the monstrous serpent is praised for
his prudence. The effect of this story on the surrounding narratives is two-fold:
first, it illustrates that temptation is not necessarily personified as female;
second, it reveals that the monstrous is not necessarily equated with either femininity or with evil. Thus, it may be less that Diana is rendered monstrous by
associating her with the Gorgons and the Sirens, than that the Gorgons and the
Sirens are elevated to the status of rational beings by being discussed in the
context of Diana and Aspidis. But equally important in this context is the fact
that Gower has Genius hold men accountable for their own deeds, making it
clear that self-control (and especially control of the senses) is paramount.
Indeed, the substantial Latin commentary to the 'Tale of Acteon' (at I.334) points
towards the earnest moral behind this slight and flippantly related *exemplum*.
Acteon is rightly punished because he does not turn his view away from the
naked Diana, who is bathing and playing in the flood in the company of her
nymphs. Perseus literally shields his eyes, and is thus able to slay Medusa and
her sisters. Ulysses and his men block their hearing, and escape the lure of the
Sirens. The autonomous 'phallic' women described in the first book of the
*Confessio* (Diana, the Gorgons, Medusa and the Sirens) are only dangerous
because of the weakness of men.

Genius's take on sexual sin is a complex one. Subjects like male sodomy,
bestiality and self-abuse remain taboo. Rape is unacceptable. Incest is viewed
with some ambivalence. Female same-sex desire and sexual transformation are
not condemned. In these tales, the distinction between the natural and the
unnatural, between virtue and vice, becomes blurred. But despite this, the poem
gives clear moral guidance, which applies to both sexes. Genius treats women as
rational beings not only by exculpating them but also, on occasion, by judging

58 On the sexuality of Artemis/Diana, see Downing, *Myths and Mysteries*, pp. 210–12; and also
Simons, 'Lesbian (In)visibility', pp. 81–122; esp. pp. 94–109; and Traub, 'The Perversion of
"Lesbian" Desire', pp. 23–49.

and punishing them according to their intentions and actions. When the punishment is unjust or too extreme, as in the case of Canace, this is allowed to stand out. The central ethical message of the sequence involving Aspidis, Acteon, Perseus and Ulysses is that men have to act responsibly and will be made to suffer for their own failures. The central ethical message of the *Confessio Amantis* as a whole is that the responsibility for sin or error falls firmly on the individual who commits it, male or female.

# 12

## *The Politics and Psychology of Governance in Gower: Ideas of Kingship and Real Kings*

### RUSSELL A. PECK

In one of the more important essays written on John Gower, George R. Coffman argued that to appreciate Gower's work we must keep in mind its political significance.[1] Writing at the end of the second World War, Coffman perceived astutely the impact of social disorder on literary consciousness, suggesting that social concerns, particularly in times of chaos, take priority over aesthetic concerns in literary production. In this regard Coffman was several decades ahead of his time in breaking away from the stipulations of textual and aesthetically oriented criticism:

> More than any other single writer, [Gower] mirrors directly the whole social range of that cosmic and chaotic period [of the late fourteenth century]. . . . In a large and significant sense it may be more important to study him as a recipient of the heritage of certain ideas which he adapts to a functional end than as a writer who assimilates his materials for the purposes of literary art.[2]

Coffman goes on to see a 'guiding principle' that runs through all of Gower's writings, a principle akin to what G.R. Owst called a 'social gospel' that cuts across all segments of class within society.[3] At the heart of this 'guiding principle' is a consistent thesis that, regardless of station or birth, 'Of al the comun poeple aboute,/ Withinne Burgh and ek withoute,/ . . ./ O lawe mot governe hem alle' (VII.1689–96).[4] For Gower, 'Ech hath his propre duete' (VII.2711), a duty which, regardless of estate, connotes a coherent, interconnected social discipline to which the individual responsibility attendant upon free choice is the linchpin. You can have good people without a good state, but you cannot have a good state without good people.

Two decades later John H. Fisher followed up on Coffman's lead, adding:

---

1  George R. Coffman, 'John Gower in his Most Significant Role', *Elizabethan Studies and Other Essays in Honor of George F. Reynolds*, University of Colorado Studies Series B. Studies in the Humanities, Vol. II, no. 4 (Boulder, CO, 1945), pp. 52–61.

2  Ibid., p. 52.

3  Ibid., p. 53, and G.R. Owst, *Literature and the Pulpit in Medieval England* (Cambridge, 1933), pp. 230–1.

4  All citations from the *Confessio Amantis* are taken from G.C. Macaulay, ed., *The English Works of John Gower*, EETS, es nos. 81 and 82 (London, 1900–1901).

'The most striking characteristic of Gower's literary production is its single-mindedness.'[5] What struck Fisher most about Gower was 'his absolute integrity, his coherent grasp of the values and ideals of his day, and his fearless expression of the moral judgements growing out of these ideals'.[6] The most single-minded of Gower's themes is the self-governance of the wise man. In this regard he well deserves the epithet of 'moral Gower' that Chaucer bestowed upon him at the end of *Troilus and Criseyde* (V.1856). Indeed, the whole of Gower's writings concern themselves with humankind's personal responsibility to rule well.

Gower conceived of wise rule in two ways: personal (psychological) and political (social). Always, both components of this hypostatic dyad are simultaneously present in Gower's ethic. Gower puts the matter succinctly at the end of the *Confessio Amantis*:

> For conseil passeth alle thing
> To him which thenkth to ben a king;
> And every man for his partie
> A kingdom hath to justefie,
> That is to sein his oghne dom.
> If he misreule that kingdom,
> He lest himself, and that is more
> Than if he loste Schip and Ore
> And al the worldes good withal:
> For what man that in special
> Hath noght himself, he hath noght elles,
> Nomor the perles than the schelles.  (VIII.2109–20)

Here Gower conceives of the hypostasis between the personal and social through images of kingship, domain, and right rule.[7] Each – the social and the personal – is contingent upon the other and operates through metaphoric interdependence. The king of England is akin to the king of the soul; the state of England is linked to one's sense of personal domain; and right rule is mirrored simultaneously through both sides of the equation. In such a reciprocal ontology, the one sees itself through the other. Each side, the personal and the social, has a king, with the other as counsellor, who, in the exchange, is nearly as crucial as the king himself: 'For conseil passeth alle thing/ To him which thenkth to ben a king' (VIII.2109–10). A healthy king needs healthy counsellors – counsellors who help justify the terms of existence for the whole metaphoric kingdom. But the bottom line of 'kingdom' (its rhyme correspondent, so to speak) is one's 'oghne dom' (VIII.2113–14), where 'oghne' (ownness, ownership, possession) and 'dom' (domain, judgement, place) locate in the self the jurisdiction of right rule or 'misreule' (VIII.2114), those tendentious relationships dependent upon personal choice. Good counsel is important if reasonable balance is to prevail. But the

---

5   John H. Fisher, *John Gower: Moral Philosopher and Friend of Chaucer* (New York, 1964), p. 135.
6   Ibid., p. v.
7   For an extended analysis of *Confessio Amantis* in terms of kingship, rule, and domain, see Russell A. Peck, *Kingship and Common Profit in Gower's Confessio Amantis* (Carbondale, IL, 1978).

king must do the choosing if the treasury of the kingdom – that priceless pearl alluded to in VIII.2120 – is to remain secure.

Both society and self are defined through interrelationships. Gower understands the bond between aspects of self (the political and the personal) in terms of reason and law. Because order is contingent upon relationship, for Gower law is more basic than king. As he explains in Book VII of the *Confessio Amantis* (that great book devoted to the education of the king):

> What is a lond wher men ben none?
> What ben the men which are al one
> Withoute a kinges governance?
> What is a king in his ligance,
> Wher that ther is no lawe in londe? . . .
> For wher the lawe mai comune
> The lordes forth with the commune,
> Ech hath his propre duete;
> And ek the kinges realte
> Of bothe his worschipe underfongeth,
> To his astat as it belongeth,
> Which of his hihe worthinesse
> Hath to governe rihtwisnesse,
> As he which schal the lawe guide. (VII.2695–2717)

Gower regularly places the crown at the top of the social order. In this respect he is profoundly monarchist. But for Gower the monarch does not have *absolute* power. His authority may, with impunity, reach beyond positive law, but it does not extend beyond natural or divine law. Wise counsel, situated in piety and humility, always reminds the king of his rightful place within divine order so that he may 'the lawe guide' for the common profit of the whole estate.

Gower is perpetually an idealist. Although there are plenty of passages in his writings indicative of a dark side to his vision, a gloom that in a few instances reaches to despondency (indeed, he sees little hope for broad social reform; vast numbers of people seldom have a moral awakening sufficient to make much difference in social revolution), he, nonetheless, never wavers in his belief in the power of God, the ultimate king, to guide his people through just laws. And among men, though the ranks will be few, there is always the possibility for the one good person to find repose in the peaceful, well-ordered estate of divine grace.

But Gower is not a theologian. His vision is acutely focused on human behaviour here and now, in all its consequences. This fact explains why the 'social gospel' Owst spoke of is always immanent in Gower. Much of his optimism is contingent on his belief in the possibilities of a just law that is beyond the reach of selfish opportunists. Opportunists may manipulate the law for selfish ends, but their effort ultimately damages them:

> If lawe stonde with the riht,
> The poeple is glad and stant upriht.
> Wher as the lawe is resonable,
> The comun poeple stant menable,

And if the lawe torne amis,
The poeple also mistorned is. (VII.2759–64)

To 'stant menable' is to have legal rights, to be accountable, to have domain. This
failure to be accountable is precisely the point upon which Gower will turn
against King Richard in the latter part of that king's reign. Reasonable maintenance of just laws makes accountability possible. Being (i.e. self) is a mere fiction
without accountability; and so too it is for kings. If the common profit is put
aside in favour of self-interest, the hypostasis of the social and personal is
broken: the king is no king, the kingdom is divided, and war and chaos ensue
with a chilling inevitability. Such disintegration is the circumstance, Gower
insists, of England in his own day:

> the regnes ben divided,
> In stede of love is hate guided,
> The werre wol no pes purchace,
> And lawe hath take hire double face,
> So that justice out of the weie
> With ryhtwisnesse is gon aweie. (Prol. 127–32)

For Gower, division is the cause of all forms of psychological, social, ethical,
linguistic and political disjunction. Division is the 'modor of confusioun' (Prol.
852), and, in crucial ways, it imposes upon the kingdom the deadliest of circumstances.[8] Good rule, for Gower, always involves balanced negotiation amidst
uncertainty and shifting terms; the wise ruler is a helmsman who learns to navi-
gate amidst such confusion.

### Good Kingship, Good Rule

All of Gower's longer poems and several of the shorter address the ethics of
kingship. One of the most striking passages defining good rule occurs in his
earliest major poem, the *Mirour de l'Omme*, where Gower uses King David as his
exemplar of kingship, citing six tropes of behaviour which all rulers should
embody: (1) King David was a shepherd; (2) King David was a harper; (3) King
David was a knight; (4) King David in his Psalter was a prophet in praise of God;
(5) though King David erred, he did penance in sorrow and tears; and (6) he was
a king who tried to reign as a mirror of good behaviour for others (*MO* lines
22,873–84). These aspects of good rule define the 'guiding principles' of which
Fisher and Coffman speak. In the Prologue to the *Confessio Amantis*, for example,
after the prophet Daniel's analysis of Nebuchadnezzar's dream and the evils of
division, Gower tells the story of Arion who, though not technically a king, is, in
his 'oghne dom', a model of good rule. Though cast into the sea, he survives

---

8   In the *Confessio* Gower places his discussion of the evil of division and its dire political conse-
    quences at the end of his account of Nebuchadnezzar's prophetic dream, which he presents as
    an allegory of the degeneration of time. The present age is like the feet of the disintegrating
    statue, a mingling of earth and steel, which lacks the strength to support the statue (Prol.
    585ff.). On the corrosive evil of division itself see, Prol. 849–1052.

with God's grace and, with his 'harpe of such temprure' that he can make 'the bestes wilde . . . tame and milde' (Prol. 1086), he, like a true shepherd, takes control of his circumstances and lives at rest in his peaceable kingdom:

> The Hinde in pes with the Leoun,
> The Wolf in pes with the Moltoun,
> The Hare in pees stod with the Hound;
> And every man upon this ground
> Which Arion that time herde,
> Als wel the lord as the schepherde,
> He broghte hem alle in good acord;
> So that the comun with the lord,
> And lord with the comun also,
> He sette in love bothe tuo
> And putte awey malencolie.  (Prol. 1059–69)

Arion's music, like David's, heals divisions even within the animal kingdom; he helps all to overcome 'the comun drede' (Prol. 1082) that stands at every man's door to disrupt repose in a peaceful life to which mankind should and can aspire, once strife and dissension have been put aside.

*Confessio Amantis* is a poem about good and bad rule. To explore the disruptive effects of division upon the human psyche,[9] Gower projects a youthful lover, Amans, who, in the chaos of his lovesickness, is sent to a confessor, Genius, who will attempt, through therapeutic questioning and catechist instruction, to teach the woeful lover by means of dozens of *exempla* to reclaim a more balanced view of himself and the world around him.[10] By examining the patterns of life embedded in tales exemplary of aspects of the Seven Deadly Sins, Genius tries to help Amans become a capable ruler within his own domain.[11] He attempts to heighten Amans' consciousness of law.[12] Law in all its forms – divine, natural, positive – regulates Gower's scheme, because more than any

---

[9] See Hugh White, 'Division and Failure in Gower's *Confessio Amantis*', *Neophilologus* 22 (1988), pp. 600–16, for an astute analysis of the ethics of division as it affects Amans and the rather dark conclusion to the poem. White developed his argument at greater length in *Nature, Sex, and Goodness in a Medieval Literary Tradition* (Oxford, 2000), where he demonstrates Gower's sophisticated ideas about the inevitable failure of his pedagogical plot because of the rawness of human sexuality and the distorted integrity of the human will as it perpetually makes self-interested choices and, given the ambiguous deceits of nature, lacks the fundamental capacity to become fully reasonable.

[10] For an excellent discussion of the role of *exempla* in Genius's instructive scheme see Charles Runacres, 'Art and Ethics in the *Exempla* of *Confessio Amantis*', *Gower's* Confessio Amantis: *Responses and Reassessments*, ed. A.J. Minnis (Cambridge, 1983), pp. 106–34.

[11] One of the most successful analyses of the therapeutic components of the poem is in James Simpson, *Sciences and the Self in Medieval Poetry: Alan of Lille's Anticlaudianus and John Gower's Confessio Amantis* (Cambridge, 1995). Simpson who sees Amans and Genius as two sides of a single entity attempting to restore a healthy, 'enformed' relationship with nature. See also *Confessio Amantis*, ed. Russell A. Peck, Vol. I (Kalamazoo, 2000), pp. 7–15.

[12] See Kurt Olsson, 'Natural Law and John Gower's *Confessio Amantis*', *Medievalia Humanistica: Studies in Medieval and Renaissance Culture*, n.s. 11 (1982), pp. 229–61, and also his important study, *John Gower and the Structures of Conversion: A Reading of the Confessio Amantis* (Cambridge, 1992).

single social function, law helps the individual get outside private interest to see objectively.

The *Confessio* is loaded with tales about good and bad rule that complement the overall plot, as Amans, that woeful 'caitif' who lies despondent in the wood (I.161ff.), ultimately puts aside his desire to live by some special law to become instead 'John Gower', a self-possessed man who prays for the welfare of England (VIII.2908ff.). Dozens of tales could be used to demonstrate the components of good rule that characterise Gower's utopic philosophy of the hypostatic individual as his personal psyche learns to live in lawful harmony with its public, social self, but let these three suffice: 'The Tale of the Three Questions' (I.3067–3402); 'The Tale of Lycurgus' (VII.2917–3025); and 'The Tale of Apollonius' (VIII.271–2008).

(1) 'The Tale of the Three Questions' is a summary tale at the end of Book I. A young king loves wisdom and trains himself rigorously: 'Of depe ymaginaciouns/ And strange interpretaciouns,/ Problemes and demandes eke/ His wisdom was to finde and seke;/ Wherof he wolde in sondri wise/ Opposen hem that weren wise' (I.3069–74). One of the king's brightest knights dares to challenge him, and, in 'an Envie' (I.3083), the king tyrannically decides to destroy his opponent by giving him a riddle he cannot answer. The penalty for a wrong answer will be death. The knight returns home, grief-stricken at his presumption. His fourteen-year-old daughter, whom he has trained to reason well, notices her father's anxiety. When she learns the cause she asks the privilege of answering in her father's place. She answers correctly, and the king is so charmed that he grants her a wish, allowing that if she were of noble birth he would marry her. She does not choose for herself, but rather asks that her father be made an earl. The king, pleased at her lack of selfishness, grants her wish. She then reminds him of his earlier observation about marriage, pointing out that she is now an earl's daughter. He, charmed even further by her wit, gladly takes her as wife.

The tale works in several ways to exemplify Gower's ideas of good rule. The king values wisdom; he also values those who are wise. Although he becomes proud and, momentarily, plays the envious tyrant, he adjusts his thinking in the presence of true wit and humbles himself before the knight by taking his daughter as his wife. The tale celebrates the education of the young and also their ability to learn. In Book VII, devoted to the education of the king, Genius instructs Amans (even as Aristotle instructed King Alexander) in five points of good policy – Truth, Liberality, Justice, Pity, and Chastity (VII.1699ff.). The 'Tale of the Three Questions' exemplifies admirably all five points; as the young king turns his envy into liberality and pity, truth is made evident through the girl's thoughtful response to the riddle, a response that enables all to see how they might benefit mutually from the other. The woman and man gain marriage partners through chaste behaviour, and justice is served for all – justice well suited to their wit. Though no harps are played, the story shines luminously in terms of the six exemplary points embodied in King David, of which Gower had spoken in the *Mirour*. The knight exemplifies the virtue of penance; the daughter, the powers of the prophet and good shepherd, as she guides the two competitive men toward a happy solution to the problem that they, in their pride, created. The young king shows all the benefit of using wit well, especially to make up for his errors. The three young people of the tale, in fact, behave so admirably in solving their dilemmas that they are given names at the end of the story, to mark their achievement of good rule.

(2) 'The Tale of Lycurgus' deals with quite different issues, but ones, nonetheless, that are crucial to Gower's views on kingship. As king, Lycurgus established in Athens so good a rule that there was no city in the world so blessed with just laws and 'the trouthe of governance' (VII.2925). Lycurgus's laws guide the people toward the mutual benefits of the common good:

> Ther was among hem no distance,
> Bot every man hath his encress;
> Ther was withoute werre pes,
> Withoute envie love stod;
> Richesse upon the comun good
> And noght upon the singuler
> Ordeigned was, and the pouer
> Of hem that weren in astat
> Was sauf: wherof upon debat
> Ther stod nothing, so that in reste
> Mihte every man his herte reste.  (VII.2926–36)

With such good laws in place he calls together his parliament and 'in audience of grete and smale' (VII.2951) he humbly tells his people the origin of the law, that it came from the god Mercurius – 'It was the god and nothing I' (VII.2971). He then tells how he must undertake a journey, but before he leaves he gets all to consent to abide by the laws. He then leaves and 'schop him nevere to be founde' (VII.3003). Thus Athens was forever bound to abide by good law set upon common profit.

The tale exemplifies as well as any in the *Confessio* the importance of common profit to good rule and the value of good laws which, if understood and consented to, are even more important than any specific king. Lycurgus succeeds because he creates just laws and finds a means whereby the people will consent to abide by those laws. As king he guides his people to rule in their 'oghne dom'. His greatness lies in the fact that the whole kingdom shares in his wisdom and enjoys the peace that ensues. In his piety he acknowledges that he has let the god work through him, which is quite different from a tyrant hanging about to play god. That he has made himself superfluous is his triumph.

(3) But the most intricate study of good rule in the *Confessio* is 'The Tale of Apollonius'. Like 'The Tale of the Three Questions' it serves a summary purpose, not just for a single book, but for the whole of the *Confessio*. Like the other two tales it examines education, riddle-solving, penance, responsible and responsive behaviour, community values, ego-control, generosity and self-fulfilment. Moreover, apropos the *Mirour*, this story, like the 'Tale of Arion' in the Prologue to the *Confessio*, demonstrates the value of a king's skill at playing the harp. It is a longer, more complex tale, but it is all the more satisfying because of that. Indeed, it is one of the great romances of all times. In brief, Prince Apollonius, who 'hath to love a gret desire' (VIII.376), sets out to see the world.

He comes to Antioch where he learns of a beautiful princess whose hand might be won in marriage if the suitor can answer a riddle; if he fails he will be killed. Apollonius figures out the answer, which reveals that the girl is her father's sexmate, and answers in a riddling way so that the king knows that he knows the truth. Apollonius returns to Tyre and, knowing that Antiochus will attempt to murder him, he takes a shipload of grain and goes into exile. He comes to Tharse where a rich burgess, Strangulio, and his wife, Dionise, take him in. The grain saves the city from famine. But, when he learns that he is pursued by an assassin, the prince sets to sea again. Fortune shipwrecks him near Pentapolim. Sole survivor of the wreck, he is found by fishermen who nurse him back to life. Artestrathes, King of Pentapolim, stages athletic games which the mysterious stranger wins. At the victory feast he meets the princess, whom he teaches to play the harp. When it is time for her to marry, she will wed no one but her music teacher. The king and queen agree to their daughter's choice because they have been impressed by the youth's *gentilesse* and because they know their daughter is a good judge of people. Word comes that Antiochus is dead and his daughter with him. The people of Tyre declare Apollonius king; he reveals his true identity to Artestrathes, and he and his now-pregnant wife set out for home. A great storm comes up; the wife goes into labour and dies giving birth to a daughter. The woman is buried at sea, and Apollonius returns to Tharse to leave the helpless baby in the care of Strangulio and Dionise. He then returns to Tyre, grief-stricken. The wife's coffin is born to Ephesus where it washes ashore. A great physician, Maister Cerymon, discovers that she is still alive, and nurses her back to health. She, thinking her husband and child dead, enters a convent. Meanwhile, the child, named Thaise, grows up. Dionise, jealous that Thaise is more admired than her own daughter, plots her murder. But just as the executioner is about to do the deed by the seashore, pirates strike and carry the girl away. Dionise announces to the public that the girl is dead and sets up a monument for the deceased. The pirates sell their prize at Mitelene to Leonin, master of a bordello. But Thaise is so wise, articulate, and beautifully innocent that none of Leonin's patrons dare touch her. So Leonin attempts to bereave her of her maidenhead himself, but she convinces him that he would make more money were he to set up a school in which she might teach others to read and write. The school becomes famous. Apollonius returns to Tharse to claim his now grown daughter, only to learn that she is dead. In despair he sets out to return to Tyre, only to be caught once more in a storm that bears him to Mitelene. Athenagoras, king of the town, calls upon the wise Thaise to see if she can help the mute Apollonius as he lies in despair in the ship's hold. She plays her harp and touches him. He strikes her, but she responds that he would not do that if he knew that she was really a princess. She identifies herself and tells her story. In mutual amazement they discover that their stories are one: the daughter has rescued her father, and the father found his daughter. In joy Apollonius weds Thaise to Athenagoras, which pleases Thaise. But first he asks that she accompany him to Tharse to settle matters with Strangulio and Dionise. On the way they stop at Ephesus to give prayers of gratitude to Diana, where they discover that the abbess, praise be to God, is the lost wife and mother. The villains at Tharse are executed according to the law. The reunited family stops at

Pentapolim, only to learn that Artestrathes has died. Parliament names Apollonius king of all the cities, a well-grounded choice:

> For he hath ferst his love founded
> Honesteliche as forto wedde
> Honesteliche his love he spedde
> And hadde children with his wif,
> And as him liste he ladde his lif.  (VIII.1994–8)

Others may take example of his good life, Genius concludes, but in Antiochus they see the vengeance that befalls one who behaves 'ayein kinde' (VIII.2007).

This tale marks the culmination of Gower's thoughts on kingship and good rule. It features two David-like kings (Apollonius and Artestrathes) who shepherd their people, love music, and heed wise counsel. They are good fathers, honest and loving, who value the wisdom of their daughters. They respect law and listen to evidence in cases before them. They act with discretion, always with an eye toward the common good. They are pious and respect the rights of their citizens. They appreciate harmony within the state but can, when occasion demands, make hard decisions and exact justice.

The tale also provides examples of bad kings and bad fathers: Antiochus is near-sighted. When his wife dies he rapes his daughter (VIII.293–304) and feeds upon her like an animal (VIII.309–11). He then makes special statutes to protect himself – laws that destroy worthy people (VIII.348–67). We are also given examples of good and bad mothers: Dionise follows her ambition and, in an effort to advance her daughter, destroys her whole family. Thaise's mother and grandmother, on the other hand, consider carefully the needs of the child and do what they can to offer support. They are chaste and work in the service of God.

The tale is much concerned with education as a factor of good rule. It teaches its audience the ambiguities of Fortune, how to ride out a storm or to survive piracy, brothels, even death, and it respects human nature. The tale teems with decent common folk who go about their business, trying to make their way. Theolous, the executioner assigned by Dionise to murder Thaise, hesitates to strike the blow, whereupon providence provides pirates to save the day. Even Leonin, the brothel-keeper, has moral qualms and changes from whoremaster to head of the schoolboard as Thaise brings respect and honour to the community. The world is not a bad place, only a trying one. We are impressed, in a most Gowerian way, with the abiding governance of providence. It may be that in real life things do not work out as they do in this tale (Gower, in fact, has a very tentative view of the politics of nature in the fallen world),[13] but the tale conveys a positive message that supports the prayerful conclusion of the poem. In its respect for the precepts of good rule figured in the reign of King David, it helps to position discrete judgement in the rule of an actual state.

---

[13] On the dark side of nature in the fallen world in Gower see White, *Nature, Sex, and Goodness*, pp. 188–219, and *Confessio Amantis*, ed. Russell A. Peck, Vol. II (2003), pp. 10–17.

*Gower and his Three Kings: Edward III, Richard II, and Henry IV*

Gower formulated his ideas of good and bad kingship during the reign of
Edward III. Though I think it likely that he had had legal training, and thus
would have known Justinian and Gratian,[14] in his poetry he shapes his political
ethics largely from books on princely rule, such as Giles of Rome's *De Regimine
Principum* on the king's rule of himself and his kingdom,[15] and commonplace
sources such as the *Secretum Secretorum*, Brunetto Latini's *Trésor*, and Valerius
Maximus's *Memorabilia*. Throughout his canon Gower directs the legal common-
places of these manuals toward real and immediate social concerns. He may be
ideologically royalist, but when the king misbehaves, he is steady and insistent
in his critique. For example, the *Mirour de l'Omme* was written during the latter
part of Edward's reign at a time when the king, having suffered reversals of
fortune in France, attempted to bolster revenues by taxation of the clergy. His
principal counsellor in this matter was his son, John of Gaunt, who used the
reformer John Wyclif against the moneyed establishment of the church.[16] Gower
himself was vigorously critical of churchmen abusing pastoral responsibilities;[17]
but he consistently opposed the first estate's overstepping its bounds to fill its
war coffers at the expense of the church and, thus, the poor. When that happens,
the king becomes tyrant and ceases to be shepherd or a model king among
kings. He creates divisions which undermine the church and his own estate as
well. For Gower, a good king is one who, rather than pillage a misguided
church, works to reform churchmen that they might become better shepherds.
The king 'should observe complete uprightness', he had argued in the *Mirour*,
and should 'defend Holy Church', not plunder it for personal wars abroad. It is

14  Legal terminology is prominent throughout *CA*, especially in the Latin apparatus of the
   poem. Fisher first made a strong case for Gower's legal affiliations, noting the reference in
   *MO* 21,774 to his wearing of striped sleeves ('Ainz ai vestu la raye mance'), the vestuary mark
   of a man of law, along with records of the poet's many legal dealings (*John Gower*, pp. 54–8,
   135–203). 'Gower's description of the training of the lawyer', Fisher observes, 'the degree of
   coif, and the privileges of serjeancy (*MO* 24,373), and his technical description of the functions
   of *plaidour, client, tort, deslayment, cas* (*MO* 24,206), *advocat* (*MO* 24,258), *president, apprentis,
   attourné* (*MO* 24,794) accord well with the early state of the profession' (p. 57).
15  See *The Governance of Kings and Princes: John Trevisa's Middle English Translation of the De
   Regimine Principum of Aegidius Romanus*, ed. David C. Fowler, Charles F. Briggs and Paul G.
   Remley (New York; London, 1997).
16  On Wyclif and taxation see Richard G. Davies, 'Richard II and the Church in the Years of
   Tyranny', *Journal of Medieval History* 1 (1975), pp. 329–62; and Nigel Saul, *Richard II* (New
   Haven, 1997), pp. 293–7.
17  See especially *MO* 18,421–21,780 on simony and the failure of cardinals, bishops, archdea-
   cons, priests, annuellers, clercs, possessioners and friars to fulfil their offices; and *VC* Book III,
   chapters 1–29, on greed amongst clergy, their immoderate yearning after luxury, wealth, and
   fleshly lasciviousness, their anger and warlike aggression, their avarice, deceit, neglect, and
   spiritual perversity; and *VC* Book IV, chapters 1–24, on monastic and confraternal corruption
   and lechery. See also Heinrich Gebhard, *Langlands und Gowers Kritik der Kirchlichen
   Verhältnisse ihrer Zeit* (Strassburg, 1911); Ruth Mohl, *The Three Estates in Medieval and Renaissance Literature* (New York, 1937); and Jill Mann, *Chaucer and Medieval Estates Satire: The Literature of Social Classes* (Cambridge, MA, 1973), which includes discussion of Gower on church
   corruption in *MO* and *VC*.

up to the king to 'keep the law with justice and equity throughout the realm'.[18] If churchmen misbehave they should be held accountable according to law, not plundered by a king who shares in their misbehaviour. Because the king has power, he is 'all the more accountable towards God' (MO 23,111–12).[19]

Gower was highly critical of Edward's war policies. The *Mirour* articulates forcefully the wise king's preference for peace over war, a position much developed in the *Confessio*, which, finally, culminates in his last poem, *In Praise of Peace*. A love of peace does not equate with negligence, of course. In the *Vox* Gower clearly admires the Black Prince, Edward's eldest living son, for some deeds in his war with France:

> Peace excels over every good, but when our tried and tested rights call for war, it should be waged. There is a time for war and there are likewise times for peace, but keep your self-control in all your actions. While Hector and Alexander were very noble, they could not stand firm upon uneven wheels. Surpass your father's deeds and you will be called greater than he.[20]

The Black Prince may defend English rights. But Gower is troubled by the brutalities of plunder, and, in the *Confessio*, speaks out strongly against foreign wars – even the crusades – which do nothing to advance the faith or the common good. Most war is simply a devious means for powerful people to become more rich.[21] The only true prince is the Prince of Peace.

Even before the Black Prince's death and the crises of state that followed close upon it, Gower looked upon Edward's morally lax rule as the real problem within the state. The once strong king had become a negligent king. In the *Vox* Gower repeatedly cries out against royal privilege that flourishes amidst bribery, favouritism and intimidation. 'Nowadays', he laments, 'the good man is punished and the wicked man is pardoned for gold' (VC VI.7.471–2, Stockton, p. 230). If the king is weak, the problems are compounded: 'A weak head makes

---

18 *Mirour de l'Omme*, lines 22,226–36, trans. William Burton Wilson, rev. Nancy Wilson Van Baak (East Lansing, MI, 1992), p. 295.

19 This idea that the king should promote church reform through education is most fully articulated in his last English poem, *In Praise of Peace*, addressed to Henry IV, concerning the cultural impact of an upright leader. It is worth observing that at the time of his deposition, Richard was reported by Sir William Bagot to have insisted that protection of the church was one of the essential duties of kingship and iterated 'a lively awareness of the spiritual prestige – and *many good confessors* – of the Plantagenet line'. See Simon Walker, 'Richard II's Views on Kingship', *Rulers and Ruled in Late Medieval England*, ed. Rowena E. Archer and Simon Walker (London, 1995), p. 51. But such public piety when hard pressed must be taken with a grain of salt. In practice, Richard did not differ much from his grandfather, but took pleasure in humiliating great churchmen and aggressively sought their revenues at every opportunity.

20 *Vox Clamantis* VI.13, trans. Eric W. Stockton, *The Major Latin Works of John Gower* (Seattle, 1962), p. 242; part and line numbers from G.C. Macaulay, ed. *The Complete Works of John Gower*, 4 vols (Oxford, 1899–1902). In *CA* Gower mentions Hector only once, and that in connection with lovers rather than warriors (VII.2526); but Alexander he uses prominently as a figure of a king who, in choosing war over peace, rushes headlong to his own destruction.

21 See especially *CA* III.2251–2621, where the unnaturalness of war is exposed – the burning of churches, slaying of priests, raping of women and destruction of law. Covetousness is said to be the main cause of war (III.2308), where conscience is either blind or put aside, and people become tyrants and pillagers to their own ruination, as the tales of Alexander and the Pirate and the War and Death of Alexander show. Even crusades are declared unlawful and wretched perversions of Christ's faith for the sake of homicide.

the members suffer. If the leader loses the way, his followers among the people go astray. . . . If a king is wicked, God . . . wills to punish him, since the law cannot' (*VC* VI.7.497–8, Stockton, p. 231). In the voice of the prophet crying in the wilderness,[22] he insists that 'the greater a man is, the greater his crimes are. When he falls from his lofty position, he is harmed the more as a result. I see many guilty men, but those who are lawgivers and yet remain lawless are guiltier than them all' (*VC* VI.7.512, Stockton, p. 231). England needs strong rule. But that rule must come from leaders who, like Lycurgus, uphold just laws.

As Edward declined into what many saw as dotage, Gower blamed him for his loss of discretion, but he also blamed his counsellors. He accuses Edward of surrounding himself with greedy 'yes-men' and, worse, of placing his rule under the control of his mistress, Alice Perrers. In *Mirour* 22,802ff., Gower speaks directly to the matter:

> A king should cherish truth and obey it above all things. . . . And yet nowadays we see a king who hates all those who speak the truth; but those who are willing to blandish him become influential. He speaks the truth who says that woman is powerful, and that is visible nowadays. May God save us from these evils, for it is in discord with the laws that a woman should rule in the land and should subject the king to serve her. A king is much deceived by women when he loves them more than his God so that he abandons honor for wantonness. This king will not be feared who thus is willing to give up his shield and seek battle in bed. Of King David I find written that he was basely discomfited because of his carnal appetite for Bathsheba. No king will be perfect who is vanquished by his frail flesh.
>
> (pp. 297–8)

David, of course, sought penance for his imperfections. Edward did not; he simply persisted in them. Although Gower is less outspoken against the king than the monk of St Albans in his *Chronicon Angliae*,[23] his position on the scandals surrounding Alice Perrers is akin to popular opinion, whether in London, the church, or parliament. And his position does not change.[24] Alice was banished from the king's presence by the Good Parliament, but after Gaunt retaliated against those decisions, Alice returned to the king.[25] Again Gower picks up the refrain, now in the *Vox Clamantis*. That a king's moral failures resonate through the whole of the state is a central proposition in Gower's ethic of good rule.[26] Gower pins the blame directly on the king's dependence on Alice Perrers:

[22] The title of the treatise, *Vox Clamantis*, refers to John the Baptist's reference to the voice crying in the wilderness, the prophetic voice announcing the coming of Christ and Judgement, which the people do not heed. See Matthew 8:1–3; Mark 1:2–3; and Luke 3:3–6.

[23] See *Chronicon Angliae ab anno domini 1328 usque ad annum 1388. Auctore monacho quodam Sancti Albani*, ed. Edward Maunde Thompson, Vol. LXIV (London, 1874), pp. 95–100, 103–5, 130–1, 136–9, 142–5, 171.

[24] On Gower's concern in *MO* with the king's alliance with Alice Perrers see Gardner Stillwell, 'John Gower and the Last Years of Edward III', *Studies in Philology* 45 (1948), pp. 454–71. For a more objective account of Dame Alice's role in English politics in 1370 than that given by Gower or the St Alban's *Chronicle*, see F. George Kay's fine study, *Lady of the Sun: The Life and Times of Alice Perrers* (London, 1966).

[25] G. Holmes, *The Good Parliament* (Oxford, 1975), pp. 103–6, 136–9, 160.

[26] In *VC* Gower writes at length against the incompatability of good rule and sexual promis-

> Above all, O king, avoid letting blind lust of the flesh arouse you towards its al-
> lurements. . . . You as a husband should enjoy your own wife according to law,
> and not deprive your holy marriage of honorable praise. No ancient writings
> about kings show that an appeased Venus and a kingdom stand together for
> long. (*VC* VI.12, Stockton, p. 240)

As in the *Mirour*, Gower seems to have the example of David and Bathsheba in
mind as he harkens back to 'ancient writings' for guidance on kingly deport-
ment.

One of the poet's anxieties with regard to the old king's decline concerns the
effect that a lack of moral rectitude might have on Edward's young grandson
Richard. With the death of the Black Prince and the threat that John of Gaunt
might position himself to become king upon Edward's death, parliament
insisted that Richard be named Prince of Wales.[27] The move was reassuring, in
that it seemed to secure an orderly succession, but it was also troubling, given
the youth of the prince. In the latter days of Edward's life and in the early years
of young Richard's reign, Gower focused his critique on the education of the boy
king. He worried especially about the child's fragmented upbringing, now that
the throne was his:

> The king, an undisciplined boy, neglects the moral behavior by which a man
> might grow up from a boy. Indeed, youthful company so sways the boy that he
> has a taste for nothing practical, unless it be his whim. The young men associated
> with him want what he wants; he enters into a course of action and they follow
> him. Vainglory makes these youthful comrades vain, for which reason they
> vainly cultivate the royal quarters more and more. They abet the boy king in his
> childish behavior, whereby he wields the authority of virtue the less.
>
> (*VC* VI.7, Stockton, p. 232)

It is a passage such as this that underlies the central motif of the *Confessio*, that
culminates in Book VII as the poet tries to educate the young lover who would
be king, at least of his 'oghne dom'.

Gower is not alone in recognising the problem. McKisack notes the anxiety
clearly audible in the Parliament of November 1381 concerning the need to
attend to the young king's education and the difficulty of doing so with him
surrounded by favoured courtiers:

> Complaints about the outrageous numbers preying on the resources of the royal
> household (with special reference to the king's confessor, Thomas Rushook),
> were linked with demands for a commission headed by the duke of Lancaster, to
> investigate both the household and the 'estate and governance' of the king's
> person.[28]

cuity. 'What honour shall a conqueror have if a woman's love can conquer him. . . . The end
will bring nothing but inevitable folly upon the man for whom Venus initially leads the way
to arms. . . . A woman does not often release a man whom she has ensnared so that he may
escape. . . . The man who is once free and subjugates himself voluntarily ought to be reckoned
more idiotic than an idiot' (*VC* VI.1, Stockton, pp. 196–7). It is not hard to see the shadow of
the court lurking behind such observations, though as before in *MO* and later in *VC* Gower
avoids naming names.
27 Saul, *Richard II*, p.17.
28 May McKisack, *The Fourteenth Century 1307–1300* (Oxford, 1959), p. 426.

By the end of the session Michael de la Pole and Richard, Earl of Arundel (whom Richard came to detest), were appointed 'to attend the king in his household and to counsel and govern his person'.[29]

Gower's insights into problems concerning the young king's education, expressed in *Vox Clamantis* VI.7, were shrewd – even prophetic. It was one thing for Burley, the boy's tutor, to introduce him to ethics and the arts, another for someone to attempt to indoctrinate a headstrong young king, devoted to self-dramatisation and the pleasures of flattery from a self-appointed, admiring audience. It seemed to Gower later in the 1390s that Richard never did learn self-discipline; that, in basic ways, Richard remained a boy who never grew up. The charge that he lacked taste for anything practical and that his rule of thumb was to indulge his every whim lingered until his dying day.

One of the most telling retrospective critiques of the young king's court is found in *Richard the Redeless*,[30] a political satire written about the time that Gower wrote his *Cronica Tripertita*. The critique of Richard is worth citing in that it accords well not only with the *Cronica* but also with Gower's criticisms of courtly behaviour in his earlier writings. The *Redeless*-author presents Richard's entourage as a fashion parade, where vanity courts vanity, as Gower put it in the *Vox* VI.7 (cited above), and courtiers 'strut'[31] and vie with each other to display ostentatious attire: unless 'the slevis slide on the erthe,/ Thei woll be wroth as the wynde and warie hem that it made' (*Redeless* III.152–3). The poet describes a Gower-like wise old man named Wit who, dressed in his homely, old-fashioned 'ray',[32] is pushed aside into 'an herne at the halle ende' (III.211). Neither the king nor his knights know the man, and they mock him as the sleeves of their gowns – sleeves slashed to pieces with 'wondir coriouse crafte', that would take 'sevene goode sowers six wekes' to hem all the seams (III.163–6) – whisper against him and drive him out of the hall. As the porter, armed with his pike, ushers him out, the sleeves cry: 'Let sle him!' while 'the berdles burnes [i.e. Richard's insolent young courtiers] bayed on him evere' (III.234–5). The poet's critique of the newfangledness of folly displacing the wise old ways of the past harkens back to Gower's analysis of the problem.

The evil of royal self-indulgence is a theme perpetually on Gower's mind. The suggestion is not simply that Richard lacked good counsel in his youth, but that he turned his peers into sycophants, whereby he received no sound apprenticeship whatsoever for adulthood. In the *Confessio*, as we have seen, Gower specialises in good counsel, especially in family relationships – children in the

---

29 See *Rot. Parl.* iii.100–4, as cited by McKisack, *The Fourteenth Century*, p. 426.

30 See James M. Dean, ed., *Richard the Redeless and Mum and the Sothsegger* (Kalamazoo, 2002), pp. 7–74; or Mabel Day and Robert Steel, eds., *Mum and the Sothsegger*, EETS, os no. 199 (Oxford, 1936), which presents *Richard the Redeless* as part of the other poem.

31 'Stroute' and 'strouutynge' recur repeatedly (*Richard the Redeless* III.121, III.134, III.177, III.189) as these 'strie [arrogant] strouters' (III.269) invent new devices each day, for all their 'witte in [their] wede ys wrappid forsothe' (III.122). Pernell praises the numbers of pleats in his garb and boasts of the cost which he does not pay; the ladies follow the men's cue and 'joied of the jette and gyside hem therunder' (III.159), while Felice vociferously objects if any fault be found in the 'makynge' (III.160).

32 The stripes (*ray*) of his 'holsom gyse' suggest *bona fide* legal training that sets him apart from the vain, witless youths who now fill the court.

care of their parents, or, in converse, parents in the care of their children (as in 'The Tale of Three Questions' and 'The Tale of Apollonius'), or children without or separated from their parents, learning their way by whatever counsel they can find, often with disastrous results (e.g. 'The Tale of Rosemund and Albinus', 'The Tale of Canace', or 'The Tale of the False Bachelor'). 'It sit well every king to have/ Discrecion', Gower writes (VII.2115–16) – discretion learned in youth. Those children who learn, through good counsel, to distinguish rightly usually fare well, witness Petronella, Thaise and young Apollonius. Parents and tutors may do their best, but even so it may not be enough, witness the stories of Alexander. But this theme of growing from childhood to maturity, of becoming a worthy 'king' over one's own estate, is seldom far removed from any moment of the *Confessio*. It is a topic Gower pondered intently for the better part of a decade before he began writing the poem, and it must have been at the centre of his thinking when young Richard, just across the river, was becoming so recurrently a presence in the public consciousness.[33]

Early in Richard's reign, Gower's response to the young king seems to have been positive. Although he makes no mention in the *Vox* of young Richard's role in bringing the uprising of 1381 to its conclusion, we might imagine that Gower admired the boy's courage in facing the mob at Smithfield.[34] Certainly, the account of the king inviting Gower to join him in his boat on the Thames in the first recension of the Prologue to the *Confessio Amantis* offers a favourable view of the young king.[35] Richard would have been about eighteen to twenty-two years old at the time, and Gower would have been about sixty. Gower reports that young Richard asked him to write 'som newe thing . . ./ That he himself it mihte loke/ After the forme of my writynge' (Prol. lines 51–3*). But regardless of whether the poet recorded an actual event, it must have amused old Gower – doubtless, like Wit in *Richard the Redeless*, in conservative dress – to think of shaping 'som newe thing' like a love-lorn courtier about the age of this king,

---

[33] For an excellent discussion of the tensions surrounding the headstrong young king's reign following the Revolt of 1381, particularly what chroniclers perceived as his greed and extravagant behaviour, his arrogant advancement of young favourites, and his irresponsible taxation of all estates, see McKisack, ch. 14: 'Richard II, his Friends and his Enemies (1381–8)', *The Fourteenth Century*, pp. 424–61.

[34] The Peasant's Revolt occurred near the end of the time that Gower was writing the *Vox*. In response to the carnage he wrote the prophetic prologue to his moral treatise (now Book I), which gives the most vivid account that we have of the bloody events that terrorised the city. The horrors are presented as an allegorical nightmare, but no mention is made of Richard's role in quelling the mob. When the poet/persona awakens we are told only that 'the madmen had been subdued under the law of old and that a new mode of law had repaired the broken course of events' (*VC* I.21, Stockton, p. 94).

[35] I am working from the hypothesis that such a meeting actually took place. Frank Grady, 'Gower's Boat, Richard's Barge, and the True Story of the *Confessio Amantis*: Text and Gloss', *Texas Studies in Literature and Language* 44 (Spring, 2002), pp. 1–15, suggests the story is only a rhetorical flourish, not history, on the grounds that a poet's representation of his patron 'is always a fiction' (p. 3). Certainly, Gower's assertion is sophisticated in its rhetoric, but Richard was not Gower's patron, nor does the passage function in that way. It does serve a useful purpose thematically in the Prologue, but that does not necessarily preclude the possibility of such an event's having, in fact, taken place.

notorious for his newfangled fashions and extravagant playmates, with all their *courant* enthusiasms.[36]

If the event on the Thames did in fact occur, it must have happened either in the mid 1380s, before 1387,[37] or, later, in 1388–89, in which case the passage would have been added after much of the poem had been written. This latter date is perhaps the preferable option in that, following the Merciless Parliament, Richard seemed to be sincerely devoted to the pursuit of peace abroad and at home, healing wounds left by the Merciless Parliament and promoting unity between factions – all benevolent themes that Gower features prominently in the *Confessio*. Foreign trade was once again flourishing, the king's relationship with the city of London was good, and Richard, with Chaucer as clerk of the king's works, was promoting the arts through the pageantry of grand public events.[38] This was a time when the king's behaviour accorded well in some ways with Gower's vision of what the state should be.

But Gower's responses to Richard's kingship were never comfortable. We get some sense of his concern over the struggles between the king and parliament in his criticisms of division within the land in the Prologue to the *Confessio*, which must have been written around the time of the Merciless Parliament (1387).[39] That concern is reiterated later, at the end of his writing career, in the *Cronica*

---

[36] Gower's account of the royal commissioning of the poem is fascinating in other ways. Although he speaks well of the king, it is important to notice the attention given to the poet's perfect allegiance as he addresses Richard: 'To whom belongeth my ligeance/ With al myn hertes obeissance /In al that evere a liege man /Unto his king may doon or can' (Prol. 25–8*). The point is not so much that Gower is boasting of his loyalty in an attempt to flatter his patron as it is to show the harmonious workings of the state. Gower seems to give his reader a bit of autobiography, but mainly he dramatises an ideal lord/vassal exchange that underscores the need for unity rather than the divisions that so harm all three of England's estates. Grady, 'Gower's Boat', makes a somewhat similar point (p. 9), though I arrived at my observations from a quite different route. Grady cites Anne Middleton's important essay, 'The Idea of Public Poetry in the Reign of Richard II', *Speculum* 53 (1978), pp. 94–114, to note that 'the king is not the main imagined audience, but an occasion for gathering and formulating what is on the common mind' (p. 107), which is an excellent point. But I quite agree with Grady that 'there are aesthetic as well as political motives for Gower's [subsequent] revisions' of the passage (p. 15, n. 25).

[37] One might imagine that the event took place around 1385–86, about the time that Chaucer was part of the queen's household at Eltham and Sheen, when he was beginning work on *The Legend of Good Women* and thinking about the *Canterbury Tales*, when the ambiance of Richard's court provided 'a congenial setting for courtly dalliance' and before the king's political life disintegrated (see Michael J. Bennett, 'The Court of Richard II and the Promotion of Literature', *Chaucer's England: Literature in Historical Context*, ed. Barbara A. Hanawalt (Minneapolis, 1992), pp. 3–20 (p. 9)); that is, prior to the Wonderful Parliament, when the Duke of Gloucester evicted Richard's chancellor and tutor, Michael de la Pole, to form a new government; and certainly before the proceedings in 1387 that led to the blood bath of the Merciless Parliament.

[38] On the stability of Richard's rule in 1388–89 and the promotion of the arts, see McKisack, *The Fourteenth Century*, pp. 464–6, and Bennett, 'The Court of Richard II', pp. 8–13. See also V.J. Scattergood, 'Literary Culture at the Court of Richard II', *English Court Culture in the Later Middle Ages*, ed. J.A. Burrow, V.J. Scattergood, and J.W. Sherborne (New York, 1983), pp. 29–43, and Gordon Kipling on Richard's sumptuous pageantry in note 50, below.

[39] On Gower's response to the political fall-out of these events see Andrew Galloway, 'The Literature of 1388 and the Politics of Pity in Gower's *Confessio Amantis*', *The Letter of the Law: Legal Practice and Literary Production in Medieval England*, ed. Emily Steiner and Candace Barrington (Ithaca, NY, 2002), pp. 67–104.

*Tripertita*, where he singles out 1387[40] as the beginning of the conflict between Richard and the rest of England, as 'Richard forsook loving-kindness' and began to transgress laws (I.4, Stockton, p. 290) in a move toward a defiant absolutist view of monarchy that ultimately became his undoing.[41] In the *Cronica* the effect is quite different from the critique in the *Confessio*, since in retrospect Gower could see how the transgressions ended in the destruction of the kingdom and Richard's kingship. But to use the *Cronica Tripertita*, written in 1399–1400 as a tribute to King Henry IV, to assess Gower's feelings about Richard and the throne in the 1380s would be a distorted anachronism.[42]

Whether Gower sympathised in the 1380s with the king, his advisers, and the moneyed interests of London represented by Nicholas Brembre, or whether he even then was as strongly in support of the Appellants as he seems to be in the *Cronica*, we do not know. Certainly he would have been concerned with the legal issues of the bloody dispute, and, given his strong emphasis on peace and reasonable behaviour as a proper goal for all in power, he must have been deeply disturbed by the rash of executions. But in the *Cronica* he insists that the victims deserved their fate. For example, of Robert Tresilian, Chief Justice of the King's Bench, one of the first to be executed, he writes, with his characteristic sense of ironic justice:

> This scoundrel stirred up the nobles and often harassed them, for which reason the wicked man finally perished, harassed himself. Because of a crime outstripping what he had committed before, he was stretched on the gallows and overcome by hanging there. The sorry fate of hanging befell those dying men upon whose hands men's justice used to hang. (I.164–9, Stockton, p. 296)

Likewise, somewhat surprisingly, I think, he defends Gloucester's execution of Simon Burley, the boy Richard's tutor. Burley had been a soldier in the command of the Black Prince, but also a man of letters who, like his older acquaintance Richard de Bury, was admired for his humanism and love of books.[43] In the

---

[40] See *Cronica Tripertita* I.1–2, where the date of the upheaval is defined as a riddle: 'Take the first letter of *mundus* and add to it C three times repeated, and take six periods of five years; and afterwards add ten times five, plus seven' (Stockton, *Major Latin Works*, p. 290). All references to the *Cronica* are identified by part and line numbers from Macaulay's edition (*Complete Works*, Vol. IV, pp. 314–42) and page number in Stockton's translation.

[41] See C.M. Barron, 'The Tyranny of Richard II', *Bulletin of the Institute of Historical Research* 41 (1968), pp. 1–18, and R.H. Jones, *The Royal Policy of Richard II: Absolutism in the Later Middle Ages* (Oxford, 1968), pp. 71–87 ('The Prerogative Restored') and pp. 88–99 ('Richardian Absolutism').

[42] See G.B. Stow, 'Richard II in John Gower's *Confessio Amantis*: Some Historical Perspectives', *Mediaevalia* 16 (1993), pp. 3–31.

[43] Though a soldier of irascible disposition who fought alongside the Black Prince at Najera, Simon Burley came from a distinguished intellectual background. His kinsman Walter Burley, one of Bradwardine's circle, a student of Ockham and close friend of Richard de Bury, had been tutor to young Edward the Black Prince, when he was twelve. Author of *De Deo Natura et Arte* (see H. Shapiro, *Medievalia et Humanistica* 15 [1963]: 86ff.), Walter was doubtless an influence on young Simon's intellectual interests and a factor in Edward's naming of Simon to tutor his son and heir Richard (Jones, *The Royal Policy of Richard II*, pp. 160–1). Both Walter and Simon had copies of Giles of Rome's *De Regimine Principum* in their libraries, a book upon which Richard seems to have modelled his theory, if not his practice, of good rule.

*Cronica*, Gower is severe in his remarks about Burley,[44] though one would think that in 1388 he might have been more kind-hearted. To young Richard, Burley, a hero who had fought at the side of the Black Prince, his father, must have been a shining example of knighthood. More than any other, Burley may have been responsible for instilling in his charge a love of the arts that led to such acts of kindness toward men of letters as his verbal commissioning of the *Confessio*.[45] If we are to believe Gower's notion of what an ideal ruler should be – namely, an Arion-like harper of such eloquence that he could calm wild beasts and, like-wise, a man of reason who understands the intentions of right law, a person schooled in old books – then Gower, one would think, would have sympathised with Burley's plan for bringing up the king.[46] Gower might even have sensed a kinship between himself, Burley, and his Aristotle figure in Book VII of the *Confessio*, as he trained the prince Alexander (and, implicitly, Amans) in rhetoric, law, and the five points of policy (VII.1699ff.). When Queen Anne herself pleaded piteously before parliament for Burley's life, she spoke to the heart of Gower's agenda of pity and good rule.

But though Gower might have admired the goals of the Simon Burley of Rich-ard's childhood, as the 1390s got under way and Richard began his insidious retaliation against the Appellants of the Merciless Parliament, his sympathy with Richard waned. In 1389 Richard declared his majority and assumed the rule of England in his own right, free of any regency. It was shortly thereafter that his rule assumed increasingly absolutist postures, behaviour that in the early 1390s, long before Henry's overthrow of the king in 1399, must have been alarming to Gower. In 1392, only two years after Gower had issued the first recension of the poem, with its recounting of his meeting with Richard on the Thames, he changed the dedication of the *Confessio* from Richard to Henry of

---

44  Gower singles out Burley, the king's chamberlain, as one who, despite his striped garment (i.e. legal training) 'fell to the fate of the sword'. Rather than defend him, as so many did in 1388, including the queen who pleaded on bended knee for his life, Gower concludes: 'When it is not virtuous, old age is the more to be blamed: even while the tears of the Queen implored medical aid [for him], the fallen man brought on his own destruction and lost his head' (I.140–3, Stockton, *The Major Latin Works*, p. 295). Perhaps Gower brings up this particular death in 1400 because, as he is defending Gloucester whom Richard had exiled and had murdered, he wishes to sway sympathy toward the duke by negating that moment when sympathy for him had been lowest. Stockton reports that Burley, Richard's tutor, had helped negotiate the marriage of Richard and Anne, but that he was 'disliked for his irritable temper' (p. 474n).

45  On Richard's cultivation of the arts see Bennett, 'The Court of Richard II', pp. 3–20; and Scat-tergood, 'Literary Culture at the Court of Richard II', pp. 29–43. Both studies take their cue from John A. Burrow's influential study, *Ricardian Poetry: Chaucer, Gower, Langland and the Gawain-Poet* (London, 1971) and Gervase Mathew, *The Court of Richard II* (New York, 1968), pp. 12–52. In a twisted way, I suppose, one might argue that it was Richard's penchant for such matters as the *newe style* that contributed to his extravagant taste for newfangled fashion, which the author of *Richard the Redeless* attacked. That is, his commissioning of the *Confessio* might have been part of that same syndrome that Richard's enemies found to be irre-sponsible.

46  The fact of the matter is that Richard studied many of the same texts that Gower studied, perhaps Giles of Rome, but certainly versions of the *Secreta secretorum*. See Walker, 'Richard II's Views on Kingship', p. 52, and Richard F. Green, *Poets and Princepleasers: Literature and the English Court in the Late Middle Ages* (Toronto, 1980), pp. 140–2, on the popularity of the *Secreta secretorum* and its derivatives.

Lancaster ('myn oghne lord,/ Which of Lancastre is Henri named' – Prol. 86–7) and removed his prayer for Richard from the conclusion of the poem ('my worthi king . . ./ Richard by name the Secounde,/ In whom hath evere yit be founde/ Justice medled with pite,/ Largesce forth with charite' – VIII.2986–90*). Some have felt that this revision is simply an expedient move by Gower as he prepared a presentation copy of his poem for another great man. But such a view obscures more than it enlightens. The change of dedication and the events of 1392 involving Richard and the city of London are not, to my mind, simply coincidence.[47]

As the new decade progressed Richard became increasingly extravagant, perhaps even hoping to be named Holy Roman Emperor. He needed more money and he was not subtle about getting it. In his perceived need for wealth to support his lavish style Richard increased taxes, made deals with foreign merchants, and demanded loans from the city.[48] When the London merchants were 'unable' to pay, the king punished the city by removing the Court of Common Pleas from London to York; he then removed from the metropolis the chancery, the rolls of the king's bench, the Fleet prison, and the exchequers of accounts, pleas, and of receipt.[49] It was in this politically charged atmosphere that the city was forced to submit to the king in a lavishly punitive public ceremony on 21 August, 1392.[50] As he manipulated the import trade, increased

[47] Certainly Henry's acknowledgement of the poet's gift in 1393, the year following the change in dedication, suggests that the poem was being taken seriously in a new light, when Henry, still Earl of Derby, gave Gower an honorary collar of S's (which perhaps signified the Swan, affiliated with Gloucester; see John Anstis, *The Register of the Garter* (1724), as cited by Fisher, *John Gower*, p. 342n). If the collar does signify the Swan (i.e. Gloucester), it might well mean that Gower, even as early as 1393, was supportive of Gloucester and the Appellants. That Henry looked upon the collar as something affiliated with his distinguished family is evident by his ordering a replacement, which he instructed his clerk of the wardrobe to supply. See Fisher, *John Gower*, p. 68. Apparently this was the collar that the effigy of the poet wears on the Gower monument in the chapel of St John the Baptist in the priory church of St Mary Overie, now St Saviour's, Southwark.

[48] See Paul Strohm, 'Trade, Treason, and the Murder of Janus Imperial', *Journal of British Studies* 35 (1996), pp. 1–23.

[49] See T.F. Tout, *Chapters in the Administrative History of Mediaeval England*, Vol. III (1928; rpt. Manchester, 1967), pp. 481–2; and David R. Carlson, Introduction to Richard Maidstone, *Concordia (The Reconciliation of Richard II with London)*, ed. David R. Carlson, with Latin translation by A.G. Rigg (Kalamazoo, 2003), pp. 4–5. Carlson notes, 'such offices returned to London only in early 1393' (p. 5).

[50] Richard's extravagant abuse of royal prerogatives would have been utterly obscene to Gower. The most detailed account of the day is Maidstone's *Concordia*, ed. Carlson, a poem of 546 Latin lines by Richard's confessor. See also an epistolary report's equally graphic account of the processional where public figures of London beg mercy of the king on their knees, offering him expensive gifts, or moments when angels bless Richard and the queen (see Helen Suggett, 'A Letter Describing Richard II's Reconciliation with the City of London, 1392', *English Historical Review* 62 (1947), pp. 212–13; *The Westminster Chronicle 1381–1394*, ed. and trans. L.C. Hector and Barbara F. Harvey (Oxford, 1982), pp. 502–7; Knighton's *Chronicle 1227–1396*, ed. and trans. G.H. Martin (Oxford, 1995), pp. 546–8; The Brut Continuation (in Middle English) in *The Brut, or, The Chronicles of England*, EETS, os no. 136 (London, 1906), pp. 347–8; Thomas Walsingham, *Historia Anglicana*, ed. Henry Thomas Riley, Rolls Series 28/1 (London, 1864), II.210–11. Carlson includes Maidstone and all other accounts in his edition. See also Gordon Kipling, 'Richard II's "Sumptuous Pageants" and the Idea of the Civic Triumph', *Pageantry in the Shakespearian Theatre*, ed. D.M. Bergeron (Athens, GA, 1986), pp. 83–103.

234        RUSSELL A. PECK

taxation and demanded greater and greater loans, the relationship between
Richard and the city of London rapidly deteriorated. Nicholas Brembre, a former
mayor of London, had been the wealthiest member of an elite moneyed group
who had favoured the king.[51] With his execution by the Merciless Parliament,
Richard attempted to play mercantile factions against each other. There were
tensions between the merchant-capitalists, whose wealth was derived from
trade, and the artisans and small masters whose wealth was based on production,[52] and those tensions weakened the king's coffers. In August of 1392
Richard moved against the city with a dramatic pageant designed to humiliate
and force officials, ecclesiasts, and merchants into submission to his will.
Carlson puts the matter succinctly: 'The conflict was financial: King Richard
needed money; the corporation of the city of London and various eminent citizens were believed to have it' (p. 1). But it was also about ego – the king's ego –
and who held what power.

From Gower's point of view, the king's behaviour epitomised the essence of
tyranny, the kind of pomp, arrogance, and splendour that he had deemed the
ruination of Babylon, Troy, and Rome (see *Vox* VI.2, Stockton, p. 228). In the 'reconciliation pageant', Richard presented himself as a god exacting penance from
disobedient disciples. Townspeople were required to appear in livery desig-
nating their rank and affiliation, to pay homage and taxes for their infidelities.
Designed as a coronation pageant, the event bore overtones of a triumphal entry
into a fallen city, as the king reclaimed his kingdom and sat in judgement over
the guilty. It was as if he, in his mercy, was giving the unfaithful one last chance
to correct their ways. The pageantry echoed key moments of Christ's ministry:
Jesus' entrance into Jerusalem, with angels descending from heaven giving him
crowns and jewels (see *Concordia*, lines 276–316, 379–96); the baptism of Christ,
as John the Baptist asked the crowd to 'Behold, the Lamb of God' (see *Concordia*,
lines 357–72); the wedding at Cana, where Christ turned water into wine (in
Richard's pageant, as he approached one fountain wine poured forth, instead of
water); and apocalyptic judgement where Christ/Richard redeems or condemns
at will.[53] At one point he interrupted the procession to pardon a thief who had

---

51  For Gower's later condemnation of Brembre for his sanction and support of the 'plottings of
   the king', a man whom the king had cherished 'like a consort', see *Cronica Tripertita* (I.154–9,
   Stockton, *Major Latin Works*, p. 296).
52  See Pamela Nightingale's two essays, 'Capitalists, Crafts and Constitutional Change in Late
   Fourteenth-Century London', *Past and Present* 124 (1989), pp. 3–35; and 'The Growth of
   London in the Medieval English Economy', *Progress and Problems in Medieval England: Essays
   in Honour of Edward Miller*, ed. Richard Britnell and John Hatcher (Cambridge, 1996),
   pp. 89–106. Caroline M. Barron, 'The Tyranny of Richard II', pp. 1–18; Ruth Bird, *The Turbulent
   London of Richard II* (London, 1949); and Gwyn A. Williams, *Medieval London: From Commune to
   Capital* (London, 1963), especially chapters 5 and 6 ('The Mercantile Interests' and 'The Rise of
   the Crafts'), pp. 106–95, are also useful in reconstructing the fiscal issues of the political crisis
   that Richard foisted upon the city in August of 1392. But see especially the Introduction and
   Bibliography to Carlson's edition of Richard Maidstone, *Concordia*, pp. 1–49, to which I am
   much indebted.
53  See Kipling, 'Richard II's "Sumptuous Pageants" ', on the ritual nature of such royal
   pageantry. Kipling compares the pageantry of 1392 with that of Richard's coronation in 1377
   and Queen Anne's in 1382. In 1392 Richard is presented as the Lamb of God in the Gospels,
   the bridegroom (*sponsus*) once rejected but now returning to his bridal chamber, as in Song of
   Songs, and the judge of the Second Coming in Apocalypse. On traditional casting of medieval

just been sentenced to death.[54] That Richard's acts were arbitrary simply proved his autocracy, a greatness that extended over life and death. But although officials bowed and paid homage in the form of expensive gifts and money, their sentiment was not one of pious gratitude but, rather, disaffection.

Seven years later, when Gower excoriates Richard's self-indulgent egomania in the *Cronica Tripertita* (see especially III.1–27, Stockton, p. 312), he alludes to the mystery plays, comparing Richard to Herod (III.9) and the Prince of Hell as they rant and strut about the stage (III.21) threatening to oppress honest people. The comparison accords with what Gower's response must have been to Richard's theatrical staging of his reconciliation with the citizens of London. As the king, at every stop along the processional way, required city officials and guildsmen to address prayers of supplication to him and the queen, he was more like Herod or a fiend than Christ entering the holy city.[55]

Allegiance is a potent pledge. When freely given it provides the very basis of a king's power. But Richard's dazzling displays and staged pardons were coercion, not the liberality becoming a king. In the eyes of the chroniclers, his bullying in August 1392 made a mockery of allegiance. His behaviour at that time was not too different from his behaviour later in the decade, when he transgressed his own sumptuary laws to assemble his liverymen of Chester as his private retinue to make sure the king got his way, regardless of law. The principal charges levied against Richard at the time of his dethronement are the very things Gower had warned him about in the Prologue and Book VII of the *Confessio*.

The new dedication of the *Confessio* to Henry of Lancaster was only the first of several literary gestures that Gower made to Henry. The second, the *Cronica Tripertita*, written shortly after Henry was crowned, celebrates the new king as the redeeming hope for a nation nearly destroyed by the evil practices of Richard. Echoing a theme of the *Confessio*, the *Cronica* begins: 'It is the work of man to pursue and seek out peace' (marginal headnote, Stockton, p. 289). The main thrust of the *Cronica* is against Richard's arrogant disregard of law. Part I reviews the decline of the nation in the last decade of Richard's reign. Richard's 'obdurate heart' is declared the cause of divisions in the land, perpetrating a kingdom divided against itself. Instead of heeding wisdom, Richard took 'immature counsel of fools to himself' and rejected the principles of older, wiser men (I.13–18, Stockton, p. 290).[56]

---

rulers as saviours, benefactors and gods, see Sabine McCormack, 'Change and Continuity in Late Antiquity: The Ceremony of Adventus', *Historia* 21 (1972), pp. 724–8.

[54] There are several instances in the 1390s when Richard arbitrarily used a public forum to pardon people condemned to death. On this occasion in 1392 one motive may have been compassion, another to exhibit his God-like authority beyond the ministrations of law. But it may also have been an in-your-face gesture to remind the people of Gloucester's cruelty, and of the Merciless Parliament's brutal disregard of the queen's appeal for mercy on behalf of Simon Burley. One is struck by the number of instances on this occasion in which Richard staged the city's atonement by forcing suppliants to plead their case before the queen at his side.

[55] See note 50. On the subsequent hostilities that stemmed from Richard's egoistic extravaganza see Ruth Bird, 'The "Taking of the City into the King's Hand" and the Coming of Henry of Lancaster', *The Turbulent London of Richard II* (London, 1949), pp. 102–113.

[56] A good parallel text to study in conjunction with the *Cronica Tripertita* is the Middle English poem contemporaneous with it, *Richard the Redeless*, an alliterative poem closely akin to *Piers*

By means of beast allegory this first part details the lawless crimes of Richard and the justness of the Appellant cause against him and his courtiers. The second part, which the Preface defines as a profane work of hell, tells how Richard disturbed the peace and slew just men: 'woe unto my pen, since I am to write of hellish deeds!' (II.10, Stockton, p. 299). Here the allegory tells how Richard surreptitiously murdered even his own kinsmen, ignored or manipulated the laws deceitfully, banished good people, and confiscated their properties. Part II ends with a eulogy for Richard's victims.

The third part of the *Cronica* proclaims the intervention of Christ, as God sends Henry to depose the haughty Richard. Richard had banished Henry to France. The contrast between Henry's return to England and Maidstone's account of the staged piety of Richard's reconciliatory entry into London in 1392 is instructive. Gower presents Henry, the true king, as one filled with piety and humility, not arrogant self-vindication:

> Disembarking first, the Duke placed his foot upon his own soil, worshipped God on bended knee, and first prayed with devotions of sincere intent, with palms outstretched to heaven, that he might win the palm of victory. In order that he might rise above the heinousness of war, he implanted a kiss upon the earth, and there the Duke made many devotions and pious prayers. He arose from prayer, and taking up his cross he found shelter for himself. And then what happy days he began to enter upon: When his native land knew that the Duke had returned safe, everybody ran to him, rejoicing everywhere. (III.150–9, Stockton, p. 316)

The humble dignity of Henry demonstrates for Gower an allegiance to God by a king worthy of loyal subjects. Richard, in his absolutist egotism, preferred to play Christ. But, when taken by Henry's followers and confronted with his crimes, he was utterly lacking in dignity. He behaved as a 'hare' (III.160), not the lion of his namesake: 'the full-grown King broke out into much blubbering' (III.164–4, Stockton, p. 316). For Gower, Henry admirably faced his responsibilities as Richard never did. Although a man of peace, he accepted duties manfully, executing Richard's false counsellors, Scrope, Green and Bushy. Although some still opposed him, Henry worked in an orderly manner: he freed Warwick and Cobham and then assembled parliament. When timid Richard 'completely renounced his title to the Crown' (marginal gloss at III.285, Stockton, p. 320), parliament elected Henry the rightful king: 'Then Henry, the glory of the English and the best of good men, was chosen King, since it was fitting' (III.298–9, Stockton, p. 320). Throughout Gower's presentation the emphasis is on the legality of Henry's actions and the piety with which he undertook them.[57]

---

*Plowman*, which I cited earlier. The criteria that Gower lays out for good kingship in *Confessio* work well as a key to both satires, as they delineate the evils of Richard's rule.

[57] Gower is not alone in his strategy of celebrating Henry's qualities and legal claim to the throne. (See *Cronica Tripertita* III.332–5, Stockton, *Major Latin Works*, p. 321, on Henry's three-fold right.) Most of the chronicles and works like *Richard the Redeless* and *Mum and the Sothsegger* emphasise, even as Gower does, the illegality of Richard's behaviour over the last dozen years of his rule, while making the point that Henry is a king who does not put himself above and beyond the reaches of law. Like Chaucer, who addresses Henry in 'The Complaint of Chaucer to his Purse', the legitimacy of his rule is defined by conquest, 'lyne and free eleccion' (lines 22–3).

A third work that Gower wrote in celebration of Henry's kingship is the shorter poem *In Praise of Peace*, Gower's last English poem. Just as *Cronica Tripertita* is presented as the conclusion to *Vox Clamantis*, *In Praise of Peace* reads like a coda to the *Confessio*.[58] 'O worthi noble kyng, Henry the ferthe' (line 1),[59] it begins, as the poet reiterates Henry's just claim to the throne through the benefits of 'glade fortune' (line 2), the 'worschipe of this lond' (line 5), the affirmation of 'the londes folk', the rights of his 'ancestrie', and 'the highe god of his justice allone' who has 'declared' it so (lines 8–14). Henry is the wise king Gower yearned for in *Confessio* Book 7, a king knowledgeable of 'olde bookes' in which 'y wot wel thow art lerned' (lines 24–5). He, like King Solomon, 'ches wisdom unto the governynge/ Of goddis folk, the which he wolde save' (lines 31–2), rather than following other licentious cravings. His rule is founded 'thurgh his wit', whereby he 'gat him pees and reste unto the laste' (lines 35–6). In the *Confessio*, Gower had emphasised that although Alexander had all the benefits of Aristotle's good instruction, he still became a tyrant and died wretchedly in exile. Gower warns Henry to avoid the errors of Alexander, who won the world by conquest and tyranny: 'Al was vengance and infortune of sinne' (line 49). As Gower had made emphatic in the *Cronica*, England has recently witnessed the folly of such tyranny in Richard's vengeful acts against his English kinsmen. Gower allows that Henry has the privilege to 'make werre upon his right' to claim his 'rightful heritage' (lines 59–65), but he insists that 'the lawe of riht schal noght be leid aside' (line 56) and that God himself will: 'Afferme love and pes betwen the kynges,/ Pes is the beste above alle erthely thinges' (lines 62–3). If a king has a choice between war and peace, 'betre is the pees, of which may no man lese' (line 70); it is 'the chief of al the worldes welthe' (line 78). In the latter part of the poem Gower advises the king to choose his counsellors well and to put aside warmongers, reminding him that Christ gave the world peace, the foundation of which is charity. The whole point of the crucifixion is peace and a new law superior to the laws of Moses (lines 187ff.). He then outlines the principal concerns facing the new king: the avaricious Pope who has brought division within the church, along with the promulgation of false belief. The priesthood needs help, which a good king can bestow by opposing church corruption. The poem concludes by turning to Cassiodorus, who emphasised the importance of pity. The final pleas and prayers address 'My worthi liege lord, Henri be name' (line 358), in whom God has planted peace 'in thi conscience' (line 368) sufficient for him to 'among the seintz be take into memoire/ To the loenge of perdurable gloire' (lines 370–1). Like David, he is a model to other kings, a keeper of the state and its laws, but also a keeper of the church. 'Sette ek the rightful Pope upon his stalle,/ Kep charite and draugh pite to honde,/ Maintene lawe, and so the pes schal stonde' (lines 383–5). One who adhered to such policy would be a wise king indeed.

Gower lived and wrote in turbulent times. The turbulence focused upon the king and the nation's leadership. Gower saw the crux of good rule figured in the crown itself. In Book VII of the *Confessio*, in his discussion of Truth, the first point

---

[58] See the *Explicit* to *Vox* that announces the *Cronica* (Stockton, p. 288).
[59] See Macaulay, *English Works*, Vol. II, pp. 481–92.

of good policy, Genius speaks of the crown as a symbol of what kingship *should* be (VII.1751ff.): the gold of the crown signifies excellence, for the good king must be the most excellent of people in order that the people revere him with allegiance. 'For if men scholde trouthe seche/ And founde it noght withinne a king,/ It were an unsittende thing' (VII.1734–6). The stones on the crown have a triple virtue: that they are hard signifies constancy; likewise, the gems in their clarity signify honesty, for the king's word must be true; and the bright colours of the gems betoken fame, for the king's 'goode name' should shine as a bright example of virtue. Finally, the crown is a circle that signifies the whole extent of the land that stands under his hierarchy, that he should 'wel kepe and guye' (VII.1774). Like the music of David's harp in the *Mirour*, the circle signals the guiding principle of orderly containment and good rule that enables both the head of state and the head of the individual to co-exist hypostatically within a single premise. The king should be the embodiment of the crown, wedded to his people, as Chaucer implies in 'Lak of Stedfastnesse'. But if he does not heed the *sentence* of the crown, then the voices of those divorced from its good rule are likely to cry out in their exile and search for a true king. That would be – and was, indeed – 'an unsittende thing' (VII.1736).

# 13

## Gower's Poetic Styles

JOHN BURROW

The variety of languages employed by Gower in his writings is more than matched by the variety of styles which they display. In his Latin works, the plain prose of the sidenotes to *Confessio Amantis* contrasts sharply with the elaborate and difficult manner of the elegiac couplets and Leonine hexameters of its headnotes; and these verses themselves contrast, though less sharply, with the rather easier couplets and Leonines of the longer Latin poems, *Vox Clamantis* and *Cronica Tripertita*.[1] In his French writings, Gower has a more leisurely and expansive manner in his *balades* than in the octosyllabic lines of the *Mirour de l'Omme*. In English, too, his way of writing in the rhyme royal stanzas of *In Praise of Peace* and the 'Supplication of Amans' contrasts with the plainer short-couplet manner familiar to all readers of *Confessio Amantis*. In his discussion of the *Confessio* in *The Allegory of Love*, C.S. Lewis remarks on this stylistic adaptability. He cites a rhyme royal stanza from the Supplication, and comments: 'No doubt, the different quality of these lines is largely due to the different metre; but if Gower can thus adapt himself with equal felicity to the two metres, and use two differing styles, then the style of his octosyllables is art, not nature – or is nature in such a way as not to be the less art.'[2]

Art or nature? Art, certainly, according to those who admire the *Confessio*. So far as the language and style of the poem are concerned, they have singled out qualities which all imply a spirit of active critical discrimination on the part of its author. The first printer of the *Confessio*, Thomas Berthelette, spoke of Gower as a model for a modern writer, 'that shall as a lanterne gyue hym lyghte to wryte counnyngly'; and another sixteenth-century reader, John Leland, praised him as 'the first polisher of our native language' ('primus patriae linguae expolitor'), before whose time no English writer had produced work 'worthy of a discriminating reader' ('eleganti lectore dignum').[3] A somewhat similar comment, expressed in the idiom of a later age, may be found in Thomas Warton's *History*

1 See A.G. Rigg, *A History of Anglo-Latin Literature, 1066–1422* (Cambridge, 1992), pp. 292–3. Also S. Echard and C. Fanger, *The Latin Verses in the* Confessio Amantis: *An Annotated Translation* (East Lansing, MI, 1991), p. xxxv.
2 C.S. Lewis, *The Allegory of Love: A Study in Medieval Tradition* (Oxford, 1936), pp. 204–5. See also R.F. Yeager in his essay ' "Oure englisshe" and Everyone's Latin: The *Fasciculus Morum* and Gower's *Confessio Amantis*', *South Atlantic Review* 46 (1981), pp. 41–53 (pp. 47–50).
3 T. Berthelette's edition of *Confessio Amantis* (1532), aaii[v], cited from N.F. Blake, 'Early Printed Editions of *Confessio Amantis*', *Mediaevalia* 16 (1993), pp. 289–306 (p. 299). J. Leland,

*of English Poetry* (1774–81): 'If Chaucer had not existed, the compositions of John Gower, the next poet in succession, would alone have been sufficient to rescue the reigns of Edward the Third and Richard the Second from the imputation of barbarism. His education was liberal and uncircumscribed, his course of reading extensive, and he tempered his severer studies with a knowledge of life. By a critical cultivation of his native language, he laboured to reform its irregularities, and to establish an English style.'[4] Correctness and regularity appealed less to the tastes of the following century; but the themes have been taken up again in the modern academy, first by G.C. Macaulay. In his meticulous edition, published in 1900, Macaulay had every occasion to notice what he calls Gower's 'finished mastery of expression', specifying 'his admirable management of the verse paragraph, the metrical smoothness of his lines, attained without unnatural accent or forced order of words, and the neatness with which he expresses exactly what he has to say within the precise limits which he lays down for himself'.[5] In his admiring and admirable review-essay on Macaulay's edition, W.P. Ker echoes such comments: ' "Correctness" is his poetical virtue, his title of honour', he writes; and again, 'it may be doubted whether even Pope is more of an artist than Gower'.[6] In *The Allegory of Love*, Lewis also invokes the Augustans, though in somewhat different terms. Gower, he says, 'is our first considerable master of the plain style in poetry. . . . He stands almost alone in the centuries before our Augustans in being a poet perfectly well bred.'[7] Following Lewis, Donald Davie offers Gower (not Chaucer) as the first English master of the 'purity of diction' which Davie finds chiefly in eighteenth-century poets: 'the perfection of the common language', 'prosaic strength, exactness and urbanity'.[8]

These comments raise three related issues, which I shall consider in turn: 'correctness', 'purity of diction', and the 'plain style'.

A writer can hardly be called 'correct' unless in his time there were recognised standards of correctness to which he might conform; and the difficulty of applying the term to a Ricardian poet lies in knowing what, for a writer of English at that time, such standards would have been. The fourteenth century has left very little evidence of any public discourse about the rights and wrongs of English writing, quite unlike that golden age of correctness, the eighteenth century.[9] Thus, we can know what, for an Augustan writer, it meant to spell

---

*Commentarii de Scriptoribus Britannicis* (c. 1540), ed. A. Hall (Oxford, 1709), pp. 414–15, cited from R.F. Yeager, *John Gower's Poetic: The Search for a New Arion* (Cambridge, 1990), p. 4.

4  T. Warton, *The History of English Poetry*, revised edition (London, 1824), Vol. II, p. 305.

5  G.C. Macaulay, *The English Works of John Gower*, EETS, es nos. 81and 82 (London, 1900–1901), I.xvi. Also p. xviii: 'We feel that we have to do with a literary craftsman who by laborious training has acquired an almost perfect mastery over his tools.'

6  W.P. Ker, *Essays on Medieval Literature* (London, 1905), pp. 104, 111.

7  Lewis, *Allegory of Love*, p. 201.

8  D. Davie, *Purity of Diction in English Verse* (London, 1952), referring to Gower on pp. 32, 59n., 68. P. Fison describes Gower as very like Dryden in 'his controlled and effortless smoothness that prefers to sacrifice an individual beauty rather than to upset the balance of the whole': 'The Poet in John Gower', *Essays in Criticism* 8 (1958), pp. 16–26 (p. 21). For a survey of the history of Gower's reputation, see D. Pearsall, 'The Gower Tradition', in *Gower's* Confessio Amantis: *Responses and Reassessments*, ed. A.J. Minnis (Cambridge, 1983), pp. 179–97; as well as the Introduction and chapters 5 and 6 of this volume.

9  For eighteenth-century evidence, see the anthology by S.I. Tucker, *English Examined* (Cambridge, 1961).

correctly; but the 'exactness and consistency' observed by Macaulay in the spelling of Gower's English remains something of a mystery.[10] Was he conforming to some orthographical standard, as yet unidentified? Or did he, as it were privately, fix upon forms for his own use, as representations of the English which he himself spoke?[11]

Yet it is clear that in his handling of metre, at least, Gower fully met the conditions required for correct writing at the time. Here standards were indeed set for him, albeit by French rather than English poets. In the remarkably faithful Fairfax manuscript, taken by Macaulay as the base text for his edition, Gower can be seen to conform closely to the metrical practice of such French writers as Guillaume de Machaut. He observes the principles of the syllable-count in his octosyllabic and decasyllabic lines very strictly – more strictly than Chaucer does, if the Chaucer manuscripts are to be trusted. Indeed, Macaulay observes that 'there are hardly more than three or four lines in the *Confessio Amantis* where a superfluous syllable stands unaccounted for'.[12] In the matter of rhyming technique, too, Gower conforms to the best Middle French usage. His rhymes are themselves exact, and he can on occasion match the virtuoso rhyming feats of his continental masters. The *Confessio* has many examples (notably at V. 79–90) of that kind of punning rhyme or *rime equivoque* so highly recommended by late medieval French Arts of Poetry; and there is another Gallic subtlety in the twelve rhyme royal stanzas of the 'Supplication of Amans', where not one of the thirty-six rhyme sounds is repeated.[13]

Guillaume de Machaut would, admittedly, have heard something of a foreign tune in Gower's verse, for the English poems represent 'a consistent and for the moment a successful attempt to combine the French syllabic with the English accentual system of metre'.[14] Yet here too there is a kind of correctness, for, as Macaulay again observes, 'the natural accent of words is preserved far better in Gower's verse than in Chaucer's'.[15] Gower makes sure, that is, that ordinary linguistic stresses coincide with the beats of the English iambic line (allowing the usual licences such as trochaic inversion in the first foot). This is the main reason why Gower even allows himself on occasion to depart from the customary correctness of his English usage, misplacing the conjunction *and*, as in the second line here:

[10] Macaulay, *English Works*, I.xciv
[11] See M.L. Samuels and J.J. Smith, 'The Language of Gower', in Samuels and Smith, *The English of Chaucer and his Contemporaries* (Aberdeen, 1988), pp. 13–22. They remark that 'the orthographical system attested by the Fairfax and Stafford MSS is very regular and consistent' (p. 17); but they show that the spellings of these manuscripts reflect Gower's own idiosyncratic mixture of Kent and Suffolk forms, there being no orthographical standard at the time to which he might have conformed (p. 20).
[12] Macaulay, *English Works*, I.cxxi. See generally pp. cxx–cxxvii. On metrical correctness in the *Confessio*, see also Yeager, *John Gower's Poetic*, pp. 16–24, and C.A. Owen, 'Notes on Gower's Prosody', *Chaucer Review* 28 (1994), pp. 405–13. On the regularity of Gower's French verse, see Macaulay, *French Works* in *The Complete Works of John Gower* (Oxford, 1899–1902), Vol. IV, pp. xliv–xlv.
[13] Observed by Owen, 'Notes on Gower's Prosody', pp. 406–7. On *rime equivoque*, see E. Langlois, ed., *Receuil d'arts de seconde rhétorique* (Paris, 1902), Index under *Equivoques*.
[14] Macaulay, *English Works*, I.xix.
[15] Ibid., I.cxxvi.

> And thus wepende sche compleigneth,
> Hire faire face and al desteigneth. (I.965–6)

The second line scans easily as it stands: x / x / x / x / x . What the eccentric
placing of *and* avoids is 'And hire faire face al desteigneth', a line which would
have thrown the two stressed syllables of 'faire face' (/ x /) into odd rather than
even positions: xx /x / /x / x.[16]

Grammar and syntax are the other areas, besides metre, where Gower may be
understood as conforming to available standards of correctness in his English
writings. It is from grammars of the Latin language that he would have been
familiar with the rules. His own word for the general principle involved is
*congruite*, which requires correct agreement between the constituents of a
sentence.[17] What grammar teaches, he says, is 'to speke upon congruite' (VII.
1531), and elsewhere he observes that 'the ferste reule of Scole' for the composition of Latin is that 'every word in his degre/ Schal stonde upon congruite'
(IV.2642–6). For a writer in English, the demands of congruity bear, not upon the
easy agreement of adjectives or verbs with nouns, but upon the construction of
sentences, and especially long ones. Macaulay, who has an eye for such things,
notices about a dozen places in the *Confessio* where Gower's syntax fails to be
congruous: sentences 'broken off and finished in a different manner'.[18] Such
disruptions are commonly caused by hypertrophy in parenthetical or subor-
dinate clauses:

> This enderday, as I forthferde
> To walke, as I yow telle may, –
> And that was in the Monthe of Maii,
> Whan every brid hath chose his make
> And thenkth his merthes forto make
> Of love that he hath achieved;
> But so was I nothing relieved . . . (I.98–104)

Yet the fact that Macaulay – quite as much judge as advocate of his author –
should find so few examples in such a long poem stands to the credit of the
poet's fidelity to 'the ferste reule of Scole'. Syntactic correctness of this kind,
sustained over many thousand lines, hardly lends itself to illustration except by
examples themselves rather untypically strong; but here is one such. Amans is
confessing to *Schadenfreude*:

> Of these lovers that loven streyte,
> And for that point which thei coveite
> Ben poursuiantz fro yeer to yere

---

16  Compare III.1415, V.7429, VII.2671. The displacement may also serve the syllable count by
    facilitating elision, as at II.851, 1301, 1556. Macaulay, *French Works*, pp. xl–xli, notes similar
    displacements of *et* in *Mirour de l'Omme*, lines 100, 415, 4523, 7860, etc. See also his note on *que*
    in Latin verses, *English Works*, I.468 (note to I.v.1).
17  MED *congruite* n. (b), also *congruli* adv. (b); OED *Congruity* 4, also *Congrue* a. 2, *Congruely* adv.,
    *Congruent* a. 3, *Congruous* a. 4, *Congruously* adv. 3.
18  Prol. 34*–42*, I.98–107, I.2946–53, III.1593–7, III.2608–16, IV.3197–211, V.1043–54, V.1335–47,
    V.7195–202, VI.1795–1803, VII.3627–39. See Macaulay's notes to these places.

> In loves Court, whan I may hiere
> How that thei clymbe upon the whel,
> And whan thei wene al schal be wel,
> Thei ben doun throwen ate laste,
> Thanne am I fedd of that thei faste,
> And lawhe of that I se hem loure.  (II.237–45)

The subordinating *whan* of line 240 and its verb *hiere* govern both the nested sub-ordinate clauses which precede it ('Of these lovers . . .') and those which follow ('How that thei . . .'); and the whole *whan*-complex is firmly coupled to the ensuing main clauses by the *Thanne* at line 244. Such command of periodic syntax cannot be taken for granted even in educated writers of the time, as the example of John Lydgate demonstrates. Perhaps it was the discipline of writing also in Latin which sharpened Gower's awareness of the grammarians' demand for 'congruity'. Certainly Ben Jonson, a writer of high classical taste, could accept him as a model of correct English, for in the second book of his *English Grammar*, 'Of Syntaxe', Jonson quotes more examples from Gower than from any other English writer.[19]

I turn now to the diction of the *Confessio*. This is a subject about which rather little is known at present, pending exploitation by scholars of the *Concordance* to the poem.[20] To speak of a writer's diction (as against his vocabulary) is to direct attention to his choices of words, selecting some and rejecting others, from the general language of his day. In his study of purity of diction, Donald Davie cites Gower as his single medieval instance of such selectivity, but without pursuing the matter himself. One promising starting point might be the study by E.T. Donaldson of the way Geoffrey Chaucer excludes from serious use what Donaldson describes as the 'idiom of popular poetry' – some of the diction, that is, of Middle English love-lyric and metrical romance.[21] It seems that Gower avoids certain expressions of this 'popular' kind at least as carefully as does Chaucer. Indeed, unlike Chaucer, he almost completely abstains from addressing his audience in his own person, after the fashion of Middle English popular romance writers.[22] He strikes that note only once, in fact, at the moment when he first embarks on his story:

> Now herkne, who that wol it hiere,
> Of my fortune how that it ferde.

---

[19] Ben Jonson, *The English Grammar*, pp. 453–553 in Vol. VIII (Oxford, 1947) of the edition of *Works* by C.H. Herford, P. and E. Simpson. The three most frequently cited English writers are Gower (29x), Chaucer (26x), and Thomas More (15x).

[20] J.D. Pickles and J.L. Dawson, eds, *A Concordance to John Gower*s Confessio Amantis* (Cambridge, 1987).

[21] E. Talbot Donaldson, 'Idiom of Popular Poetry in *The Miller's Tale*', *English Institute Essays 1950* (1951), pp. 116–40, reprinted in Donaldson, *Speaking of Chaucer* (London, 1970), pp. 13–29.

[22] See R. Crosby, 'Chaucer and the Custom of Oral Delivery', *Speculum* 13 (1938), pp. 413–32, with Chaucer examples on p. 415. A.T. Gaylord speaks of the absence of any 'allusion to occasions when the author might be addressing a company of listeners' in the *Confessio*, with the bookish Gower 'suppressing almost entirely any minstrel associations': ' "After the Forme of my Writynge": Gower's Bookish Prosody', *Mediaevalia* 16 (1993), pp. 257–88 (pp. 259, 283).

> This enderday, as I forthferde
> To walke, as I yow telle may . . . (I.96–9)

It is as if, to get his narrative under way, Gower draws for once upon the ener-gies of oral narrative: 'Now herkne . . .'. He follows this up with an introductory formula also commonly used by other narrative and lyric poets: 'This enderday, as I forthferde . . .'.[23] Nowhere else in the *Confessio*, I believe, does Gower extend such generous hospitality to the 'idiom of popular poetry', though he does quite often allow himself another convenient narrative formula from the romances, 'And so bifell upon a dai', with minor variations in the first three words.[24] Although Chaucer has similar expressions, he reserves the plainest form, 'And so befell upon a day', for his imitation of old-fashioned metrical romance, 'Sir Thopas' (VII.748, and compare line 918 there).

Donaldson in his essay identified certain items of contemporary poetic diction which Chaucer used only with his tongue in his cheek, marking them off, evidently, as worn-out, déclassé, or the like: *hende*, *derne* (of love), *gent*, *love-longynge*, *ore* (mercy). Gower simply excludes some of these altogether: no one in the *Confessio* is ever *gent*, nor do the many lovers there ever suffer from *love-longynge* or pray for the *ore* of their mistresses. The other two words identi-fied by Donaldson, *hende* (as in 'hende Nicholas') and *derne*, are each used once only by Amans, in rhyme on both occasions: he refers to his lady as 'that hende' (IV.644) and speaks of Love as 'of himself so derne,/ It luteth in a mannes herte' (I.1932–3).[25] Further evidence of what Warton called Gower's 'critical cultiva-tion' of his English may be seen in the sparing employment of poetic alliterative formulae.[26] Typical examples are those wheeled out by Chaucer in his 'rym I lerned longe agoon': 'bright in bour', 'game and glee', and 'worly under wede' ('Sir Thopas', VII.742, 840, 917). These particular phrases are absent from the *Confessio*, along with others of the same sort, such as 'stiff in stour' and even 'red as rose'. The purge is only partial, however. Gower will on occasion speak of 'cares colde' (III.299), have a horseman 'prike and prance' (VI.1191), or speak of a hero as 'war and wys' (VIII.696). Yet one may guess that a suitably qualified reader – an *elegans lector* from the London intelligentsia, perhaps – would have been impressed by the relative absence of such commonplace English poeticisms. That reader might indeed have received the very impression

---

23 Texts beginning 'This ender day' (or 'night') are numbers 3593–9 in C. Brown and R.H. Robbins, *The Index of Middle English Verse* (New York, 1943). Gower employs the formula on one other occasion, in the narrative of Paris: 'This ender day, as I gan fare' (V.7400).
24 See II.300 and III.1694; II.1310, V.6748 and VIII.374; also III.2368, V.676, VII.3474. The word *day* may be replaced as rhyme or context dictate: by *tide* (I.349, V.5573), *nyht* (V.2170, V.3957), *chaunce* (III.789), or *cas* (IV.458).
25 Donaldson relies upon 'ironical contexts' to identify such diction in Chaucer. Since Gower does not deal in stylistic ironies, further study of this aspect of his language must look, in the *Concordance*, for poetic words simply not used at all, or rarely, in the *Confessio*.
26 J.P. Oakden gives a list of alliterative phrases in the *Confessio*, drawing on a German thesis; but many of them belong to common parlance, not poetic usage, like 'lord and lady' or 'come to court': *Alliterative Poetry in Middle English: A Survey of the Traditions* (Manchester, 1935), pp. 368–71.

described by Davie in his account of 'pure' diction: 'the sense of English words thrusting to be let into the poem and held out of it by the poet'.[27]

But how, more generally and positively, is one to characterise the style of *Confessio Amantis*? I take a cue from C.S. Lewis's description of Gower as 'our first considerable master of the plain style in poetry'. What does it mean, though, to call him a 'master of the plain style'? In the case of later masters, such as Ben Jonson, scholars can draw upon a wealth of contemporary critical discourse, which helps with the understanding of their way of writing.[28] In the case of Gower, by contrast, evidence for such a critical context is scanty; nor does the poet himself offer much guidance. At the beginning of Book I, he declares his intention of changing 'the Stile of my writinges' (I.8), but this single occurrence of the word *stile* refers to the content, not the manner, of what is to follow (MED *stile* n.(2), sense (b)). One may glean something, however, from his frequent uses of the word *plein* itself. On occasion, the word denotes fullness of utterance (Latin *plenus*), as at VII.521–6; but more often it denotes direct, unadorned speech or writing (Latin *planus*).[29] When people in the *Confessio* refer to this, they speak of using words 'trewe and plein' (VII.1731), 'pleine and bare' (VII.2350), or 'pleine and expresse' (VIII.2185). It is an ideal exemplified in the Gospels (VI.977), a moral ideal to be set against equivocation: 'frounces' (II.392, VII.1594), 'colours' (VII.1625), and 'double speche' (VII.1733). Fine language, says Genius, is to be avoided in confession:

> it mot be plein,
> It nedeth noght to make it queinte,
> For trowthe hise wordes wol noght peinte.  (I.282–4)

According to Genius, again, the arts of logic and rhetoric both favour plain speaking. Logic distinguishes between the true and the false in 'pleine wordes' (VII.1532–4); and rhetoric, more surprisingly, teaches a man 'in what wise he schal pronounce/ His tale plein withoute frounce' (VII.1593–4). Bearing these passages in mind, one may see a little more than mere conventional self-deprecation in Gower's concluding apology for the 'lak of curiosite' in his book:

> For thilke scole of eloquence
> Belongith nought to my science,
> Uppon the forme of rethoriqe
> My wordis forto peinte and pike,
> As Tullius som tyme wrot.
> Bot this y knowe and this y wot,
> That y have do my trewe peyne
> With rude wordis and with pleyne,

---

[27] Davie, *Purity of Diction in English Verse*, p. 5.

[28] See W. Trimpi, *Ben Jonson's Poems: A Study of the Plain Style* (Stanford, CA 1962). Trimpi draws on Classical and Renaissance thinking about plain style to explicate Jonson's verse. He recognises, but sets aside, a distinct native tradition of plainness among medieval poets (p. 119).

[29] The two senses are sometimes difficult to distinguish, as lexicographers remark (MED *plain(e* adj. and *plein(e* adj.). The one sense often entails the other: one way of covering a topic fully is to write about it plainly.

In al that evere y couthe and myghte,
This bok to write as y behighte. (VIII.3115–24)

Gower was in reality well acquainted with the 'scole of eloquence'; nor does
he, of course, confine his diction to 'rude' and 'pleyne' words. Some of his
French-derived vocabulary is indeed distinctly *recherché*: 'devolte apparantie'
(I.636), 'duistres' (I.1027), 'femeline' (V.5550), 'aspirementz' (VII.256), 'deduit'
(VIII.2847).[30] On occasion, too, his training in rhetoric surfaces quite ostenta-
tiously in the patterning and play of words. An extreme example is the
anaphoric list of female attractions in Book V: 'Som on, for sche is whit of skin,/
Som on, for sche is noble of kin,/ Som on . . . etc.' (V.2469–81). *Repetitio* can also
take unpatterned forms, as in the cadenzas on the words *pride* (I.3297–314), *gold*
(V.234–45), and *word* itself (VII.1564–87). A more learned form of repetition,
*traductio*, rings the changes on a root word, as in the following lines about
Tiresias:

> And for he hath destourbed kinde
> And was so to nature unkinde,
> Unkindeliche he was transformed,
> That he which erst a man was formed
> Into a womman was forschape.
> That was to him an angri jape;
> Bot for that he with Angre wroghte,
> Hise Angres angreliche he boghte (III.373–80)

The wordplay here – 'kinde . . . unkinde . . . unkindeliche' and 'angri . . . Angre
. . . Angres . . . angreliche' – recalls, for once, the mannerism of Gower's Latin
verses.[31]

Such wordplay, however, plays little part in the staple style of *Confessio
Amantis*. Gower's best effects do not generally, in fact, depend upon the use of
rhetorical tropes. Simple words are used in straightforward literal senses, as in
the following lines, spoken by Amans:

> Somdiel I mai the betre fare,
> Whan I, that mai noght fiele hir bare,
> Mai lede hire clothed in myn arm (IV.1139–41)

Although 'clothed' stands in contrast to 'bare', the antithetical coupling nonetheless serves to release a suggestion of flesh beneath the sleeve; so the word itself
acquires a certain sensuality. This has prompted comparison with an epithet of
similar sound in Keats, 'the wealth of *globed* peonies';[32] yet Gower, unlike Keats,
achieves the effect without any richness of poetic diction. Like all the other
words in his lines, 'clothed' has its straight literal meaning, departing from
everyday usage only by virtue of a certain redundancy (the woman would of

---

30  See L.F. Casson, 'Studies in the Diction of the *Confessio Amantis*', *Englische Studien*, 69 (1934),
    pp. 184–207 (pp. 185–6).
31  Compare, for example, the plays on *flectere* in the Latin verses I.vi, or on *probare* in IV.vi.
32  J.A. Burrow, *Ricardian Poetry: Chaucer, Gower, Langland and the Gawain-Poet* (London, 1971),
    p. 30.

course be clothed, if he was leading her by the arm). This is the peculiar eloquence of the plain style. Christopher Ricks has noticed other places in the poem where simple words acquire, in their context, a rather mysterious potency: 'soft' in passages describing beds (I.876, IV.3019), silence (I.2564), and night ('long and softe', IV.3210), or 'gold' in the long passage about Midas (V.217ff.).[33] Elsewhere the effect may be crisp and pointed, as in:

> The daies gon, the Monthe passeth,
> Hire love encresceth and his lasseth  (IV.781–2)

Or, with another antithesis, in the question put by Amans:

> What scholde I winne over the Se,
> If I mi lady loste at hom?  (IV.1664–5)

In the Confessor's stories, plain speaking can strike a dry, laconic note, with comments such as 'He fond the meschief which he soghte' (V.5244), or 'And thoghte more than he seide' (I.2106, and again at II.895 and 2670). Sometimes a whole story will come to a head in a single line, whose power owes nothing to any verbal elaboration: 'The trompe of deth was at my gate' (I.2210), or ' "Drink with thi fader, Dame," he seide' (I.2551). These things have, as Ricks says, 'all the simplicity of literalness and all the suggestiveness of symbolism'.[34]

Yet such symbolic suggestiveness plays rather little part in the *Confessio*. The poem's prevailing mode of meaning is literal. Individual cases here – Amans himself, or the many cases recalled by Genius – are offered as literal examples of the general category to which they belong (love, pride, or whatever). For this generalising purpose the plain style is well suited, since it can handle particular cases without adventuring too much upon those singularities which, as Gower puts it, 'it needeth nought to specifie' (Prol. 33 and 866). Generic epithets, for instance, strike just the right note here: beds can be simply soft, wells fresh, and ladies' fingers long and small.

This same leaning towards the typical and the general appears also, more idiosyncratically, in Gower's peculiar uses of two very plain little words, *the* and *thing*. In his study of the definite article in Middle English, Mustanoja notices Gower's predilection for the word *the*.[35] He is fond of that generalising use which appeals to common experience, as in: 'The Wynter wol no Somer knowe,/ The grene lef is overthrowe' (VIII.2853–4); and he also employs expressions of this kind, more oddly, in describing particular occasions. Thus, in the tale of Constance, after a murderous banquet:

---

33  C. Ricks, 'Metamorphosis in Other Words', in Minnis, *Responses and Reassessments*, pp. 25–49 (pp. 28–30, 34–8).
34  Ricks, p. 40. Another example is the pennon embroidered with three fishes in the story of Ulysses and Telegonus, VI.1391ff.
35  T.F. Mustanoja, *A Middle English Syntax*, Part I 'Parts of Speech' (Helsinki, 1960), pp. 232–59, with frequent references to Gower. Mustanoja suspects French influence in some cases, as when the definite article is used with an abstract noun: 'the charite goth al unknowe' (Prol. 319, cited on p. 257).

> The Dissh forthwith the Coppe and al
> Bebled thei weren overal.  (II.699–700)

Or again, in the tale of Narcissus:

> The houndes weren in a throwe
> Uncoupled and the hornes blowe:
> The grete hert anon was founde.  (I.2297–9)

'The Dissh' and 'the Coppe' stand, of course, for numerous items of the same sort; and 'the grete hert' (not previously referred to) represents what a reader might expect in such a hunt. So this frequent little trick of style directs singulars or particulars towards the general categories to which they belong, in keeping with the poem's overall mode of meaning, literal exemplification. A similar set towards the general and, in this case, the abstract marks Gower's liking for *thing*, a word which the *Concordance* records no less than 570 times in the *Confessio*. It has a remarkable range of reference, to every kind of behaviour and action, to episodes and stories, and even to the poem itself ('som newe thing', Prol. 51*). The general effect is one of distancing, as may be seen in the prayer of Cephalus to Phoebus. Cephalus speaks of love as 'a thing' which is most at home in darkness (IV.3201), and he uses the same word again shortly after:

> And thus whan that thi liht is faded
> And Vesper scheweth him alofte,
> And that the nyht is long and softe,
> Under the cloudes derke and stille
> Thanne hath this thing most of his wille.  (IV.3208–12)

Ricks quotes these lines to illustrate 'the power of abstracting and generalising' exerted by the word in the *Confessio*.[36] He also refers to a remarkable use of *thing* by Venus, advising Amans to abandon the pursuit of love:

> The thing is torned into was;
> That which was whilom grene gras,
> Is welked hey at time now.
> Forthi my conseil is that thou
> Remembre wel hou thou art old.  (VIII.2435–9)

*Confessio Amantis* has made very few contributions to English dictionaries of quotations. The extraordinary line, 'The thing is torned into was', would be unintelligible out of context, despite the simple words of which it is composed; and the poem has rather few isolable high moments such as the cry of Cephalus to the Sun: 'Withdrawgh the Banere of thin Armes' (IV.3220). The paucity of such richly poetic strokes no doubt helps to explain why the *Confessio* failed to appeal to readers in the Romantic period. Coleridge confessed to a scorn for 'the almost worthless Gower', classing him among 'the lengthy poets who . . . make drossy

---

36  Ricks, 'Metamorphosis in Other Words', pp. 28–30.

lead as ductile as pure gold'.[37] It is certainly the case that the virtues of correctness, pure diction and the plain style cannot guarantee writers against dullness. The *Rhetorica ad Herennium*, then ascribed to Cicero, distinguished three levels of style, giving a positive account of the lowest of these as 'composed of correct and well-chosen words' ('puris et electis verbis'). Yet the treatise also warns those cultivating such 'elegant simplicity of diction' that they should beware of producing 'a dry and bloodless kind of style' ('aridum et exsangue genus orationis').[38] Readers will differ about how much of the *Confessio* can justly be described as dry and bloodless; but Gower's short-couplet style, like that of his French masters, certainly has dullness as its characteristic fault. The dullnesses of the *Confessio*, like its beauties, are hard to illustrate without extensive quotation; but a few lines from the story of Apollonius of Tyre may call them to mind:

> He sih the wepinge al aboute,
> And axeth what the cause was,
> And thei him tolden al the cas,
> How sodeinli the Prince is go.
> And whan he sih that it was so,
> And that his labour was in vein,
> Anon he torneth hom ayein,
> And to the king, whan he cam nyh,
> He tolde of that he herde and syh,
> How that the Prince of Tyr is fled,
> So was he come ayein unsped. (VIII.522–32)

In its limitations as well as its strengths, Gower's is essentially a long-poem style, serviceable for a work of more than 33,000 lines. *Confessio Amantis* is, in fact, one of the last and most extended English examples of the very long poem in short couplets – a type developed in the twelfth century by French writers such as Chrétien de Troyes, and turned to encyclopaedic purposes later in the *Roman de la Rose* and in English poems such as *Cursor Mundi*, *Handlyng Synne* and *The Prick of Conscience*. In this respect, Gower shows himself more old-fashioned than Chaucer, who abandoned the octosyllabic couplet after leaving his *House of Fame* unfinished, perhaps because he came to consider that its rapidly recurring rhymes gave him too little scope to achieve the richer poetic effects he was finding in Italian poetry. Gower was capable of writing longer lines in rhyme royal quite as skilfully as his contemporary, but in most of his English and French verse he remained content with the octosyllable.

Very long poems like the *Confessio*, whether narrative or expository or both, have played a diminishing part in Western literature since the Middle Ages. They have proved, in particular, hardly compatible with Romantic and post-Romantic expectations of what poems ought to be like. Typical of such taste is

---

[37] Cited by J.L. Lowes, *The Road to Xanadu*, 2nd edn (London, 1951), p. 471, n. 145. Coleridge does, however, characterise his scorn as 'perverse'.
[38] *Ad C. Herennium de Ratione Dicendi*, ed. and trans. H. Caplan, Loeb Classical Library (London and Cambridge, MA, 1954), IV.xi.16. Cf. Trimpi, *Ben Jonson's Poems*, p. 56: 'Barrenness, dullness, and leanness are the faults that the plain style is most likely to fall into, according to nearly every rhetorical treatise.'

the comment by Edgar Allan Poe, responding in a letter to the prospect of a long poem from his friend James Russell Lowell: 'Poetry must eschew narrative. . . . I mean to say that *true poetry* – the highest poetry – must eschew it. The Iliad is *not* the highest. The connecting links of a narration . . . are necessarily prose, from their very explanatory nature.'[39] The functions of verse had already, by Poe's time, become quite highly specialised, and the distinction that he draws between the proper provinces of prose and poetry would not have been recognised by a medieval writer. Gower's short-couplet style had its origins in a twelfth-century type developed, precisely, for purposes of extended narration. So it is for this function that the style is adapted, as if to allow the reader (typically, readers rather than listeners) to follow the text, if they wished, quite fast.[40] The result can hardly qualify as 'the highest poetry'; but it is, in the right hands, one kind of 'true poetry'.

[39] Letter of October 1843, in J.W. Ostrom, ed., *The Letters of Edgar Allan Poe*, 2 vols (Cambridge, MA, 1948), Vol. I, p. 239.
[40] Gaylord, 'Gower's Bookish Prosody', emphasises the 'bookish' character of the *Confessio*, as a poem to be taken by the reader 'at the proper speed', that is, quickly (p. 281).

# *Appendix:*
## *A Chronology of Gower Criticism*

SIÂN ECHARD AND JULIE LANZ

> Pitty ô pitty, death had power
> Ouer Chaucer, Lidgate, Gower:
> They that equal'd all the Sages
> Of these, their owne, of former Ages.[1]

Thomas Freeman's *Epigram 14*, quoted earlier with reference to Gower's learning, is in fact, as its opening lines above show, a *memento mori*. Death has indeed left Chaucer, Lydgate, and Gower alike to the mercy of the memories and perceptions of later readers, and while I have traced the different histories of Chaucer and Gower, it is important to acknowledge that Gower has always had serious, scholarly readers. The 'Chronology of Criticism' which concludes this volume makes clear that every decade of the last century saw some important work on Gower, and many of the contributors to this volume can trace their own earliest work on Gower back several decades. The decision to offer the bibliography traditional in volumes such as these in a chronological form was taken in part because it allows a reader to see at a glance how Gower criticism has grown and changed; to see the threads of interest which I discussed in the Introduction, and to see the slow but steady increase in critical encounters with Gower's works. The increase is particularly notable from the 1980s onwards, perhaps because the methodologies of the current critical *Zeitgeist* are beginning to make it possible to see more clearly into Gower's real enterprise. Coffman and Fisher both argued that to understand Gower, one had to place him in his context. In a period which now considers social, cultural and material contexts for literature as a matter of course, it is not surprising to find Gower – political, urban and socially (if conservatively) engaged – a new object of interest. Gower's careful self-presentation throughout his works, and the subtle ironies crafted into it, have begun to be uncovered by critical interests in authorship and self-fashioning. Thus, while changes in critical practice have encouraged a renewal of interest in Gower, it is equally important that Gower justifies that interest. Some aspects of Gower's work have become available now that it is fashionable to look for them – but those aspects were always there.

A word about the comprehensiveness of the 'Chronology' is in order. While we have made every effort to represent the range and depth of Gower criticism, it is inevitable that some things will have been left out. In addition, judgements had to be made about whether or not to include works which were not primarily about Gower.

---

1   Thomas Freeman, *Rubbe, and a Great Cast: Epigrams* (London, 1614), *Epigram 14*, lines 1–4.

For the most part, we did not include studies in which Gower was merely one in a list of examples. The 'Chronology' concludes with a separate section on aids to Gower scholarship – editions, bibliographies, concordances, and the like. It is our hope that these, together with the 'Chronology' and the *Companion* itself, will provide a valuable resource to readers who seek to become further acquainted with John Gower.

> Of hem that writen ous tofore
> The bokes duelle, and we therfore
> Ben tawht of that was write tho:
> Forthi good is that we also
> In our tyme among ous hiere
> Do wryte of newe som matiere,
> Essampled of these olde wyse  (Prol. 1–8)

Items marked with an asterisk are anthologised in Peter Nicholson, ed., *Gower's Confessio Amantis: A Critical Anthology*. The two pieces originally in German – by Arno Esch and Götz Schmitz – are translated. The latter is a selection from the third chapter of Schmitz's book.

### Before 1800

Warton, Thomas, *The History of English Poetry from the Close of the Eleventh to the Commencement of the Eighteenth Century*, Vol. II (London, 1778).

### 1800–1900

Ellis, George, *Specimens of the Early English Poets, to which is prefixed an historical sketch of the rise and progress of the English Poetry and Language; in three volumes*, 2nd edn (London, 1801).

Todd, Henry, *Illustrations of the Lives and Writings of Gower and Chaucer collected from authentick documents* (London, 1810).

Nicolas, Sir Harris, 'John Gower the Poet', *Retrospective Review and Historical and Antiquarian Magazine*, second series, 2 (1828), pp. 103–17.

'John Gower and his Works', *The British Quarterly Review*, no. 53, Jan. 1 (1858), pp. 3–36.

Easton, Morton W., *Readings in Gower* (Philadelphia, 1895).

Eichinger, Karl, *Die Trojasage als Stoffquelle für John Gower's Confessio Amantis* (Munich, 1900).

Görbing, F., 'Die Ballade *The Marriage of Sir Gawain* in ihren Beziehungen zu Chaucers "Wife of Bath's Tale" und Gowers Erzählung von Florent', *Anglia* 23 (1900), pp. 405–23.

### 1901–1910

Fluegel, Ewald, 'Gower's *Mirour de l'Omme* und Chaucer's Prolog', *Anglia* 24 (1901), pp. 437–508.

Maynadier, G.H., *The Wife of Bath's Tale: Its Sources and Analogues* (London, 1901).

Stollreither, Eugen, *Quellen-Nachweise zu John Gowers Confessio Amantis* (Munich, 1901).

Gough, A.B., *The Constance Saga* (Berlin, 1902).

Ker, W.P., 'John Gower, Poet', *Quarterly Review* 197 (1903), pp. 437–58.

Kittredge, G.L., 'Chaucer and Some of His Friends', *Modern Philology* 1:1 (1903), pp. 1–18.

Hamilton, George L., 'Notes on Gower', *Modern Language Notes* 19:2 (1904), pp. 51–2.

Fowler, R. Elfreda, *Une Source Française des Poèmes de Gower* (Macon, 1905).

Hamilton, George L., 'Gower's Use of the Enlarged *Roman de Troie*', *PMLA* 20:1 (1905), pp. 179–96.

Tatlock, J.S.P., 'Milton's Sin and Death', *Modern Language Notes* 21:8 (1906), pp. 239–40.

Waltz, Gotthard, *Das Sprichwort bei Gower, mit besonderem Hinweis auf Quellen und Parallelen* (Nördlingen, 1907).

Macaulay, G.C., 'John Gower', *The Cambridge History of English Literature*, Vol. II, *The End of the Middle Ages*, ed. A.W. Ward and A.R. Waller (Cambridge, 1908), pp. 133–55.

## 1911–1920

Hamilton, George L., 'Some Sources of the Seventh Book of Gower's *Confessio Amantis*', *Modern Philology* 9:3 (1912), pp. 323–46.

Dodd, William George, *Courtly Love in Chaucer and Gower* (Boston, 1913).

Cook, Albert S., 'Dante and Gower', *Archiv für das Studium der neueren Sprachen und Literaturen* 132 (1914), p. 395.

Kuhl, Ernest P., 'Some Friends of Chaucer', *PMLA* 29:2 (1914), pp. 270–6.

Lowes, John Livingston, 'Spenser and the *Mirour de l'Omme*', *PMLA* 29:3 (1914), pp. 388–452.

Lowes, John Livingston, 'Chaucer and the Seven Deadly Sins', *PMLA* 30:2 (1915), pp. 237–371; note that this is a response to Frederick Tupper's article of the same title in *PMLA* 29:1 (1914), pp. 93–128.

Bihl, Josef, *Die Wirkungen des Rhythmus in der Sprache von Chaucer und Gower* (Heidelberg, 1916).

Knowlton, E.C., 'The Allegorical Figure Genius', *Classical Philology* 15:4 (1920), pp. 380–4.

## 1921–1930

Knowlton, E.C., 'Genius as an Allegorical Figure', *Modern Language Notes* 39:2 (1924), pp. 89–95.

Hamilton, George L., 'Studies in the Sources of Gower. I. The Latin and French Versions of "Barlaam and Jospahat", and of the Legendary History of Alexander the Great', *Journal of English and Germanic Philology* 26 (1927), pp. 491–520.

Gilbert, Allan H., 'Notes on the Influence of the *Secretum Secretorum*', *Speculum* 3:1 (1928), pp. 84–98.

Manly, John Matthews, 'On the Question of the Portuguese Translation of Gower's *Confessio Amantis*', *Modern Philology* 27:4 (1930), pp. 467–72.

## 1931–1940

Fox, George G., *The Mediaeval Sciences in the Works of John Gower* (Princeton, 1931).

Heather, P.J., 'Precious Stones in the Middle-English Verse of the Fourteenth Century', *Folk-Lore* 42 (1931), pp. 217–64, 345–404.

Street, Ethel, 'John Gower', *London Mercury* 24 (1931), pp. 230–42.

Casson, Leslie F., 'Studies in the Diction of the *Confessio Amantis*', *Englische Studien* 69 (1934), pp. 184–207.

\*Lewis, C.S., *The Allegory of Love: A Study in Medieval Tradition* (Oxford, 1936), see pp. 198–222.

Kleineke, Wilhelm, *Englische Fürstenspiegel vom Policraticus Johanns von Salisbury bis zum Basilikon doron König Jakobs I* (Halle, 1937).

### 1941–1950

Dilts, Dorothy A., 'John Gower and the *De Genealogia Deorum*', *Modern Language Notes* 57:1 (1942), pp. 23–5.

Heather, P.J., 'The Seven Planets', *Folk-Lore* 54 (1943), pp. 338–61.

Henkin, Leo J., 'The Carbuncle in the Adder's Head', *Modern Language Notes* 58:1 (1943), pp. 34–9.

\*Coffman, George R., 'John Gower in his Most Significant Role', *Elizabethan Studies and Other Essays in Honor of George F. Reynolds* (Colorado, 1945), pp. 52–61.

Callan, Norman, 'Thyn Owne Book: A Note on Chaucer, Gower and Ovid', *Review of English Studies* 22:88 (1946), pp. 269–81.

Bland, D.S., 'The Poetry of John Gower', *English* 6 (1948), pp. 286–90.

Stillwell, Gardiner, 'John Gower and the Last Years of Edward III', *Studies in Philology* 45 (1948), pp. 454–71.

Thorpe, Lewis, 'A Source of the *Confessio Amantis*', *Modern Language Review* 43 (1948), pp. 175–81.

Bennett, J.A.W., 'Caxton and Gower', *Modern Language Review* 45 (1950), pp. 215–16.

### 1951–1960

Dwyer, J.B., 'Gower's *Mirour* and its French Sources: A Re-examination of Evidence', *Studies in Philology* 48 (1951), pp. 482–505.

Bloomfield, Morton W., *The Seven Deadly Sins: An Introduction to the History of a Religious Concept, with Special Reference to Medieval English Literature* (East Lansing, MI, 1952).

Neville, Marie, 'Gower's Serpent and the Carbuncle', *Notes and Queries* 197 (1952), pp. 225–6. See Henkin above.

Dulak, Robert E., 'Gower's "Tale of Constance" ', *Notes and Queries* 198 (1953), pp. 368–9.

Legge, Dominica, ' "The Gracious Conqueror" ', *Modern Language Notes* 68:1 (1953), pp. 18–21.

Sullivan, William L., 'Chaucer's Man of Law as a Literary Critic', *Modern Language Notes* 68:1 (1953), pp. 1–8.

Wickert, Maria, *Studien zu John Gower/ Studies in John Gower*, trans. Robert J. Meindl (Cologne/Washington, 1953/1982).

Coffman, George R., 'John Gower, Mentor for Royalty: Richard II', *PMLA* 69:4 (1954), pp. 953–64.

Beichner, Paul E., 'Gower's Use of *Aurora* in *Vox Clamantis*', *Speculum* 30:4 (1955), pp. 582–95.

Goolden, P., 'Antiochus's Riddle in Gower and Shakespeare', *Review of English Studies*, n.s. 6:23 (1955), pp. 245–51.

Raymo, Robert R., 'Gower's *Vox Clamantis* and the *Speculum Stultorum*', *Modern Language Notes* 70:5 (1955), pp. 315–20.

Siegmund-Schultze, Dorothea, 'John Gower und seine Zeit', *Zeitschrift für Anglistik und Amerikanistik* 3 (1955), pp. 5–71.

Peter, John, *Complaint and Satire in Early English Literature* (Oxford, 1956).

Raymo, Robert R., '*Vox Clamantis*, IV, 12', *Modern Language Notes* 71:2 (1956), pp. 82–3.

Eisner, Sigmund, *A Tale of Wonder: A Source Study of The Wife of Bath's Tale* (Wexford, 1957).

Fison, Peter, 'The Poet in John Gower', *Essays in Criticism* 8 (1958), pp. 16–26.

Isaacs, Neil D., 'Constance in Fourteenth-Century England', *Neuphilologische Mitteilungen* 58 (1958), pp. 260–77.

## 1961–1970

Fisher, John H., 'Wyclif, Langland, Gower, and the Pearl Poet on the Subject of Aristocracy', *Studies in Medieval Literature in Honor of Professor Albert Croll Baugh*, ed. MacEdward Leach (Philadelphia, 1961), pp. 139–57.

Russell, P.E., 'Robert Payn and Juan De Cuenca, Translators of Gower's *Confessio Amantis'*, *Medium Aevum* 30:1 (1961), pp. 26–32.

Murphy, James J., 'John Gower's *Confessio Amantis* and the First Discussion of Rhetoric in the English Language', *Philological Quarterly* 41 (1962), pp. 401–11.

Kanno, M., 'Some Characteristics of the Verbal Substantive in Gower's *Confessio Amantis'*, *Hiroshima Studies in English Language and Literature* 9:1–2 (1963), pp. 90–8.

Fisher, John H., *John Gower: Moral Philosopher and Friend of Chaucer* (New York, 1964).

Jochums, Milford C., ' "As Ancient as Constantine" ', *Studies in English Literature* 4 (1964), pp. 101–7.

McNally, J.J., 'The Penitential and Courtly Tradition in Gower's *Confessio Amantis'*, *Studies in Medieval Culture*, ed. J.R. Sommerfeldt (Kalamazoo, MI, 1964), pp. 74–94.

Spriggs, Gereth M., 'Unnoticed Bodleian Manuscripts Illuminated by Herman Scheere and his School', *Bodleian Library Record* 7:4 (1964), pp. 193–203.

Ferguson, A.B., *The Articulate Citizen and the English Renaissance* (Durham, NC, 1965).

Miller, Robert P., 'The Wife of Bath's Tale and Mediaeval *Exempla'*, *English Literary History* 32:4 (1965), pp. 442–56.

Weber, Edwart, *John Gower: Dichter einer ethisch-politischen Reformation* (Bad Homburg, 1965).

*Bennett, J.A.W., 'Gower's "Honeste Love" ', *Patterns of Love and Courtesy: Essays in Memory of C.S. Lewis*, ed. John Lawlor (London, 1966), pp. 107–21.

Lawlor, John, 'On Romanticism in the *Confessio Amantis'*, *Patterns of Love and Courtesy: Essays in Memory of C.S. Lewis*, ed. John Lawlor (London, 1966), pp. 122–40.

Pearsall, Derek, 'Gower's Narrative Art', *PMLA* 81:7 (1966), pp. 475–84.

Schueler, Donald, 'Some Comments on the Structure of John Gower's *Confessio Amantis'*, *Explorations of Literature*, ed. Rima D. Reck (Baton Rouge, LA, 1966), pp. 15–24.

Weber, Edwart, *John Gower: Zur literarischen Form seiner Dichtung* (Bad Homburg, 1966).

Blake, N.F., 'Caxton's Copytext of Gower's *Confessio Amantis'*, *Anglia* 85 (1967), pp. 282–93.

David, Alfred, 'The Man of Law vs. Chaucer: A Case in Poetics', *PMLA* 82:2 (1967), pp. 217–25.

Schueler, David, 'The Age of the Lover in Gower's *Confessio Amantis'*, *Medium Aevum* 36 (1967), pp. 152–58.

*Esch, Arno, 'John Gowers Erzählkunst', *Chaucer und seine Zeit: Symposion für Walter F. Schirmer*, ed. Arno Esch (Tübingen, 1968), pp. 207–39.

Hoffman, Richard L., 'An Ovidian Allusion in Gower', *American Notes and Queries* 6 (1968), pp. 127–8.

Ito, Masayoshi, 'Gower's Use of rime riche in *Confessio Amantis*: As Compared with his Practice in *Mirour de L'Omme* and with the Case of Chaucer', *Studies in English Literature* 46 (1969), pp. 29–44.

Iwasaki, H., 'A Peculiar Feature in the Word-Order of Gower's *Confessio Amantis*', *Studies in English Literature* 45 (1969), pp. 205–20.
Pearsall, Derek, *Gower and Lydgate* (London, 1969).
Regan, Charles L., 'John Gower and the Fall of Babylon: *Confessio Amantis*, Prol. 11. 670–686', *English Language Notes* 7 (1969), pp. 85–92.
Bauer, Gero, *Studien zum System und Gebrauch der 'Tempora' in der Sprache Chaucers und Gowers* (Vienna, 1970).
Byrd, David, 'Gower's *Confessio Amantis*, III.585', *Explicator* 29, item 2 (1970).
*Economou, George D., 'The Character Genius in Alain de Lille, Jean de Meun, and John Gower', *The Chaucer Review* 4 (1970), pp. 203–10.

**1971**

Burrow, John A., *Ricardian Poetry: Chaucer, Gower, Langland, and the Gawain Poet* (London, 1971).
Gilroy-Scott Neil, 'John Gower's Reputation: Literary Allusions from the Early Fifteenth Century to the Time of *Pericles*', *Yearbook of English Studies* 1 (1971), pp. 30–47.
Ito, Masayoshi, 'Gower and Rime Royal', *Bulletin of College of General Education, Tohoku University* 12:2 (1971), pp. 47–65.
Scattergood, V.J., *Politics and Poetry in the Fifteenth Century* (London, 1971).
Warren, Michael J., 'A Note on *Pericles*, Act II, Chorus 17–20', *Shakespeare Quarterly* 22:1 (1971), pp. 90–2.

**1972**

Harbert, Bruce, 'The Myth of Tereus in Ovid and Gower', *Medium Aevum* 41 (1972), pp. 208–14.
Mainzer, Conrad, 'John Gower's Use of "Mediaeval Ovid" in the *Confessio Amantis*', *Medium Aevum* 41 (1972), pp. 215–29.
Schueler, Donald G., 'Gower's Characterization of Genius in the *Confessio Amantis*', *Modern Language Quarterly* 33 (1972), pp. 240–56.
Williams, Michael, 'The Linguistic and Cultural Frontier in Gower', *Archaeologica Cambrensis* 121 (1972), pp. 61–9.

**1973**

Clogan, Paul M., 'From Complaint to Satire: The Art of the *Confessio Amantis*', *Medievalia et Humanistica*, n.s. 4 (1973), pp. 217–22.
Pickford, T.E., '"Fortune" in Gower's *Confessio Amantis*', *Parergon* 7 (1973), pp. 20–9.

**1974**

Farnham, Anthony E., 'The Art of High Prosaic Seriousness: John Gower as Didactic Raconteur', *The Learned and the Lewed: Studies in Chaucer and Medieval Literature*, ed. Larry D. Benson, David Staines and McKay Sundwall (Cambridge, MA, 1974), pp. 161–73.
*Schmitz, Götz, *The Middel Weie: Stil- und Aufbauformen in John Gowers Confessio Amantis* (Bonn, 1974).

**1975**

Byrd, David, 'Gower's *Confessio Amantis*, VI.145', *Explicator* 33, item 35 (1975).
Cowling, Samuel T., 'Gower's Ironic Self-Portrait in the *Confessio Amantis*', *Annuale Mediaevale* 16 (1975), pp. 63–70.

Economou, George D., 'The Two Venuses and Courtly Love', *In Pursuit of Perfection: Courtly Love in Medieval Literature*, eds. Joan M. Ferrante and George D. Economou (Port Washington, NY, 1975), pp. 17–50.

Gallacher, Patrick J., *Love, the Word and Mercury: A Reading of John Gower's Confessio Amantis* (Albuquerque, NM, 1975).

Hatton, Thomas, 'The Role of Venus and Genius in John Gower's *Confessio Amantis*: A Reconsideration', *Greyfriar* 16 (1975), pp. 29–40.

Ito, Masayoshi, 'Gower's Knowledge of *Poetria Nova*', *Studies in English Literature* 162 (Tokyo, 1975), Eng. no. 3–20.

Kirk, Elizabeth D., 'Chaucer and his English Contemporaries', *Geoffrey Chaucer: A Collection of Original Articles*, ed. George D. Economou (New York, 1975), pp. 111–27.

Nitzsche, Jane Chance, *The Genius Figure in Antiquity and the Middle Ages* (New York, 1975).

Theiner, Paul, 'The Man of Law Tells his Tale', *Studies in Medieval Culture* 5 (1975), pp. 173–9.

## 1976

Baker, Denise, 'The Priesthood of Genius: A Study of the Medieval Tradition', *Speculum* 51:2 (1976), pp. 277–91.

Ito, Masayoshi, *John Gower, the Medieval Poet* (Tokyo, 1976).

Kelly, Henry A., *Love and Marriage in the Age of Chaucer* (Ithaca, NY, 1976).

Weiher, Carol, 'Chaucer's and Gower's Stories of Lucretia and Virginia', *English Language Notes* 14 (1976), pp. 7–9.

Wetherbee, Winthrop, 'The Theme of Imagination in Medieval Poetry and the Allegorical Figure of "Genius" ', *Medievalia et Humanistica*, n.s. 7 (1976), pp. 45–64.

## 1977

Boni, John, 'Gower's "Custom" in *Pericles*: Shakespeare's Hand?', *American Notes and Queries* 16 (1977), pp. 35–6.

Burke, Linda Barney, 'Women in John Gower's *Confessio Amantis*', *Medievalia* 3 (1977), pp. 239–59.

Dean, James, 'Time Past and Time Present in Chaucer's *Clerk's Tale* and Gower's *Confessio Amantis*', *English Literary History* 44:3 (1977), pp. 401–18.

Fisher, John H., 'Chancery and the Emergence of Standard Written English in the Fifteenth Century', *Speculum* 52:4 (1977), pp. 870–99.

Friedenreich, Kenneth, '*Volpone* and the *Confessio Amantis*', *South Central Bulletin* 37 (1977), pp. 147–50.

Gradon, Pamela, 'John Gower and the Concept of Righteousness', *Poetica* 8 (1977), pp. 61–71.

Harder, Henry L., 'Livy in Gower's and Chaucer's Lucrece Stories', *Publications of the Missouri Philological Association* 2 (1977), pp. 1–7.

Olsson, Kurt O., 'The Cardinal Virtues and the Structure of John Gower's *Speculum Meditantis*', *Journal of Medieval and Renaissance Studies* 7 (1977), pp. 113–48.

Olsson, Kurt O., 'Rhetoric, John Gower, and the Late Medieval *Exemplum*', *Medievalia et Humanistica*, n.s. 8 (1977), pp. 185–200.

Phelan, Walter S., 'Beyond the Concordance: Semantic and Mythic Structures in Gower's *Tale of Florent*', *Neophilologus* 61 (1977), pp. 461–78.

Theiner, Paul, 'The Literary Uses of the Peasants' Revolt of 1381', *Actes du VIe Congres de l'Association Internationale de Litterature Comparée/Proceedings of the 6th Congress of the International Comparative Literature Association*, ed. Michel Cadot et al. (Stuttgart, 1977), pp. 303–6.

## 1978

Cherniss, Michael D., 'The Allegorical Figures in Gower's *Confessio Amantis*', *Res Publica Litterarum* 1 (1978), pp. 7–20.

Hamm, R. Wayne, 'A Critical Evaluation of the *Confisyon del Amante*, the Castilian Translation of Gower's *Confessio Amantis*', *Medium Aevum* 47 (1978), pp. 91–106.

Mainzer, Conrad, 'Albertano of Brescia's *Liber Consolationis et Consilii* as a Source-Book of Gower's *Confessio Amantis*', *Medium Aevum* 47 (1978), pp. 88–90.

Middleton, Anne, 'The Idea of Public Poetry in the Reign of Richard II', *Speculum* 53:1 (1978), pp. 94–114.

Parkes, M.B., and A.I. Doyle, 'The Production of Copies of the *Canterbury Tales* and the *Confessio Amantis* in the Early Fifteenth Century', *Medieval Scribes, Manuscripts and Libraries: Essays Presented to N.R. Ker*, ed. M.B. Parkes and A.G. Watson (London, 1978), pp. 163–210.

Peck, Russell A., *Kingship and Common Profit in Gower's Confessio Amantis* (Carbondale, IL, 1978).

Regan, Charles Lionel, 'John Gower, John Barleycorn, and William Langland', *American Notes and Queries* 16 (1978), p. 102.

## 1979

Burnley, J.D., *Chaucer's Language and the Philosophers' Tradition* (Cambridge, 1979).

Ito, Masayoshi, 'Gower's Use of *Vita Barlaam et Josaphat* in *Confessio Amantis*', *Studies in English Literature* 162 (Tokyo, 1979), Eng. no. 3–18.

Stevens, Martin, 'The Royal Stanza in Early English Literature', *PMLA* 94:1 (1979), pp. 62–76.

Strohm, Paul, 'Form and Social Statement in *Confessio Amantis* and the *Canterbury Tales*', *Studies in the Age of Chaucer* 1 (1979), pp. 17–40.

Woolf, Rosemary, 'Moral Chaucer and Kindly Gower', *J.R.R. Tolkien, Scholar and Storyteller: Essays in Memoriam*, ed. Mary Salu, Robert T. Farrell and Humphrey Carpenter (Ithaca, NY, 1979), pp. 221–45.

## 1980

Burke, Linda Barney, 'The Sources and Significance of the *Tale of King, Wine, Woman and Truth* in John Gower's *Confessio Amantis*', *Greyfriar* 21 (1980), pp. 3–15.

Burnley, J.D., '*Fine Amor*: Its Meaning and Context', *Review of English Studies* 31:2 (1980), pp. 129–48.

Green, Richard Firth, *Poets and Princepleasers: Literature and the English Court in the Late Middle Ages* (Toronto, 1980).

*Minnis, Alastair J., 'John Gower, Sapiens in Ethics and Politics', *Medium Aevum* 49:2 (1980), pp. 207–29.

## 1981

Burrow, John A., 'The Poet as Petitioner', *Studies in the Age of Chaucer* 3 (1981), pp. 61–75.

Coleman, Janet, *English Literature in History, 1350–1400: Medieval Readers and Writers* (London, 1981). See the chapter 'John Gower's Complaint', pp. 126–56.

Collins, Marie, 'Love, Nature, and Law in the Poetry of Gower and Chaucer', *Court and Poet: Selected Proceedings of the Third Congress of the International Courtly Literature Society, Liverpool, 1980*, ed. Glyn S. Burgess et al. (Liverpool, 1981), pp. 113–28.

Cresswell, Julia, 'The Tales of Acteon and Narcissus in the *Confessio Amantis*', *Reading Medieval Studies* 7 (1981), pp. 32–40.

Gardiner, Eileen, 'The Recension of the *Confessio Amantis* in the Plimpton Gower', *Manuscripta* 25:2 (1981), pp. 107–12.

Manzalaoui, M.A., ' "Noght in the Registre of Venus": Gower's English Mirror for Princes', *Medieval Studies for J.A.W. Bennett, Aetatis Suae Lxx.*, ed. P.L. Heyworth (Oxford, 1981), pp. 159–83.

Samuels, M.L., and J.J. Smith, 'The Language of Gower', *Neuphilologische Mitteilungen* 82:3 (1981), pp. 295–304.

Yeager, Robert F., '"Our Englisshe" and Everyone's Latin: The *Fasciculus Morum* and Gower's *Confessio Amantis*', *South Atlantic Review* 46:4 (1981), pp. 41–53.

## 1982

Beidler, Peter G., ed., *John Gower's Literary Transformations in the Confessio Amantis: Original Articles and Translations* (Washington, DC, 1982). Contents:

Peter G. Beidler, 'The Tale of Acteon', 'The Tale of Acis and Galatea' and 'Diabolical Treachery in the Tale of Nectanabus'

Carole Koepke Brown, 'The Tale of Deianira and Nesus' and 'The Tale of Pygmalion'

Judith C.G. Moran, 'The Tale of Pyramus and Thisbe' and 'The Tale of Midas'

Natalie Epinger Ruyak, 'The Tale of Phebus and Daphne' and 'The Tale of Neptune and Cornix'

Nicolette Stasko, 'The Tale of Iphis' and 'The Tale of Iphis and Araxarathen'

Karl A. Zipf, Jr., 'The Tale of Icarus' and 'The Tale of Echo'

John B. Gaston, 'The Tale of Ceyx and Alceone' and 'The Tale of Leucothoe'

Douglas L. Lepley, 'The Tale of Argus and Mercury' and 'The Tale of Tereus'

Patricia Innerbichler De Bellis, 'Thomas of Kent's Account of the Birth of Alexander: Text and Translation'

Edna S. deAngeli, 'Julius Valerius' Account of the Birth of Alexander: Text and Translation'

Goodall, Peter, 'John Gower's *Apollonius of Tyre*: *Confessio Amantis*, Book VIII', *Southern Review* 15:3 (1982), pp. 243–53.

Harrison, Anne Tukey, 'Echo and her Medieval Sisters', *The Centennial Review* 26:4 (1982), pp. 324–40.

Hoeniger, F. David, 'Gower and Shakespeare in *Pericles*', *Shakespeare Quarterly* 33:4 (1982), pp. 461–79.

*Olsson, Kurt, 'Natural Law and John Gower's *Confessio Amantis*', *Medievalia et Humanistica* n.s. 11 (1982), pp. 229–61.

Strohm, Paul, 'A Note on Gower's Persona', *Acts of Interpretation: The Text in Its Contexts, 700–1600: Essays on Medieval and Renaissance Literature in Honor of E. Talbot Donaldson*, ed. Mary J. Carruthers and Elizabeth D. Kirk (Norman, OK, 1982), pp. 293–8.

Yeager, Robert F., 'John Gower and the *Exemplum* Form: Tale Models in the *Confessio Amantis*', *Mediaevalia* 8 (1982), pp. 307–35.

## 1983

Aers, David, 'Representations of the "Third Estate": Social Conflict and its Milieu around 1381', *Southern Review: Literary and Interdisciplinary Essays* 16:3 (1983), pp. 335–49.

Braswell, Mary Flowers, *The Medieval Sinner: Characterization and Confession in the Literature of the English Middle Ages* (Rutherford, NJ, 1983).

Green, Richard Firth, 'The *Familia Regis* and the *Familia Cupidinis*', *English Court Culture in the Later Middle Ages*, ed. V.J. Scattergood, J.W. Sherborne and J.A. Burrow (New York, 1983), pp. 87–108.

Harris, Kate, 'John Gower's *Confessio Amantis*: The Virtues of Bad Texts', *Manuscripts and Readers in Fifteenth-Century England: The Literary Implications of Manuscript Study*, ed. Derek Pearsall (Cambridge, 1983), pp. 26–40.

Ito, Masayoshi, 'Gower's *Diogenes and Alexander* and its Philosophic-Literary Tradition', *Poetica* 16 (1983), pp. 66–77.

Minnis, Alastair J., ed., *Gower's Confessio Amantis: Responses and Reassessments* (Cambridge, 1983). Contents:
J.A. Burrow, 'The Portrayal of Amans in *Confessio Amantis*'
Christopher Ricks, 'Metamorphosis in Other Words'
Alastair Minnis, '"Moral Gower" and Medieval Literary Theory'
Paul Miller, 'John Gower, Satiric Poet'
Charles Runacres, 'Art and Ethics in the *Exempla* of *Confessio Amantis*'
Elizabeth Porter, 'Gower's Ethical Microcosm and Political Macrocosm'
Jeremy Griffiths, '*Confessio Amantis*: The Poem and its Pictures'
Derek Pearsall, 'The Gower Tradition'

Ronberg, Gert, 'Two North-West Midland Manuscripts Revisited', *Neophilologus* 67:3 (1983), pp. 463–7.

Samuels, M.L., 'Chaucer's Spelling', *Middle English Studies Presented to Norman Davis in Honour of his Seventieth Birthday*, ed. Douglas Gray and E.G. Stanley (Oxford, 1983), pp. 17–37.

Scattergood, V.J., 'Literary Culture at the Court of Richard II', *English Court Culture in the Later Middle Ages*, ed. V.J. Scattergood, J.W. Sherborne and J.A. Burrow (New York, 1983), pp. 29–43.

Shaw, Judith Davis, 'John Gower's Illustrative Tales', *Neuphilologische Mitteilungen* 84:3 (1983), pp. 437–47.

Smith, Jeremy J., 'Linguistic Features of Some Fifteenth-Century Middle English Manuscripts', *Manuscripts and Readers in Fifteenth-Century England: The Literary Implications of Manuscript Study*, ed. Derek Pearsall (Cambridge, 1983), pp. 104–12.

Waterhouse, Ruth, and John Stephens, 'The Backward Look: Retrospectivity in Medieval Literature', *Southern Review* 16:3 (1983), pp. 356–73.

## 1984

Benson, C. David, 'Incest and Moral Poetry in Gower's *Confessio Amantis*', *The Chaucer Review* 19:2 (1984), pp. 100–9.

Braswell, Mary Flowers, 'Poet and Sinner: Literary Characterization and the Mentality of the Late Middle Ages', *Fifteenth Century Studies* 10 (1984), pp. 39–56.

Diller, Hans Jürgen, ' "For Engelondes Sake": Richard II and Henry of Lancaster as Intended Readers of Gower's *Confessio Amantis*', *Functions of Literature: Essays Presented to Erwin Wolff on his Sixtieth Birthday*, ed. Ulrich Broich, Theo Stemmler, and Gerd Stratmann (Tübingen, 1984), pp. 39–53.

Glasser, Marc, ' "He Nedes Moste Hire Wedde": The Forced Marriage in "The Wife of

Bath's Tale" and its Middle English Analogues', *Neuphilologische Mitteilungen* 85:2 (1984), pp. 239–41.

Kinneavy, Gerald, 'Gower's *Confessio Amantis* and the Penitentials', *The Chaucer Review* 19:2 (1984), pp. 144–63.

Minnis, Alastair J., *Medieval Theory of Authorship: Scholastic Literary Attitudes in the Later Middle Ages* (London, 1984).

Nicholson, Peter, 'Gower's Revisions in the *Confessio Amantis*', *The Chaucer Review* 19:2 (1984), pp. 123–43.

Payne, Robert O., 'Late Medieval Images and Self-Image of the Poet: Chaucer, Gower, Lydgate, Henryson, Dunbar', *Vernacular Poetics in the Middle Ages*, ed. Lois Ebin (Kalamazoo, 1984), pp. 249–61.

Shaw, Judith Davis, '*Lust* and *Lore* in Gower and Chaucer', *The Chaucer Review* 19:2 (1984), pp. 110–22.

Yeager, R.F., 'Aspects of Gluttony in Chaucer and Gower', *Studies in Philology* 81:1 (1984), pp. 42–55.

Yeager, R.F., 'John Gower and the Uses of Allusion', *Res Publica Litterarum* 7 (1984), pp. 201–13.

Yeager, R.F., ' "O Moral Gower": Chaucer's Dedication of *Troilus and Criseyde*', *The Chaucer Review* 19:2 (1984), pp. 87–99.

### 1985

Boffey, Julia, *Manuscripts of English Courtly Love Lyrics in the Later Middle Ages* (Cambridge, 1985).

Fischer, Olga C.M., 'Gower's "Tale of Florent" and Chaucer's "Wife of Bath's Tale": A Stylistic Comparison', *English Studies* 66:3 (1985), pp. 205–25.

Hillman, Richard, 'Shakespeare's Gower and Gower's Shakespeare: The Larger Debt of *Pericles*', *Shakespeare Quarterly* 36:3 (1985), pp. 427–37.

Hiscoe, David, 'The Ovidian Comic Strategy of Gower's *Confessio Amantis*', *Philological Quarterly* 64:3 (1985), pp. 367–85.

Shaw, Judith Davis, 'An Etymology of the Middle English Coise', *English Language Notes* 22:4 (1985), pp. 11–13.

Siberry, Elizabeth, 'Criticism of Crusading in Fourteenth-Century England', *Crusade and Settlement*, ed. Peter W. Edbury (Cardiff, 1985), pp. 127–34.

### 1986

Dove, Mary, *The Perfect Age of Man's Life* (Cambridge, 1986).

Gittes, Katharine S., 'Ulysses in Gower's *Confessio Amantis*: The Christian Soul as Silent Rhetorician', *English Language Notes* 24:2 (1986), pp. 7–14.

Levin, Rozalyn, 'The Passive Poet: Amans as Narrator in Book 4 of the *Confessio Amantis*', *Proceedings of the Illinois Medieval Association* 3 (1986), pp. 114–30.

Nicholson, Peter, 'The "Confession" in Gower's *Confessio Amantis*', *Studia Neophilologica* 58:2 (1986), pp. 193–204.

Olsen, Alexandra Hennessey, 'The Literary Impact of the Pun in Middle English Poetry', *In Geardagum: Essays on Old and Middle English Language and Literature* 7 (1986), pp. 17–36.

Wetherbee, Winthrop, 'Genius and Interpretation in the *Confessio Amantis*', *Magister Regus: Studies in Honor of Robert Earl Kaske*, ed. Arthur Groos (New York, 1986), pp. 241–60.

Wright, Stephen K., 'Gower's Geta and the Sin of Supplantation', *Neuphilologische Mitteilungen* 87:2 (1986), pp. 211–17.

Zambreno, Mary Frances, 'Gower's *Confessio Amantis* IV, 1963–2013: The Education of Achilles', *Proceedings of the Illinois Medieval Association* 3 (1986), pp. 131–48.

### 1987

Cherniss, Michael D., *Boethian Apocalypse: Studies in Middle English Vision Poetry* (Norman, OK, 1987).

Goodall, Peter, ' "Unkynde abhomynaciouns" in Chaucer and Gower', *Parergon* n.s. 5 (1987), pp. 94–102.

Lawton, David, 'Dullness and the Fifteenth Century', *English Literary History* 54:4 (1987), pp. 761–99.

Nicholson, Peter, 'Poet and Scribe in the Manuscripts of Gower's *Confessio Amantis*', *Manuscripts and Texts: Editorial Problems in Later Middle English Literature*, ed. Derek Pearsall (Cambridge, 1987), pp. 130–42.

Olsen, Alexandra Hennessey, 'In Defense of Diomede: "Moral Gower" and *Troilus and Criseyde*', *In Geardagum: Essays on Old and Middle English Language and Literature* 8 (1987), pp. 1–12.

Olsen, Alexandra Hennessey, 'Literary Artistry and the Oral Formulaic Tradition: The Case of Gower's *Apollonius of Tyre*', *Comparative Research on Oral Traditions: Memorial for Milman Parry*, ed. John Miles Foley and Albert Bates Lord (Columbus, OH, 1987), pp. 493–509.

Olsson, Kurt, 'John Gower's *Vox Clamantis* and the Medieval Idea of Place', *Studies in Philology* 84:2 (1987), pp. 134–58.

White, Hugh, 'The Naturalness of Amans' Love in *Confessio Amantis*', *Medium Aevum* 56:2 (1987), pp. 316–22.

Yeager, R.F., 'English, Latin, and the Text as "Other": The Page as Sign in the Work of John Gower', *Text: Transactions of the Society for Textual Scholarship* 3 (1987), pp. 251–67.

Yeager, R.F., 'Pax Poetica: On the Pacifism of Chaucer and Gower', *Studies in the Age of Chaucer* 9 (1987), pp. 97–121.

### 1988

Alvar, Manuel, 'El Clerc de John Gower y su Polivalencia en Juan de Cuenca', *Hispanic Studies in Honor of Joseph H. Silverman*, ed. Joseph V. Ricapito (Newark, DE, 1988), pp. 1–13.

Bunt, G.H.V., '*Exemplum* and Tale in John Gower's *Confessio Amantis*', *Exemplum et Similitudo: Alexander the Great and Other Heroes as Points of Reference in Medieval Literature*, ed. W.J. Aerts and M. Gosman (Groningen, 1988), pp. 145–57.

Harbert, Bruce, 'Lessons from the Great Clerk: Ovid and John Gower', *Ovid Renewed: Ovidian Influences on Literature and Art from the Middle Ages to the Twentieth Century*, ed. Charles Martindale (Cambridge, 1988), pp. 83–97.

Juby, W.H., 'A Theves Dede: A Case of Chaucer's Borrowing from Gower', *American Notes and Queries* 1:4 (1988), pp. 123–5.

Lynch, Kathryn, *The High Medieval Dream Vision: Poetry, Philosophy, and Literary Form* (Stanford, 1988), especially 'John Gower's Fourteenth-Century Philosophical Vision', pp. 163–98.

Nicholson, Peter, 'The Dedications of Gower's *Confessio Amantis*', *Mediaevalia* 10 (1988), pp. 159–80.

Samuels, M.L., and J.J. Smith, *The English of Chaucer and his Contemporaries* (Aberdeen, 1988). Includes 'The Language of Gower', 'The Trinity Gower D-Scribe and His

Work on Two Early *Canterbury Tales* Manuscripts', 'Spelling and Tradition in Fifteenth-Century Copies of Gower's *Confession Amantis*'.

Simpson, James, 'Ironic Incongruence in the Prologue and Book I of Gower's *Confessio Amantis*', *Neophilologus* 72:4 (1988), pp. 617–32.

White, Hugh, 'Division and Failure in Gower's *Confessio Amantis*', *Neophilologus* 72:4 (1988), pp. 600–16.

Zaerr, Linda Marie, 'Duke or Duck: Reading the Stories in John Gower's *Confessio Amantis*', *Willamette Journal of the Liberal Arts* 4:1 (1988), pp. 1–9.

## 1989

Edwards, A.S.G., and Derek Pearsall, 'The Manuscripts of the Major English Poetic Texts', *Book Production and Publishing in Britain, 1375–1475*, ed. Jeremy Griffiths and Derek Pearsall (Cambridge, 1989), pp. 257–78.

Gittes, Katharine S., 'Gower's Helen of Troy and the Contemplative Way of Life', *English Language Notes* 27:1 (1989), pp. 19–24.

Green, Eugene, 'Speech Acts and the Art of the *Exemplum* in the Poetry of Chaucer and Gower', *Literary Computing and Literary Criticism: Theoretical and Practical Essays on Theme and Rhetoric*, ed. Rosanne G. Potter (Philadelphia, 1989), pp. 167–87.

Hanna, Ralph III, 'Sir Thomas Berkeley and his Patronage', *Speculum* 64:4 (1989), pp. 878–916.

Hatton, Thomas J., 'John Gower's Use of Ovid in Book III of the *Confessio Amantis*', *Mediaevalia* 13 (1989), pp. 257–74.

Hiscoe, David W., 'Heavenly Sign and Comic Design in Gower's *Confessio Amantis*', *Sign, Sentence, Discourse: Language in Medieval Thought and Literature*, ed. Julian N. Wasserman and Lois Roney (Syracuse, 1989), pp. 228–44.

Pearsall, Derek, 'Gower's Latin in the *Confessio Amantis*', *Latin and Vernacular: Studies in Late-Medieval Texts and Manuscripts*, ed. A.J. Minnis (Cambridge, 1989), pp. 13–25.

Pearsall, Derek, 'Interpretative Models for the Peasants' Revolt', *Hermeneutics and Medieval Culture*, ed. Patrick J. Gallacher and Helen Damico (Albany, NY, 1989), pp. 63–70.

Shaw, Judith Davis, 'The Role of the Shared Bed in John Gower's Tales of Incest', *English Language Notes* 26:3 (1989), pp. 4–7.

Yeager, R.F., ed., *John Gower: Recent Readings* (Kalamazoo, MI, 1989). Contents:
Hugh White, 'Nature and the Good in Gower's *Confessio Amantis*'
James Dean, 'Gather Ye Rosebuds: Gower's Comic Reply to Jean de Meun'
Linda Barney Burke, 'Genial Gower: Laughter in the *Confessio Amantis*'
Winthrop Wetherbee, 'Constance and the World in Chaucer and Gower'
Götz Schmitz, 'Gower, Chaucer, and the Classics: Back to the Textual Evidence'
R.F. Yeager, 'Did Gower Write *Cento*?'
Robert M. Correale, 'Gower's Source Manuscript of Nicholas Trevet's *Les Cronicles*'
Russell A. Peck, 'John Gower and the Book of Daniel'
Michael P. Kuczynski, 'Gower's Metaethics'
David G. Allen, 'God's Faithfulness and the Lover's Despair: The Theological Framework of the Iphis and Araxarathen Story'
Kurt Olsson, 'Aspects of *Gentilesse* in John Gower's *Confessio Amantis*, Books III–V'
Peter C. Braeger, 'The Illustrations in New College MS. 266 for Gower's Conversion Tales'

Patricia Eberle, 'Miniatures as Evidence of Reading in a Manuscript of the
*Confessio Amantis* (Pierpont Morgan MS. M. 126)'

## 1990

Axton, Richard, 'Gower – Chaucer's Heir?', *Chaucer Traditions: Studies in Honour of
Derek Brewer*, ed. Ruth Morse, Barry Windeatt and Toshiyuki Takamiya
(Cambridge, 1990), pp. 21–38.
Hillman, Richard, 'Gower's Lucrece: A New Old Source for the Rape of Lucrece', *The
Chaucer Review* 24:3 (1990), pp. 263–70.
Minkova, Donka, 'Adjectival Inflexion Relics and Speech Rhythm in Late Middle
and Early Modern English', *Papers from the 5th International Conference on English
Historical Linguistics, Cambridge, 6–9 April 1987*, ed. Sylvia Adamson, Vivien Law,
Nigel Vincent and Susan Wright (Amsterdam, 1990), pp. 313–36.
Olsen, Alexandra Hennessey, *'Betwene Ernest and Game': The Literary Artistry of the
Confessio Amantis* (New York, 1990).
Yeager, R.F., *John Gower's Poetic: The Search for a New Arion* (Cambridge, 1990).

## 1991

Archibald, Elizabeth, ed. and trans., *Apollonius of Tyre: Medieval and Renaissance
Themes and Variations, Including a Text and Translation of the 'Historia Apollonii Regis
Tyri'* (Cambridge, 1991).
Bertolet, Craig, 'From Revenge to Reform: The Changing Face of "Lucrece" and its
Meaning in Gower's *Confessio Amantis*', *Philological Quarterly* 70:4 (1991), pp.
403–21.
Blake, Norman F., 'Gower's Vocabulary as a Guide to his Imaginative World', *The
Medieval Imagination. L'imagination médiévale: Chaucer et ses contemporains*, ed.
André Crépin (Paris, 1991), pp. 177–206.
Copeland, Rita, *Rhetoric, Hermeneutics, and Translation in the Middle Ages: Academic
Traditions and Vernacular Texts* (Cambridge, 1991). Final chapter is on Chaucer and
Gower.
Crépin, André, 'L'imagination Amoureuse dans la *Confessio Amantis* de Gower', *The
Medieval Imagination. L'imagination médiévale: Chaucer et ses contemporains*, ed.
André Crépin (Paris, 1991), pp. 207–22.
Dean, James, 'Gower, Chaucer, and Rhyme Royal', *Studies in Philology* 88:3 (1991),
pp. 251–75.
MacAdam, Alfred J., '*Confessio Amantis*', *Revista Iberoamericana* 57 (154) (1991),
pp. 203–13.
Nicholson, Peter, ' "The Man of Law's Tale": What Chaucer Really Owed to Gower',
*The Chaucer Review* 26:2 (1991), pp. 153–74.
Santano Moreno, Bernardo, 'The Fifteenth-Century Portuguese and Castilian Trans-
lations of John Gower, *Confessio Amantis*', *Manuscripta* 35:1 (1991), pp. 23–34.
Santano Moreno, Bernardo, 'Some Observations on the Dates and Circumstances of
the Fifteenth-Century Portuguese and Castilian Translations of John Gower's
*Confessio Amantis*', *SELIM: Journal of the Spanish Society for Medieval English
Language and Literature* 1 (1991), pp. 106–22.
Yeager, R. F., ed., *Chaucer and Gower: Difference, Mutuality, Exchange* (Victoria, BC,
1991). Contents:
R.F. Yeager, 'Learning to Speak in Tongues: Writing Poetry for a Trilingual Culture'
Winthrop Wetherbee, 'Latin Structure and Vernacular Space: Gower, Chaucer and
the Boethian Tradition'

Peter Beidler, 'Transformations in Gower's "Tale of Florent" and Chaucer's "Wife of Bath's Tale" '

Carolyn Dinshaw, 'Rivalry, Rape and Manhood: Gower and Chaucer': see also in Anna Roberts, ed., *Violence against Women in Medieval Texts*, entry under Dinshaw in 1998

A.J. Minnis, 'De Vulgari Auctoritate: Chaucer, Gower, and the Men of Great Authority'

Peter Nicholson, 'Chaucer Borrows from Gower: The Sources of *The Man of Law's Tale*'

Chauncey Wood, 'Chaucer's Most Gowerian Tale'

Zeeman, Nicolette, 'The Verse of Courtly Love in the Framing Narrative of the *Confessio Amantis*', *Medium Aevum* 60:2 (1991), pp. 222–40.

## 1992

Bennett, M.J., 'The Court of Richard II and the Promotion of Literature', *Chaucer's England: Literature in Historical Context*, ed. B.A. Hanawalt (Minneapolis, MN, 1992), pp. 3–20.

Burrow, John A., 'The Griffin's Egg: Gower's *Confessio Amantis* I.2545', *Chaucer to Shakespeare: Essays in Honour of Shinsuke Ando*, ed. T. Takamiya and R. Beadle (Cambridge, 1992), pp. 81–5.

Chandler, Katherine R., 'Memory and Unity in Gower's *Confessio Amantis*', *Philological Quarterly* 71:1 (1992), pp. 15–30.

Crépin, André, 'Human and Divine Love in Chaucer and Gower', *A Wyf Ther Was: Essays in Honour of Paule Mertens Fonck*, ed. Juliette Dor (Liege, 1992), pp. 71–9.

Dinshaw, Carolyn, 'Quarrels, Rivals, and Rape: Gower and Chaucer', *A Wyf Ther Was: Essays in Honour of Paule Mertens Fonck*, ed. Juliette Dor (Liege, 1992), pp. 112–22.

Fisher, John H., 'A Language Policy for Lancastrian England', *PMLA* 17 (1992), pp. 1168–80.

Levine, Robert, 'Gower as Gerontion: Oneiric Autobiography in the *Confessio Amantis*', *Mediaevistik* 5 (1992), pp. 79–94.

Minnis, Alastair J., 'Authors in Love: the Exegesis of Late-Medieval Love-Poets', *The Uses of Manuscripts in Literary Studies: Essays in Memory of Judson Boyce Allen*, ed. Charlotte C. Morse, Penelope B. Doob and Marjorie C. Woods (Kalamazoo, MI, 1992), pp. 161–91.

Olsson, Kurt, *John Gower and the Structures of Conversion: A Reading of the* Confessio Amantis (Cambridge, 1992).

Ronnick, Michele Valerie, 'Capa Furrata and Nuda Iura: Vox Clamantis, 4.601–2', *Notes and Queries* 39 (237) (4) (1992), pp. 444–5.

Sanders, Arnold A., 'Ruddymane and Canace, Lost and Found: Spenser's Reception of Gower's *Confessio Amantis* 3 and Chaucer's *Squire's Tale*', *The Work of Dissimilitude: Essays from the Sixth Citadel Conference on Medieval and Renaissance Literature*, ed. David G. Allen and Robert A. White (Newark, 1992), pp. 196–215.

Santano Moreno, Bernardo, 'Reflexiones en Torno a la Presensia de *Confessio Amantis* de John Gower en la Peninsula Iberica', *Fifteenth Century Studies* 19 (1992), pp. 147–64.

Westrem, Scott D., 'Two Routes to Pleasant Instruction in Late-Fourteenth-Century Literature', *The Work of Dissimilitude: Essays from the Sixth Citadel Conference on Medieval and Renaissance Literature*, ed. David G. Allen and Robert A. White (Newark, 1992), pp. 67–80.

Wright, Sylvia, 'The Author Portraits in the Bedford Psalter Hours: Gower, Chaucer and Hoccleve', *The British Library Journal* 18:2 (1992), pp. 190–201.

**1993**

Aguirre, Manuel, 'The Riddle of Sovereignty', *The Modern Language Review* 88:2 (1993), pp. 273–82.
Astell, Ann W., 'The Peasants' Revolt: Cock-Crow in Gower and Chaucer', *Essays in Medieval Studies: Proceedings of the Illinois Medieval Association* 10 (1993), pp. 53–64.
Blake, N.F., 'Early Printed Editions of *Confessio Amantis*', *Mediaevalia* 16 (1993), pp. 289–306.
Donavin, Georgiana, *Incest Narratives and the Structure of Gower's Confessio Amantis* (Victoria, BC, 1993).
Peck, Russell A., 'The Problematics of Irony in Gower's *Confessio Amantis*', *Mediaevalia* 15 (1993 for 1989), pp. 207–29.
Yeager, Robert F., ed., *Mediaevalia* 16 (1993 for 1990); special issue. Contents:
    George B. Stow, 'Richard II in John Gower's *Confessio Amantis*: Some Historical Perspectives'
    Judith Ferster, 'O Political Gower'
    Edward Donald Kennedy, 'Gower, Chaucer, and French Prose Arthurian Romance'
    William Calin, 'John Gower's Continuity in the Tradition of French *Fin' Amor*'
    Helen Cooper, ' "Peised evene in the balance": A Thematic and Rhetorical Topos in the *Confessio Amantis*'
    Anthony E. Farnham, 'Statement and Search in the *Confessio Amantis*'
    James Simpson, 'Genius's "Enfourmacioun" in Book III of the *Confessio Amantis*'
    R.A. Shoaf, '"Tho love made him an hard eschange" and "With fals brocage hath take usure": Narcissus and Echo in the *Confessio Amantis*'
    A.C. Spearing, 'Canace and Machaire'
    A.S.G. Edwards, 'Gower's Women in the *Confessio*'
    Chauncey Wood, 'Petrarchanism in the *Confessio Amantis*'
    Alan T. Gaylord, '"After the forme of my writynge": Gower's Bookish Prosody'
    N.F. Blake, 'Early Printed Editions of *Confessio Amantis*'
    Thomas A. Bestul, 'Gower's *Mirror de l'Omme* and the Meditative Tradition'
    Andrew Galloway, 'Gower in his Most Learned Role and the Peasants' Revolt of 1381'
    Charles R. Blyth, 'Thomas Hoccleve's Other Master'
    Lynch, Stephen J., 'The Authority of Gower in Shakespeare's *Pericles*'

**1994**

Bullón-Fernández, María, 'Confining the Daughter: Gower's "Tale of Canace and Machaire" and the Politics of the Body', *Essays in Medieval Studies* 11 (1994), pp. 75–85.
Galloway, Andrew, 'The Making of a Social Ethic in Late-Medieval England: From *Gratitudo* to "Kyndeness" ', *Journal of the History of Ideas* 55:3 (1994), pp. 365–83.
Owen, Charles A., Jr., 'Notes on Gower's Prosody', *The Chaucer Review* 28:4 (1994), pp. 405–13.
Peck, Russell A., 'The Phenomenology of Make Believe in Gower's *Confessio Amantis*', *Studies in Philology* 91:3 (1994), pp. 250–69.

Scanlon, Larry, *Narrative, Authority, and Power: The Medieval Exemplum and the Chaucerian Tradition* (Cambridge, 1994), especially 'Bad examples: Gower's *Confessio Amantis*', pp. 245–97.

## 1995

Bullón-Fernández, María, 'Nature or Culture? John Gower's "Tale of Apollonius", in *Proceedings of the VIth International Conference of the Spanish Society for Medieval English Language and Literature*, ed. P. Fernández Nistal and J.M. Bravo Gozalo (Valladolid, 1995), pp. 57–63.

Cortijo Ocaña, Antonio, 'La Traducción Portuguesa de la *Confessio Amantis* de John Gower', *Evphrosyne* 23 (1995), pp. 457–66.

Fredell, Joel, 'Reading the Dream Miniature in the *Confessio Amantis*', *Medievalia et Humanistica* 22 (1995), pp. 61–93.

Grady, Frank, 'The Lancastrian Gower and the Limits of Exemplarity', *Speculum* 70:3 (1995), pp. 552–75.

Olsson, Kurt, 'Love, Intimacy and Gower', *The Chaucer Review* 30:1 (1995), pp. 71–100.

Parkes, M.B., 'Patterns of Scribal Activity and Revisions of the Text in Early Copies of Works by John Gower', *New Science out of Old Books: Studies in Manuscripts and Early Printed Books in Honour of A.I. Doyle*, ed. Richard Beadle and A.J. Piper (Aldershot, 1995), pp. 81–121.

Scala, Elizabeth, 'Canacee and the Chaucer Canon: Incest and Other Unnarratables', *The Chaucer Review* 30:1 (1995 ), pp. 15–39.

Simpson, James, *Sciences and the Self in Medieval Poetry: Alan of Lille's Anticlaudianus and John Gower's Confessio Amantis* (Cambridge, 1995).

Vasta, Edward, 'Chaucer, Gower, and the Unknown Minstrel: The Literary Liberation of the Loathly Lady', *Exemplaria* 7:2 (1995), pp. 395–418.

Yeager, R.F., 'Ben Jonson's *English Grammar* and John Gower's Reception in the Seventeenth Century', *The Endless Knot: Essays on Old and Middle English in Honor of Marie Borroff*, ed. M. Teresa Tavormina and R.F. Yeager (Cambridge, 1995), pp. 227–39.

## 1996

Astell, Ann, *Chaucer and the Universe of Learning* (Ithaca, NY, 1996).

Duffell, Martin J., 'Chaucer, Gower, and the History of the Hendecasyllable', *English Historical Metrics*, ed. C.B. McCully and J.J. Anderson (Cambridge, 1996), pp. 210–18.

Ferster, Judith, *Fictions of Advice: The Literature and Politics of Counsel in Late Medieval England* (Philadelphia, 1996), especially 'O Political Gower', pp. 108–36.

Garbáty, Thomas J., 'A Description of the Confession Miniatures for Gower's *Confessio Amantis* with Special Reference to the Illustrator's Role as Reader and Critic', *Mediaevalia* 19 (1996), pp. 319–43.

Kiefer, Lauren, 'My Family First: Draft-Dodging Parents in the *Confessio Amantis*', *Essays in Medieval Studies* 12 (1996), pp. 55–68.

Machan, Tim William, 'Thomas Berthelette and Gower's *Confessio*', *Studies in the Age of Chaucer* 18 (1996), pp. 143–66.

McKinley, Kathryn, 'Kingship and the Body Politic: Classical Ecphrasis and *Confessio Amantis* VII', *Mediaevalia* 21 (1996), pp. 161–87.

Smith, Jeremy J., 'A Note on Constrained Linguistic Variation in a North-West-Midlands Middle-English Scribe', *Neophilologus* 80:3 (1996), pp. 461–4.

Tinkle, Theresa, *Medieval Venuses and Cupids: Sexuality, Hermeneutics, and English Poetry* (Stanford, 1996), especially '*Remedia Amoris*', pp. 178–97.

## 1997

Allen, Elizabeth, 'Chaucer Answers Gower: Constance and the Trouble with Reading', *English Literary History* 64:3 (1997), pp. 627–55.

Cortijo Ocaña, Antonio, '*O Livro do Amante*: The Lost Portuguese Translation of John Gower's *Confessio Amantis* (Madrid, Biblioteca de Palacio, MS II–3088)', *Portuguese Studies* 13 (1997), pp. 1–6.

Craun, Edwin D., *Lies, Slander, and Obscenity in Medieval English Literature: Pastoral Rhetoric and the Deviant Speaker* (Cambridge, 1997), especially 'Confessing the deviant speaker: verbal deception in the *Confessio Amantis*', pp. 113–56.

Echard, Siân, 'Pretexts: Tables of Contents and the Reading of John Gower's *Confessio Amantis*', *Medium Aevum* 66:2 (1997), pp. 270–87.

Essaka, Joshua, 'Chaucer's Ghoast and Gower's *Confessio Amantis*', *Notes and Queries* 44, no. (242) (4) (1997), pp. 458–9.

Kerby-Fulton, Kathryn, and Steven Justice, 'Langlandian Reading Circles and the Civil Service in London and Dublin, 1380–1427', *New Medieval Literatures* 1 (1997), pp. 59–83.

Robins, William, 'Romance, *Exemplum*, and the Subject of the *Confessio Amantis*', *Studies in the Age of Chaucer* 19 (1997), pp. 157–81.

Yeager, Robert F., '*Scripture Veteris Capiunt Exempla Futuri*: John Gower's Transformation of a Fable of Avianus', *Retelling Tales: Essays in Honor of Russell Peck*, ed. Thomas Hahn and Alan Lupack (Cambridge, 1997), pp. 341–54.

## 1998

Bowers, Robert, 'The Frame is the Thing: Gower and Narrative Entente', *In Geardagum: Essays on Old and Middle English Language and Literature* 19 (1998), pp. 31–9.

Davenport, W.A., *Chaucer and His English Contemporaries: Prologue and Tale in 'The Canterbury Tales'* (New York, 1998).

Dinshaw, Carolyn, 'Rivalry, Rape and Manhood: Gower and Chaucer', *Violence against Women in Medieval Texts*, ed. Anna Roberts (Gainesville, FL, 1998), pp. 137–60. See also in R.F. Yeager, ed., *Chaucer and Gower* (1991).

Echard, Siân, 'With Carmen's Help: Latin Authorities in the *Confessio Amantis*', *Studies in Philology* 95:1(1998), pp. 1–40.

Yeager, Robert F, ed., *Re-Visioning Gower* (Asheville, NC, 1998). Contents:
 Patricia Batchelor, 'Feigned Truth and Exemplary Method in the *Confessio Amantis*'
 Dhira B. Mahoney, 'Gower's Two Prologues to *Confessio Amantis*'
 Thomas Cable, 'Metrical Similarities between Gower and Certain Sixteenth-Century Poets'
 Russell A. Peck, 'The Phenomenology of Make-Believe in Gower's *Confessio Amantis*'
 Kurt Olsson, 'Reading, Transgression, and Judgment: Gower's Case of Paris and Helen'
 Larry Scanlon, 'The Riddle of Incest: John Gower and the Problem of Medieval Sexuality'
 María Bullón-Fernández, 'Engendering Authority: Father and Daughter, State and Church in Gower's "Tale of Constance" and Chaucer's "Man of Law's Tale" '

Gregory M. Sadlek, 'John Gower's *Confessio Amantis*, Ideology, and the "Labor" of "Love's Labor" '

Eve Salisbury, 'Remembering Origins: Gower's Monstrous Body Poetic'

David Aers, 'Reflections on Gower as "*Sapiens* in Ethics and Politics" '; reprinted in David Aers, *Faith, Ethics and Church: Writing in England, 1360–1409* (Cambridge: D.S. Brewer, 2000)

Claire Fanger, 'Magic and the Metaphysics of Gender in Gower's "Tale of Circe and Ulysses" '

Hugh White, 'The Sympathetic Villain in *Confessio Amantis*'

Siân Echard, 'Glossing Gower: In Latin, in English, and *in absentia*: The Case of Bodleian Ashmore 35'

A.S.G. Edwards, 'Selection and Subversion in Gower's *Confessio Amantis*'

Martha W. Driver, 'Printing the *Confessio Amantis*: Caxton's Edition in Context'

## 1999

Aers, David, '*Vox Populi* and the Literature of 1381', *The Cambridge History of Medieval English Literature*, ed. David Wallace (Cambridge, 1999), pp. 432–53.

Astell, Ann W., *Political Allegory in Late Medieval England* (Ithaca, 1999), especially 'Gowers Arion and "Cithero" ', pp. 73–93.

Dimmick, Jeremy, ' "Redinge of Romance" in Gower's *Confessio Amantis*', *Tradition and Transformation in Medieval Romance*, ed. Rosalind Field (Cambridge, 1999), pp. 125–37.

Echard, Siân, 'Designs for Reading: Some Manuscripts of Gower's *Confessio Amantis*', *Trivium* 31 (1999), pp. 59–72.

Emmerson, Richard K., 'Reading Gower in a Manuscript Culture: Latin and English in Illustrated Manuscripts of the *Confessio Amantis*', *Studies in the Age of Chaucer* 21 (1999), pp. 143–86.

Grinnell, Natalie, 'Medea's Humanity and John Gower's Romance', *Medieval Perspectives* 14 (1999), pp. 70–83.

Hanning, R.W., '"And Countrefete the Speche of Every Man/ He Koude, Whan He Sholde Telle a Tale": Toward a Lapsarian Poetics for *The Canterbury Tales*', *Studies in the Age of Chaucer* 21 (1999), pp. 29–58.

Mast, Isabelle, 'Rape in John Gower's *Confessio Amantis* and Other Related Works', *Young Medieval Women*, ed. Katherine J. Lewis, Noël James Menuge and Kim M. Phillips (Stroud, 1999), pp. 103–32.

Schutz, Andrea, 'Absent and Present Images: Mirrors and Mirroring in John Gower's *Confessio Amantis*', *Chaucer Review* 34:1 (1999), pp. 107–24.

Simpson, James, 'Breaking the Vacuum: Ricardian and Henrician Ovidianism', *Journal of Medieval and Early Modern Studies* 29:2 (1999), pp. 325–55.

Summers, Joanna, 'Gower's *Vox Clamantis* and Usk's *Testament of Love*', *Medium Aevum* 68:1 (1999), pp. 55–62.

Watt, Diane, 'Literary Genealogy, Virile Rhetoric, and John Gower's *Confessio Amantis*', *Philological Quarterly* 78:4 (1999), pp. 389–415.

Wetherbee, Winthrop, 'John Gower', *The Cambridge History of Medieval English Literature*, ed. David Wallace (Cambridge, 1999), pp. 589–609.

Yeager, Robert F., 'The Body Politic and the Politics of Bodies in the Poetry of John Gower', *The Body and the Soul in Medieval Literature*, ed. Anna Torti and Piero Boitani (Cambridge, 1999), pp. 145–65.

## 2000

Aers, David, *Faith, Ethics and Church: Writing in England, 1360–1409* (Cambridge, 2000). Includes (as chapter 5) 'Reflections on Gower' (Yeager, 1998).

Ashton, Gail, 'Her Father's Daughter: The Re-Alignment of Father-Daughter Kinship in Three Romance Tales', *Chaucer Review* 34:4 (2000), pp. 416–27.

Balestrini, Maria Cristina, 'A Proposito del Prologo de la Confesion del Amante', *Letras* 40–41 (1999–2000), pp. 100–6.

Bullón-Fernández, María, *Fathers and Daughters in Gower's Confessio Amantis: Authority, Family, State and Writing* (Cambridge, 2000).

Dean, Paul, 'Pericles' Pilgrimage', *Essays in Criticism* 50:2 (2000), pp. 125–44.

Echard, Siân, 'House Arrest: Modern Archives, Medieval Manuscripts', *Journal of Medieval and Early Modern Studies* 30:2 (2000), pp. 185–210.

McCarthy, Conor, 'Love and Marriage in the *Confessio Amantis*', *Neophilologus* 84:3 (2000), pp. 485–99.

Meecham-Jones, Simon, 'Prologue: The Poet as Subject: Literary Self-Consciousness in Gower's *Confessio Amantis*', *Betraying Our Selves: Forms of Self-Representation in Early Modern English Texts*, ed. Henk Dragstra, Sheila Ottway and Helen Wilcox (Houndmills, England, 2000), pp. 14–30.

Meecham-Jones, Simon, 'Questioning Romance: Amadas and Ydoine in Gower's *Confessio Amantis*', *Parergon* 17:2 (2000), pp. 35–49.

Pearsall, Derek, 'The Rede (Boarstall) Gower: British Library, MS Harley 3490', *The English Medieval Book: Studies in Memory of Jeremy Griffiths*, ed. A.S.G. Edwards, Vincent Gillespie and Ralph Hanna (London, 2000), pp. 87–99.

Penhallurick, Robert, 'On Gower English, Dialect and Metaphor', *The Celtic Englishes*, Vol. II, ed. Hildegard L.C. Tristram (Heidelberg, Germany, 2000), pp. 303–13.

Staley, Lynn, 'Gower, Richard II, Henry of Derby, and the Business of Making Culture', *Speculum* 75:1 (2000), pp. 68–96.

Sylvester, Louise, 'Reading Narratives of Rape: The Story of Lucretia in Chaucer, Gower and Christine de Pizan', *Leeds Studies in English* 31 (2000), pp. 115–44.

White, Hugh, *Nature, Sex, and Goodness in a Medieval Literary Tradition* (Oxford, 2000), especially 'Gower', pp. 174–219.

Yeager, Robert F., 'Politics and the French Language in England During the Hundred Years' War: The Case of John Gower', *Inscribing the Hundred Years' War in French and English Cultures*, ed. Denise N. Baker (Albany, NY, 2000), pp. 127–57.

## 2001

Bratcher, James T., 'Gower and Child, no. 45, 'King John and the Bishop', *Notes and Queries* 48:1 (2001), pp. 14–15.

Echard, Siân, 'Dialogues and Monologues: Manuscript Representations of the Conversation of the *Confessio Amantis*', *Middle English Poetry: Texts and Traditions: Essays in Honour of Derek Pearsall*, ed. Alastair Minnis (York, 2001), pp. 57–75.

Edwards, A.S.G., and T. Takamiya, 'A New Fragment of Gower's *Confessio Amantis*', *Modern Language Review* 96:4 (2001), pp. 931–6.

Harris, Kate, 'The Longleat House Extracted Manuscript of Gower's *Confessio Amantis*', *Middle English Poetry: Texts and Traditions: Essays in Honour of Derek Pearsall*, ed. Alastair Minnis (York, 2001), pp. 77–90.

Kerby-Fulton, Kathryn, and Steven Justice, 'Scribe D and the Marketing of Ricardian Literature', *The Medieval Professional Reader at Work : Evidence from Manuscripts of Chaucer, Langland, Kempe, and Gower*, ed. Maidie Hilmo and Kathryn Kerby-Fulton (Victoria, BC, 2001), pp. 217–37.

Krummel, Miriamne Ara, ' "The Tale of Ceix and Alceone": Alceone's Agency and Gower's "Audible Mime" ', *Exemplaria* 13:2 (2001), pp. 497–528.

Watt, Diane, 'Sins of Omission: Transgressive Genders, Subversive Sexualities, and Confessional Silences in John Gower's *Confessio Amantis*', *Exemplaria* 13:2 (2001), pp. 529–51.

Yeager, Robert F., 'John Gower's Images: "The Tale of Constance" and "The Man of Law's Tale" ', *Speaking Images: Essays in Honor of V.A. Kolve*, ed. Robert F. Yeager and Charlotte Morse (Asheville, NC, 2001), pp. 525–57.

## 2002

Arner, Lynn, 'History Lessons from the End of Time: Gower and the English Rising of 1381', *Clio* 31:3 (2002), pp. 237–55.

Coleman, Joyce, 'Lay Readers and Hard Latin: How Gower May Have Intended the *Confessio Amantis* to be Read', *Studies in the Age of Chaucer* 24 (2002), pp. 209–35.

Donavin, Georgiana, 'Taboo and Transgression in Gower's "Apollonius of Tyre" ', *Domestic Violence in Medieval Texts*, ed. Eve Salisbury, Georgiana Donavin and Merrall Llewelyn Price (Gainesville, FL, 2002), pp. 94–121.

Epstein, Robert, 'Literal Opposition: Deconstruction, History, and Lancaster', *Texas Studies in Literature and Language* 44:1 (2002), pp. 16–33.

Galloway, Andrew, 'The Literature of 1388 and the Politics of Pity in Gower's *Confessio Amantis*', *The Letter of the Law: Legal Practice and Literary Production in Medieval England*, ed. Emily Steiner and Candace Barrington (Ithaca, NY, 2002), pp. 67–104.

Grady, Frank, 'Gower's Boat, Richard's Barge, and the True Story of the *Confessio Amantis*: Text and Gloss', *Texas Studies in Literature and Language* 44:1 (2002), pp. 1–15.

Hanrahan, Michael, 'Speaking of Sodomy: Gower's Advice to Princes in the *Confessio Amantis*', *Exemplaria* 14:2 (2002), pp. 423–46.

Rytting, Jenny, 'In Search of the Perfect Spouse: John Gower's *Confessio Amantis* as a Marriage Manual', *Dalhousie Review* 82:1 (2002), pp. 113–26.

Scala, Elizabeth, *Absent Narratives, Manuscript Textuality, and Literary Structure in Late Medieval England* (Houndsmills, Basingstoke, 2002), especially ' "Hic quasi in persona aliorum": the Lover's Repression and Gower's *Confessio Amantis*'.

Watt, Diane, 'Oedipus, Apollonius, and Richard II: Sex and Politics in Book 8 of John Gower's *Confessio Amantis*', *Studies in the Age of Chaucer* 24 (2002), pp. 180–208.

## 2003

Butterfield, Ardis, 'Articulating the Author: Gower and the French Vernacular Codex', *Yearbook of English Studies* 33 (2003), pp. 80–96.

Echard, Siân, 'Gower's Books of Latin: Language, Politics and Poetry', *Studies in the Age of Chaucer* 25 (2003), pp. 123–56.

Echard, Siân, 'Last Words: Latin at the End of the *Confessio Amantis*', *Interstices*, ed. Richard Firth Green and Linne Mooney (Toronto, 2004), forthcoming.

Watt, Diane, *Amoral Gower: Language, Sex, and Politics* (Minneapolis, MN, 2003).

*Editions, Translations, Anthologies and Guides*

**Editions and Selections**

Caxton, William, *This Book is Intituled Confessio Amantis* (London, 1483).

Berthelette, Thomas, *Jo. Gower de Confessione Amantis* (London, 1532, 1554).

Chalmers, Alexander, *The Works of the English Poets, from Chaucer to Cowper; including the Series Edited with Prefaces, Biographical and Critical, by Dr. Samuel Johnson: and The Most Approved Translations*, Vol. II (London, 1810).

Sutherland, Lord George Granville Leveson-Gower, *Balades and other Poems by John Gower* (London, 1818). Presented to the Roxburghe Club by Earl Gower.

Coxe, Henry Octavius, ed., *Poema quod dicitur Vox Clamantis necnon Chronica Tripartita* (London, 1850).

Pauli, Reinhold, ed., *Confessio Amantis of John Gower: Edited and Collated with the Best Manuscripts by Dr. Reinhold Pauli*, 3 vols (London, 1857).

Stengel, Edmund, *John Gower's Minnesang und Ehezuchtbüchlein: LXXII Anglo-normannische Balladen, aus Anlass der Vermählung seines Lieben Freundes und Collegen Wilhelm Vietor neu hrsg. von Edmund Stengel* (Marburg, 1886).

Morley, Henry, ed., *Tales of the Seven Deadly Sins being the Confessio Amantis of John Gower* (London, 1889).

Macaulay, G.C., ed., *The Complete Works of John Gower*, 4 vols (Oxford, 1899–1902). The *Confessio* is also reprinted as *The English Works of John Gower*, EETS, es nos. 81 and 82 (London, 1900–1901).

Bennett, H.S., ed., *Confessio Amantis: Selections* (Cambridge, 1927). Cambridge Plain Texts series volume. Based on Pauli.

Howard, Edwin J., ed., *John Gower's Confessio Amantis: Selections* (Oxford, OH, 1964).

Peck, Russell, ed., *Confessio Amantis* (New York, 1968, rpt Toronto, 1980).

Bennett, J.A.W., ed., *Selections from John Gower* (Oxford, 1968).

Weinberg, Carole, ed., *Selected Poetry: John Gower* (Manchester, 1983).

Peck, Russell, ed., *Confessio Amantis*. With Latin translations by Andrew Galloway. Vol. I (Kalamazoo, MI, 2000).

**Translations**

Stockton, E.W., trans., *The Major Latin Works of John Gower* (Seattle, 1962).

Tiller, Terence, ed., *Confessio Amantis (The Lover's Shrift)* (Harmondsworth, Middlesex, 1963).

Echard, Siân, and Claire Fanger, trans., *The Latin Verses in the Confessio Amantis: An Annotated Translation* (East Lansing, MI, 1991). With Preface by A.G. Rigg.

Wilson, William Burton, *Mirour de l'Omme (the Mirror of Mankind), by John Gower*, ed. Nancy Wilson Van Baak (East Lansing, MI, 1992).

**Bibliography**

Yeager, Robert F., 'A Bibliography of John Gower Materials through 1975', *Mediaevalia* 3 (1977), pp. 261–306.

Yeager, Robert F., *John Gower Materials: A Bibliography through 1979* (New York, 1981).

Yeager, Robert F., 'The Poetry of John Gower: Important Studies, 1960–1983', *Fifteenth-Century Studies: Recent Essays*, ed. R.F. Yeager (Hamden, CT, 1984), pp. 3–28.

Fisher, John H., R. Wayne Hamm, Peter G. Beidler and Robert F. Yeager, 'John

Gower', *A Manual of the Writings in Middle English: 1050–1500*, ed. Albert E. Hartung, vol. VII (New Haven, CT, 1986).

Nicholson, Peter, *An Annotated Index to the Commentary on Gower's 'Confessio Amantis'* (Binghamton, NY, 1989).

Nicholson, Peter, ed., *Gower's Confessio Amantis: A Critical Anthology* (Cambridge, 1991).

## Concordances

Pickles, J.D., and J.L. Dawson, eds., *A Concordance to John Gower's Confessio Amantis* (Cambridge, 1987).

Yeager, Robert F., Mark West, and Robin L. Hinson, eds., *A Concordance to the French Poetry and Prose of John Gower* (East Lansing, MI, 1997).

## Newsletter

The *John Gower Newsletter*, published by the John Gower Society, includes short descriptions of papers, dissertations and publications concerning Gower.

# Index to Appendix

The *Chronology of Criticism* is presented in chronological order so that the development of Gower studies can be traced at a glance. Here we provide as well an alphabetical index to the Chronology, so that authors can be found quickly by name as well as by date. Many of the authors represented in the *Chronology* are of course also named in the essays in the *Companion*, and those contributions are indicated through references in the main Index.

# Index of Manuscripts

# General Index